BIOGRAPHICAL MEMOIRS OF FELLOWS, VI

PROCEEDINGS OF THE BRITISH ACADEMY · 150

BIOGRAPHICAL MEMOIRS OF FELLOWS VI

Published for THE BRITISH ACADEMY
by OXFORD UNIVERSITY PRESS

Oxford University Press, Great Clarendon Street, Oxford OX2 6DP

Oxford New York
Auckland Bangkok Bogotá Buenos Aires Cape Town Chennai
Dar es Salaam Delhi Hong Kong Istanbul Karachi Kolkata
Kuala Lumpur Madrid Melbourne Mexico City Mumbai Nairobi
São Paulo Shanghai Singapore Taipei Tokyo Toronto

British Library Cataloguing in Publication Data
Data available

978–0–19–726423–2
ISSN 0068–1202

Typeset in Times
by J&L Composition, Filey, North Yorkshire
Printed in Great Britain
on acid-free paper by
Antony Rowe Limited,
Chippenham, Wiltshire

The Academy is grateful to Professor P. J. Marshall, CBE, FBA
for his editorial work on this volume

Contents

PETER BIRKS

Peter Brian Herrenden Birks
1941–2004

PETER BIRKS, WHO WAS ELECTED to the Academy in 1989, was one of the most influential legal scholars of his generation. He owed that influence to the admiration in which his rigorous and innovative thinking was held by lawyers and judges not only in this country but throughout the Commonwealth and in Europe too. He was most widely known through his writings, but in Oxford, in particular, his reputation also rested on his teaching, especially in the famous restitution seminars which he conducted with various colleagues over three decades. His meticulous and sympathetic supervision of his doctoral students turned pupils into friends and fellow enthusiasts who are the first to acknowledge the continuing impact of his thinking on their work.

In a very real sense Peter's life centred on the colleges and universities in which he worked—University College London, Brasenose College, Oxford, Edinburgh, Southampton and Oxford again, this time in All Souls. For those in legal or university life who knew him as a passionate, generous and entertaining colleague and friend it comes as something of a shock to realise that in his *Who's Who* entry he did not record his school, either of his first two marriages or the existence of three of his four children. Nor did he keep in contact with friends from his schooldays or from outside the university world. Uncomfortable or not, the truth seems to be that, being very deeply committed to the work which he was doing, more often than not—and not least in the last years—Peter would give it priority over competing personal and family concerns. Settled back in Oxford for the last fifteen years of his life, he was interested in the Law Faculty and his college and with everything that went on there. In an uncomplicated way, he loved the usual sights and sounds—

Proceedings of the British Academy, **150**, 3–34. © The British Academy 2007.

the buildings, the choirs, walking in Christ Church meadow, cycling back and forth to his home on Boar's Hill. As a result, he could have a somewhat blinkered attitude to the challenges and opportunities of life outside the academic world. On one occasion this led him to make some spectacularly unwise public remarks when his younger daughter, Laura Bailey, who had a first-class degree in English, chose a career as a highly successful supermodel. The predictably derisive comments in the press he found hard to handle. Fortunately, in the weeks before he died, Peter saw his first wife, all his children and his three grandsons and heard about two more grandchildren who were on the way.

We make these points to explain why this memoir will concentrate almost exclusively on Peter's life within the academic and legal worlds. Nor, due to the limitations of space, shall we repeat in detail what we have said elsewhere.[1] After an outline of his career, we first examine his work on Roman law and then turn to his work on restitution and unjust enrichment.

Career[2]

Peter was born in Hassocks on the South Downs on 3 October 1941. His father, who was a doctor, was abroad in the army till the end of the war. During that time Peter lived with his mother, who was of Welsh descent. After the war, his father decided not to join the family medical practice but to move the family instead to Assam in India. Peter's brother was born there. Peter went to school in Assam until he was seven when he was sent home to Aymestrey House Preparatory School where he remained until the age of 13. Since he was able to return to India only twice and spent his holidays, unhappily, as a paying guest with a family (usually a clergyman's family), during those long years the school represented an element of stability. While in India, his father had become obsessed with trying to find a cure for a condition which he associated with drinking tea. As a result he lost money and, when the family returned to this country and Peter's sister was born, they were in bad financial straits. Peter was taken out of education for a whole year, during which he and his father

---

[1] In the Memorial Addresses reproduced in A. Burrows and Lord Rodger of Earlsferry (eds.), *Mapping the Law: Essays in Memory of Peter Birks* (Oxford, 2006), pp. vii–xv.
[2] An outline, which includes a list of degrees and honours, is given at the very front of *Mapping the Law* (n. 1).

lived in a series of guest houses. Eventually, the family were reunited and his father settled into a medical practice. In October 1956 Peter became a pupil at Chislehurst & Sidcup Grammar School where he remained until 1960. He studied Latin and Greek. Being academically gifted, good at both rugby and cricket and taking part in school plays, he was held up to more junior boys as an ideal all-rounder. After leaving school, he spent a year teaching Latin at his old prep school. His success as a teacher was acknowledged in an appreciative letter from the school which Peter kept among his papers.

Although he briefly contemplated a career as a classics teacher, when Peter went up to Trinity College, Oxford, on a State scholarship in October 1961 it was to study law. He was awarded a minor scholarship in 1963. One of the law tutors at the college was John Kelly, a lively and high-spirited Irishman who had written a thesis on Roman law at Heidelberg with the renowned Romanist Wolfgang Kunkel. At the time, not only was Roman law one of the three subjects in the first-year examination, Law Moderations, but in the final examination, Schools, there was also a compulsory paper on the Roman law of contract and a popular paper on the Roman law of delict. These subjects, in particular, gave scope for Kelly's imagination and, with his classical background, Peter much enjoyed his teaching. Peter gained a first in the Final Honours School of Jurisprudence in 1964.

It appears that Peter did, briefly, consider going into practice, but was told by a partner in a City law firm that he seemed 'a bit of an egg-head'. In any event, by the time he left Oxford for a junior teaching post in the Northwestern Law School in Chicago, he had settled on a career in academic law. When he returned to this country he became a lecturer at University College London where Tony Thomas was the Professor of Roman Law. A superb teacher and dedicated scholar, he was, for Peter and many others, 'a dazzling and magnetic figure'.[3] In the junior ranks of the Law Faculty Peter found himself among colleagues whom he liked and admired, in particular, the legal historian, John Baker—later Sir John Baker, the Downing Professor at Cambridge—and Paul Mahoney, who became the Registrar of the European Court of Human Rights and President of the European Union Civil Service Tribunal. Peter taught a variety of subjects and participated in the LL M seminar on restitution. But at this time his principal academic interest, which Thomas

---

[3] 'Obligations: One Tier or Two?' in P. G. Stein and A. D. E. Lewis (eds.), *Studies in Justinian's Institutes in memory of J. A. C. Thomas* (London, 1983), pp. 18–38, at 19.

encouraged, was Roman law. He was an enthusiastic participant in meetings of the Roman Law Group, known informally as the *grex*, which Thomas established to rival the *gremium* in Cambridge. Peter was equally at home in the sessions in a local pub and in the dinners which always followed the meetings and which helped to form lasting friendships among the participants. While still at UCL in 1971, when the Bar qualification rules were about to be made stricter, Peter and Paul Mahoney decided to cram for the exams. But finding the grind repulsive, after two weeks he abandoned the effort to obtain what would have been, for him, a useless formal qualification as a barrister.

Peter had married while still at Oxford and he had a daughter, Zillah, by that marriage. But by about 1967 he and his wife had separated. As a result, he lived a somewhat unsettled existence, loyally supported at (not infrequent) times of crisis by Paul and Parvin Mahoney. Fortunately, he was an enthusiastic and skilful cook, as well as a lover of good wine. Still, the lack of a fixed base in London added to the attractions of a post in Oxford, to which Peter was always keen to return. But he had published relatively little—and that mostly on Roman law. Especially with the changes in the Oxford syllabus, which saw the end of the compulsory paper on Roman law in Schools and the introduction of new subjects, such as administrative law and family law, Peter may not have seemed to be offering the ideal range of subjects for a tutorial fellow. At any rate, more than one application for a fellowship was turned down before he was appointed to Brasenose College in 1971. At about the same time he remarried.

When he arrived at Brasenose, Barry Nicholas was a long-established fellow of the college. The following year, while remaining a fellow of Brasenose, he became Professor of Comparative Law. In 1973 Herbert Hart became Principal. The other law tutor was John Davies, an exceptionally successful teacher. In due course they were joined by Hugh Collins. Peter could not have found himself in more congenial company and surroundings. He proved to be an excellent, if demanding, tutor[4] and a loyal servant of the college. Peter was devoted to Nicholas,[5] a fellow Romanist, who in due course succeeded Hart as Principal. Nicholas, who had always valued quality over quantity in publications, would reassure

---

[4] For a description of a tutorial, see Burrows in *Mapping the Law* (n. 1), pp. vii–viii.

[5] As is apparent from the fine memoir which he wrote for these Proceedings: 'John Kieran Barry Moylan Nicholas (1919–2002)', *Proceedings of the British Academy*, 124 (2004), 219–39. Peter also edited a Festschrift for Nicholas: *New Perspectives in the Roman Law of Property: Essays for Barry Nicholas* (Oxford, 1989).

Peter if he ever worried that he was not publishing enough. It was during his time at Brasenose that he and Jack Beatson (later Mr Justice Beatson, but then a law don at Merton) began teaching in the restitution seminars which Guenter Treitel and Derek Davies had started some time before. These seminars were to be the arena in which, week by week, Peter hammered out his ideas on the subject. The series of sixteen two-hour seminars was not only a source of immense pleasure to Peter personally but soon established itself as a 'must' for serious BCL and M Jur. students from all over the world. In short, 'Peter adored it and the students adored him.'[6]

But after he had been at Brasenose for a few years Peter's private life was in chaos once more as his second marriage, by which he had two children, Laura and Ben, broke down. A bitter divorce followed. Forced to move back to live in college and with pressing financial demands, he nevertheless revealed little of his difficulties to his colleagues. Even during a period of sabbatical leave, however, Peter found himself unable to give his full attention to the *Introduction to the Law of Restitution* which he was contracted to write for the Clarendon Press. Around this time he even contemplated giving up his work as a law teacher and becoming a college bursar. In the end, because of the pressures in his private life, he accepted the invitation to apply for the Chair of Civil Law at Edinburgh which had become vacant when Alan Watson left for Pennsylvania in 1979.

Despite the invitation to Peter, certain prominent members of the Edinburgh Law Faculty were opposed to the appointment of another scholar of ancient Roman law who, it was argued, would contribute little to the education of modern Scots lawyers. They would have preferred someone with an interest in the *ius commune* or modern Roman-Dutch law. Moreover, relations with the Faculty of Advocates, which still had a say in appointments to the chair, were somewhat strained. Despite these very real difficulties, Peter—who was in reality the outstanding candidate—was appointed. Happily, he quickly established himself within the faculty, doing much, in particular, to encourage the other members of his department to undertake research.[7] Peter soon became an admirer of the

---

[6] Burrows in *Mapping the Law* (n. 1), p. viii.

[7] Along with Grant McLeod, he wrote an important article on the Roman law background to Lord Mansfield's judgment in *Moses v McFerlan* (1760) 2 Burr 1005: 'The Implied Contract Theory of Quasi-Contract: Civilian Opinion Current in the Century before Blackstone', *Oxford Journal of Legal Studies*, 6 (1986), 46–85. They also prepared a new translation of Justinian's Institutes: *Justinian's Institutes* (London and Ithaca, NY, 1987). Although Birks had eventually to withdraw, he was involved in securing the publication of the linked volume edited by his

Scottish institutional writers who, he felt, had laid a foundation for the analysis of Scots law which English law lacked but which Scots lawyers tended to neglect.[8] Most importantly, two brilliant articles published in 1985 cut through the bewildering terminology of the Scots law of unjust enrichment and, in due course, set the law off on a new course.[9] Nothing could better have answered those who had doubted the wisdom of appointing a real Roman law scholar to the Chair.

In 1984 Peter had married for the third time. This marriage was to last and to make him profoundly happy. His new wife, Jackie, continued to live and work in Oxford, while Peter lived in a rather spartan flat in the Trinity district of Edinburgh. During term, he regularly worked late into the evenings during the week and then, roughly every second weekend, he would travel from Edinburgh to London by the overnight coach and then go on to Oxford where he would teach restitution and take Roman law tutorials for Brasenose, while snatching some time at home. Then it was back by coach to Edinburgh on Sunday night.

Eventually, with his second son, Theodore, on the way, Peter decided to apply for the Chair of Law at Southampton. By this time, particularly with the publication of *An Introduction to the Law of Restitution* in 1985, Peter was, of course, a star and he was immediately appointed. But he was to spend only seven terms in Southampton. Tony Honoré retired from the Regius Chair of Civil Law in Oxford in 1988. The appointment fell to be made on the nomination of the Prime Minister, Mrs Thatcher. She took a personal interest in the matter and recommended that the Queen should appoint Peter with effect from 1989. Now aged 48 and in his prime, he was back in Oxford, where he had always wanted to be, and in a college, All Souls, which provided a setting in which he could get on with his work.

Now followed perhaps his most productive years. The ferment of developments in the law of restitution inevitably claimed most of his attention and he was able to find less time than he would have wished to

---

doctoral pupil, Ernie Metzger: *A Companion to Justinian's Institutes* (Oxford, 1998). See the Preface, pp. xiii–xiv.

[8] 'The Foundation of Legal Rationality in Scotland' in R. Evans-Jones (ed.), *The Civil Law Tradition in Scotland* (Edinburgh, 1995), pp. 81–99; 'More Logic and Less Experience: The Difference between Scots Law and English Law' in D. L. Carey Miller and R. Zimmermann (eds.), *The Civilian Tradition and Scots Law: Aberdeen Quincentenary Essays* (Berlin, 1997), pp. 167–90.

[9] 'Restitution: A View of the Scots Law', *Current Legal Problems*, 38 (1985), 57–82 and 'Six Questions in Search of a Subject', *Juridical Review* (1985), 227–52.

work on publications in Roman law—his last article on the subject proper appeared in 1998.[10] However many new restitution cases came to his attention, Peter always had a complete mastery of the facts and the nuances of the judgments. As the new judgments arrived, cries of joy or howls of despair were soon to be heard and, in due course, acute observations would appear, *inter alia* in the articles which he and Bill Swadling prepared for the All England Reports Annual Reviews from 1996 to 2000. It all seemed so effortless that it was easy to forget that, as his closely written bound notebooks indicated, his bravura performance was based on a vast amount of sheer hard work.

Within the Oxford Law Faculty, Birks was a charismatic and dynamic figure renowned not only for the brilliance of his teaching and scholarship but also for his dedication to the faculty in various administrative roles. He went far beyond the call of duty in responding to any demand to serve or chair a faculty committee or examining board; and he spearheaded new faculty initiatives, such as the Clarendon Law Lecture series. He was particularly interested in developing postgraduate teaching and delighted in the success of the M Jur. degree which attracted excellent students from Civil Law countries. He was the driving force behind the creation in 1994 of the Oxford Institute of Legal Practice—the initiative to which he, at least, would probably have attached the most importance. His dream, that this would engender a more rigorous intellectual approach to training practitioners and so stimulate research into very practical areas of law, has yet to be realised.

Much of Peter's time, in the late 1980s and early 1990s, was devoted to legal education at the national level. He became a member of the Lord Chancellor's Advisory Committee on Legal Education but did not find their deliberations to his taste. The main focus of his efforts centred, however, on another of his passions: the Society of Public Teachers of Law (now the Society of Legal Scholars). He was concerned that academic lawyers were not given the status they merited and he saw the SPTL as a means to promote the interests of academic law on a national stage. To bring that about, a considerable shake-up of the Society was needed and as Honorary Secretary between 1989 and 1996 that is what he took it upon himself to achieve. Although his agenda, that all practising lawyers

---

[10] 'Can we get Nearer to the Text of the *Lex Aquilia*?' in B. C. M. Jacobs and E. C. Coppens (eds.), *Een Rijk Gerecht* (Nijmegen, 1998), pp. 25–41. An article on 'Roman Law in Twentieth-Century Britain' appeared posthumously in J. Beatson and R. Zimmermann (eds.), *Jurists Uprooted: German-Speaking Emigré Lawyers in Twentieth-Century Britain* (Oxford, 2004), pp. 249–68.

should have a law degree, was one which he could never realistically hope to have accepted by the professions at that time, his structural reforms of the Society, and the profile he gave to it during those years, made him one of the greatest figures in its history. Fittingly he was its President in 2002–3, his year of office culminating in the annual conference in his beloved (and sunny) Oxford.

In about 2003 Peter began to experience difficulties with his health. He attended his general practitioner and was sent for various specialist investigations. Diabetes was diagnosed and treated, but he continued to suffer disturbing symptoms. He was persuaded to go for further investigations and, eventually, in March 2004 he was diagnosed as suffering from cancer of the oesophagus. Characteristically, in a telephone call the following morning about the diagnosis, he appeared more concerned to discuss an event in the world of Oxford law which had particularly annoyed him. It was believed that the tumour would be operable after a course of chemotherapy, but eventually the cancer spread before the operation could be carried out. Throughout all these problems with his health, Peter continued to work—doing his normal load of teaching and administration, finishing his book on *Unjust Enrichment* in September 2003 and then, when his cancer had been diagnosed, furiously preparing a new edition which the Oxford University Press had agreed to publish unusually quickly because of the alarming number of misprints in the first edition. Peter showed amazing bravery in the face of his illness. For instance, one evening in May 2004, he presided over dessert in All Souls, calmly conversed with the guests, helped them to coffee and liqueurs, then strolled round the quadrangle and talked about a range of subjects—before revealing that, earlier that day, he had unexpectedly learned that the cancer had spread and that the outlook was now probably hopeless. Except for a few days he spent in hospital, Peter continued to go into college and, despite increasing frustration as the illness progressed, he worked on his book right up until about ten days before he died, at home, on 6 July 2004. His funeral service took place in the chapel of All Souls and, in November, a memorial service was held in the University Church which was packed not only with his Oxford colleagues but with delegations and friends from all over the world.

While Peter's fame and influence derived, for the most part, from his work on restitution or unjust enrichment, his first love, and the mainspring of much of his thinking, was Roman law. So, in giving an account of his work, we start with Roman law.

Roman Law

Although Birks attended David Daube's lectures on Roman law for Moderations, he did not do any more advanced work with him—never even attending the smaller classes which Daube gave on *condictiones* for the BCL. This was a recurring source of regret to Birks who some-times imagined that by not doing a doctorate he had somehow excluded himself from the authentic Oxford line of Roman law scholarship. Not the least of Barry Nicholas's services was to still those doubts. Of course, any regrets Birks may have had on this score did not diminish the grati-tude which he felt towards John Kelly and Tony Thomas for their teach-ing. Typically, he gave very practical expression to this gratitude. For many years he placed articles in the *Irish Jurist* edited by Kelly. Then, after Kelly's death, he travelled to Dublin to give lectures on Roman law. Similarly, he contributed many lectures to the Current Legal Problems series published by University College London. It is indeed somewhat curious that, in his entire career, he published only three articles in spe-cialist Roman law journals and none in the (leading) *Savigny Zeitschrift*.[11] This probably meant that his work reached a smaller international audience than it deserved.

The fact that Birks's teachers were John Kelly and Tony Thomas, who came from outside the mainstream of Oxford Roman law scholarship, may help to explain what is otherwise a somewhat surprising aspect of some of his work. For more than a century the study of Roman law has been bedevilled by uncertainty about the extent to which the texts which appear in the Digest under the names of jurists from the first two cen-turies AD have in fact been altered—'interpolated'—so as to incorporate later changes in the law. To begin with, the prevailing view was that there were many interpolations, but in the last forty years or so opinion has become more conservative. As it happens, Kelly and, more particularly, Thomas remained disposed to the more radical approach. And—despite the conservative stance adopted by Nicholas—especially in his later arti-cles Birks too argued for more far-reaching changes in the texts than most scholars would nowadays accept.[12] As a result those articles received a

---

[11] 'The Early History of *Iniuria*', *Tijdschrift voor Rechtsgeschiedenis*, 37 (1969), 163–208; 'A Point of Aquilian Pleading', *IVRA*, 36 (1985), 97–107 and 'Wrongful Loss by Co-Promisees', *Index*, 22 (1994), 181–8 (a special volume comprising a festschrift for Peter Stein).

[12] See, for instance, 'Other Men's Meat: Aquilian Liability for Proper User', *Irish Jurist*, NS 16 (1981), 141–85, the radical approach in which he modified, but did not entirely abandon, in 'Ulpian 18 *ad Edictum*: Introducing *Damnum Iniuria*' in R. Feenstra and others (eds.), *Collatio*

somewhat mixed reception, even though they often contained valuable insights.[13]

While a lecturer at UCL, Birks did a part-time LL M course and in 1967 he was awarded the degree with distinction. His thesis was on 'The Development of the Law of Delict in the Roman Republic' and, in part, it covered the early period of Roman law, down to roughly the second century BC. The sources for that period are sparse and difficult to interpret so that use has to be made of non-legal works such as the plays of Plautus and Terence. Not surprisingly, therefore, it is not a field in which scholars have found it easy to produce a convincing account of the way the law developed.

Nevertheless, particularly because of his interest in work being carried on in the field of English legal history, Birks was attracted to this period. In the late 1960s Toby Milsom was Professor of Legal History at the London School of Economics. Sir John Baker has recalled how Peter would go to his classes and return from the Aldwych 'freighted with new ideas and already turning in his mind the possibilities for applying the new insights to the history of Roman law'.[14] So, even before the publication of Milsom's *Historical Foundations of the Common Law* in 1969, his work was greatly affecting Birks's thinking about the way that Roman law might have developed.

Following Milsom, Birks noted, for example,[15] that in English law the change from disputes being decided by divine adjudication to disputes being decided by juries was unlikely to have been sudden, since quite often one side would have an interest in arguing that the old ways should continue to be followed. Similarly, even if the procedural rules for bringing a dispute before the court were relatively well understood, to begin with, there would have been no rules of substantive law to which a tribunal could refer in order to decide the dispute. These rules would emerge only very gradually—and in English law the judges were able to postpone deciding many questions by putting the general issue to the jury.

Iuris Romani: Études dédiées à Hans Ankum à l'occasion de son 65e anniversaire (Amsterdam, 1995), vol. 1, pp. 17–36. This article also contains (p. 20 n. 18) a rather precipitate rejection of the text of D.9.2.29.6.

[13] See, for instance, R. Feenstra, 'L'application de la loi Aquilia en cas d'homicide d'un homme libre, de l'Époque classique à celle de Justinien', in H. Ankum, R. Feenstra *et al.* (eds.), *Mélanges Felix Wubbe* (Fribourg, 1993), pp. 141–60, at 149, criticising the first of the articles in n. 12 above.

[14] J. Baker, 'Bezoar-Stones, Gall Stones, and Gem-Stones: A Chapter in the History of the Tort of Deceit', in *Mapping the Law* (n. 1), pp. 545–59, at 545.

[15] 'English Beginnings and Roman Parallels', *Irish Jurist*, NS 6 (1971), 147–62.

Arguing by analogy, Birks suggested that in Roman law the vital change from the old *legis actio* procedure to the formulary procedure should also be seen as a gradual process during which, so long as the law permitted it, litigants would seek to exploit any advantages which one or other of the procedures offered. In the *Lex Aebutia*, he suggested, the legislature intervened to remove the advantages of the option of using the old procedure.[16] More generally, and contrary to the commonly held view, Birks argued that, just as in English law, so in early Roman law the main focus of attention would not have been on reforming procedures, but on trying to develop a body of law by which to decide the substance of disputes. Since in the early stages there would be no pre-existing body of rules, it is anachronistic, he maintained, to think of there then being a great divide between the *ius civile* and the law developed by the praetor. The idea of the praetor developing a distinct body of law to supplement or correct the old *ius civile*—which is the picture in the classical period of Roman law—could not have emerged until a stage when the general body of law had developed to such an extent that it was recognised as an entity, complete in itself, which might require such supplementing or correcting from another source.[17] Birks sought to apply this general approach in tracing the development of particular aspects of the substantive law, such as the *condictio*,[18] *iniuria*[19] and theft.[20]

There is no doubt that the approach which he advocates in these early articles, and which is perhaps his most distinctive contribution to the subject, is attractive. This is so even though it is vulnerable to an obvious objection of which Birks himself was very conscious: that the pattern of developments in English law is not necessarily any guide to the way that Roman law developed.[21] Moreover, however sound, an approach which draws on analogies with English law is never likely to be taken up by Romanists in other countries who are unfamiliar with English legal history. Despite these drawbacks, Birks remained convinced that, while one had indeed to be cautious about drawing on the experience of English law, with further detailed work his approach would produce valuable

---

[16] 'From *Legis Actio* to *Formula*', *Irish Jurist*, NS 4 (1969), 356–67.

[17] *Irish Jurist*, NS 6, 147, 155.

[18] *Irish Jurist*, NS 6, 147, 156–9.

[19] 'The Early History of *Iniuria*', *Tijdschrift voor Rechtsgeschiedenis*, 37 (1969), 163; 'Lucius Veratius and the *Lex Aebutia*' in A. Watson (ed.), *Daube Noster: Essays in Legal History for David Daube* (Edinburgh, 1974), pp. 39–48. He dealt with later stages in the development of liability for *iniuria* in '*Infamandi Causa Facta* in Disguise', *Acta Juridica* (1976), 83–104.

[20] 'A Note on the Development of *Furtum*', *Irish Jurist*, NS 8 (1973), 349–55.

[21] See, for instance, *Irish Jurist*, NS 6, 147 and 162.

results. So, even though he never got round to producing the larger work in which his thinking might have been developed systematically, he always spoke of coming back to the question—in an email dated 26 May 2004, after he had been told that the cancer had spread, he said, 'I wanted to end with a Milsomian version of the R L of Delict, but that won't be possible.' As that message suggests, curiously enough, Milsom probably had a greater impact than any Romanist on Birks's thinking about Roman law.

Birks appears to have stopped working consistently on early Roman law about the time he moved to Oxford in 1971, since the flow of articles dried up about that time. Indeed he published relatively little in the next few years. By contrast, after his appointment to the Edinburgh chair, he produced a large amount of work on Roman law, but mostly on the classical and Justinianic periods, including a masterly analysis of the Roman concept of ownership[22] and, significantly for his work on English law, translations of the very difficult books 12 and 13 of the Digest dealing with what amounts to the Roman law of unjust enrichment.[23] During this time too, he engaged in a bitter public dispute with his predecessor in the chair, Alan Watson, over Watson's intemperate criticisms of Tony Honoré's work.[24]

His study of English law and legal history made Birks particularly sensitive to matters of procedure and to pleadings. He was constantly asking himself—and anyone else who would listen—what would actually have happened in front of the praetor or the *iudex*. The question is, of course, particularly difficult to answer since very few accounts of actual cases have come down to us. Birks therefore paid close attention to such little evidence as could be gleaned from the speeches of Cicero[25] and from rhetorical works.[26] But, by good fortune, two recently discovered inscriptions from Spain provided new material which he was able to exploit.

The first of these inscriptions was the *Tabula Contrebiensis*, dating from about 87 BC. Birks was to make what turned out to be the crucial

---

[22] 'The Roman Law Concept of Dominium and the Idea of Absolute Ownership', *Acta Juridica* (1985), 1–38.

[23] For A. Watson (ed.), *The Digest of Justinian* (Philadelphia, 1985; paperback reprint, 1998).

[24] See 'Honoré's Ulpian', *Irish Jurist*, NS 18 (1983), 151–81 with references to the review and correspondence. Connoisseurs of the dispute will also read D. C(ohen), 'The Battle of the Atlantic', *Rechtshistorisches Journal*, 2 (1983), 33–6, A. Watson, 'An Open Letter to D.C.', *Rechtshistorisches Journal*, 3 (1984), 286–90 and T. Honoré, 'New Methods in Roman Law', ibid., 290–305.

[25] Cf. 'The Rise of the Roman Jurists', *Oxford Journal of Legal Studies*, 7 (1987), 444–53.

[26] '*Infamandi Causa Facta* in Disguise', *Acta Juridica* (1976), 83–104.

contribution to its interpretation. Early in 1983 John Richardson, his colleague in the chair of Classics at Edinburgh, who was preparing an article on the inscription for the *Journal of Roman Studies*, consulted Birks
about it. The inscription contains the text of two formulae which had
been used to decide a dispute over water rights between two communities
in an area near the modern city of Zaragoza. Very few examples of the
formulae—in effect, the pleadings—used in actual cases have been preserved and so the find was potentially extremely important. Birks, who
was busy with other matters, noted, almost casually, that one of the formulae contained a fiction—something which the Spanish scholars who
had previously studied the inscription had completely missed. Although,
to begin with, Birks appeared not to realise this, his insight totally transformed the translation and interpretation of the text. Once persuaded—
in an alcohol-fuelled discussion of the text that went on in his flat until
three o'clock one Saturday morning—to give the matter his full attention, Peter immersed himself in the inscription and in its implications for
our understanding of the formulary system of procedure. The result was
not just that Richardson's draft article was radically altered,[27] but that the
following year a further joint article was published which has become the
standard study on the subject.[28] Remarkably, Birks was able to accom-
plish all this at a time when he was working to complete his *Introduction
to the Law of Restitution.* Birks's work on the fiction in the *Tabula
Contrebiensis* undoubtedly paved the way for his valuable article comparing the use of fictions in Roman and English law—very much to the
advantage of the Roman system.[29]

The other new inscription, discovered in 1981 and published in 1986,[30]
contains much of the text of the so-called *Lex Irnitana.* This statute,
which dates from the first century AD, regulated the affairs of the *municip-
ium* of Irni in the south of Spain. For students of Roman law it is of enormous interest because chapters 84 to 93 give not only the details of the

[27] J. Richardson, 'The Tabula Contrebiensis: Roman Law in Spain in the Early First Century BC',
Journal of Roman Studies, 73 (1983), 33–41. See especially 33 n. 1.

[28] P. Birks, A. Rodger, J. S. Richardson, 'Further Aspects of the *Tabula Contrebiensis*', *Journal of
Roman Studies*, 74 (1984), 45–73. Although discussed with the other authors, Part III was very
largely Birks's work—and would have been even more detailed and far-reaching if space had
permitted. By this time he had triumphantly switched to a word processor and dot matrix printer
which spewed forth sheet after connected sheet of text.

[29] 'Fictions Ancient and Modern' in N. MacCormick and P. Birks (eds.), *The Legal Mind: Essays
for Tony Honoré* (Oxford, 1986), pp. 83–101.

[30] J. González, 'The Lex Irnitana: a New Copy of the Flavian Municipal Law', *Journal of Roman
Studies*, 76 (1986), 147–243.

jurisdiction of the magistrates of Irni but the procedures to be followed by litigants. Certain aspects of these chapters have proved difficult to interpret, however, and Birks participated in a valuable colloquium organised by John Crook in Cambridge in March 1987 to stimulate thinking on the topic.[31] The following year Birks published an article on the appointment of *iudices* which draws on the new material.[32]

The same attention to the detail of what would have happened in court is apparent in a series of articles which Birks wrote on the *Lex Aquilia*, the Roman statute relating to property damage—a subject which he taught for many years to candidates for Schools and the BCL. Here he used various hypothetical arguments, which the parties might have deployed to gain an advantage in court, in order to try to choose between a number of possible versions of the text of the statute[33] and of the wording of the pleadings.[34] While not all of his suggestions are likely to win acceptance, the articles, especially on the formulae, highlighted questions which had been wrongly neglected. In particular, his suggestion[35] that the rubric of the relevant title in the Praetor's Edict was *de damno iniuria* rather than *ad legem Aquiliam* is both acute and potentially important.

Although Birks was, therefore, an active contributor to the specialist literature on ancient Roman law, he regarded it as anything but a subject of purely antiquarian interest. In a university environment where Roman law often seemed to be regarded as of no relevance to the study of modern law, Birks was passionate in his defence of its continuing importance in the education of modern lawyers. The decision of the Oxford Law Board to make Roman law optional in Law Moderations shocked and saddened him, but also made him more determined than ever to assert the case for Roman law. He was justly proud that, despite determined hostile propaganda in some quarters, a majority of undergraduates always opted

---

[31] See J. A. Crook, D. E. L. Johnston and P. G. Stein, 'Intertiumjagd and the Lex Irnitana: a Colloquium', *Zeitschrift für Papyrologie und Epigraphik*, 70 (1987), 173–84. Some of the suggestions made by Birks during the colloquium are specifically identified in the report.

[32] 'New Light on the Roman Legal System: The Appointment of Judges', *Cambridge Law Journal*, 47 (1988), 36–60.

[33] 'Can we get Nearer to the Text of the *Lex Aquilia*?' in *Een Rijk Gerecht* (n. 10), 25

[34] 'A Point of Aquilian Pleading', *IVRA*, 36 (1985), 97–107; 'The Model Pleading of the Action for Wrongful Loss', *Irish Jurist*, NS 25–7 (1990–2), 311–28, at 327. Birks argued that there was only one model for both chapter 1 and chapter 3. See also 'Doing and Causing to be Done' in A. D. E. Lewis and D. J. Ibbetson (eds.), *The Roman Law Tradition* (Cambridge, 1994), pp. 31–53, at 32.

[35] 'The Edictal Rubric "ad legem Aquiliam"' in R. Pérez-Bustamante (ed.), *Estudios de Historia del Derecho Europeo: Homenaje al Professor G. Martínez Díez* (Madrid, 1994,) vol. 1, 81–9, at 83, and *Collatio Iuris Romani* (n. 12), vol. 1, 17, 23–4.

to take Roman law in Mods. The reintroduction of a revised course of Roman law as a compulsory subject in Mods in 2006 would not only have delighted him but was, in part at least, a vindication of his stand.

More persuasive in that battle than any mere words could have been was, perhaps, the very obvious fact that Birks's seminal work on the law of restitution owed much to his work on Roman law. In 1969, one of his very first articles—on quasi-delicts in Roman law[36]—gave early notice of his interest in questions of classification. It was precisely because he regarded Gaius' 'short but brilliant exposition of the law'[37] for students as having made a major contribution to the kind of analysis of the law which Birks regarded as essential that he would go back to the Institutes again and again. Nevertheless, on this particular matter, he pointed to the 'very imperfect truth' of Gaius' statement in Institutes 3.88 that all obligations arise either from contract or from delict. Referring to a passage in Lord Chancellor Haldane's speech in *Sinclair v Brougham*,[38] Birks remarked that 'Statements of that kind typify the worst effects of the twofold classification of obligations. Quasi-contractual obligation, which should be based on the redress of unjust enrichment, becomes contaminated by contractual doctrine.'[39] Sixteen years later he returned to the passages in Gaius and Justinian as the starting-point of his argument that English lawyers would have to abandon the misleading terminology of quasi-contract if the law were ever to develop rationally and coherently.[40] Eighteen years after that, when his thinking on questions of classification had been progressively refined in a stream of publications,[41] in his book on *Unjust Enrichment* Birks still devoted space to a careful discussion of the relevant passages of Gaius and Justinian.[42] Moreover, his familiarity with the Roman texts on unjust enrichment undoubtedly eased his way

---

[36] 'The Problem of Quasi-Delict', *Current Legal Problems*, 22 (1969), 164–80. He can be seen still worrying away at the topic but now also drawing on Scots Law and the writings of Austin in 'Obligations: One Tier or Two?' in *Studies in Justinian's Institutes in memory of J. A. C. Thomas* (n. 3), p. 18.

[37] 'The Foundation of Legal Rationality in Scotland' in *The Civil Law Tradition in Scotland* (n. 8), pp. 81, 88.

[38] [1914] AC 398, 415.

[39] *Current Legal Problems*, 22 (1969), 164, 165.

[40] P. Birks, *An Introduction to the Law of Restitution* (Oxford, 1985; paperback edn., 1989), pp. 29–31.

[41] Including 'Definition and Division: A Meditation on *Institutes* 3.13' in P. Birks (ed.), *The Classification of Obligations* (Oxford, 1997), pp. 1–36.

[42] *Unjust Enrichment*, 1st edn. (Oxford 2003), pp. 28 n. 11 and 230–1; 2nd edn. (Oxford, 2005), pp. 30 n. 15 and 268–70.

into the Continental, especially German, work on the subject. As we shall see, this was eventually to revolutionise his own thinking.[43]

Restitution and unjust enrichment

While Peter's first love was Roman law, the subject for which he was best known, and on which he had the greatest impact, was unquestionably the law of restitution or (as he latterly preferred to call most of it) the law of unjust enrichment. By the time of his death, he had become the world's leading academic authority on the topic. It was indeed to this area that he most successfully applied his deeply held beliefs about the law. That it should be transparently rational, coherent and elegant; that rigorous classification of the divisions within the law was crucial to orderly thinking; that confusing language and, even worse, legal fictions[44] should be excised; and that the law should be described in analytically precise language that illuminated, rather than obfuscated, its essential elements. Since Birks devoted so much of his working life to revising and refining his thinking on the subject, our account of his work must be correspondingly more detailed.

The long-neglected and little explored English law of restitution provided the perfect raw material for his approach. When Birks first became interested in the subject in the late 1960s, the first book on the English law of restitution, *The Law of Restitution* by Robert Goff (sometime Fellow of Lincoln College, Oxford, and later to become a Lord of Appeal in Ordinary) and Gareth Jones (Fellow of Trinity College, Cambridge) had only just been published (in 1966). They had seen and shown that underpinning a mass of apparently disparate cases, both in common law and in equity, was the principle that the unjust enrichment of a defendant at the expense of a claimant should be reversed. In other words, in line with Civil Law jurisdictions and as recognised in 1937 in the United States *Restatement of Restitution*, Goff and Jones persuasively argued that, while it was rare for the judges expressly to acknowledge that this was what was happening, English law did grant restitution of unjust enrichments. Even though it also included aspects of property law, the law of restitution was therefore a third major category of the law of obligations, alongside contract and tort.

---

[43] See below section 4, 'The Civilian Conversion'.
[44] See above, n. 29.

If Goff and Jones could justifiably be said to have 'created' the subject in England, it was Birks's work, especially in providing a rigorous and illuminating conceptual structure for the subject, which triggered the huge modern academic interest in it. His work in a rapidly developing area of law also brought him into contact with, and to prominence among, judges and practitioners, most of whom had not previously encountered his work as a Roman law scholar. While Peter had no wish to join them, he found this direct contact with members of the practising profession stimulating. It also meant that his message on the merits of transparent rationality in the law had a wider and significantly different audience than if it had been confined to the classroom and the groves of academe.

Birks's writings on the law of restitution/unjust enrichment were, by any standards, prolific albeit that, by today's RAE-induced expectations, he started slowly. In retrospect, his publications in this area can be conveniently divided into four main phases: (1) early exploration (1971–82); (2) the unjust factors and quadration scheme (1983–97); (3) the misnomer and multi-causality adjustments (1998–2002); (4) his civilian conversion (2003–5).

(1) Early exploration (1971–82)

Birks's publications on restitution in this early period were almost exclusively the published versions of public lectures delivered in the Current Legal Problems series at University College London. There were five of these, published in 1971, 1972, 1974, 1980, and 1982.[45] Birks's interest in the law of restitution was initially kindled by George Webber, who taught the subject at UCL. So, for this reason as well as his original connection with UCL, it is not surprising that Birks was such a regular contributor to the Current Legal Problems series. In contrast, it is a surprise, especially in the light of his later prodigious publication output, that, with only one exception (a 1976 article on the unrequested payment of another's debt, co-authored with Jack Beatson)[46] he did not initially

---

[45] 'Negotiorum Gestio and the Common Law', Current Legal Problems, 24 (1971), 110–32; 'The Recovery of Carelessly Mistaken Payments', Current Legal Problems, 25 (1972), 179–99; 'Restitution for Services', Current Legal Problems, 27 (1974), 13–36; 'Restitution from Public Authorities', Current Legal Problems, 33 (1980) 191–211; 'Restitution for Wrongs', Current Legal Problems, 35 (1982), 53–76.

[46] 'Unrequested Payment of Another's Debt', Law Quarterly Review, 92 (1976), 188–212.

publish on restitution other than through a Current Legal Problems lecture.

The first three Current Legal Problems lectures in the early 1970s follow a similar pattern. We see Birks's desire to articulate a clear scheme that rationally links decided cases back to unjust enrichment; his careful use of legal history; his reliance on analogical reasoning, most especially in arguing that what applies to the restitution of money must also apply to the restitution of the value of services; and his willingness to offer rational reinterpretations of past cases (e.g. the novel argument in his 1972 article on 'Negotiorum Gestio and the Common Law'[47] that *Craven-Ellis v Canons Ltd*[48] was best understood as a case on necessary services and inevitable expense saved). By the third of the articles we have Birks's first fully articulated conceptual scheme, which drew a distinction in the common law between 'weak quasi-contract' and 'strong quasi-contract'. The former dealt with non-contractual requested or freely accepted services; the latter with payments and other benefits that were, objectively, unequivocally beneficial. Weak quasi-contract was thought to be closer than strong quasi-contract to contract, because it did rely to an extent on the defendant's 'will'. There was no possibility of arguing that strong quasi-contract was part of contract whereas, at this stage in his thinking, Birks thought that it might be plausible to regard weak quasi-contract as contractual: hence the labels 'weak' and 'strong'.

As we have already mentioned, Birks was by now (the mid-1970s) teaching restitution on the Oxford BCL course along with Jack Beatson. Their co-authored article[49] argued that a debt is not automatically discharged by an unrequested payment, unless paid by compulsion (or probably by necessity) or if there has been free acceptance by the debtor. The then recent decision in *Owen v Tate*[50] was the particular focus of attention. This article contains the last published reference to Birks's 'strong' and 'weak' quasi-contract scheme. As this early scheme is less well-known than others that Birks devised in later years, it is worth setting out the succinct explanation of it in that article:

> This restitutionary right [for compulsory discharge of another's debt] is based on the conjunction of two elements, first, that the debtor defendant has received an unequivocal benefit; second, that the benefit was not conferred voluntarily by the intervener-plaintiff. It is a right whose genesis is wholly independent of

---

[47] *Current Legal Problems*, 24 (1971), 110–32.
[48] [1936] 2 KB 403.
[49] See above, n. 46.
[50] [1976] QB 402.

the will of the defendant and which is incapable of contractual analysis. It should be contrasted with the right, which a voluntary intervener has against an assenting debtor, which depends on the will of the defendant, manifested in his assent, and which will frequently be capable of analysis in terms of genuine implied contract. To facilitate the contrast between these differently generated rights, one of us has suggested the labels 'strong quasi-contract' for the former and 'weak quasi-contract' for the latter. It is a serious criticism of *Owen v Tate*, even if its result be right, that it does not adequately distinguish between these two different bases of the appellant's case.[51]

Although elements of that early scheme were to remain important to Birks's thinking, especially in deciding whether a defendant had been benefited, the division between weak and strong quasi-contract was in due course abandoned. This was no doubt because Birks came to see it as misleading, not only because of the fictional connotations of 'quasi-contract' but also because the scheme focused only on the common law and excluded equity. In view of his later strong advocacy of the need to see common law and equity juxtaposed within the same books,[52] it is perhaps surprising that in this early period he focused purely on the common law half of the picture. His early preoccupation with just the common law of restitution is further reflected in the fact that he approached the publishers of the Modern Legal Studies series in the early 1970s with the idea of a book on 'quasi-contract'. No doubt, in hindsight he would have regarded the publishers' rejection of that inadequately titled proposal as a blessing in disguise.

As we have already noted, perhaps because of his problems in his private life, in terms of publications the late 1970s were remarkably unproductive for Birks. Indeed he produced only one article in a four-year period (1977–80) and that was the written version of his Current Legal Problems lecture on 'Restitution from Public Authorities'.[53] In that article, Birks skilfully and persuasively exposed the inadequacies of the duress explanation of restitution from public authorities although, in contrast to his later, hugely influential, work on this topic, at this stage he stopped just short of advocating a full-blown right of a citizen to restitution of money demanded *ultra vires* by a public authority.

The last of Birks's publications in this early exploratory era was the most important. It was another Current Legal Problems lecture—this

---

[51] *Law Quarterly Review*, 92 (1976), 188, 207–8.
[52] See, e.g., his final book review in *Law Quarterly Review*, 120 (2004), 344–8.
[53] *Current Legal Problems*, 33 (1980), 191–211.

time on 'Restitution and Wrongs'.[54] Here we see an ever more confident Birks forging the distinction, which was to become so central to his thinking, between restitution of unjust enrichment by subtraction and restitution for wrongs. Prior to that article many had realised that 'waiver of tort' was a misleading description because in waiving a tort a claimant rarely excuses it. Few, however, had realised, with the clarity that Birks's account brought, that waiver of tort covered two fundamentally different routes to restitution. The first and usual way of 'waiving the tort' was to found one's claim to restitution by establishing the tort and then seeking restitution rather than the more usual response of compensation. The second was to found one's claim not on the tort but rather on unjust enrichment as an independent cause of action. At this stage Birks saw both areas as underpinned by the generic conception of unjust enrichment and as therefore falling within the law of restitution, the distinction between them turning on the different meanings of 'at the expense of': by committing a tort (or other wrong) to the claimant; and by subtraction from the claimant. As we shall now see, this was to be one of the central themes of the book that was to make his name.

(2) The unjust factors and quadration scheme (1983–97)

By the early 1980s Birks had devised and, in his teaching on the BCL, had tested out a sophisticated and elegant scheme for understanding the English law of restitution, both at common law and in equity. Now all he had to do was to write it down. The completion of this task, which he had begun while still at Brasenose, preoccupied him in the hours which he could devote to the subject during his early years in Edinburgh.[55]

The end product was his highly acclaimed *An Introduction to the Law of Restitution* published by the Clarendon Press in 1985. Birks was riddled with self-doubt as to its worth and told friends that he had seriously contemplated throwing the manuscript off the Forth Road Bridge. He need not have worried. The book was a huge success. As Derek Davies said in his review, 'The book is intended to be, and is, seminal'.[56] Up to this time, while Birks had built a reputation as a brilliant and challenging teacher, especially on the BCL restitution course, he was principally known among the academic fraternity as a Roman law scholar. His writ-

---

[54] *Current Legal Problems*, 35 (1982), 53–76.
[55] For his large output on Roman law at this time, see the text accompanying nn. 22–32 above.
[56] J. D. Davies, Review, *Lloyd's Maritime and Commercial Law Quarterly* [1986], 540, 541.

ten output on restitution had been relatively modest and his articles in *Current Legal Problems* did not have the wide readership of articles in journals such as the *Law Quarterly Review*, the *Cambridge Law Journal* or the *Modern Law Review*. His name was not well-known to most students or to the judges or practising profession. The book changed all that. Before long, his dramatic and unique style of prose and his search for rational transparency were capturing the imagination of scholars, students and judges all over the world. As Professor Robert Chambers, a Canadian who was later to write a D.Phil. under Birks, has expressed it: 'I had never before encountered a book like it. Although I had received a good basic legal education, it was on a minor scale: an understanding of particular rules in particular contexts. No one had asked the big questions about the organisation of the law as a whole and the relationships between the constituent parts. No one had analysed the law with such clarity and logic.'[57]

The book took the raw material of the law of restitution, painstakingly unearthed by Goff and Jones, and gave it a clear and readily understandable conceptual structure. This involved separating out three main questions. (1) Was the defendant enriched (the 'benefit' question)? (2) Was the enrichment at the claimant's expense (the 'at the expense of' question)? (3) Was the enrichment at the claimant's expense unjust (the 'unjust' question)? Each of those three questions was then linked back to the black letter law in the cases by clearly articulated, and freshly labelled, concepts.

So on the first question, because a defendant can 'subjectively devalue' objective benefits, it was important to establish either that the defendant had been 'incontrovertibly benefited' or that he had 'freely accepted' the benefit. In relation to the 'at the expense of' question, there was a fundamental division between the 'subtractive' and the 'wrongdoing' senses: and within the former, one needed to recognise 'interceptive' as well as direct subtraction. Finally, and most importantly, the unjust question was to be answered by the claimant establishing an 'unjust factor'. In respect of restitution for wrongs, the unjust factor was the wrong. For the bulk of restitution, where one was concerned with unjust enrichment by subtraction, the unjust factors were divided into three main types. First, and principally, there were unjust factors that vitiated or qualified the claimant's voluntariness or consent in making a transfer. These included mistake, compulsion, and failure of consideration. Secondly, there was

---

[57] 'Resulting Trusts' in *Mapping the Law* (n. 1), pp. 247, 248.

the unjust factor of 'free acceptance'. This meant that a defendant had stood by, allowing a benefit to be conferred on him, knowing that the claimant expected to be paid for it. Free acceptance was unique in operating both as an unjust factor and as a test of benefit. Finally, there were unjust factors which led to 'policy-motivated restitution'. These unjust factors were miscellaneous policies dictating restitution such as 'no taxation without Parliament' and 'discouragement of illegal conduct'.

It can be seen that the scheme, using fresh and analytically tight labelling, was logical, simple and clear. It covered both common law and equity and it enabled one to see easily how the 'generic conception' of unjust enrichment brought together, through a layer of more specific principles and concepts, the black letter law in the cases. For Birks, the unjust enrichment was 'downward-looking' in the sense that he saw it primarily as an organising tool for the existing law rather than as an 'upward-looking' principle for the development of the law.

Birks's willingness to use new precise language to explain what the judges were doing, even if they had not expressed it in the same way as he did, is a hallmark of his book and indeed of all his later work. Some critics disliked it, arguing that it produced a jargon understood only by those steeped in the Birksian scheme. In reality, while new, it was straightforward and illuminating language that cut through some of the traditional obscure terminology used by the judiciary. Time has proved those critics wrong, for much of his distinctive terminology is now in standard use not only among academics but also among judges and practitioners.

The devising of a new scheme for understanding this area of the law captured the imagination of many lawyers, for whom the necessary combination of traditional doctrinal skills and a pioneering spirit proved irresistible. There was a shared belief that a new subject was being created which the English judges would soon inevitably have to recognise. Birks captured the spirit of the times, with the following passage written on the fly-sheet of his book:

> Restitution is an area of the law no smaller and no less important than, say Contract, Tort, or Trusts. A series of intellectual and historical accidents has, however, scattered its raw material to the fringes of other subjects. Homes have been found for it under dishonest or opaque labels; quasi-contract . . . constructive trust, money had and received, and so on. Dispersed in this way, Restitution has escaped the revolution in legal learning which has happened over the past century. It has been the age of the textbook. Successive editions have settled the case-law of other subjects into well-tried and now familiar patterns. The case-law of Restitution remains disorganized: its textbooks have only just begun to be written . . . It is the last major area to be mapped and in some

sense the most exciting subject in the modern canon. There is everything to play for.

Two features of the scheme stand out. The first is that the unjust question was answered by the claimant needing to establish an unjust factor. Birks saw this as the distinctive approach of the common law in contrast to civilian systems where, once it was established that there was an enrichment at the claimant's expense, restitution would follow unless the defendant could show that there was a 'juristic basis' for the enrichment. In this he was very much reflecting the approach in Goff and Jones and what he saw as a list of some unjust factors first referred to by Lord Mansfield in *Moses v Macferlan*.[58] The second outstanding feature is that unjust enrichment and restitution were two sides of the same coin. There was a 'quadration' between them. Unjust enrichment did not generate any responses other than restitution. One could therefore refer equally appropriately to the law of restitution or to the law of unjust enrichment.

Once the book was published, and with his personal life now stable and happy, Birks's output of articles, case notes and essays on restitution soared.[59] He published his views, often almost immediately, on virtually every new restitutionary development; and areas of the law that had escaped his detailed attention in the book were now addressed in articles. It was as if he were on a missionary-like crusade to convert sceptics to the newly accessible, long-neglected, creed of restitution; and it was all tremendously exciting, not least because judges too had caught the restitutionary bug.

In 1989 he produced a revised paperback version of his book. Unusually, this was not a second edition. Rather, the original text was left untouched apart from the correction of an unseemly number of typographical errors. Perhaps not altogether successfully, changes in the law were collected in a series of endnotes.

Still awaited was a case that would enable the House of Lords authoritatively to recognise in England the new law of restitution based on unjust enrichment. The opportunity came, and was taken, in *Lipkin Gorman v Karpnale Ltd*[60] in 1991 with, fittingly, the leading speech being given by Lord Goff.

---

[58] (1760) 2 Burr 1005.

[59] Between 1987 and 1997 he published on restitution alone a book, some 14 contributions to edited books and some 38 articles and case-notes. See 'The Publications of Peter Birks' compiled by Eric Descheemaeker in *Mapping the Law* (n. 1), pp. 641–51.

[60] [1991] 2 AC 548.

From his deluge of publications in this period, there are two articles that merit special mention. The first was his masterly examination of the law on 'knowing receipt', as it had conventionally been called, in his 1989 article, 'Misdirected Funds: Restitution from the Recipient'.[61] This was a prime example of the force of his analytical and analogical reasoning in creatively linking together apparently disparate cases in common law and equity. A restitutionary analysis of this area had not been attempted previously, but the article showed for the first time that, whatever other claims there might be, at the core of the facts in a knowing receipt case is the defendant's unjust enrichment at the claimant's expense, with the unjust factor being ignorance. Hence there was no good reason for insisting on fault-based liability. Rather, the facts were analogous to a mistaken payment and logic dictated that, as with that central restitutionary claim, liability for the receipt of misdirected funds should be strict, subject to protecting the recipient by recognising a change of position defence. Although English law still does not recognise that the recipient of misdirected funds should be strictly liable to make restitution, Birks's thesis has been essentially accepted by eminent judges writing extra-judicially.[62] It seems only a matter of time before it will be accepted authoritatively by the courts.

A second article of especial importance was his contribution to a seminar on Restitution organised by Professor Paul Finn in Canberra in September 1989. Birks's essay, 'Restitution from the Executive: a Tercentenary Footnote to the Bill of Rights',[63] boldly argued that a citizen was entitled, as of right, to restitution of money demanded *ultra vires* by a public authority. At the time when he wrote, *Woolwich Building Society v IRC*[64] had reached the Court of Appeal. The reversal of the decision by the House of Lords owed much to the Birks essay, as Lord Goff generously acknowledged in the leading speech. The decision in *Woolwich* therefore constituted a rare example of judges and jurists working very closely together to produce a significant advance in the common law. Birks believed passionately in co-operative enterprise and that belief lay behind the series of Saturday seminars on various subjects, and involving academics, judges and practitioners, which he selflessly organ-

---

[61] *Lloyd's Maritime and Commercial Law Quarterly*, [1989] 296–341.

[62] See, e.g., Lord Nicholls, 'Knowing Receipt: The Need for a New Landmark' in W. R. Cornish *et al.* (eds.), *Restitution: Past, Present and Future: Essays in Honour of Gareth Jones* (Oxford, 1998), pp. 231–50.

[63] P. Finn (ed.), *Essays on Restitution* (North Ryde, NSW, 1990), pp. 164–205.

[64] [1989] 1 WLR 137, CA.; [1993] AC 70, HL.

ised in All Souls under the aegis of the SPTL.[65] Although he was too modest to see it in these terms, *Woolwich* was a glorious triumph for him.

Two further publications from his prodigious output in the early 1990s should be highlighted. The first was his short book, *Restitution—The Future*, which was largely conceived and written while he was visiting Australia and Hong Kong in 1990 and 1991. It pulled together developments in Birks's thinking on some central themes in the law of restitution. In particular, we see, in the first chapter, Birks forging an ever sharper distinction between restitution of unjust enrichment ('In time, this is what will be called, for short, Unjust Enrichment')[66] and restitution for wrongs.

The second of these publications was his initial analysis of the swaps cases that were to dominate restitutionary litigation in England from 1993 to the end of the decade and were not only to be a rich source of interest for academics but were also to lead to several important developments in the law (especially the removal of the mistake-of-law bar). Writing in 1993,[67] Birks criticised the idea, put forward at first instance by Hobhouse J in *Westdeutsche Landesbank Girozentrale v Islington BC*,[68] that 'absence of consideration' was an unjust factor. He argued that that was merely masking the truth that restitution was being granted for mistake or failure of consideration. As something of an afterthought he added to footnote 137 a comment to the effect that mistake could not justify restitution in a 'closed swap' (fully executed on both sides) because the effect of the mistake had by then been spent and there was no prejudice to the payor. By now Birks was held in such high esteem that when the first swaps case—the *Westdeutsche* case—reached the House of Lords, their Lordships spent a considerable time discussing that footnote before ultimately rejecting it.[69]

The early and mid-1990s were golden years for Birks. Restitution was the sexy academic subject in English private law and new case law was coming thick and fast. Birks was at the centre of it all. His ideas were being debated not only on the BCL and in other courses around the globe but also in the courts. In 1995 his importance to the world of practice was appropriately recognised by his appointment as an honorary Queen's

---

[65] The contributions were published in various volumes which Birks edited for the Oxford University Press, e.g. *The Frontiers of Liability*, vols. 1 and 2 (Oxford, 1994).

[66] *Restitution—The Future* (Annandale, NSW, 1992), p. 2.

[67] 'No Consideration—Restitution after Void Contracts', *University of Western Australia Law Review*, 23 (1993), 195–234.

[68] [1994] 4 All ER 890.

[69] [1996] AC 669.

Counsel. Catching the mood, Birks persuaded Francis Rose to set up a new journal dedicated to restitution, the *Restitution Law Review*. The first edition was published in 1994 and contained Sir Peter Millett's article on the restitution of bribes which was almost immediately cited by the Privy Council in *Attorney General for Hong Kong v Reid*[70]—something of a record for a new publication. Some academics found all the attention being paid to the law of restitution difficult to understand. It was predicted by some—inaccurately as it turned out—that it was a South Sea Bubble that was about to burst.

More seriously, Birks's work attracted fierce critics, the most vociferous of whom was Steve Hedley, then a don at Cambridge, who derided Birks and those who supported him as rule-formalists seeking to impose unnatural order on open-textured legal reasoning.[71] Birks met such criticisms head-on and continued to argue the case for rational transparency and coherence in the law with his unique brand of learned, logical and passionate argument.

(3) The 'misnomer' and 'multi-causality' adjustments (1997– 2001)

Birks had always been deeply interested in the taxonomy of the law. Gaius' Institutes had been instrumental in drawing him to restitution[72] and he increasingly found inspiration from modern civilian law, especially the law of Germany, where matters of doctrinal classification were taken much more seriously than had been usual in the common law system. So it was that, looking across English private law as a whole, he became convinced that the fundamental division he had drawn between restitution for unjust enrichment and restitution for wrongs meant that the two were not best regarded as part of the same subject. The 'generic conception' of unjust enrichment cut across what he had come to regard as the crucial and illuminating division between 'events' that happened in the world and legal 'responses' (by the creation of rights) to those events. Unjust enrichment was an event. Restitution was a response. The traditional way of classifying the law—and for Birks the best way—was by event. Increasingly his writings came to emphasise a four-fold categorisation of events in English private law into 'consent, wrongs, unjust enrich-

---

[70] [1994] 1 AC 324.
[71] See, e.g., 'Unjust Enrichment', *Cambridge Law Journal*, 54 (1995), 578–99.
[72] See the text accompanying nn. 37–42 above.

ment and others'.[73] Responses, in contrast, included compensation, punishment and restitution.

Moreover, Birks came to the view that it was incorrect to regard restitution as triggered only by unjust enrichment and wrongs. Rather, restitution could be triggered by consent (as where one promises to pay back a loan that one has received) or by other miscellaneous events.

In the light of these developments in his thinking, two vital adjustments were needed to the scheme set up in *An Introduction to the Law of Restitution*.

First, the name of the subject, and of the book, was incorrect. As an independent subject, it was the event of unjust enrichment that one was concerned with, not the response of restitution. The subject should therefore be called 'unjust enrichment'. Originating in the United States *Restatement of Restitution* in 1937, and followed through by Goff and Jones and by himself, restitution had been the wrong choice of name.

Secondly, unjust enrichment and restitution did not quadrate. His 'quadration thesis', described in section (2) above, was misleading and should be abandoned. Although unjust enrichment triggered only restitution, restitution was 'multi-causal' and could be triggered by consent, wrongs and a variety of other events as well as by unjust enrichment.

In 1997 a conference was held in Cambridge to mark the imminent retirement of Professor Gareth Jones. Birks chose that occasion, packed with 'restitution lawyers', not least Goff and Jones, to present the two major adjustments to his scheme in his paper 'Misnomer'.[74] Those who attended the conference will recall the dramatic impact of Birks, now the guru of the subject, passionately arguing that, along with just about all those present, he had been talking about the wrong subject. It is hard to disagree with Mitchell McInnes's nomination (at the meeting of the Society of Legal Scholars in 2003)[75] of 'Misnomer' as the most important article on the law of restitution of the previous decade.

Many could not see that these adjustments really mattered. Surely this was all a question of terminology? There were mutterings that Birks was becoming too obsessed for his own good with taxonomy. After all, we all knew what we meant by the law of restitution. However, for Birks correct

---

[73] This four-fold classification was actually first put forward by him when discussing rights *in rem* in *An Introduction to the Law of Restitution*, p. 53. For the full picture of his thinking on this, see e.g., his Introduction to *English Private Law* (Oxford, 2000), xli–xlii, and *Unjust Enrichment*, 2nd edn. (Oxford, 2005) ch. 2.

[74] In *Restitution: Past, Present and Future* (n. 62), p. 1.

[75] M. McInnes, 'Misnomer: a Classic', *Restitution Law Review* [2004], 79–95.

classification was essential to orderly reasoning. It mattered a great deal that one's concepts were accurately and precisely labelled. Muddle and confusion would otherwise follow and, in turn, incorrect decision-making, even if only occasionally, would be the inevitable consequence. If the map was wrong, it had to be redrawn before someone got lost.

In the publications which followed that article, as he had done in the previous period, Birks took every opportunity to preach the merits of the 'multi-causal misnomer' message in the context of his 'consent, wrongs, unjust enrichment and others' picture of the events triggering rights in English private law. Indeed, branching out from unjust enrichment, his wider map of English private law led on to the ambitious project of producing a multi-authored two-volume overview of the principles of English law, structured in line with a classification that had its roots in Gaius' Institutes. Published under his general editorship in 2000, *English Private Law* (and its sister volume *English Public Law*) is a magisterial work that deserves wider acclaim than it has so far been afforded.

One other development in his thinking on unjust enrichment during this period is also worthy of mention. 'Free acceptance' as an unjust factor had been controversial from the outset and had been attacked by several academics. Having initially tried to defend it as based on 'unconscientious receipt', Birks came to think that it was best confined to its role as a test of benefit. This broke the final link with his early idea of 'weak quasi-contract'.[76] All the law of unjust enrichment except 'policy-motivated restitution' was 'claimant-sided' and sharply distinct from liability based on the will of the defendant. Abandoning free acceptance made the scheme of *An Introduction* even more elegant and straightforward: unjust factors either went to non-voluntariness (you must repay because 'I didn't mean it') or were policy reasons (you must repay because 'Mother says so').[77]

The most refined statement of Birks's adjusted scheme for unjust enrichment and its relationship to restitution was set out in six lectures which he gave as Visiting Fellow at Wellington in 1999 and published as a short book, *The Foundations of Unjust Enrichment*, in 2002.

One particular jurisdiction that Birks thought it important to try to convert to his adjusted scheme was the United States. After decades of neglect, work had begun on a new *Restatement of Restitution* under the

---

[76] See above section 1, Early exploration.
[77] For Birks's use of this nursery language, to stress how simple his scheme was, see P. Birks and R. Chambers, *The Restitution Research Resource*, 2nd edn. (Oxford, 1997), p. 2.

leadership of the chief reporter, Professor Andrew Kull. In 2001 a conference was convened in Texas largely, it would seem, to enable Birks to
argue his case, which he did with customary vigour in his paper 'Unjust
Enrichment and Wrongful Enrichment'.[78] This was followed a couple of
years later with 'A Letter to America'.[79] It was a disappointment to Birks
that those responsible for the *Restatement* did not accept his arguments
or at least did not think that they were sufficiently crucial to necessitate
the abandonment of language that had been used ever since the first
Restatement. It seems likely that the only concession to Birks's thinking
will be to adjust the title of the *Third Restatement*[80] so that it includes
both restitution and unjust enrichment. For Birks that would have
represented an unsatisfactory muddle.

(4) The civilian conversion (2003–5)

One might have thought that Birks's adjustments to the scheme in *An
Introduction* were dramatic enough. They were to be dwarfed, however, by
the final stage of the Birks story. At one time he had been contemplating
putting together a large practitioners' textbook. Instead, he decided to
write a book, in the Clarendon Law Series (of which he had become the
general editor), but under what he now saw as the correct title of 'Unjust
Enrichment'. It would appear that he initially intended to set out his
adjusted scheme along the lines of *The Foundations of Unjust Enrichment*
(the short book referred to above). Comparative law would be used to
show how the common law 'unjust factors' approach and the civilian
'absence of basis' approach reached similar results. However, in the
course of writing the book in 2002 and 2003, Birks became convinced
that a version of the civilian approach was better and more truly
explained the cases than did the unjust factors scheme that he had spent
the best part of thirty years perfecting. So it was that he announced himself a convert to 'absence of basis'. Indeed—and not necessarily correctly—he went further and argued that in the swaps cases the English
courts had already switched to that approach. In his now famous, or infa-
mous, preface to the first edition of *Unjust Enrichment*, published in 2003,
we see him facing up squarely to the enormity of his change of sides:

---

[78] 'Unjust Enrichment and Wrongful Enrichment', *Texas Law Review*, 79 (2001), 1767–94.
[79] *Global Jurist Frontiers*, 3 (2003).
[80] This is due for completion in 2010.

> Almost everything of mine now needs calling back for burning. St Paul was rel-atively lucky. In one flash of blinding light he knew that he must change sides. In the university the awful sense of having been wrong comes on more slowly and with it the still more awful realization that one must befriend those whom one has persecuted and persecute those who are one's friends. But universities are for getting to the bottom of things, come what may. Public apostasies may ruin a reputation and thus cost a merit point or two, but that cannot be helped. I dare not say that I am finally error-free, but in my view, for whatever it may still be worth, this butterfly, although it could certainly have been better depicted by another hand, is very beautiful and its emergence from the chrysalis of restitution is something to celebrate.

The book displays all the great features of Birks's writings: original ideas, depth of learning, rigorous reasoning and clarity of vision—and all in his unique succinct style of prose. In the months following publication, he continued to work on, and to refine, his new ideas, defending them with characteristic robustness not only in his BCL seminars but also at a specially convened academic symposium in Oxford in January 2004.[81] As we have seen,[82] this led to his decision that, despite ever-failing health, he must produce a slightly revised version of the new scheme. So it was that, a few days before his death, he completed a second edition that was published posthumously in 2005.

It remains to be seen whether the new Birksian scheme will be accepted by the courts. At the time of writing, academic argument rages over whether Birks Mark 2 (the 'New Testament') is to be preferred to Birks Mark 1 (the 'Old Testament').[83] In particular, 'absence of basis' can be criticised as superficially elegant and simple but as in practice throwing up a range of difficulties that are not encountered, or have already been solved, on the 'unjust factors' approach. As Professor Rose has written, 'The book is a cliff-hanger. Only time will tell whether this new world has been correctly predicted or will be built along these lines. If it is not, we shall never know whether theory might have been turned into practice by the force of Birks's intellect and personality.'[84] Certainly, past experience shows that Birks would have followed up the book with a torrent of articles and notes as he sought to explain further (and, yes, to refine still more) his new approach. He would perhaps have taken heart from *obiter*

---

[81] The papers were published in *Restitution Law Review*, [2004], 260–89
[82] At the end of our account of his career.
[83] These are labels commonly used by those teaching on the BCL Restitution course.
[84] 'The Evolution of the Species' in *Mapping the Law* (n. 1), pp. 13, 29.

dicta of Lord Walker of Gestingthorpe in the recent major restitution case, *Deutsche Morgan Grenfell Group plc v IRC*.[85] In paying fulsome tribute to Birks's contribution to the law of restitution, Lord Walker expressed tentative support for drawing the common law and civil law approaches together, using 'no basis' as a single unifying principle.[86]

Birks had an enormous impact on the law of restitution/unjust enrichment both in the universities and in the courts. Nevertheless, it is strongly arguable that his legendary reputation suffered because of his willingness to change his views. For example, at least one eminent judge, who greatly admired Birks, indicated nervousness about applying his opinions lest he should later depart from them, leaving the judge stranded. Birks recognised the problem but saw it as a necessary evil on the way to a better version of the truth. After all, he was an academic with a markedly different role from that of a judge—even though he greatly supported co-operation between judge and jurist. One wonders, however, whether at times his drive for clarity and his excitement at discovering and teaching new insights led him to overstate his changes of mind. In other words, if one stands back and looks at his work in this area as a whole, the changes are perhaps not as dramatic as Birks portrayed them to be. It is at least arguable that they were, by and large, incremental developments from, rather than reversals of, previously espoused positions. So it was that his early scheme, of strong and weak quasi-contract, led through to his unjust factors scheme which led in turn to his version of 'absence of basis'. It might have been possible for Birks not to risk losing the faith of the judges in the co-operative enterprise by presenting his final enthusiasm for the civilian approach as a development of the scheme of unjust factors rather than as a rejection of them. Indeed, although it is not reflected in the tone elsewhere, in one part of his book[87] he did try to set out a 'limited reconciliation' using the image of a pyramid with unjust factors at the bottom and 'absence of basis' at the top.

Birks was a truly great scholar. Apart from the advances that he himself made, his work inspired many other academics to follow in his footsteps. The 'Birksian school of thought' has pursued, and will continue to pursue, rational transparency and elegant coherence in legal reasoning not only in the law of restitution but across English private law generally.

---

[85] [2006] UKHL 49, [2006] 3 WLR 781.
[86] At para. 158. See also Lord Hoffmann at paras. 21 and 28.
[87] *Unjust Enrichment*, p. 116.

That is his greatest legacy and the one for which he would most have wanted to be remembered.

ALAN RODGER
Fellow of the Academy

ANDREW BURROWS
Fellow of the Academy

Note. We are grateful for the information provided by Brenda Allen, the Office Manager at Chislehurst & Sidcup Grammar School, by Clare Hopkins, the Archivist of Trinity College, Oxford, and by the Faculty of Laws, University College London. We would also wish to thank, in particular, Jackie Birks, Paul Mahoney and Bill Swadling for commenting on earlier drafts of the text and for providing us with their recollections.

WILLIAM FREND

William Hugh Clifford Frend
1916–2005

WILLIAM HUGH CLIFFORD FREND was born on 11 January 1916, the second son of the Revd E. G. C. Frend, Vicar of Shottermill in Surrey.[1] His mother, Edith née Bacon, was the daughter of a progressive general practitioner, one of the first to have a telephone installed. A sister of his mother was the first woman to become an alderman in Leeds. William Frend 1757–1841,[2] a great great-uncle, was deprived of his fellowship at Jesus College, Cambridge, because of his Unitarian and generally left-wing views at the time of the French Revolution,[3] though he continued to receive the income of the fellowship until he got married. Whether genes running through the Frend family had anything to do with it or not, the theme of dissent was always central to Frend's projects of research. The themes investigated by him usually involved controversy over the nature of the Church and its dealing with diversity, above all the question whether the Church should set itself to be a society of saints, a 'gathered Church' as he called it, or a society of both saints and sinners living in the

---

[1] In 1932, when he found Shottermill getting too much, he opted for the livings at Tyneham and Steeple in the Isle of Purbeck, where he stayed for the remaining four years of his life.

[2] The father of this William Frend was a wine merchant and twice mayor of Canterbury.

[3] He was author (among much else that was both radical and interesting) of: *An address to inhabitants of Cambridge and of its neighbourhood, exhorting them to turn from false worship of three persons to the worship of the one true God*, 1st edn. (St Ives, 1788); *Scarcity of bread, a plan for reducing the high price of this article in a letter addressed by William Frend to William Devaynen* (London, 1795); *Peace and union recommended to the associated bodies of republicans and anti-republicans* (Cambridge, 1793). See *The trial of William Frend MA, fellow of Jesus College, Cambridge in the vice chancellor's court for publishing a pamphlet entitled peace and union, by John Beverley, proctor of the vice chancellor's court* (Cambridge, 1793). A biography: Frida Knight, *University Rebel: the Life of William Frend 1751–1841* (London, 1971).

Proceedings of the British Academy, **150**, 37–54. © The British Academy 2007.

world and making compromises with it. He was obviously also very much interested in different attitudes taken by individual Christians and by different groups of Christians towards 'the powers that be'.

William Frend was the youngest by seven years of a family of four children (two sisters and two brothers). In his biographical notes he wrote: 'I never heard a rough word between my father and my mother, and while I was a bit of an outsider, the rest of the family, plus cousins, were very united . . . I had a French governess when I was four . . . I was also beginning to be interested in archaeology. This was partly due to the age gap separating me from other members of the family. At times my parents had little idea what to do with me when the rest of the family was at home. The museum (at Haslemere) was the answer.' The curator was E. W. Swanton, who had transformed a miscellaneous collection of flints and stuffed birds into a museum with stimulating displays illustrating geological time and world history from the Mesolithic to the expansion of Britain in the nineteenth century. It fired Frend's imagination.

Frend was educated as a boarder at Fernden Peparatory School, Haslemere, a school to which he later felt that he owed an enormous debt, and then went on to Haileybury 1929–34, where he won an exhibition, and later a scholarship. He remembered his form-master J. Hampden Jackson, 'a genius as a teacher and an inspiring, rather leftward, personality', who was an expert on Central Europe and Finland, and knew a great deal about economic history. Frend appreciated the freedom senior boys were given at that school. He was allowed to excavate in the garden of the local station master, and he and Christopher Mayhew circulated as a discussion paper for the sixth form, a left-wing, anti-public school journal called *Out of Bounds*. Frend's school record was not particularly distinguished, but in 1934 he won an open scholarship to Keble College.

Looking back, Frend felt that the scholarship had been the turning point in his life. In addition to his study for Honours Schools, in 1934 and 1935 Frend took part as a volunteer in Mortimer Wheeler's dig at Maiden Castle. He duly gained a first class in Modern History with examiners' congratulations in 1937. He decided to go on to take a D.Phil. This was the time of the Spanish Civil War and Frend sided strongly with the republican government. So there need be no surprise that he chose as his subject the Donatists of Roman North Africa, with his sympathies favouring the supposed heretics as against St Augustine their great opponent. Hugh Last and Norman Baynes were his supervisors. Baynes became a friend, and his advice to the budding academic was remembered: 'Be generous but not lavish with footnotes. Always give credit where it is due. End a critical review on a positive note. Our students have first call on our assistance. Research must seek to meet the needs of each new generation of scholars.' Frend's father died in 1937, the year he graduated, and he and his mother were left on slender resources. Frend now depended on grants and scholarships. Haileybury helped with a grant of £200. However, he also managed to win a Craven Fellowship which enabled him to gain wider experience and background knowledge for his research by travelling. It was on the advice of Baynes that he spent the year 1937–8 in Berlin studying under Hans Lietzmann.

In Berlin Frend lived with a Jewish family while attending the Friedrich Wilhelm, now Humboldt, University as a *Gasthörer*. Lietzmann was at that time the leading representative of the German tradition of ecclesiastical history established by A. von Harnack. In his last book, *From Dogma to History: how an understanding of the Early Church developed* (London, 2003), Frend expressed his gratitude to von Harnack and Lietzmann,

> Theirs was a movement from Dogma to History. My work has been decisively influenced by these scholars . . . I have attempted to build on their foundations, to integrate the study of the mission and thought of early Christian Churches into the social and political movements of the day . . . I have taken Adolf von Harnack (1851–1930) as the founder of the new approach to early Church history. He was a scholar who cut through some of the niceties of Lutheran ecclesiastical law to a truth based on a minimum of credal statements, and on acceptance, as he put it, of the fatherhood of God and the brotherhood of man revealed in the New Testament . . . He believed that a scholar should also be a 'doer' in the service of his Church.

The Harnack tradition held a strong but non-dogmatic allegiance to Christianity. It sought religious truth, or more exactly the values and the essential nature of religion, through historical research. The approach was conservative and patriotic, but at the same time also called for a strong social conscience. It was obviously extremely congenial to one side of Frend's personality, a side which complemented the radical and rebellious instincts which he shared with his eighteenth-century great great-uncle.

Lietzmann did Frend another important service: he gave him a letter of introduction to his friend Louis Poinssot, the Director General of Antiquities for Tunisia, who later introduced him to André Berthier.[4]

---

[4] Cf. Frend's review of A. Berthier and colleagues, *Les vestiges du Christianisme antique dans la Numidie centrale,* in *Journal of Roman Studies,* 34 (1944), 152–3.

Frend visited many archaeological sites in Tunisia and later in Algeria, and also was given the opportunity to do some archaeological work himself. In this way he gained first-hand experience of the archaeological remains which were to figure so largely in his book on the Donatists, and at the same time he was impressed by the way French archaeologists from Gsell to Berthier applied archaeology to history. Frend came to feel that archaeological evidence was enormously important to counterbalance the overwhelming 'orthodoxy' of the surviving written sources.[5] In a report to the Foreign Office the British consul in Tunis wrote that Frend was an atheist and a Marxist. This was almost certainly no longer true. The consul, like many others later, failed to see the mischievous twinkle which often used to lighten Frend's argumentative conversation.[6] Frend also spent part of 1939 at the Sorbonne. By now he had started to publish in learned journals.[7]

Frend was in the Cadet Reserve, but he stood down in September 1939 to complete his thesis. He received his D.Phil. in 1940 on the day Paris fell. In 1940 he had a medical prior to call-up and was classified 'D', because he had still not fully recovered from a duodenal ulcer he had suffered in 1935. Thereupon, Frend was directed by the Ministry of Labour and National Service to the War Office (F.1) as Assistant Principal. Among other duties he wrote a report on water supplies in North Africa for the Inter Service Intelligence Survey. In April 1941 he was seconded to the Cabinet Office, and from then until August 1942 he served as Secretary to two Cabinet Committees dealing with Free French Forces, and with Allied supplies. He was then transferred to Political Intelligence in the Foreign Office, then stationed at Woburn Abbey. His task was to compile intelligence reports for use in propaganda in North Africa, mainly directed against the Vichy authorities. In August 1943 he was transferred to North Africa. In November he was promoted to be Head of 'D' Section (Intelligence) for the Psychological Warfare Branch in North Africa with his centre at Tunis. Frend recalls:

---

[5] *Saints and Sinners in the Early Church, differing and conflicting traditions in the first six centuries* (London, 1985), p. 176.

[6] See below, p. 52.

[7] His earliest publications were a review of Y. Allais, *Djemilla*, in *Journal of Roman Studies*, 28. 2 (1938), 254–5; 'The *memoriae apostolorum* in Roman North Africa', *Journal of Roman Studies*, 30 (1940), 32–49; and signifying the direction of his interests 'A note on the Berber background in the Life of Saint Augustine', *Journal of Theological Studies*, 43 (1942), 179–81 and 'The revival of Berber art', *Antiquity*, 15 (1942), 342–52.

The problems were obvious. By and large the Tunisians had favoured Rommel . . . Even after the surrender contact with influential Tunisians was a necessity. This meant Habib Bourguiba and his Neo-Destour . . . For five months all went well . . . but the French were suspicious . . . I found my position difficult . . . I was moved over to the German section of PWB. I always believe that my efforts helped secure good relations, which have continued to the present, with a progressive Arab state.

In April 1944 Frend was transferred to Italy. He served at Allied Forces Headquarters as Intelligence Officer in the German Section, successively at Caserta, Rome and Florence. After the capture of Rome, Frend took part in some extremely interesting and informative conversations with the staff of the German embassy, which led to von Weizsäcker, the German ambassador to the Vatican, cooperating with the allies, and to the embassy staff staying in Rome instead of being sent back to Germany.[8] Subsequently Frend served in the 5th Army PWB Combat Unit, with the US 92nd Division. His task was to broadcast front-line propaganda at the German 148th division opposite. This division had been recruited in Silesia and consequently included many Poles. Frend's propaganda persuaded significant numbers of these men to come over, and to join General Anders' army. As Intelligence Officer, among other duties, Frend had to interrogate German prisoners of war, including generals. Some of them suggested that Britain should now take over Germany and run it like its Empire.[9]

When Frend left Intelligence in 1946 he was uncertain about his future career. He applied for a place in the Foreign Office. A perceptive interviewer asked him whether he would not prefer to become a don. Frend's answer that this was certainly an idea evidently did not go down well, for he did not get in. He was, however, given a temporary job on the board responsible for editing German Foreign Ministry Documents 1947–51.[10] While engaged on this work in Berlin he spent spare time converting his D.Phil. thesis into the book which became *The Donatist Church.* When he was no longer needed for the editing of German documents the career of a don beckoned, though he may have hankered after a career in politics, for as late as 1966–7 he was chairman of the Cambridge City Liberal

[8] The British authorities were careful to prevent these conversations from turning into negotiations, which the Germans evidently hoped that they would. See Frend's account in *History Today*, 54.12 (2004), 62–3.

[9] After the war Frend held a territorial commission in the Queen's Royal Regiment from 1947 to 1967. He was awarded the TD in 1959, and a clasp in 1967.

[10] *Documents on German Foreign Policy*, Ser. C and D (London, HMSO, 1950–), special responsibility for vols. iii and iv in Series D.

Party, and Liberal candidate for the Market Ward. Whether he had such hankerings or not, in 1951 Frend applied for and obtained a research fellowship at Nottingham University.[11] There he did research on Manichaeism in North Africa, and revived a moribund archaeological society for staff and students.

On 2 June 1951 William Frend married Mary Grace, daughter of E. A. Crook FRCS. Mary was a very stable and sensible partner. She was perhaps more traditionally religious than her husband. She kept the home-fires burning, and her husband in order with good humour. They had a son (Simon) and a daughter (Sally). In 1952 Frend published *The Donatist Church*, probably his most influential book.[12] He had been engaged with this theme—on and off—since 1937. The book is remarkable for the lucid explanation of the surviving Donatist texts, and presents sympathetic portraits of the Donatist leaders, especially Donatus, Parmenian and Tyconius. It was a pioneering work in the way it relates the development of a religious movement to its political, social and economic contexts, as well as in the full use Frend made of the rich archaeological evidence from the Africa of the High Plains that had been revealed by the work of French archaeologists from Gsell to Berthier. Frend was now able to put into practice his conviction of the fundamental importance of archaeological research for understanding the spread and material culture of early Christianity, a conviction which informed not only all his subsequent writings, but also the teaching he gave to his students. *The Donatist Church* remains a model of how a subject of this kind should be treated.

Why, Frend asked, did a contested episcopal election to the see of Carthage create so profound and lasting a division in the African Church? Frend studied the geographical prevalence of the schism, and tried to relate the strength of its appeal to the ethnic, social, economic and cultural background of its followers, including what he thought were the linguistic divisions of the region. He decided that the principal division was between the peasants on the inland plains of Numidia, who were Donatists, and the inhabitants of the cities and towns nearer the coast, who were Catholics. He concluded that Donatism reflected the aspir-

---

[11] Memoir: 'Richard, Patrick, Crossland Hanson 1916–1988', *Proceedings of the British Academy*, 76 (1990), 411–22, on p. 416.
[12] Professor D. F. Wright comments on the title: 'The fact that he called *The Donatist Church*, what traditionally had been devalued as a "schism", points to another distinctive contribution, sympathetic attention to dissident, even under-dog movements, and the highlighting of the diversity, not to say divisiveness, of what is too often neatly referred to as "the Church".'

ations of the African under-privileged, that is of the relatively un-Romanised and, as he thought, self-consciously and linguistically Berber population, while Catholicism represented the Romanised bourgeoisie of the cities and the great landowners.

This clearly is a class-war model, and it is not surprising that many readers, like the consul at Tunis earlier, decided that Frend was a Marxist. The ethnic and social aspects of Frend's explanation of Donatism have been criticised with strong arguments.[13] In the words of Peter Brown: 'The issue at stake is not the protest of a particular group, but the autonomy of a provincial tradition of Christianity. . . . It was Constantine who provoked the struggle by allying the Empire with the universal Catholic Church.'[14] The idea that Donatism was basically a protest against an imposed urban and Latin civilisation cannot account for the fact that the Donatist leaders wrote in classical rhetorical Latin, and that it was led from thoroughly Roman centres like Carthage, Cirta and Timgad.[15] Frend never retracted his ethnic, social and political interpretation of Donatism,[16] but it is the case that in his later references to the subject Berbers and antagonism to Latin urban civilisation figure less prominently, and resistance to the imposition of the orthodoxy of the transmarine churches is given much greater emphasis.[17]

Frend's sociological model inevitably reflects the contemporary intellectual atmosphere. The view of an exploitative, and therefore hostile, relationship between classical city and the country is of course ultimately derived from Marx, but it was widely accepted among Frend's contemporaries. The theme of exploitation of the peasants by the landowners of the Graeco-Roman city ('idle mouths') is also prominent in A. H. M Jones's *Later Roman Empire*,[18] as also in the writings of M. I. Finley,[19]

---

[13] See (among others) Peter Brown, 'Religious dissent in the later Roman empire: the case of North Africa', *History*, 46 (1961), 83–101 = *Religion and Society in the Age of St Augustine* (London, 1972), pp. 237–59; R. A Markus, 'Christianity and dissent in Roman North Africa: changing perspectives in recent work', in D. Baker (ed.), *Studies in Church History, 9: Schism, Heresy and Religious Protest* (Cambridge, 1972), pp. 21–36 = *From Augustine to Gregory the Great*, Variorum Reprints (London, 1983), no. VIII.

[14] Brown, 'Religious Dissent', 97 = *Religion and Society*, p. 255.

[15] Markus, 'Christianity and dissent', 30; Peter Brown, 'Christianity and local culture in Late Roman North Africa', *Journal of Roman Studies*, 58 (1968), 85–95 = *Religion and Society*, pp. 279–300.

[16] *The Rise of Christianity* (London, 1984), pp. 654–5.

[17] *Saints and Sinners in the Ancient Church* (London, 1985), pp. 95–117.

[18] *The Later Roman Empire, a Social and Administrative Survey* (Oxford, 1964), esp. vol. 2, pp. 767–823.

[19] e.g. *The Ancient Economy* (London, 1973), pp. 86–93, 138–141.

who developed and simplified Max Weber's model of the 'consumer city'.[20] But when Frend was writing *The Donatist Church*, the most eloquent presentation of the conflict model of the relations between city-dwellers and peasants was that of Michael Rostovtzeff, in his famous *Social and Economic History of the Roman Empire,* where this model provides an explanation for the disaster of the third-century crisis.[21] Whatever the extent of the direct influence of Rostovtzeff, Frend's treatment of ecclesiastical history from a social and economic point of view is much closer to the manner of Rostovtzeff than to that of any of Frend's own contemporaries. Far from being a Marxist, Rostovtzeff was of course a refugee from the Marxist revolution. Frend was not a Marxist either, but his point of view differed from that of Rostovtzeff in that his sympathies were with what he thought were the rural protesters against an imposed Roman culture. One might add that Frend's account of Berber 'nationalism' was surely influenced by his experience of Neo-Destour in Tunisia, and of the various other independence movements which were at that time hastening the end of the European empires.

In the same year as he published *The Donatist Church*, Frend was elected a Fellow of the Society of Antiquaries. In the following two years (1952–3) Caius College awarded Frend an S. A. Cook Bye Fellowship, which enabled him to widen his archaeological knowledge by travel in Asia Minor.[22] In 1953 he was appointed Cambridge University Assistant Lecturer in Divinity.[23] In 1956 he was elected Fellow of Caius College, and he was Director of Studies in Archaeology and Ancient History from 1961–9. He served as University Pro-proctor for the years 1961–2 and 1967–8. Meanwhile Frend maintained his practical interest in archaeology by conducting a rescue excavation on the Arbury Road estate in 1953–4.[24] From 1956 to 1960 he was director of the excavations of a fifth-century church at Knossos under the auspices of the British School at

---

[20] Max Weber, *Economy and Society*, translated and edited by G. Roth and C. Wittich (New York, 1968), vol. 3, pp. 1215–17. The first edition of the posthumous German original, *Wirtschaft und Gesellschaft*, was edited by Marianne Weber and published at Tübingen in 1922. For Frend on Max Weber, see 'Die Bedeutung von Max Webers Aufsatz für die Untersuchung der frühen christlichen Sektenbewegung', in W. Schluchter (ed.), *Max Webers Sicht des antiken Christentums* (Frankfurt a. Main, 1985), pp. 466–88.

[21] *The Social and Economic History of the Roman Empire* (Oxford, 1926), pp. 442–8.

[22] 'A third-century inscription relating to *Angareia* in Phrygia', *Journal of Roman Studies*, 46 (1956), 46–56.

[23] His lectures became *The Early Church* (London, 1965), which is still much read, and annotated, by students.

[24] 'A Romano-British Settlement at Arbury Rd, Cambridge', *Proceedings Cambridge Antiquarian Society*, 48 (1955), 10–43; 'Further finds at Arbury Rd.', ibid., 49 (1956), 25–9.

Athens,[25] and during his sabbatical year 1963–4 he was Associate Director of the Egypt Exploration Society's excavation at Q'asr Ibrim, Nubia. Frend again took part in the excavation of that site in 1972 and 1974.[26]

It was Hugh Last who proposed that Frend should make the persecution of the Christians his next project, following up Last's own article on the legal aspects of the Persecutions (*Journal of Roman Studies*, 37 (1937), 80–92). Frend discussed the matter over tea with Norman Baynes, who was just recovering from a broken hip. It was their last meeting. Frend left Baynes with a sense of gratitude, and his mind made up.[27] So he started the research which was to lead to *Martyrdom and Persecution*. Frend's handling of the subject is closer to the manner of Baynes than to the legal and constitutional approach of Last, but essentially different from either. The book is in a sense an expansion of *The Donatist Church*. Instead of looking for an explanation of the Donatist schism in Africa, he now looked for roots of that controversy in the earlier history of Christianity, and its links with Judaism. The book offers a vast panorama. The concept of martyrdom as a primary means of salvation is traced back to the Jewish literature of the Maccabaean revolt. Frend suggests a parallel between the experience of the Jewish rigorists in Palestine and that of the rural protesters of North Africa, and of other Christian sectarians, above all the Phrygian Montanists. He argues that a strong Jewish presence in North Africa was a precondition for the rapid expansion of Christianity. Another Semitic religion appealed to the Berbers whose own religion had been Phoenician.

Alongside the Christian—and Jewish—traditions of protest and separation, Frend traces alternative Christian—and Jewish—traditions which saw no unbridgeable gap between themselves and the dominant Graeco-Roman society: he contrasts the separatist Maccabees, the Qumran Sect, Tatian, Tertullian, Cyprian and the Donatists with the more world-open Philo, Justin, Clement of Alexandria and Origen. He goes on to suggest that the eventual historical division between Eastern and Western Christianity had its roots in these two opposite

---

[25] 'A Byzantine Church at Knossos', *Papers of the British School at Rome*, 56 (1961), 186–238.
[26] 'Q'asr Ibrim 1963–64 Expedition', in *Acts of VII Congress of Christian Archaeology*, held at Trier 1965 (Rome, 1965), pp. 531–8; 'The podium at Q'asr Ibrim', *Journal of Egyptian Archaeology*, 60 (1974), 30–60; 'Recently discovered materials for writing the history of Christian Nubia', *Studies in Church History*, 11 (1975), 19–30; *The Archaeology of Early Christianity* (London, 1996), pp. 306–13.
[27] See *From Dogma to History*, p. 166.

traditions. The puritan and rigorous traditions of Africa contributed to the negative attitude to 'the World' which has generally characterised the Church in the West, while the Eastern Church has remained closer to the traditions of Clement and Origen.[28]

In a thorough, and in part critical, review Fergus Millar points out the vast amount of factual material worked into Frend's book. He draws attention to the range of subjects covered: Rome's attitude to foreigners and foreign cults, the early development of the Church and its conflicts with orthodox Judaism as well as with Graeco-Roman society, the history of the persecutions, the triumph of the Church under Constantine.

> No lesser man would have attempted it. Nor would a more cautious man. Frend rushes in vigorously where generations of scholars have trod with care . . . he has traced with profound historical sense and sympathy the way in which the different intellectual and social traditions and the various theologies current in the early Church found their various expressions in the responses early Christians made to the hostility of their environment, the pressure of the state and the ultimate threat of death. In doing that he has shown, in a way not to be achieved by any number of scholarly histories of the early Church, or learned treatments of early dogmatics, how the development of Christianity, and the application of its beliefs in real life, is a central element in the history of that period. Frend like Rostovtzeff will provide an easy target for lesser men. The book does indeed contain an immense number of mistakes, not all just the products of haste. . . . These defects do not alter my view that this is the most important book on the first three or four centuries of the Empire to be published for many years.[29]

In 1965 Frend was visiting scholar at Grahamstown University in South Africa. In 1969 he left Cambridge on being appointed Professor of Ecclesiastical History at the University of Glasgow. From 1972–5 he was Dean of the Faculty of Divinity. His politics had moved to the right. In the years 1977–9 he was Chairman of the Conservative Party in the Buchanan–Drymen area, and Vice-Convenor of the local Community Council. Characteristically, his service as Conservative chairman overlapped with a spell as Chairman of AUT Scotland during the years 1976–8.

Meanwhile Frend had begun work on another project. Having been elected Birkbeck Lecturer in Ecclesiastical History for the academic year 1967–8, he used this opportunity to give a course of lectures on the his-

---

[28] See Peter Brown, 'Approaches to the religious crisis of the third century', *English Historical Review*, 83 (1968), 542–58 = *Religion and Society*, pp. 74–93, esp. pp. 84–93.

[29] Fergus Millar's review: *Journal of Roman Studies*, 56 (1966), 231–6.

tory of the Monophysite Movement (431–641), which was to form the basis of his third major work, *The Rise of the Monophysite Movement*. The book was published at Cambridge in 1972, seven years after the appearance of *Martyrdom and Persecution in the Early Church*. It received an unfavourable review from L. R.Wickham. 'The book is over-supplied with events and narratives. The wood disappears in a multitude of trees. Analysis and explanation give way to chronicle. Interest is unlikely to be kindled by the narrative, not constructed from primary sources, but rendered down from secondary sources.'[30] Wickham points out numerous inaccuracies. Frend was greatly hurt by this criticism.[31] The criticism is not without some justification, but nevertheless completely misses the point of the book,[32] which in fact tells a dramatic story of how a religious controversy split the Church in the East, and in the end undermined the structure of the Empire itself, even though none, or at least only very few, of the participants had intended this outcome.

The medium is narrative but a narrative which covers a wide range of topics, developments, in theology of course, but also in ecclesiastical and secular politics, and those both at local and imperial level. Most of the elements which figured prominently in Frend's previous work reappear: the emperor, the relations of Church and state, the problem of accommodating dissent within the Church, conflicting regional loyalties, the dichotomy of town and country, with the latter given new and forceful champions in the monks, and, last but not least, the interaction of religious coercion and of group loyalties. The abundance of facts may sometimes seem confusing to a reader trying to get through the book too quickly. But this book was certainly more difficult to write than either *The Donatist Church* or *Martyrdom and Persecution*. The sources are not only in Latin and Greek but also in Syriac and Coptic, and the archaeology of a region stretching from Egypt to Armenia is very much more complex and much less known than that of North Africa. Neither the literary sources nor the archaeology had at that time received anything like as much scholarly attention as those for North Africa. To make a comprehensive synthesis of the evidence bearing on the story of the Monophysites cannot have been an easy task, and as far as I know, no other author writing in English had even attempted it.

---

[30] *Journal of Theological Studies*, NS 24 (1973), 591–9.
[31] ' "The Monophysites": a rejoinder on a recent issue', *Modern Churchman*, NS 16 (1974), 100–6.
[32] See Dom Frederick Hockey, for a much more perceptive review in *Revue d' Histoire Ecclésiastique*, 68 (1973), 851–4.

Frend's treatment of the interaction of religious and secular factors has in fact become more subtle. He no longer treats the religious controversy as simply an expression of underlying ethnic and social conflicts.[33] Instead he shows a much more complex interaction of a multitude of factors, undermining old, and creating new allegiances and identities, in both religious and secular spheres. Monophysitism was not an expression of Syrian or Coptic ethnicity, but the rise of Monophysitism in Egypt, Syria and Armenia led to the creation of literatures in local languages, and thus also to the growth of new regional identities, and in Nubia and Ethiopia to the consolidation of new kingdoms.

After *The Rise of the Monophysite Movement,* Frend remained productive. He published far more articles than can be mentioned in this memoir.[34] Some repeat earlier work, but most of them are both original and interesting. The titles of two volumes of collected papers in the Variorum series sum up Frend's special interests: *Religion, Popular and Unpopular in the Early Christian Centuries* (London, 1975); *Town and Countryside in the Early Christian Centuries* (London, 1980). In 1984 he published *The Rise of Christianity,* pp. xv+1022 (London). This is essentially a comprehensive but readable textbook, intended both for students and a wider readership. Frend had always believed that the results of scholarship should be passed on to the widest possible audience. The book once more displays Frend's enormous knowledge. It also shows how Frend saw the significance of his own work in relation to ecclesiastical history as a whole.

Frend was now internationally recognised as one of the leading historians of the Early Church. In 1974 he received an honorary DD from Edinburgh University. In 1979 he was elected Fellow of the Royal Society of Edinburgh. The year 1976 was spent by him as Visiting Professor at the University of South Africa, Pretoria. From 1976 to 1978 Frend was a member of the University of Michigan's team on the 'Save Carthage' Project. He was also on the managing committee of the project, owing his place to the Tunisian authorities. His main task with the Michigan team was to collate evidence for the growth of Christian churches in Carthage, and especially to record any that had been discovered since Vaultrin's

---

[33] See for instance p. xiii: 'At the outset, however, except in Egypt, it would be hazardous to see monophysitism as an expression of regionalism on the part of non-Hellenistic provincials . . .. It is not true . . . that at an early period in their history the Monophysites and Nestorians attracted to themselves the Semitic population of the eastern provinces of the Roman Empire who found adherence to a schismatic church an opportunity for expressing hatred of foreign rule.'

[34] A bibliography submitted to the British Academy in December 2002 lists around 313 items.

work in the 1930s.[35] In the course of his investigations, Frend learnt about a baptistery standing on its own at Bir Messaouda, Carthage. He studied the site and published his observations.[36] In 1997 (or 1998) he heard that Richard Miles was taking an interest in the site of the baptistery. They discussed it over tea at a Classical seminar. Others had told Miles that Bir Messaouda was unpromising, but Frend encouraged him to continue. Miles did, and Frend became a staunch patron for Miles's project, speaking up for it at every opportunity. Frend was proved right. Miles made important discoveries from the Vandal and Byzantine periods, including the largest church so far discovered at Carthage.[37] It transpired that the remains had narrowly escaped destruction to make room for a car park.

Further honours followed. From 1980 to 1983 Frend was President of the *Comité international d'histoire ecclésiastique comparée*, and thereafter *Président d'honneur*. In 1981 he became Vice-President of the Association Internationale d'Études Patristiques. In the academic year 1981–2 he was Visiting F. and M. Tuohy Professor in Interreligious Studies at John Carrol University, Cleveland. His lectures were published as *Saints and Sinners in the Early Church* (London, 1985). In 1983 Frend was elected a Fellow of the British Academy, after having been nominated by the historians. He spent 1984 as a Senior Fellow at Dumbarton Oaks. In the same year he became Emeritus Professor of Glasgow University. In 1991 friends and colleagues presented him with a festschrift, *Early Christianity*, which had been edited by Ian Hazlett.

He had long been active in the service of the Church of England. As a boy Frend had been impressed by his father's dedication to the work of his parish. He later recalled that he had experienced a phase of atheism, to the horror of his mother, but that he had got over this by the time of his father's death. When he became established at Cambridge he evidently decided that he must give some practical expression to his commitment to Anglicanism. His account of this decision is rather light-hearted. He claims that he joined the divinity faculty at Cambridge because he did not want to be just a 'research bod' in the history faculty. Once in the divinity faculty he felt that he had to do something practical, so he had himself licensed as a Lay Reader in the diocese of Ely in 1956, and served as

[35] 'The early Christian Church in Carthage', in *Excavations at Carthage 1976, conducted by the University of Michigan*, vol. 3, ed. J. H. Humphrey (Ann Arbor, 1978), pp. 21–41.
[36] 'A two period baptistery at Carthage', *Bulletin CEDAC*, 6 (Carthage, 1985), 42–3; amplified by N. Duval, *Revue d'Études Augustiniennes*, 34, 1 (1988), 86–92.
[37] R. Miles, 'British excavations at Bir Messaouda, Carthage 2000–2004: the Byzantine basilica', *BABesch (Bulletin Antieke Beschaving)*, 81 (2006), 199–226.

Editor of the *Modern Churchman* from 1963–82. The Revd Simon
Tebbutt wrote the following comment on his editorship:

> Frend's long association with the Modern Churchman's Union (Frend had
> joined as long ago as 1935) had to do with its being open to revise its under-
> standing of scripture and theology as modern learning discovered new truths
> that are being revealed by science and archaeology. He was a typical Broad
> Churchman and was not much inclined to turn his understanding into either
> Liturgy or Worship. . . . [As editor he felt it to be] his duty to inform serious
> theologians and historians of current thinking among academics in the Church.

He criticised David Jenkins, Bishop of Durham, for his dismissal of the
Christmas event as 'so much mythology'.

Frend was ordained deacon in the Scottish Episcopal Church at Perth
in 1982, and priest in 1983,[38] serving as a non-stipendiary priest in the
parish of Aberfoyle. The ministry provided an outlet for his still abundant
energy in his retirement. Douglas Feaver, Bishop of Peterborough, who
had once been on an archaeological dig with Frend in North Africa,
offered him the rectorship of Barnwell together with Thurning and
Luddington, in the diocese of Peterborough. When he told his Scottish
bishop about the offer the latter was shocked that someone with so little
experience should have such an appointment: 'You should not touch it
with a barge pole, William'. That was a challenge and naturally Frend was
determined to prove the bishop (and others) wrong. According to Simon
Tebbutt, Frend found liturgy difficult but took his pastoral duties very
seriously. The confidence which he had displayed in the lecture theatre
seemed to desert him as a parish priest. He was hopeless with vestments,
and from the word go dispensed with them in whatever parish he was in.
Tebbutt was told: 'William is loved by all in the village—he and Mary
have captured our hearts'. William wore his learning lightly—his job now
was pastor and friend. He took particular pains to get the full life story
of those he buried. Eventually he came to love preaching. Mary classified
her husband's sermons as either 'a one sermon' or 'a two sermon' according to whether it contained the material that was right for a single sermon, or enough for two. Frend used his huge knowledge of life in the
ancient world to make his sermons on biblical texts 'incredibly interesting'. Parishioners lacking the historical background tended to find the
Bible difficult. Frend brought it alive. He was a member of the
Peterborough diocesan synod from 1988 to 1990. He served at Barnwell

---

[38] Mary was not in favour. According to Frend's tape, she thought that her husband, who in this
context describes himself 'as a not very religious person', was not up to it.

from 1984–90. After 1990 he helped as honorary assistant priest in the Fulbourn group of parishes in the Ely diocese.

Frend was now again able to visit Cambridge regularly, to frequent the library, take part in seminars, and to argue with colleagues who disagreed with his scholarly theories. From 1992 to 1996 he served as supply lecturer in the Divinity Faculty. In 1995 he was elected a Member by the New York Academy of Sciences, and an Overseas Member by the American Association for the Advancement of Science. Publications continued to appear.[39] In 1996 Frend published *The Archaeology of Early Christianity, a History.* The book contains a mass of fascinating information about forgotten archaeologists and their excavations. The development of Christian archaeology is related to its historical background, so that the reader is made aware how the ebb and tide of archaeological activity has been related to missionary zeal, nationalism, wars, and above all the rise and fall of the European empires. In 1997 Caius College, which had already given him membership of its SCR in 1991, awarded him another Bye Fellowship. Frend still exercised his practical enthusiasm for archaeology,[40] and was still publishing. In 2001 he published 'Great Historians of the Early Church: Adolf von Harnack'.[41] Another Variorum volume of collected studies, *Orthodoxy, Paganism and Dissent in the Early Christian Centuries*, appeared in 2002.

In the same year Mary died and left Frend bereft and lonely. In his last years he was not very mobile. But he kept busy. He took two church services a month. His amazing memory was intact and he could and did write. *From Dogma to History: how an understanding of the Early Church developed* (London, 2003), is dedicated to Mary. The book is an account of great scholars of earlier generations to whom Frend felt indebted.

In personality Frend was very, almost quintessentially, English; at the same time he was profoundly influenced by both German and French scholarship. He saw early Christian archaeology as an international force for bringing together scholars from all over the world. Not very much interested in theology or even religious philosophy, yet paradoxically, and unlike many positivist historians, as for instance A. H. M. Jones, the great

[39] 'Edward Gibbon (1737–94) and early Christianity', *Journal of Ecclesiastical History*, 44.4 (1993), 661–72.
[40] With A. Cameron, 'Survey excavation on the Long Field at Rookery Farm, Great Wilbraham', *Proceedings of the Cambridge Antiquarian Society*, 81 (1992), 5–13; with J. A. Hadman, 'A deposit of Roman lead from North Lodge Farm, Barnwell, Northants', *Britannia*, 25 (1994), 224–6.
[41] *Journal of Ecclesiastical History*, 52.1 (2001), 83–102.

historian of Late Antiquity, Frend was very much concerned with the history of ideals and ideas, and above all the interrelation of ideas and their background in individual or collective experience. Although it is rooted in French and German scholarship, Frend's very individual kind of ecclesiastical history really has no precedents either in French or in German, and regrettably few ecclesiastical historians have tried their hands at it since. Frend had a visual memory, which enabled him to retain, not always altogether accurately, an immense knowledge of evidence both textual and archaeological. It was in his bringing together of archaeological and literary evidence that he made his great contribution as a historian. As an archaeologist Frend's biggest strength was his enthusiasm. His digging methods were a little primitive, but he knew an incredible amount about North African Christianity, which allowed him quickly to place his discoveries into a historical context. Following the French, he was one of the first scholars of early Christianity to use archaeological material in a 'scientific' way.

Everyone who met him was struck by his enthusiasm and boundless energy. It was this which inspired numerous pupils. He took an interest in their careers and rejoiced at their successes. They liked and admired him, but did not find him easy to know. Frend was rather touchy. He resented that an age bar prevented him from being elected on to the committee of the Patristic Conference at the age of 75, and also the fact that in spite of his life-long interest in North Africa the British Academy did not elect him on to its Tunisian Committee. In his last years he was very disappointed, indeed felt that he had been unjustly treated, when an application to get him a public honour, which had the support of some very well-known scholars, was rejected by the patronage commission. Frend certainly sometimes irritated colleagues. In his capacity as member of the editorial board of the *Journal of Ecclesiastical History* Frend was a pertinacious defender of the Early Church, and seeing himself as its only defender he proved difficult and disruptive to a succession of chairmen. He was very sure of his opinions, and not ready to change them under criticism. While he was open-minded about receiving new thought, he could be distinctly prickly about colleagues who disagreed with him. But he did not bear grudges, and as G. R. Evans noted in *The Church Times*, there was profound humility under his sometimes seemingly over-self-confident and even bumptious exterior, and above all he always had a great sense of humour.

Frend expressed some worries over the future of his subject. Here are some of his reasons for concern. Interest, especially in the United

Kingdom, in the history and doctrine of the Early Church has declined seriously. One main cause is the lack of training in Greek and Latin in schools. A second reason is the decline in importance of the first four councils, and particularly of the Council of Chalcedon with its Christological definitions, in the thinking of the Anglican Church. The creeds and definitions remain the title deeds of the Church, but an understanding of their meaning and why they were framed the precise way in which they were would be restricted to a minority. The divinity faculties in Britain have not developed either a centre for the study of Antiquity and Christianity on the lines of the *J. D. Dölger Institut für Antike und Christentum,* or an organisation for the publication of a long and continuing series of translated and annotated patristic texts, as achieved by the *Sources Chrétiennes* or the *CSEL* in Vienna. Without these or similar outlets there is little to encourage theological research students to embark on a career devoted to the early history and doctrine of the Church.[42]

But Frend's naturally optimistic spirit was aware of a positive side: the greatly increased involvement of classicists and archaeologists in the study of late antiquity, and the steady flow of new evidence being revealed by discoveries in the fields of archaeology and papyrology. Characteristically, he did his best to the end to help the positive factors to prevail. In 1982 he presented the Society of Antiquaries with the 'Frend Medal', in order to encourage young British archaeologists to take an interest in overseas archaeology. In 1999 he founded a travel scholarship for young persons at the beginning of their career. In the words of Rosemary Cramp, former President of the Antiquaries: 'Frend is a man of abounding good will, who has used his intellectual and financial resources with great generosity for the benefit of others.' Near the end of his life Frend had begun to work on a book about the early life of St Augustine. He died on 12 August 2005. A week earlier, in hospital, he told his vicar, the Revd Rhiannon Jones, that he was not afraid of dying; he did, however, want to finish off a few footnotes for his latest book.

WOLFGANG LIEBESCHUETZ
Fellow of the Academy

---

[42] Shortened from *From Dogma to History,* pp. 169–71.

Note.   In preparing this memoir I have been assisted by Frend's daughter Mrs Sally McIntyre, the Revd Rhiannon Jones, the Revd Simon Tebbutt, Professor Pauline Allen, Professor Gerald Bonner, Professor Rosemary Cramp, Dr Richard Duncan-Jones, Dr Peter Linehan, Professor Robert Markus, Dr Richard Miles, Professor Malcolm Schofield, Professor Frances Young, the anonymous obituaries of *The Times* and *Daily Telegraph,* and the obituary in *The Church Times,* written by Professor G. R. Evans. I have also used the biographical and bibliographical material deposited by William Frend with the British Academy, and two tapes in the possession of his daughter, in which Frend, interviewed by David Talbot, describes his experiences during the war and immediately after.

JACK GALLAGHER

John Andrew Gallagher
1919–1980

JOHN ANDREW GALLAGHER, ALWAYS KNOWN AS 'JACK', was born on 1 April (a date to which he liked to draw attention) in 1919. He was the only child of Joseph and Mary Adeline Gallagher. Jack was born in Birkenhead, a fact not irrelevant to his later career as an historian of empire. Birkenhead lay across the Mersey from Liverpool, a short ferry or train ride away. It was a boom town of the nineteenth century, flourishing with the growth of Merseyside as the gateway to Britain's main industrial districts in Lancashire, Yorkshire and the Midlands. Its waterfront was dominated by the great shipbuilding firm of Cammell Laird, and seamed with the railway lines serving its industrial plants and processing industries. It was the largest slaughtering and meat-distributing centre in Britain and the greatest milling centre in Europe.[1] Much of its population, like that of Liverpool, was of Irish origin. At the time of Jack's birth, its most famous son was Frederick Smith, Lord Birkenhead, Lord Chancellor in Lloyd George's coalition government, and before 1914, a vociferous champion of Ulster's struggle against Home Rule. For most of Jack's early life Birkenhead's economy was in steep decline, hard-hit by the slump in shipbuilding and the contraction of overseas trade. But there were, perhaps, few better places to stimulate the imagination on the causes of Britain's rise to world power in the nineteenth century and its subsequent fall.

---

[1] For Birkenhead's development and industrial history, S. Marriner, *The Economic and Social Development of Merseyside* (London, 1982), pp. 9, 34, 77, 132–3; P. J. Waller, *Democracy and Sectarianism: a Political and Social History of Liverpool 1868–1939* (Liverpool, 1981); W. Hewitt, *The Wirral Peninsula* (1922).

Jack's origins were modest. His father Joseph had migrated to Canada before the the First World War, but returned to fight in the First Canadian Contingent. At the time of Jack's entry into secondary school in 1929, his occupation was listed as 'railway checker', counting the 'foreign' rolling stock for whose use of the line a charge would be levied. But it would be a mistake to assume that Jack was brought up in poverty in a back-to-back tenement. The family address in 1929 was 35 Dingle Road, a small semi-detached house (assuming no change in the street number since then) not a terraced house. As a small boy he attended Woodchurch Road Elementary School. Then in 1929 he entered Birkenhead Institute on a free scholarship at a time when only 11 per cent of Birkenhead children proceeded to a secondary school.[2]

An agreeable myth, retailed in Richard Cobb's evocative memoir[3] and deriving, no doubt, from Jack's own mischievous imagination, portrays Jack's schooling as a Dickensian travail, with touches of Hollywood. Jack was educated by 'rough Irish fathers' denouncing the atheism of 'Jean Jakes Rewso', to prepare for his vocation as a Catholic priest—his mother's wish. In fact, Birkenhead Institute was not a Catholic school at all. It was a grammar school founded in 1889 by a group of Birkenhead businessmen with the support of two leading Liverpool figures, Henry Tate (of the sugar firm) and Philip Holt, the ship-owner. The school was to be non-denominational. It served a growing middle-class population who could not afford the fees of Birkenhead School. The parents listed in the school records included 'window-cleaner' and 'locomotive fitter' as well as those of more solidly middle-class occupations.[4] At the time of Jack's arrival, its most famous 'old boy' was the poet Wilfred Owen, killed in the First World War. Like many grammar schools it deferred to the public school model, using a 'house' system, and replacing plebeian football with middle-class rugby in 1934. Jack throve in the school, winning scholarships and prizes. He was secretary of the Sixth Form Literary and Debating Society ('the artful appeals to imperialist and anti-fascist sentiment made by Williams and Gallagher won an overwhelming victory' its minutes recorded in 1936); editor of the school magazine, the *Visor* ('articles dealing with original topics will be scrutinised with uncommon tenderness' declared an editorial); and 'headmaster's prefect'. In 1936, no doubt with the encouragement of the headmaster, a Cambridge graduate,

[2] Waller, *Democracy and Sectarianism*, p. 298.
[3] R. Cobb, 'Jack Gallagher in Oxford', *Cambridge Review*, 7 Nov. 1980.
[4] Birkenhead Institute Records, held at Birkenhead Reference Library. I am grateful to Mrs Pauline Black for help with these.

he applied to Trinity College, Cambridge. At the age of seventeen, he won a major scholarship to the College (the only history student in that year to do so),[5] as well one of the two hundred 'state studentships' awarded in England and Wales to help meet the fees of impecunious applicants. It was a glittering prize. A photograph in the *Birkenhead Advertiser* shows a quizzical-looking Jack, already bespectacled, being 'chaired' by his peers.

Jack liked to recall his days as an undergraduate historian as a solitary commoner among the idle offspring of dukes, whose essays were as hereditary as their titles. This was an embellishment. 'Life up here is charmingly inconsequent', he reported to the *Visor* a few weeks after arriving in Trinity. 'One can be just Bohemian enough for it to be interesting and not uncomfortable.' Academically, Jack amply fulfilled the promise of his scholarship, winning more prizes and gaining a First in Part One of the Historical Tripos in 1939. What he learned from the historians in Trinity is unclear. One 'upheld the tradition of conviviality . . . when one went to his room with an essay, he would be found in an armchair, gouty limbs swathed in bandages, half the floor covered in bottles'. Another 'lectured on medieval constitutional history—unaided by any notes—with ardour and gusto . . .'.[6] A more important influence may have been George Kitson Clark. It was Kitson Clark who sent him off to buy a dinner jacket at his expense.[7] But perhaps the crucial thing about Jack's education in Cambridge was its interruption by war.

At the outbreak of war, Jack joined the Royal Tank Regiment, perhaps because the 'Greasers', as the cavalry called them, lacked the snobberies of older formations. It is sometimes suggested that he served in one of the 'special forces' or intelligence, but there is no evidence for this (the writer has not had access to his military record). Jack did fight in North Africa, Italy and Greece. For whatever reason, he did not become an officer: it is said that he refused the promotion. But there can be no doubt that the war had a powerful impact on his imagination and personality. Jack wanted his memorial to read 'tank soldier and historian'. He returned to Cambridge as a well-travelled twenty-six year old, not a callow youth from Birkenhead. Above all, perhaps, from his time in Cairo he had seen at first hand what he was later to stress as an historian of empire, the importance of Egypt in British world strategy. Jack never

---

[5] Records of Trinity College, Cambridge, courtesy of Jonathan Smith.

[6] See V. G. Kiernan, 'Herbert Norman's Cambridge', in R. W. Bowen (ed.), *E. H. Norman: his life and scholarship* (Toronto, 1984).

[7] I owe this anecdote to Ms Katharine Whitehorn.

ceased to complain at the neglect of Egypt by British historians. 'It must be because it's too important', he used to say.

Having secured a First in Part Two in 1946, Jack was awarded a Holland Rose Studentship by the University and embarked on a thesis. He was part of a remarkable post-war generation of research students in History at Cambridge, including Maurice Cowling, John Fage, Harry Ferns, George Grun (a close friend of Jack's), Eric Hobsbawm, Oliver MacDonagh, Roland Oliver, Henry Pelling, John Pocock, Ronald Robinson, and Eric Stokes. Jack's topic was listed as 'British Colonial Policy in West Africa 1830–1886'.[8] In fact, he never completed a doctoral thesis, having been elected to a prize fellowship at Trinity in 1948. To win that fellowship, he had written, at breakneck speed (parts of the later chapters were submitted in what looks like ball-point pen), a dissertation entitled 'British Penetration of West Africa, 1830–1865'. It was written with astonishing assurance and sardonic wit. 'Only explorers understand the feelings of explorers', we are told on page three. 'Disraeli sailed down the Nile in search of ideas, Flaubert wandered over North Africa in search of debauchery.' The choice of subject was not accidental, nor was its theme. As a schoolboy in Birkenhead, Jack would have looked across the river to Liverpool, then still the commercial capital of British West Africa. He would have seen the monuments erected by its merchant princes, including the Picton Library where he did much of his research. In Birkenhead itself, the Cammell Laird works was a reminder of the importance of the Laird family in the growth of the city, and of the leading part played by Macgregor Laird in the effort to open the Niger to British trade and influence. In Jack's dissertation it is not officials and governments who take centre stage, but the 'palm oil ruffians', the mercantile chancers who were struggling to build a new trade in palm oil to replace the old one in slaves. The decisions that mattered were made not in London but Liverpool. The major argument that emerges is the reluctance of governments at home to extend their commitments or to act at all except in moments of crisis. Here was the germ of the thesis set out on a global scale some five years later.

To read the dissertation is also to be struck by two other characteristics. The first is Jack's delight in the larger-than-life personalities who turned up on the West African coast, refugees from scandal, bankruptcy or an ill-starred affair: 'the desperate characters, broken men and men with quick fortunes to make'. The motives, stratagems, delusions and

---

[8] *Cambridge Historical Journal*, 9 (1949), 371.

emotions, real and imagined, of the historical actors are shrewdly and entertainingly analysed. Here was that quizzical, amused view of life already apparent in the seventeen-year-old boy. The second is the absence of overt ideological influence. The point is worth making because, in several accounts, Jack appears as a youthful adherent of the Communist party. 'I was a Communist', wrote the Canadian Harry Ferns, a historian at Trinity in the year above Jack. 'And so was Jack Gallagher.'[9] Victor Kiernan, then a research fellow at Trinity, taught Jack for a time before leaving in 1938. He remembered him as 'going through a spell as a Marxist'.[10] In pre-war Cambridge, Indian students were subject to a form of official surveillance and those of Communist sympathies were discreetly organised as a 'colonial group' by Kiernan and then by other history students in Trinity, including Ferns and Jack. Given Jack's working-class origins in a deeply depressed town, the intellectual glamour of Marxism in 1930s Cambridge and the sense of impending struggle with Fascism, it is not hard to imagine the appeal that Communism might have held. But it seems unlikely that it survived Jack's time in the army. When Ferns met him again in 1949, he 'told a few jokes that showed that he had long since left the Communist Party and had begun to question the basic truths of Marxism'.[11] A remark in his dissertation makes that scepticism explicit: 'It is possible, but it is fruitless, to beat industrialism with any stick that comes to hand.' Yet, as we will see in a moment, the influence of Marx, or more precisely of Lenin, on Jack's view of empire was pervasive and subtle.

Meanwhile he had begun to lecture (the medium in which he came to excel), first on 'Europe and West Africa' in 1948–9. When his thesis supervisor, J. W. Davidson, left Cambridge for Canberra in 1950, Jack succeeded him as Lecturer in Colonial Studies (from 1950–3 as an 'Assistant Lecturer'), combining this in the Cambridge fashion with his Trinity fellowship. A vast field beckoned. In 1945, perhaps in response to the intellectual shock of the war, the Cambridge History Faculty inaugurated a new paper, 'The Expansion of Europe', to deal with 'the political, economic and cultural contacts of the principal countries of Europe—including Russia—with the remainder of the world in the period since

---

[9] H. S. Ferns, *Reading from Left to Right* (Toronto, 1983), p. 74.
[10] Communication from Professor Victor Kiernan, 7 Feb. 1999.
[11] Ferns, *Reading from Left to Right*, p. 316.

1400'.[12] 'The subject shall include', the rubric declared, 'exploration; missionary, humanitarian and political movements; the development of overseas trade and investment; the reaction of extra-European countries to European influence, including the effects on peasant economy of the opening of international markets; . . . the foundation of colonial empires; . . . the problems of native self-government; international relations in the colonial sphere, with the relevant military and naval history'.[13] By 1953, Jack was giving the main lecture course in the subject for the period to 1850, covering, as he put it, the 'Tipperary to Tokyo group of civilisations'. From 1954 his partner in this enterprise was Ronald Robinson (on post-1850). By that time they had published under the title of 'The Imperialism of Free Trade', a manifesto of startling originality on the pattern of British expansion in the nineteenth century, and the way that it ought to be studied.[14]

It would be otiose to précis the arguments of what is perhaps the most widely read essay on modern imperialism, whose phrases and concepts have been bandied about not just by historians but by sociologists, political scientists and students of international relations for the last forty years. But it may be useful to trace their intellectual roots. The essay insisted that the driving force behind Victorian Britain's expansion was the search for markets. Free trade was the weapon to open new regions to the products of Britain's industrial economy. Far from being limited to those parts of the world annexed as colonies, British economic ambition was world-wide. But in some places it faced much tougher resistance to the idea of an open economy than it did in others. When and where that occurred, and when the chance was offered, the British did not hesitate to act aggressively to force their way in and impose a commercial regime that was more to their taste. The key to British expansion was a common commercial purpose, but a willingness to use the most economical method to achieve the aim: 'informal' influence where possible, but, if necessary, rule. It was a brilliant insight. But, in its global sweep, and in its stress upon industrialisation as the dynamic of imperialism, it drew upon Marxism, not as political doctrine but as an account of world history. It was Europe's industrial revolution that triggered the change in its place in

[12] R. Hyam, 'The Study of Imperial and Commonwealth History at Cambridge, 1881–1981: Founding Fathers and Pioneer Research Students,' *Journal of Imperial and Commonwealth History*, 29, 3 (2001), 80.
[13] Ibid.
[14] J. Gallagher and R. Robinson, 'The Imperialism of Free Trade', *Economic History Review*, Second Series, 6, 1 (1953), 1–15.

the world. This view of world history would have been familiar to Jack's near contemporaries in pre-war Cambridge and he would have heard it from the Indian Marxists in the 'colonial group'. By the 1930s, however, the most influential version of Marx's thinking on empire was its famous reworking by Lenin to explain how imperialism had delayed the collapse of capitalism. In *Imperialism: the Highest Stage of Capitalism*, Lenin had insisted that imperialism was not just a matter of colonies, but of imposing economic domination under a wide variety of political conditions: imperialism was not only, or simply about territorial possession. Jack's own work on West Africa, Harry Ferns's on Argentina (eventually published as *Britain and Argentina in the Nineteenth Century* (Oxford, 1960)) and Michael Greenberg's on China (*British Trade and the Opening of China 1800–1842* (Cambridge, 1951)) showed the wide range of methods that the British employed to gain their economic objectives.

There were other influences somewhat closer to home than Lenin or Marx. Gallagher and Robinson would have been very familiar with the second large volume of the *Cambridge History of the British Empire* published in 1940. It contained a chapter by Charles Ryle Fay on the 'Movement towards Free Trade 1820–1853'.[15] Fay presented a panoptic view of commercial and imperial expansion, in which the search for markets carried British merchants far beyond the old limits of empire. He invented the term 'informal empire' that was central to the idea of free trade imperialism. He characterised the period of his chapter as 'an age of free trade and imperial increase'. 'We think of free trade as planless and passive. They [the merchants and manufacturers], by aid of free trade, took empire in their stride. By free trade they secured political empire, and something more, which we may call economic empire. Although imperialism was at a discount, empire itself was at a premium'.[16] Here, in embryo, were some of the key arguments that Gallagher and Robinson deployed to refute the supposed 'anti-imperialism' of the mid-Victorian age. A second prime influence may have been that of J. W. Davidson, the supervisor whose help Jack had acknowledged in the preface to his dissertation. Davidson was a New Zealander who had arrived in Cambridge in 1938, completing a Ph.D. in 1941 titled 'European Penetration of the South Pacific 1779–1842' (the similarity to Jack's own title may have been no coincidence). It was Davidson who stressed the

---

[15] J. Holland Rose, A. P. Newton and E. A. Benians (eds.), *The Cambridge History of the British Empire Vol. II: The New Empire 1783–1870* (Cambridge, 1940), pp. 388–414.
[16] Fay, 'Free Trade', p. 414.

importance of relating the 'imperial factor' to its non-imperial setting, of seeing European expansion 'in the round'. 'The Imperial Historian forgets at his peril', he remarked in the preface to his Ph.D. thesis, 'that the cattle ranching of Uruguay and Australia, the fruit-growing of Honduras and Samoa, the experiments in governing non-European peoples in Java, Mexico and Uganda, and the investment of capital in India and China all form part of one great [if disorderly] movement'.[17] The similarity, even in phrasing, to the global setting evoked by Gallagher and Robinson in the 'Imperialism of Free Trade' is immediately striking. Both Gallagher and Robinson, who helped Davidson with his book on the *Northern Rhodesian Legislative Council*,[18] and was also at St John's, had good reason to be familiar with Davidson's ideas.

In the end, however, 'The Imperialism of Free Trade' cannot be reduced to the sum of other men's arguments. The crispness and rigour with which it was written extracted a thesis from rich raw materials: the essential continuity of British expansion over the long nineteenth century. It added three new inventions of extraordinary significance for the study both of British imperialism and the 'expansion of Europe'. The first was the idea of 'collaboration' as the connecting rod between British expansion and the society and economy of the regions it encroached on. The terms on which the British 'collaborated' with the indigenous elites, were, Gallagher and Robinson insisted, the key to the nature of the imperial regime. Where cooperation was forthcoming and mutual advantage was perceived, Britain's interests were best served by the invisible dominance of its merchants, bankers and diplomats: this was 'informal empire', whose purpose was the same, and whose benefits similar to, the 'formal' empire of rule. Where it was lacking, an injection of force, or even of rule, was meant to induce the minimum of compliance that British interests required in any particular place or time. Implicit in this was a novel conception of colonial politics as a series of shifting and unstable bargains that might at some point unravel completely—an insight that was to reshape profoundly the study of colonial nationalisms over the next two decades. Secondly, Gallagher and Robinson advanced a much more flexible definition of the rogue word 'imperialism' than was current at the time. They famously rejected its association with territorial acquisition (here the debt to Lenin was obvious) in favour of treating it as the (variable) political input needed to secure essentially economic objectives.

---

[17] Quoted Hyam, 'Imperial and Commonwealth History', 82.
[18] Published in 1948.

Imperialism could now be detected as much in Britain's Near Eastern diplomacy in the 1830s and 1840s, or the negotiation of treaty ports in China, as in the invasion of the Punjab or the annexation of New Zealand. Thirdly, from their attempt to explain the baffling pattern of British interference—the willingness to leave zones of great economic importance in virtual independence while imposing colonial rule on tracts of desert or rock—Gallagher and Robinson deduced an imperial logic or system. Those who decided in London on the form and extent of Britain's commitments in any particular place were guided by their notion of Britain's *world* interests, by the vision of Britain as a global power with a 'world-system' to manage. They acquired 'barren rocks' or annexed empty sea coasts not for their intrinsic value but as the defences and out-works of the more valuable regions where trade and investment were greatest. It followed from this that an 'intra-mural' approach to a colony's history could make little sense. A colony's politics and economics were bound to be shaped by external forces and interests, by disturbance or upsets in far-distant places, or by an invisible shift in geopolitical equilibrium. Colonial history could not be written (this was one of Jack's favourite phrases) 'like the annals of a parish'. It had to be linked up to the larger movements of global and imperial history.

'The Imperialism of Free Trade' was thus a manifesto for the study of empire in a post-colonial age. Its attitude to Britain's own imperial era was neither sentimental nor celebratory. Its global compass was attuned to a post-war world whose political geography had been transformed by the revolution in East Asia, the independence of India and the spread of cold war. Its stress on 'collaboration' (perhaps an odd term to choose so close to the years of Nazi occupation) stripped away the pretence that colonial rule could be seen as purely the province of white men, or that black men had been the passive victims of fate. As a reinterpretation of Britain's nineteenth-century empire, it drew a critique, the fiercest of which came from D. C. M. Platt, an historian of Latin America, who derided the suggestion that British mercantile influence in Argentina (Gallagher and Robinson's main Latin American case) reached the level of dominance implied in the language of 'informal empire'.[19] As a master-narrative of British imperialism, perhaps its chief influence was delayed until the mid-1960s, when some of those trained in Cambridge in the 'Expansion of Europe' began to teach in their turn, when new funding arrived for 'area studies' in Asia, Africa and Latin America, and when

[19] Platt's views are most fully set out in his *Finance, Trade and Politics* (Oxford, 1968).

the all-but final collapse of Europe's colonial empires ignited wide interest in their rise and fall.

By that time Jack, again in partnership with Ronald Robinson, had produced the book that was to make both their names. His fellowship dissertation remained unpublished. Some of its findings made their way into his first published article on 'Fowell Buxton and the New African Policy 1838–1842'.[20] This displayed an interest in the role of lobbies and interests in the making of policy (heavily discounted in his later writing), a mistrust of 'enthusiasm' (a recurrent theme both academic and personal) and a taste for carefully wrought prose. Jack also contributed part of a chapter on Europe's economic relations with Asia and Africa to the *New Cambridge Modern History* (printed insouciantly under the name J. Galla*c*her) that drew on his earlier work on the West African slave trade.[21] Africa remained at the centre of his interests. In the early 1950s he and Ronald Robinson embarked on a study of the partition of Africa. It was, perhaps, an obvious choice (Ronald Robinson's doctorate had been on Central Africa). In the 'Imperialism of Free Trade', they had argued that much of Britain's formal empire of rule had been acquired not for the sake of its economic rewards, which were absent or lacking, but as a way of protecting more valuable regions. The grandest example of this safety-first syndrome was tropical Africa. In the history of British expansion, it was an after-thought, taken up reluctantly when the failure to do so threatened Britain's grip on the places that mattered. Africa was thus an ideal test-case for their larger theory. What made it all the more fascinating (and, as a project, all the more viable) was the electric speed with which most of tropical Africa had been reconnoitred, invaded, shared out and annexed in less than two decades. Africa was not the only case of a colonial 'scramble', but it was the most dramatic and the most complete.

Africa and the Victorians (1961) was a large-scale assault on the conventional history of the African Scramble and of European imperialism more generally. It ridiculed the claim that it was tropical Africa's wealth that attracted the attention of European governments, the British especially. It was scathing about the influential thesis, much favoured by diplomatic historians, that Africa had served as the safety-valve for the pressures and tensions of Europe's power politics. It dismissed as absurd

---

[20] J. Gallagher, 'Fowell Buxton and the New African Policy 1838–1842', *Cambridge Historical Journal*, 10 (1950), 36–58.

[21] See J. O. Lindsay (ed.), *New Cambridge Modern History Vol. VII: The Old Regime 1713–1763* (Cambridge, 1957), ch. 24: 'Economic relations in Africa and the Far East', pp. 566–79.

the suggestion that British statesmen acquired an empire in Africa to please their importunate voters, or, as J. A. Hobson had once claimed, to drown the voice of domestic grievance with the raucous echo of imperial triumph. It argued instead that Britain's part in the Scramble was the outgrowth of crisis in two African regions whose real importance to Britain derived from the fact that both lay across the sea-road to India. After 1880, British influence in Egypt and South Africa came under strain from political change. Egypt's modernisation under its own local rulers had ended in bankruptcy. The onerous terms imposed from outside to restore the state's credit sparked a revolt which, so London reasoned, threatened Britain's use of the Suez Canal. In South Africa, the rapid development of the Witwatersrand goldfields endowed Kruger's troublesome Transvaal republic with the means to disrupt Britain's grip on Cape Colony (the majority of whose whites were Afrikaners or 'Dutch') thus breaking its hold on the Southern African littoral and the main route to India. Fear of a 'proto-nationalist' regime in Egypt led to a unilateral British occupation in 1882. Fear of an all-powerful and anti-British Transvaal led London to try to squeeze it into submission as part of a 'British South Africa' and step-by-step towards the South African War of 1899–1902. It was these forward movements that alarmed and enraged the other European powers who had previously regarded their African interests with something less than enthusiasm. The result was the rush to partition the tropical hinterlands whose value had so recently seemed to governments in London, Paris and Berlin to be practically negligible.[22]

This sweeping revision of the entrenched historiography was underpinned intellectually by three powerful ideas, each of considerable methodological significance. The first was the emphasis that the argument gave to events 'on the ground' not in Europe but Africa: this was the 'local crisis'. The origins of the crises in Egypt and South Africa were not to be traced to decisions made in Europe or the new assertiveness of the European powers. They sprang from the breakdown of local regimes under the stress of economic and social change. The peculiar trajectory along which Africa entered the gravitational field of the global economy imposed intolerable pressures on many pre-colonial states. The result was not one but a whole chain of explosions that destroyed the pre-partition equilibrium. The historian in search of the causes of imperial expansion was thus better advised to sift local evidence and explore local archives

[22] See also their 'The Partition of Africa' in F. H. Hinsley (ed.), *New Cambridge Modern History Vol. XI: Material Progress and World Wide Problems* (Cambridge, 1962).

than to place too much faith in the explanatory power of metropolitan sources. The second was the idea of the 'official mind', the collective mentality ruling in Whitehall. This was the source for the routine assumptions that guided officialdom in its advice to ministers on foreign, colonial or Indian policy. It drew on a peculiar departmental 'historiography' of what had gone right and what had proved wrong. It handed down from one generation to the next the 'cold rules for national safety'[23] ignored at their peril. It was largely indifferent to purely commercial concerns, except as an adjunct to Britain's power in the world. In *Africa and the Victorians,* the 'official mind' is the calculating machine in which the costs and benefits of British intervention are soberly added up, the 'black box' from which the decisions emerged to annex or occupy, appease or delay. Its secrets were revealed in the private correspondence in which ministers debated with each other, or with their advisers, on what course to take. It was from the archive of the 'official mind' that Gallagher and Robinson claimed to deduce the primacy of strategic over economic motives in Britain's part in the Scramble.

The third key idea, already explicit in 'The Imperialism of Free Trade', was the defensive mood of late-Victorian policy-makers, and their obsession with protecting Britain's mid-Victorian gains against external rivals and internal assailants. London cared little about the small change to be earned in the tropical back-waters of African commerce. But it cared a great deal about the links in its chain of 'imperial defence', the system of naval and military power that safeguarded its spheres of commercial expansion. Annexations were tiresome, but they were often the means to avert the attrition of British world power. By the 1880s this defensive obsession was fixated on India, Britain's grandest possession, an indispensable source of military power, and the stronghold from which British trade and diplomacy could command southern Asia. This was the real arena for the struggle of empires. Seen in this light, the partition of Africa could hardly be cast as the climax of British or European imperialism. It was really a side-show. Gallagher and Robinson captured this thought in a mischievous phrase: the African Scramble was a gigantic footnote to Britain's conquest of India.

The nature of the intellectual collaboration involved in the making of *Africa and the Victorians* has been memorably recorded by Jack's two

---

[23] R. Robinson and J. Gallagher, *Africa and the Victorians* (1961), p. 463.

closest academic partners, Ronald Robinson and Anil Seal.[24] A visitor from Oxford in 1953 saw 'the Great Collaborators at work . . . in Jack's room. Jack head down at a kneehole desk piled with volumes beavering away at his scribbling . . . RER leaning back in a lordly proprietary way in a chair tipped back with his RAF boots on the desk with Jack sitting the other side . . . '.[25] By all accounts, Jack's penchant for travel and his dislike of getting up before noon meant that it was Alice Denny (Ronald Robinson's wife) who became the main driving force behind the book's actual completion. Much of its impact can be said to derive from the remarkable fusion of its conceptual framework with a vivid prose style, epigrammatic and witty. The deft character sketches, the evocation of mood, the depiction of place echoed the tone of Jack's dissertation. They sprang from an intense historical imagination (perhaps originally nourished by the reading of Dickens) that was fascinated by the gallery of human types and the twists of fortune that settled the fate of careers, ambitions or affairs of the heart. It was a view of life that was injected in part into Jack's teaching. In *My Friend Judas* (1959), Andrew Sinclair, one of Jack's star pupils in the late 1950s, gave a fictional portrait of Jack (thinly disguised as 'Johnson') as a tutor. 'Supervisions with Johnson are fun', says the hero Ben:

> He's really a sort of Harley Street toothman manqué. When you come he puts you in a chair, and gives you a Tio Pepe in a big glass as an anaesthetic to show you he thinks you're human and he's interested in that. Then he switches on the lamp in his cranium which must be about four hundred Whats and then some Whys. Then he leans forward and makes you open your mouth, so he can have a squint inside. He probes around with a few points from your essay, feeling out your cavities, which he's nice enough to treat as if they were depths. Then out come his pincers, but he's made you feel so the same as him, all wound-up and reasonable-doubting, that you begin to feel it *is* a wisdom-tooth he's working out of you, and that it's *yours*. And if he has to pull something all the way out of you and leave a gap, he doesn't fill up the holes with his fake teeth. He just plugs up the molars you've got with a tough lead filling so you feel they'll last out. He's a filler and a fixer like all good tutors should be.[26]

Tuition was mixed with more worldly advice. 'I am not your moral tutor', he told one moral tutee. 'I will help you out if you get into scrapes with the college. Your paternity suits are your own affair.' Always travel

---

[24] R. Robinson and A. Seal, 'Obituary: Professor John Gallagher', *Journal of Imperial and Commonwealth History*, 9, 2 (1981), 119–24.

[25] Communication from Dr A. F. Madden.

[26] Andrew Sinclair, *My Friend Judas* (1959), p. 11. I am grateful to Andrew Sinclair for discussing his memories of Jack Gallagher with me.

light but take plenty of dollars, was another injunction. Always vote against the 'unanimous' view. Keep out of the photographs. It was perhaps the willingness to be a sort of father-confessor to errant and insecure youth that made him a natural choice to be dean of the college (the 'profane not the sacred dean' he used to say), a post he held from 1960 to 1963.

In 1962, however, Jack was elected to the Beit Professorship of Commonwealth History at Oxford. He was not the first choice. The electors had wanted the New Zealander J. C. Beaglehole, the great authority on Cook's explorations. But when he declined, they agreed upon Jack, who arrived in Balliol in 1963. Oxford's History Faculty (then the 'Modern History Faculty') was very different from Cambridge's. It had far fewer teachers with interests in the extra-European world and no undergraduate course like the Expansion of Europe. It was Eurocentric, even Anglocentric. This did not deter Jack for whom Europe's history held as much fascination as that of anywhere else. His energies anyway were mainly devoted to graduate supervision: he had arrived in time for the rapid expansion of postgraduate interest in Asia and Africa and quickly acquired a large group of research students. At the weekly seminar in Commonwealth History held at Nuffield College (where Jack's principal colleagues, Freddie Madden and David Fieldhouse, were fellows) he dispensed the ideas that he and Ronald Robinson had devised over the previous decade. With this new stock of concepts, imperial history was rejuvenated. Far from being outmoded by the fall of empires, it seemed to supply the essential connection between the histories of regions, saving them from the fate (of which Jack was contemptuous) of being mere 'area studies'. Indeed, as Jack practised it, there was little distinction between imperial history and global history. Imperialism (properly defined) was the master-key to modern world history.

Even before he had arrived in Oxford, Jack's own research had begun to focus more and more upon India. This passage from African to Indian history was implicit perhaps in the central argument of *Africa and the Victorians*. The partition of Africa had revealed the British belief that India was the centrepiece of their imperial system, the quintessential component without which it would fail. Much of the rest of Jack's academic career was absorbed by the study of the Anglo-Indian connection, and its drastic impact on the shape of British world power from the late-nineteenth to the mid-twentieth century. The immediate problem was to explain the rise of the nationalist movement that had pulled down the Raj and with it the rest of the British imperium. In conventional histories, this was usually explained as the outcome of British 'reform'—the prudential concession of self-rule in doses—and the irresistible appeal of the nationalist idea under the inspirational leadership of Gandhi and Nehru. But to the historian of empire armed with the concept of 'collaboration', these were clichés at best. 'Looking in from the outside is the occupational vice which bedevils Western students of African or Asian history', Jack wrote in 1962, 'even if the road to ethnocentricity is paved with the best of intentions'.[27] If India's colonial politics were to be understood, Indian politicians would have to be studied on their own terms, and, ideally, from their own sources. From about 1960, he began to work systematically on this huge new project, initially with Anil Seal, his first research student, and then with a stream of new pupils that they recruited between them. The vast archive of the Raj in New Delhi and London (a whole continent of paper) had to be opened up. The grand apparatus of Indian administration had to be reconceived as a system not so much of rule as of collaboration. The trail of politics had to be followed down into the provinces and even the districts, where the British dealt directly with Indian notables, and the real bargains were struck.

By the late 1960s a whole team of young historians in both Cambridge and Oxford was hard at work on the provincial politics of colonial India, on Muslim politics, on Gandhi's *satyagraha*, and on the political economy that British rule had helped shape. By the mid-1970s, they had begun to produce an entirely new version of modern Indian history, which quickly attracted the label of the 'Cambridge School'.[28] Like the 'imperialism of free trade', it was iconoclastic and liberating. Indian politicians no longer appeared as the selfless champions of anti-colonial struggle. They were portrayed instead as skilled and ruthless practitioners in the games of faction and patronage, the real stuff of politics at the district and provincial levels. The provincial alliances that made up the Congress, and gave the British so much trouble after 1919, were cobbled together by political bosses in an acrid atmosphere of mutual mistrust. Gandhi's ideas were treated as the foibles of a crank by many hard-nosed Congressmen, however deferential they might be in public. The real innovation in the 'Cambridge School' history was to insist that Indian nationalism was not a spontaneous growth but a response to the changing terms

[27] In his review of L. Gann and P. Duignan, *White Settlers in Tropical Africa. Historical Journal*, 5, 2 (1962), 198.
[28] The first fruits of the 'school' were A. Seal, *The Emergence of Indian Nationalism* (Cambridge, 1968) and J. Gallagher, G. Johnson and A. Seal (eds.), *Locality, Province and Nation* (Cambridge, 1973). Jack's contribution to this volume was 'Congress in Decline: Bengal, 1930–1939'.

of Anglo-Indian collaboration. As the British made more demands on the districts—to govern them more closely and tax them more heavily— Indians banded together to protect their interests. As provincial and central government loomed larger in the localities, Indians formed provincial and then 'all-India' associations to bring local influence to bear on higher authority. The British in turn aimed to win new allies among their Indian subjects, by devolving power downwards, mobilising fresh clients in the business of rule. This was the real point of constitutional reform, much of whose meaning lay in the 'small print' where votes and seats were distributed among rival Indian 'constituencies'. Imperialism and nationalism thus marched in parallel and both sides depended upon a set of shaky alliances. Neither could risk a fight to the finish. But the moment would come (as it had by the end of the Second World War) when the British lacked the means to make the bargains they needed to defend the commanding heights of the Raj.

Jack had intended to write a history of Indian politics from the First World War to the end of the 1930s, as part of a series with Anil Seal.[29] Some of it may have been written but, for obscure reasons, left unfinished. Perhaps this was partly because Jack was also engaged in writing a more panoptic account of Britain's imperial system after the First World War, one of the first fruits of which was a remarkable paper on 'Nationalisms and the Crisis of Empire 1919–1922', written (probably) in 1968.[30] 'Once the British Empire had become world-wide', ran its opening line, 'the sun never set on its crises'. In the fourth and last of his historical enterprises he set out to explain why an empire that had reached its greatest extent in 1921 was near the end of its tether only twenty years later. The struggle to defend what Jack called the 'British world-system' was traced in the anxious debates of the policy-makers in Whitehall, oppressed by the burden of post-war debt, the dislike of the voters for costly commitments (a theme carried over from *Africa and the Victorians*), and the effects of depression on colonial politics. To make matters worse, the need to appease those that they thought of as the 'moderates' in India cut down the claim they could make on the sub-continent's resources, so long the pivot of British power in Asia. When they faced the three-cornered challenge to British world power in the late 1930s, they barely escaped catastrophic defeat. But from the interlocking of crises (a favourite image of Jack's) there was to be no real escape.

---

[29] Anil Seal's volume was meant to be the first of a series of five.
[30] It was subsequently published in *Modern Asian Studies*, 15, 3 (1981), 355–68.

The first version of this was presented in a series of papers in Cambridge in the autumn of 1973. The ideas were set out in the Ford lectures in Oxford and the Wiles Lectures at Queen's University in Belfast in 1973–4. They were published (posthumously) as *The Decline, Revival and Fall of the British Empire*,[31] a title that reflected Jack's characteristically paradoxical argument that the huge effort of wartime had brought a short-lived recovery of imperial strength but at the cost of incurring vast additional debts and exhausting what remained of British political influence, above all in India. By the time that he gave the Ford lectures, Jack had returned to Cambridge and Trinity. He had been privately told of his election to the Vere Harmsworth chair (of Imperial and Naval History), and he wrote to the Oxford Vice-Chancellor in April 1970. 'I have been very happy here . . . what is taking me to Cambridge is simply the sentimental pull of a place where I spent nearly twenty years of my life.'[32] Once back in Trinity, Jack soon became Dean, and shortly afterwards Vice-Master, grand vizier of the college whose Master was a species of constitutional monarch. For most of Jack's time, this was 'Rab' (Lord) Butler (Master 1965–77) with whom Jack got on well.[33] 'He gave rulings on discipline and decided protocol as to the manner born', Rab wrote about Jack after his death. 'With undergraduate representations he exhibited a remarkable patience which involved meetings lasting three or four hours. As a result, we had a large, relaxed and consultative student body'.[34] But this last phase of Jack's life was overshadowed by illness. He had been seriously ill while in India in 1970. In the late 1970s, his health declined sharply, and he had a leg amputated to arrest the effects of disease. He died on 5 March 1980, a few weeks before his sixty-first birthday. He had been elected a Fellow of the British Academy in 1978.

Through his intellectual partnership with Ronald Robinson (whose powerful, astringent mind was the perfect foil to Jack's imagination), but also on his own account, Jack Gallagher was the most creative and original historian of modern imperialism. One key to his influence was his verbal felicity, in speech or on paper. From his schooldays on, he displayed an intense interest in the uses of language and the craft of writing. He was an avid reader of fiction (Evelyn Waugh was a favourite, 'his jokes are so good') and also read widely in German and French. The result was

---

[31] J. A. Gallagher, *The Decline, Revival and Fall of the British Empire: The Ford Lectures and Other Essays*, ed. A. Seal (Cambridge, 1982).

[32] J. Gallagher to Vice-Chancellor, 7 April 1970, Oxford University Archives.

[33] See Mollie Butler, *August and Rab: a Memoir* (London, 1992).

[34] 'R.A.B.' in *The Times*, 11 March 1980, p. 14.

a style that was ironic and humorous, sometimes mocking and caustic, but never dull, repetitive or merely conventional. Jack's writing was meant to look round the corner and see a new view of the world, often surprising and comic. But he was also a product of Britain's post-war intellectual culture. He took the social sciences seriously, deploying sociology and social statistics alongside archival inquiry. Much of the strength of his and Ronald Robinson's work derived from the rigour and utility of its concepts. The academic citations of their original essay can be counted in thousands, far beyond the field of empire history. Jack saw himself as a professional and had little time for history's gentleman amateurs.

Jack was not a large man, and cared little about dress. But he had a solid reassuring presence. His eyes would gleam with barely suppressed humour and his conversation was punctuated with a throaty laugh. Jack was convivial and liked institutional life. He shone in company and was a raconteur of endless invention. But he could also seem lonely, and the references in his writings to disappointment in love were not entirely ironic. He could be very elusive and guarded his privacy. There is an entertaining correspondence in the Oxford University Archive in which the registrar of an Indian university inquired of his whereabouts (Jack had been sent the full dossier of a professorial appointment some months before). I am sorry, ran the reply, but Professor Gallagher has left Balliol without a forwarding address. Jack was not against order, tradition and civility: indeed quite the reverse. But he had an instinctive mistrust for claims to authority and loathed the parade of high principle or fine feeling. 'As often happens in English life', he once remarked of the critics of empire, 'some of the denunciators have been those whose private lives lie in ruins and who therefore set forth to rebuild the state'.[35] He had little regard for political pieties. 'Colonialism', he observed (this was after a visit to the Congo), 'is not the form of government hardest to endure, but the form of government safest to attack'.[36] He treated the demands of bumbledom and bureaucracy with a famous insouciance. 'Chuck them in the bin, Bert', he would tell the college porter at Balliol when the mountain of brown envelopes appeared at the beginning of term.[37]

By today's academic measuring tape, Jack's output was slim. He published in his lifetime a few short pieces under his name as well as the essay

---

[35] From his review in the *Historical Journal*, 6 (1962), 198.
[36] Ibid.
[37] Cobb, 'Jack Gallagher in Oxford', p. 21.

and book co-written with Ronald Robinson. How Jack would have fared in modern British academia, with its machine-tractor station mentality and zealous commissariat, is indeed a question. For by temperament Jack adhered to an older tradition. If he published little during his life it was partly because he spent his time prodigally in teaching and supervision. There, his influence could be drastic and in some cases life-changing. It is not to be thought of as 'delivering the syllabus' (in our inane modern phrase). To be taught by Jack was to learn how to write, to escape the familiar, and to meet a new view of life that was amused, irreverent and sceptical. 'Everybody is somebody's ghastly best friend', he would say. For many research students, it was also to find unimagined fascination in the topic they had chosen, once exposed to Jack's scrutiny. It was perhaps in the capacity to inspire the imagination of others at the highest level that Jack realised his own gifts most completely. It is for that as much as for his seminal writings that he will long be remembered.[38]

JOHN DARWIN
Nuffield College, Oxford

Note. I am most grateful to all those whose letters or conversation have helped me with the writing of this memoir.

---

[38] In addition to those mentioned above, there is a valuable memoir by Anil Seal as the introduction to *Decline, Revival and Fall.* An obituary appeared in *The Times* on 7 March 1980. An obituary of Ronald Robinson can be found in *The Independent* of 25 June 1999. A joint memoir of 'Robinson and Gallagher' appears in *Oxford Dictionary of National Biography.*

PHILIP GRIERSON   *Eaden Lilley, Cambridge*

Philip Grierson
1910–2006

I. The Cambridge don

PHILIP GRIERSON, HISTORIAN AND NUMISMATIST, died aged 95 on 15
January 2006. He was for seventy years a Fellow of Gonville and Caius
College, Cambridge, and for over sixty of them he lived in the same set of
rooms. This could be the summary of a quiet life, dedicated to the ivory
tower; in his case it was nothing of the kind. He went to Cambridge as a
student in 1929; in 1935 he became a fellow and lived in the college from
then on, from 1945 in rooms overlooking the Market Place, until his final
illness at the turn of 2005 and 2006. He was no recluse: students came to
read history essays to him and to enjoy his hospitality; friends—in later
years from all over the world—came to visit the most eminent living
expert on the coinage of medieval Europe. He also greatly enjoyed travel,
which took him to Russia, out of curiosity, in 1932, and to Germany later
in the 1930s to help a Jewish family find sanctuary; later still to Italy and
elsewhere for research and conferences; he was a lecturer, reader and professor in Cambridge, and a part-time professor of Numismatics and the
History of Coinage in Brussels, an honorary curator of Byzantine coins
in Dumbarton Oaks in Washington, DC, and a visiting professor in
Cornell University. And in all these places he enjoyed making friends and
mingling in the social life about him.

In 1987 an interview was recorded in Helsinki in which he gave the
most complete of a series of reminiscences of his life.[1] He described his

---

[1] 'A numismatic career', recorded by Knud Wallenstierna and Panu Saukkonen in 1987: see
below, p. 100, for this and other sources. The quotations which follow are from this document.

Proceedings of the British Academy, **150**, 79–104. © The British Academy 2007.

grandfather, another Philip Grierson, 'a kind and generous man but most unbusinesslike', who was in earlier life a well-to-do country gentleman who built a large country residence, Baldonnell House, near Clondalkin five miles west of Dublin; but as a landowner he lost heavily in the agricultural depressions of the late nineteenth century, and this and his extravagance compelled him to sell his house in 1903; he died 'in somewhat straitened circumstances' in 1910—a fortnight after his grandson was born in Dublin on 15 November 1910.

The second son of the elder Philip Grierson, Philip Henry Grierson, Philip's father, was born in 1859 and trained as an accountant; for some years he managed his father's estate, but 'after the Irish Land Act of 1896 he joined the Irish Land Commission', and until 1906 was a land surveyor. In the course of surveying in Donegal in 1898, 'he met and married my mother. It proved an exceptionally happy marriage, despite an age difference . . . of sixteen years.' In 1906 the Liberal government, regarding such appointments as political patronage, gave Grierson the sack, and he tried his hand at managing a small farm which had formed part of the family estate. He quickly realised that he could not rear a family in reasonable prosperity by such means, and took advantage of his training as an accountant and his exceptional numeracy to enter business. He soon acquired a reputation for financial acumen, became a director of companies, and embarked on a reasonably prosperous business career when he was already in his fifties.

Most of the friends of the younger Philip Grierson's later years came through college and university and academic contacts—and especially through the coin cabinets of the world; but he was always devoted to his family, regularly visiting his parents in Ireland while they lived—and he came from a long-lived family. By the time of his death his close relations were represented by his sister Janet, a leading Anglican deaconess, and the family of his elder sister Aileen, who had predeceased him.

Philip's mother was a doctor's daughter; and Philip himself was destined from his boyhood to be a doctor. He modestly claimed that this was because he had 'no business aptitudes'—which may have been true in a conventional sense; but hardly does justice to the way in later life he defied the iron laws of economics in building up an immensely valuable collection of medieval coins from a modest inheritance and an academic income. We may more readily accept that he had 'no inclination towards . . . the Church or the Law'. Nor was he inclined to matrimony, and he used to say that his output in research and his collection owed much to his being free of the responsibilities or costs of a family.

From the mid-1920s England became his home: first, as a schoolboy at Marlborough, then as an undergraduate. At Marlborough he specialised in the natural sciences and was preparing for a medical degree. His early scientific training was later to help him in the technical study of coins—and to inspire his love of science fiction. But in due course his interests widened; he read voraciously among the great historical classics, especially Gibbon; and when he came up to Cambridge he was eager to transfer to history. The Director of Studies in Caius was my father, Zachary Brooke, who accepted Philip (though he had nothing remotely resembling an A level in History) and supervised his studies; and he watched with delight the development of Philip's historical talents.

Philip completed his degree in 1932 with Firsts in both parts of the Tripos, and although he was later to speak modestly of his achievement, it must have made an impression on his teachers. He had already, in the spring of 1931, before taking Part I of the Tripos, been awarded the Lightfoot Scholarship for ecclesiastical history—a prize endowed by the great theologian J. B. Lightfoot as one of the moves in the early 1870s to support the study of history in the university, then a poor relation of law and moral sciences. In 1931 it involved examination papers on the whole of church history and some more specialised region; it provided him with a modest income for the next three years. In 1933 he was awarded the College's Schuldham Plate, which is given to the student with the highest marks in the Tripos.[2] Meanwhile, he was awarded the College's Ramadge Studentship in 1932, and supplemented his income with the University's Allen Scholarship (1934). In due course Philip was registered for a higher degree—an aim which, in accordance with the custom of the time, he abandoned when he had won a college fellowship (he took the Litt.D. in 1971).[3]

On 1 November 1935 he was elected to an unofficial Drosier Fellowship at Caius; he was to be a Fellow of Caius for seventy years. He remained nominally a research fellow until 1941 (after renewal in 1938); and he came into residence in the 'New Building' overlooking the Market Place in 1936, returning to it in 1945.[4] From November 1936 he was

[2] *Cambridge University Reporter*, 1930–1, p. 979 (9 May 1931); Gonville and Caius College Archives, Gesta 1929–35, p. 241.

[3] For his early research, see below, pp. 87–9.

[4] The College records show him occupying G11 and G1, St Michael's Court, both in the New Building opened in 1936, till 1939. From 1939–45 St Michael's Court was requisitioned by the Commissioners in Lunacy and Philip shared P4 Tree Court with a colleague. He moved into G6, St Michael's, in October 1945, and it was his home until his death: Gonville and Caius College Archives, Absence Books.

permitted to teach up to six hours a week; and in 1941 his fellowship became Official and he was appointed college lecturer—at first for three years, but by then he was so deeply entrenched that the College Council forgot to renew his lectureship until 1946, when a College Order of 8 February confirmed his appointment as from 1 October 1944![5]

His attempt to join the forces at the outbreak of the Second World War had been frustrated by his eyesight and some defect in his feet. Meanwhile, he became at an early age an important pillar both of the college and of the History Faculty. In 1938 he was appointed a Faculty Assistant Lecturer. In due course he shared with my father—and then took over—the outline course in medieval European history. I came to Caius as a student in 1945, the year in which Philip began collecting coins. He used to circulate a box of coins at his lectures, while freely making some such confession as: 'The Visigothic coins in the box are forgeries made to be sold to Napoleon's generals when they invaded Spain; but they give you a better idea of Visigothic art than genuine ones.' In supervision he was sparing of praise—'I've no quarrel with that' was his favourite reaction to what I thought was rather a good essay; this was not to discourage but because he treated his pupils as equals, as colleagues. We visited his rooms to read essays and to listen to his gramophone records and read his books: one of his most distinguished pupils has commented on the encouragement Philip gave him to read as widely as possible and to look at medieval artefacts. In a natural informal way his room was one of the most active social centres of the College.

In the Faculty, he was only promoted Lecturer (owing probably to wartime restrictions) in 1945—he was given a personal readership in 1959 and promoted to a personal Chair in Medieval Numismatics in 1971.[6] Meanwhile, he was a member of the History Faculty Board continuously from 1942 to 1951, and again from 1955 to 1958—and Secretary of the Faculty Board in succession to Herbert Butterfield from 1943 to 1946. This was an onerous post, as it still is, but in quite a different way. The equivalent officer today is supported by a substantial administrative and secretarial staff in a world-famous Faculty building. In the 1940s the Secretary administered the Faculty from his college rooms, with the aid of half a secretary in an office in Green Street. In about the same period, from 1945 to 1955, he was an efficient and conscientious Literary

[5] *Gesta* 1939–47, p. 296.
[6] The details which follow have been checked in the *Cambridge University Reporter*'s annual Faculty Board lists.

Director of the Royal Historical Society; and for this and his other services he was later rewarded by appointment as an Honorary Vice-President of the Society.

Philip was naturally business-like in personal administration; but Z. N. Brooke's advice to avoid college administration by never accepting a tutorship was attended to; and Philip—in spite of being invited later in his career—also avoided ever being chairman of the Faculty Board, though in his professorial years he was a conscientious member of the Degree Committee. Characteristically for a lover of books and bibliographies, he accepted the post of College Librarian in 1944, and in the same year first became a Syndic of the Cambridge University Library. He was to remain College Librarian till 1969, and Syndic—with brief intervals when he was on leave—till 1980; from 1977 to 1980 he was Chairman of the Library Syndicate.[7] In 1980 his seventieth birthday brought his terms of office to a close; but he remained much longer a frequent visitor, devoted to the Library which he had served so long. As Chairman, he was remembered for his dedication to its needs and for his informality: he was later reprimanded for encouraging a major University Syndicate to meet without gowns.

His service to the College centred on his teaching and direction of studies, in 1944–5 and (after Michael Oakeshott's departure, first to Oxford then to LSE) from 1949 for ten years or so, after which, to his great delight, he handed over the task of directing studies in history in the College to Neil McKendrick. Apart from the Library and the College Council (of which he was frequently a member), he avoided college offices: the great exception was his term as President, from 1966 to 1976. The President of Caius is second-in-command to the Master and acts as his deputy in the Master's absence—a frequent occurrence while the Master was Joseph Needham who, for all his devotion to Caius, was a dedicated globe-trotter. He must be a member of the College Council, and in practice shares with the Master much of the committee work of the College and some of the pastoral care of fellows and staff. In 1976 Needham retired as Master, and it was Philip's task to organise and preside over the election of his successor, Sir William Wade (see below, pp. 287–310). Perhaps above all, the President presides in the Combination Room, and is the central figure in its social life, with a special responsiblity for making visitors feel welcome. Philip was no bon viveur, but he was an excellent host

---

[7] From information kindly provided by Jacqueline Cox, University Assistant Archivist in the Cambridge University Library, from Cambridge University Archives ULIB 1/1/8, 1/12.

and a popular President—though he was also impatient of slow meals and liable to call colleagues to order who talked instead of eating: for his evenings after dinner were precious to him—for research or the cinema. This was one of a number of minor foibles which occasionally irritated and always entranced his colleagues; in later years he was a figure much loved by the fellowship, much admired by the students.

In course of time came many academic honours: FBA in 1958, honorary degrees at Ghent, Leeds and Cambridge; five medals, including that of the Royal Numismatic Society (1958) and the Gold Medal of the Society of Antiquaries of London (1997)—as well as a medal struck in his honour to celebrate his eightieth birthday; and several international prizes. He was besides a corresponding fellow or honorary member of seventeen international societies and academies.

In college he became a cultic figure: when he dined in hall on his birthday in his nineties he was greeted by lively cheers. For he never lost the capacity to mingle with men and women generations younger than himself. Grant Tapsell, who first met him in 1998 (when Philip was approaching his eighty-eighth birthday) enjoyed his hospitality and shared his love of films.[8]

> Philip loved movies. He even said the word 'movies' with impish relish. I used to love watching them with someone who had seen Charlie Chaplin and Buster Keaton films when they were first released. Indeed, I am tempted to say that if coins came to be at the heart of his professional career, movies were at the centre of his private life. When I first met him in 1998, Philip's local notoriety as a film-goer was already of five or six decades standing. He enjoyed recounting a notice put in the local paper in—I think—the 1940s announcing the opening of Cambridge's eighth cinema: 'Now Mr Grierson of Caius will be able to go to a different cinema every day, and two on Sundays.'
>
> Philip was single, but rarely solitary. Every academic year began with several parties for new students at Caius. The barely concealed purpose was to recruit students [to the] pleasant world of movie evenings . . ., the natural development of earlier social gatherings centred in music . . . But once the technology for the home viewing of movies came on stream there was no stopping Philip. His collector's heart was moved, and he amassed a collection of videos that numbered in the thousands rather than hundreds.
>
> Philip rather enjoyed playing the role of Methuselah to the students he met. But he was certainly a very active one, inviting many of us to movie and pizza evenings very frequently until his last years.
>
> It has to be said that his exquisite taste in coins was not always transferred to the screen. His shelves groaned under the weight of movies by such lumin-

[8] What follows is from Grant Tapsell's contribution to the Memorial Event in the Fitzwilliam Museum on 16 March 2006.

aries as Sylvester Stallone, Jackie Chan, Steven Seagal, and Arnold Schwarzenegger. In keeping with his *Who's Who*-listed interest in science fiction, there were also any number of variations on the theme of humans being hunted in space by creatures with very large teeth and even bigger appetites . . ..
But woe betide historical films that wallowed in inaccuracies or anachronisms—I remember spirited demolitions of both *Gladiator* and *Troy*. Philip was thus not a film *auteur* in the way that he was a great historian and numismatist. But that made him endlessly human and accessible, as well as quite simply a lot of fun.

Tapsell first met him in 1998; I knew him from my childhood. Real contact between us began in 1945 when I travelled to Cambridge to be interviewed for an entrance scholarship. 'I know all about you', he said 'and I have read your general paper and disagree with every idea in it.' In recognition of this I was given a major scholarship and was soon sitting at his feet in supervisions and lectures, and enjoying his gramophone records. In 1948 I was approached by two colleges, one in Cambridge, one in Oxford, as a possible candidate for a fellowship. Philip is alleged to have denounced this as 'baby-snatching'. Philip and others among the fellowship must have been active in the months that followed, since it was early in 1949 that I received a letter from the recently elected Master, Sir James Chadwick, offering me a fellowship at Caius. My chief recollection of my admission as fellow in July 1949 is seeing Philip sitting opposite to me—he only went willingly into the College chapel for the admission of fellows and masters. We thought differently on many things from religious faith to strip lighting (which he loved); but the bond of respect and affection between us was not the least affected—I am one of many who counted his friendship among the happiest experiences of our lives.

It is fitting that the last words of this part of our appreciation should be from the pen of his closest colleague in the study of medieval coins, Dr Mark Blackburn, Keeper of Coins and Medals in the Fitzwilliam Museum and so custodian of Philip's collection—whose election as a Fellow of Caius in 2005 was one of the prime comforts of Philip's declining months.

While describing Philip as collector and the meaning of his collection, he noted that:[9]

> Philip prided himself on his fitness and longevity. This was the man who in his 20s had walked back to Cambridge after an evening at the theatre in London, who in middle age rode a racing bicycle and who had regularly played squash until he was 80 . . . [and was hard at work on *Medieval European Coinage* well

[9] Also from the Memorial Event of 16 March 2006.

into his nineties. Blackburn went on to pay tribute] to a scholar, benefactor, colleague and friend who was held in the highest esteem; a private man with forthright opinions and a powerful intellect that could be intimidating; yet one who was sociable to the core with a mischievous sense of humour and a generous nature . . . He loved Caius and he loved Cambridge, yet his friends were spread across the globe.

II. The historian

Philip Grierson will be remembered above all as a numismatist. But he was a historian first, and a knowledge of medieval history—east and west, Byzantine and Latin—of extraordinary width and precision underpinned his study of coins. The switch to history from medicine when he came up to Cambridge was entirely his own decision, the fruit of wide, discursive reading, with Gibbon directing his thoughts to the Middle Ages. One of his Marlborough mentors, congratulating him on getting a First in Tripos, confessed that he had warned him he would get a Second if he transferred to history. In an interview with Edward Timms printed in *The Caian* in 1978,[10] Philip listed the Cambridge historians who had influenced him. He had been taught in Caius by Z. N. Brooke, whose concern for his welfare is witnessed by a string of surviving letters, and Michael Oakeshott—a great intellectual historian whom Philip much admired though they had little in common; most of all he confessed his debt to the supervisor of his postgraduate studies, Professor C. W. Previté-Orton.[11] He also attended G. G. Coulton's lectures, which were followed by informal seminars in Coulton's college rooms in St John's and at home; and a letter in the Coulton archives shows that the association flowered into friendship: Philip, by now a research fellow of Caius, wrote familiarly in a manner which would have been congenial to Coulton's anti-Catholic sentiments about the merits of the great American historian H. C. Lea and the weakness of a Roman Catholic defence of the Inquisition.[12] 'Otherwise I had virtually no contacts with senior members of the College or University, although I suppose I was influenced by the choice of books that lecturers suggested for further reading.'[13]

[10] *The Caian* 1977–8, pp. 33–55.
[11] Cf. *Cambridge University Reporter*, 1933–4, p. 623.
[12] St John's College Archives, Coulton Box 3, 23 July 1937—kindly communicated to me by Dr Peter Linehan.
[13] *The Caian* 1977–8, p. 34, where he also says he looked about for university scholarships and settled on the Lightfoot.

In 1931 Philip won the Lightfoot Scholarship. Z. N. Brooke had held it before him, and it would be natural to suppose that his influence lay behind Philip's interest in it; but there is another possibility, for there is one striking omission from his own list of his Cambridge mentors. The most prolific of his Cambridge correspondents (to judge from available evidence) was the kindly, eccentric, elderly Dixie Professor of Ecclesiastical History, J. P. Whitney (1857–1939): nine letters and cards from Whitney survive, ranging in date from 24 November 1930, early in Philip's second year as an undergraduate, to 13 May 1933. The first evidently related to reading for the Lightfoot Scholarship, and the Lightfoot question papers are in the archive, comprising (as always down to the 1970s) three papers on the whole of church history, a special subject and an essay. The special subject was 'The Church in the Frankish kingdom in the Eighth Century'. He was duly awarded the scholarship in May 1931. Whitney sent a card, saying Philip's success was 'not a surprise'. Z. N. Brooke also congratulated him, saying he only remembered one previous occasion when an undergraduate had won it; soon after, in congratulating him on his First in Part I of the Tripos, Brooke admitted that he had been 'a little anxious whether the Lightfoot had not taken too much of your time'.[14] After Part II, with a knowledge of the whole of church history behind him, and a detailed knowlededge of the eighth-century Frankish church for immediate background, Philip embarked on postgraduate research under Previté-Orton's supervision, on the ninth-century Archbishop Hincmar of Rheims. Philip's own account is that he was attracted to the field by Helen Waddell's *Wandering Scholars*, 'a learned and beautifully written evocation of the lives of Irish and other scholars in Western Europe between the late Roman Empire and the thirteenth century. Some of the Irish scholars had frequented the Carolingian courts, especially that of Charles the Bald', and so another Irish scholar was inspired to study the career of Archbishop Hincmar (845–82). The remaining letters from Whitney—four, ranging from 30 October 1932 to 13 May 1933—all relate to Hincmar, sometimes giving advice, sometimes asking Philip for help.

'After some months' work, however, I realised that the project was premature, for a new edition of the archbishop's letters was in progress' and he would be duplicating work elsewhere. 'Amongst his correspondents,

---

[14] These letters and exam papers are in Gonville and Caius College Archives, Grierson files. In *The Caian* interview Philip recalled the Scholarship gave him £70 a year for three years; *The Times*, 11 May 1931, announcing the award, assessed it about £78 a year.

however, was a certain Count Baldwin, who had eloped with a daughter of Charles the Bald and was to become the first count of Flanders'—and this seemed a promising field. It seems likely indeed that the shift from a primarily clerical to a primarily lay theme also reflected a shift in his own outlook and interests. And so he began to study 'the sources for the history of the Low Countries between the ninth and the twelfth centuries'.[15] He submitted fellowship dissertations on this theme, unsuccessfully in 1934, successfully in 1935. In the course of these years Philip was put in touch with the eminent Belgian historian François-Louis Ganshof of Ghent;[16] from this stemmed his long friendship with Ganshof and his family—and an association with Belgian scholars which lasted into his nineties.

Most of his early articles reflect two lines of interest: secular and ecclesiastical. Much of the material for the history of Flanders in the ninth, tenth and eleventh centuries was of its nature ecclesiastical: his first book was an edition of the annals of two major religious houses.[17] His articles[18] show Philip's delight in minute detective work, reconstructing the materials and infrastructure of Flemish and Frankish history. 'The translation of the relics of St Donatian to Bruges' is a *tour de force* of inference from tiny fragments of evidence and brilliant conjecture. His studies of the early abbots of St Peter's and St Bavo's Ghent reflect his love of lists and dates. In 'The early abbots of St Bavo's' he first laid out the fourteenth-century list of abbots, noting with relish of abbot after abbot: 'He is certainly a fictitious character'—then deploying a rather shorter, genuine list. He continued his list for St Peter's down to 941 in 'The translation of the relics of St Amalberga'.[19] Some of the materials he worked were more secular; and one can see emerging in two of the articles of 1938–9 his interest in other Carolingian lords beside the counts of Flanders. He devised a plan, frustrated by the war, to collaborate with

---

[15] From 'A numismatic career' (n. 1), pp. 7–8.

[16] From Z. N. Brooke's letters to Philip it seems clear that Ganshof had already commented on Philip's first submission in 1934; and since Brooke and Ganshof were friends it would be surprising if the former had not arranged for Philip to meet Ganshof at an earlier stage.

[17] *Les annales de Saint-Pierre de Gand et de Saint-Amand*, (Brussels, Commission royale de l'histoire de Belgique, 1937).

[18] 'The early abbots of St Peter's of Ghent', *Revue Bénédictine*, 48 (1936), 129–46; 'The early abbots of St Bavo's of Ghent' and 'The translation of the relics of St Donatian to Bruges', *Revue Bénédictine*, 49 (1937), 29–61 and 170–90.

[19] 'The translation of the relics of St Amalberga to St Peter's of Ghent', *Revue Bénédictine*, 51 (1939), 292–315. For what follows, see 'La maison d'Évrard de Frioul et les origines du comté de Flandre', *Revue du Nord*, 24 (1938), 241–66; 'L'origine des comtes d'Amiens, Valois et Vexin', *Le Moyen Age*, 49, 3rd Series, 10 (1939), 81–125.

Jean Dhondt on a book on Flanders; and he clearly planned other work now represented in print by his studies of 'La maison d'Evrard de Frioul' and the counts of Amiens, Valois and Vexin. In the mid-1940s he encouraged his pupil Janet Sondheimer to work on the early Carolingian aristocracy, which issued in an excellent thesis, never published. But after the war Philip found that Dhondt was engaged in his major study of the Carolingian aristocracy, and so felt no longer inclined to pursue this line of study. This revelation approximately coincided with his debut as a coin collector in 1945.

His work on Flanders also inspired his major article on 'The relations between England and Flanders before the Norman conquest' (1941).[20] But he was meanwhile much involved in a far wider study of the political history of medieval Europe. Already in the late 1930s, as the original *Cambridge Medieval History*—edited latterly by Brooke and Previté-Orton—drew to a close, Brooke suggested to Philip 'the idea of compiling a supplementary volume of genealogical tables. So over a period of three years or so I did a good deal of work on the family relationships of the ruling dynasties of Europe in the Middle Ages'—work which was never published, presumably owing to wartime restrictions.[21] But the drafts he compiled 'familiarised me with the primary sources and much of the secondary literature on the political history of most of Europe in the Middle Ages. I have never consequently been at a loss over references to Peter the Ceremonious or Charles of Anjou . . .'—'information . . . which every numismatist needs to have at his fingertips'. From the mid-1940s on he was regularly engaged in giving a long course of lectures, not narrow in concept but with a strong political core, on the whole of medieval history. To the 1940s belong both his article on Germanic kingship (1941) and the start of his labours in editing Previté-Orton's *Shorter Cambridge Medieval History*—on which he embarked after Previté-Orton's death in 1947, and saw into print in 1952.[22] These labours help to explain a very striking feature of his numismatic studies: that he was equally at home in early and late medieval Europe, in Byzantium and the West. To this his formidable memory made a fundamental contribution. But even more conspicuous in his later work are two preoccupations: his love of dates and lists, of the foundations of historical science;

---

[20] *Transactions of the Royal Historical Society*, 4th Series, 23 (1941), 71–112.

[21] 'A numismatic career' (n. 1), pp. 9–10.

[22] 'Election and inheritance in early Germanic kingship', *Cambridge Historical Journal*, 7 (1941), 1–22; C. W. Previté-Orton, *The Shorter Cambridge Medieval History*, ed. P. Grierson, 2 vols. (Cambridge, 1952).

and his zealous pursuit of the origins of money and coinage, and their social and economic function in the early Middle Ages.

His interest in Byzantium now appears most fruitful, no doubt, in his great Dumbarton Oaks catalogues; but it was also represented in his brilliant Spoleto lecture 'The Carolingian Empire in the eyes of Byzantium' (1979, published 1981), in which he suggested that the western empire worried observers in Byzantium a good deal less than Russia disturbed the western powers in the Cold War—and the lists of Belgian abbots were followed in 1962 by a fundamental tool for Byzantinists, 'The tombs and obits of the Byzantine emperors (337–1042)'.[23]

Philip's collection of coins and his published studies were mostly Continental; but his interest in the origins of coinage seems to have stemmed particularly from his studies of Anglo-Saxon England for the Ford Lectures in Oxford in 1957. The lectures were never published, but they played a key role in his Spoleto lecture of 1960 (published 1961), 'La fonction sociale de la monnaie en Angleterre aux VIIe–VIIIe siècles', in which he tackled the problem of how early medieval economies worked with little or no regular currencies.[24] His knowledge of English sources, and versatile use of them, also bore fruit in 'Sterling', in *English linear measures: an essay in origins* (Stenton Lecture 1971) and his article on the geld *de moneta* and *monetagium* in Domesday Book (1985).[25]

He had already extended his reading into anthropology and archaeology, and trailed his coat in his celebrated Royal Historical Lecture 'Commerce in the Dark Ages: a critique of the evidence' (1958, published 1959).[26] He carried these adventures still further in *The Origins of Money*, the Creighton Lecture in London for 1970 (published 1977), which extended his range of learning into the ancient Middle East. But the drift of all these studies is that in the early Middle Ages money and coins were

---

[23] *Settimane di studio del Centro italiano di studi sull'alto medioevo*, 27 (1981), 885–918; 'The tombs and obits of the Byzantine emperors (337–1042)', *Dumbarton Oaks Papers*, 16 (1962), 1–60.

[24] *Settimane di studio del Centro italiano di studi sull'alto medioevo*, 8 (1961), 341–85: see esp. p. 362 n. 46, where the relation to the Ford lectures is acknowledged. The typescripts of the lectures are now in the Fitzwilliam Museum.

[25] 'Sterling', in R. H. M. Dolley (ed.), *Anglo-Saxon Coins: Studies presented to F. M. Stenton on the Occasion of his 80th Birthday, 17 May 1960*, (London, 1961), pp. 266–83; *English Linear Measures: an Essay in Origins* (Stenton Lecture 1971, Reading, 1972); 'Domesday Book, the geld *de moneta* and *monetagium*: a forgotten minting reform', *British Numismatic Journal*, 55 (1985), 84–94.

[26] *Transactions of the Royal Historical Society*, 5th Series, 9 (1959), 123–40 (several times reprinted, finally in 1979, in Grierson, *Dark Age Numismatics* (London, Variorum), ch. II).

primarily for gift exchange or the payment of wergelds, with trade trailing far behind. He stimulated a lively debate, whose end is not yet.

I conclude with some examples of his range and virtuosity. In 'The Roman Law of Counterfeiting' (1956) he invaded the abstruse mysteries of Roman Law, with conspicuous success; he was to return there, in company with J. A. Crook and A. H. M. Jones, in 'The authenticity of the "Testamentum S. Remigii"' (1957) in which he overturned the doubts he had expressed the year before. In later years, from 1977 to 1987, he was Chairman of the British Academy's project on the Prosopography of the Later Roman World. In the Prothero Lecture for 1970 (published 1971), 'The monetary pattern of sixteenth-century coinage', he drew a picture of fundamental importance to the economic historian as well as the numismatist.[27] In 'The European heritage', his contribution to *Ancient Cosmologies*, edited by Carmen Blacker and Michael Loewe (1975), he revealed, perhaps, something of his own world picture. He quoted Walter Lippmann, a distinguished American publicist[28] who 'wrote of revealed religion (as Philip observed) in terms as trenchant as they were disrespectful'. Lippmann concluded: 'The modern man does not take his religion as a real account of the constitution, the government, the history, and the actual destiny of the universe. With rare exceptions his ancestors did.' 'Whatever one may think of other aspects of this judgement', Philip observed, 'in the field of cosmology it is wholly true.' The essay which followed deployed wide learning and deep understanding. Although we may suspect that Philip had a good deal of sympathy for Lippmann's own point of view, it did not deter him from devoting exceptional talents and a very long life to adding immeasurably to our knowledge of many regions of medieval history, some far removed from money and coins. But coins were paramount.

---

[27] 'The Roman Law of Counterfeiting', in *Essays in Roman Coinage presented to Harold Mattingly*, ed. R. A. G. Carson and C. H. V. Sutherland (Oxford, 1956), pp. 240–61; A. H. M. Jones, P. Grierson and J. A. Crook, 'The authenticity of the "Testamentum S. Remigii"', *Revue Belge de Philologie et d'Histoire*, 35 (1957), 356–73; 'The monetary pattern of sixteenth-century coinage', *Transactions of the Royal Historical Society*, 5th Series, 21 (1971), 45–60.
[28] Walter Lippmann, *A Preface to Morals* (London, 1929), pp. 68–9, quoted on p. 226 of P. Grierson, 'The European heritage' in C. Blacker and M. Loewe (eds.), *Ancient Cosmologies* (London, 1975), pp. 225–58.

III. Philip Grierson as numismatist

What made Philip Grierson the foremost medieval numismatist of our time, or indeed perhaps of any time?

In personal terms he was someone well equipped by nature for a long and distinguished academic career. Daily walks to the Fitzwilliam or the University Library, squash into his eighties, and a robust constitution kept him in good health until near the end of his life, and contributed to his remarkable stamina and powers of concentration. As a scholar Philip's qualities were formidable: his intellect was of the first order, combining flair and intuition with keen critical qualities, an amazing memory, and a ravenous appetite for knowledge and ideas. He combined the enthusiasm and energy of a collector with the application and thoroughness of a scholar. His aptitude for languages gave him readier access than most enjoy to the fragmented literature of medieval coinage; and amongst other things he had a wide knowledge of science, metallurgy, engineering, metrology, mathematics and even statistics. His one significant weakness (to which he readily confessed) was to allow himself to be sidetracked into studying any interesting problem or detail that he came upon.

Grierson's work on the *Cambridge Medieval History*, culminating in his production of the *Shorter History* in 1952, brought him an encyclopaedic knowledge of the political structures of medieval Europe. This gave him a much broader historical background than most historians or numismatists can command. He was equally at home in the fifth century and the fifteenth, in western Europe or the Byzantine east. Indeed, Philip was something of a numismatic polymath, for unlike most western medievalists he not only understood the essentials of oriental coinage but also, having taken Ancient History as an option in his Tripos, he gained a good working knowledge of Greek and Roman coinage. Thus, when he wanted an example of mistaken historical attribution, he chose not a medieval coin but one from fourth-century Delphi; he was joint editor of an unfinished work by his late friend Otto Morkholm on *Early Hellenistic Coinage*; and he wrote a learned article on the Roman law of counterfeiting.

It was thus with the benefit of wide historical training that Philip, at the age of 34, suddenly became aware of medieval coins and their potential as a primary source for historians. In January 1945 he was rummaging through a box of miscellaneous coins accumulated by his late father, and happened to notice a copper coin that he could not identify. When he was advised that it was a Byzantine coin of the Emperor Phocas, his interest was aroused and he thought of acquiring a few more to show his history students. He explained to Spinks, the best known of the London dealers, that he was prepared to spend up to £5 to buy a few coins, but that he was not a collector and had no intention of becoming one. But there were latent collector genes in his make-up—his father had had a taste for scholarly collecting (focused first on freshwater snails, later on stamps) of the kind that involves the keeping of careful records and a systematic effort to study and understand the material involved.

The timing of Philip's entry into the coin collecting arena was, if not absolutely ideal, at least highly favourable. The largest private collection of the twentieth century, that formed by the fifth Lord Grantley, consisting of some 50,000 coins of most countries and periods, was sold by auction in 1943–5. Of the eleven sales involved, Philip only arrived in time for the last which had few coins to interest him. But missing the others was not too much of a setback, since most of Grantley's coins had been bought for stock by London dealers as there was no competition from abroad during the war. As a result the London dealers had hundreds of coins in stock at very low prices and Philip was able to amass a sizeable collection very rapidly—within two years he had 4,000 coins, and within five, 7,000. Baldwin had sold a number of good Grantley coins to their largest client, R. C. Lockett, but Philip obtained many of these in 1956 when Lockett's own collection came onto the market. Elsewhere in Europe the coin market was more difficult in the post-war years, with travel on the Continent restricted by circumstance, and payment across national borders hampered by exchange controls. But Philip began to travel as much as he could and soon got to know most of the serious Continental dealers, as well as curators, collectors and others of the European numismatic fraternity, whose activities had been seriously dislocated by the war.

Philip's reputation as an historian of Flanders led soon to an opening in Belgium which was to become one of the major overseas commitments of his career. In the interests of restoring academic links that had been ruptured by the war he was invited through the British Council to lecture in Brussels, Liège and Amsterdam in 1948. He chose to discuss the light that could be thrown on the decline of the Roman Empire and the transition to the Middle Ages by the changes in Roman coinage of the fourth and fifth centuries. Two of the professors in his audience called on him the next day to ask if he was willing to be a candidate for the recently vacant Chair of Numismatics and the History of Money at the Université Libre in Brussels. Philip accepted without hesitation, and was to hold the post until his retirement in 1981. It involved giving fifteen lectures a year, carried a modest stipend in local currency (which was a convenience in the era of exchange controls) and led to him spending about six weeks a year in Brussels, at times which fitted in conveniently with vacations in the annual Cambridge calendar. It gave him great pleasure over the years and, quite apart from the prestige associated with the appointment, 'not the least of its services to my career was that it compelled me to take up the study of numismatics seriously'.

Philip's inaugural lecture at Brussels had an unexpected consequence. In 1951 an English version of it was published by the Historical Association under the title *Numismatics and History*. The President of the American Numismatic Society was moved by the plea it contained for more regular teaching in the subject. From this developed a plan for the Society to hold an annual summer seminar for up to a dozen selected students from American universities, to whom some visiting scholars would be asked to lecture. In its second year, 1953, Philip was invited to visit the Society for six months during which time at the suggestion of Alfred Bellinger, Professor of Classics at Yale, he went to Washington to see the coins at Dumbarton Oaks, an institution established for the furtherance of Byzantine and other studies which had recently acquired an important private collection. By this date Grierson had already made his mark as a Byzantine numismatist, largely as a result of three substantial articles on seventh-century coins that had appeared in the *Numismatic Chronicle* for 1950 and 1951, and which Madame Morrisson has described as models of clarity and logic. Bellinger and Grierson were asked to advise on how to make the best scholarly use of the coins at Dumbarton Oaks. The upshot of this was an invitation to Grierson to become honorary Adviser in Byzantine Numismatics, with a view to making the Dumbarton Oaks collection of Byzantine coins the best in the world, and then with Bellinger to publish it. Grierson set about the task of building the collection with enthusiasm. It enabled him to visit dealers and auctions all over Europe, and he greatly enjoyed 'the fun of collecting at other people's expense'. He had himself formed a collection of Byzantine coins, but in order to avoid a conflict of interest he ceased to collect the Byzantine series upon appointment and sold most of his coins to Dumbarton Oaks at an independent valuation.

For more than forty years Grierson was to spend about two months each summer at Dumbarton Oaks working on the catalogues. The first volume, on the sixth century, published in 1966, was by Bellinger alone, and consisted of a meticulous catalogue on traditional lines, without an introductory survey. Grierson, who was responsible for the massive volumes II (1968), III (1973) and V (1999), wanted his to provide the basis for a critical re-examination of the whole sequence of Byzantine coinage. His three volumes therefore included comprehensive introductions, as did volume IV (1999) by Michael Hendy, who had become involved with the project after Bellinger's death in 1978. At one time Grierson contemplated writing an introduction to Bellinger's first volume of the catalogue, but much new work on the sixth century by other scholars was being published or in preparation and he decided to concentrate on other priorities. These included a joint volume with Dr Melinda Mays, which appeared in 1992, on the fine collection of fifth-century Roman coins at Dumbarton Oaks, thus providing an overture to the volumes on the Byzantine series itself. Grierson felt that his Dumbarton Oaks prefaces, though large in scale, were 'not all that distinguished in content', but other scholars have taken a more favourable view of them. Alongside the Dumbarton Oaks volumes Grierson was, intermittently, also writing a general survey which was published in 1982 as *Byzantine Coins*, a book that contains the best available account of Byzantine coinage as a whole and is especially good on the seventh to eleventh centuries as a result of his work on the Dumbarton Oaks catalogues of that period.

After disposing of his Byzantine coins Grierson concentrated his collecting on the coins of Western Christendom from the fall of the Roman Empire to the end of the fifteenth century. The collection had initially arisen out of his own teaching interests, which were limited to the Continent. In deciding to exclude the coinages of the British Isles, he felt there were others capable of dealing with them; but also he had as early as 1949 conceived the idea of putting together a collection that would complement the Fitzwilliam Museum's, and there was already a good collection of British coins in the Museum. Although he set out initially to acquire a representative collection of Islamic coins from the more westerly provinces, these never exceeded some five hundred pieces, and from the early 1950s he made few additions—apart from coins of Norman Sicily with Arabic inscriptions and comparable issues of Italy, Spain and the Crusaders. As his European collection grew he gradually developed the idea of using it as the basis of a work of reference, as no book along those lines had been attempted since a three volume work published by Engel and Serrure in 1891–1905. His aim, since the 1950s, had therefore been to put together as representative a collection as possible of types, denominations and mints, and this objective was magnificently fulfilled over the next fifty years. Although he inherited some family money in

1970, his coins were essentially paid for out of his own earnings or pension. By the early 1990s the collection contained some 16,000 to 17,000 coins, but he continued to acquire more specimens at a rate of perhaps two or three hundred a year, and on his death they numbered in all around 20,000 pieces. He had recently estimated that they had a market value of £5–10 million. This figure could however be an underestimate, since the prices of good coins have risen strongly in the last few years and his collection contains many rarities that are no longer obtainable. Although his series of each country is surpassed by the holdings of its own national museum, Grierson was able to claim that he had the second or third best collection of almost every European country. This means therefore that overall his coins constitute by far the best and most balanced general collection of medieval European coinage anywhere. In the 1970s he made it clear that he intended to bequeath his collection to the Fitzwilliam Museum, and the provision of additional space in the Coin Department enabled him in 1979 to transfer his coins, hitherto insecurely housed in his college rooms, to the new 'Grierson Room', on loan to the Museum during his lifetime.

In 1955 Philip had been invited by the newly established British Academy Committee for the Sylloge of Coins of the British Isles to be the author of what was to become the first volume in its new series of catalogues of the major public collections. With only minor refinements, his volume on the Fitzwilliam collection (up to the Conquest) has served as a starting point and model for all subsequent authors in a project that has now reached its sixtieth volume. Although the coinages of the British Isles were not directly within Grierson's purview, he nevertheless made some typically incisive contributions in this field. These range in date from the sixth-century find of coin ornaments at St Martin's in Canterbury to the symbolism of the closed crown on the gold sovereigns of Henry VII, and include a reconstruction of the 1902 find of late ninth-century coins from Stamford in the Danelaw, and a penetrating analysis of references in Domesday Book to the geld *de moneta*. He was also struck by the fact that the only two material finds of gold coins in England from the seventh century each consisted of a round number— forty in the ship burial at Sutton Hoo and one hundred from Crondall Heath in Surrey. Grierson's suggestions that the former might have represented a sort of 'grandiose Charon's obol' for each of the forty rowers, and the latter a sum equivalent to the wergild of a Kentish ceorl have not found universal acceptance. But no one has proposed another explanation for the round numbers and Grierson had a better understanding than most that the functions of coinage in emerging societies were not entirely monetary in the ordinary sense. The theme of his 1956-7 Ford Lectures in Oxford was *Coinage and Society in Early Anglo-Saxon England*; he also wrote on the commercial and social functions of money in the Dark Ages more generally; and his interest in anthropology led him in 1970 to choose *The Origins of Money* as the subject of his Creighton Lecture in the University of London. He was the first scholar with a broad enough view to be able to look at coinage of different regions on a wide canvas, seeking to explain the movement of bullion between the Islamic, Byzantine and Western spheres in terms of metrology and gold : silver ratios, or identifying the impact, from the late fifteenth century, of African gold, of silver from the new Germanic mining areas, and of more from the New World, on the structure as well as on the volume of European coinage. Yet Grierson's wider perspectives did not preclude him from attending to the more technical areas of numismatics when he felt they could yield valuable information. Thus, for example, he compiled a corpus by dies in his study of the gold *solidi* of Louis the Pious, and analysis of die-cutting styles and features often underlies his identification of the products of different mints in the Byzantine series.

By the 1960s Grierson was beginning to think more specifically about the possible format for publication of his collection, but for many years he was too much immersed in the Dumbarton Oaks project to launch himself into a multi-volume work on western coinage. He did however produce a general survey entitled *Monnaies du Moyen Age* in 1976 which, with some additions and adjustments, was reproduced in English as *The Coins of Medieval Europe* in 1991. Western medieval coinage is extremely complex, because most of what are now modern countries had not yet developed into unitary states, and coinage rights had anyway often been ceded by rulers to ecclesiastical or other authorities, so that the number of different issuers was legion. Grierson's account of this complicated picture, which treats the subject from many angles—political, economic, cultural—is a brilliant synthesis and is written with magisterial authority. Great collectors are not often also great scholars, but Grierson regarded himself as fortunate to have gained much of his detailed knowledge of medieval coinage from his activities as a collector. He enjoyed the process of collecting, and was excited by the successful pursuit of rare items that he needed. In 1964 he bought a unique portrait denier of Charlemagne for £1,060, an acquisition that gave him a mixture of acute pleasure and a sense of guilt for what he saw as such an extravagance (it would now be worth tens of thousands).

In the early 1980s, after years of encouragement from Ian Stewart and other friends, the long-contemplated plan to publish the collection ('something to do in my retirement') at last began to become a reality. Philip was not a natural project manager, but steered by others, in particular by Christopher Brooke, in 1982 he put a proposal to the British Academy which led to its adoption as an Academy Research project. Cambridge University Press agreed to undertake the publication of *Medieval European Coinage (MEC)* in fourteen volumes, and funding was secured from the Leverhulme Trust to employ Mark Blackburn, a specialist in Anglo-Saxon coinage, as a research associate for the first three years. In 1985 conditions were favourable to secure the joint support of the Academy and of Gonville and Caius College, an arrangement that happily continued for eighteen years, the Academy's share of the funding latterly being assumed by the Arts and Humanities Research Board (later Council). The first volume, a collaborative effort of Grierson and Blackburn, appeared at the end of 1986; it covers the whole of Europe from the fifth to the mid-tenth century, but subsequent volumes were to be arranged on a regional basis. Next, therefore, they started work on the Low Countries, the region to which Grierson had devoted his early career, but its coinage, like that of the rest of the greater German Empire, is very complex; with more than a hundred authorities having issued coins, the scale of the work grew and progress was slow. On Blackburn's appointment as Keeper of Coins and Medals at the Fitzwilliam Museum in 1991, he was replaced on the *MEC* project by Dr Lucia Travaini, a specialist in the coinage of Norman Italy. Grierson had also published extensively in this field, and together they turned to the preparation of the volume for Southern Italy, which was duly published in 1998.

By 1996, with Grierson now in his mid-eighties, it had become apparent that the original concept by which he would be the principal author of all fourteen volumes was unsustainable, and he agreed to a new strategy of commissioning leading authorities in the various series to prepare appropriate volumes, supported by additional research staff based in Cambridge under his guidance. By 2000 seven new volumes had been commissioned with foreign experts, assisted by three research associates employed in the Fitzwilliam. Grierson himself returned to working on the Low Countries, while still aiming to make significant contributions to the other volumes underway. On his death he left more than a thousand pages of typescript for two substantial volumes on the Low Countries, with two volumes by other authors on the Iberian Peninsula and Northern Italy close to completion, and five more in preparation. The project will continue under the direction of Dr Blackburn, and there is every hope that most of it can be completed by the present generation of scholars. As is not unusual with ventures of this kind, the amount of work needed to produce a thorough and balanced survey of medieval coinage has proved much greater than anticipated. But this is understandable since the volumes are designed to serve as authoritative reference books for historians as well as numismatists, and nothing of this breadth and depth has ever previously been attempted.

Grierson saw it as the primary objective of the medieval numismatist to establish where, when and under whose authority the coins had been struck. With the multitude of issuers, and prevalence of imitation, this is often not a simple task. When Grierson came to the subject he discovered that relatively few professional historians in the medieval field had bothered with coins and that for the early Middle Ages they were still a largely unexploited form of evidence. Conversely, numismatists often seemed to work in a world of their own, with insufficient understanding of the general historical context. Grierson described his own approach to this situation as one of benevolent scepticism. In his first President's Address to the Royal Numismatic Society in 1962 he remarked that 'the enquiries into the validity of accepted conclusions should often be directed not at the conclusions themselves but at the means by which they were obtained'. This led him to develop a keen interest in numismatic methodology—the interpretation of the types and inscriptions of coins, the assessment of documentary evidence, the operation of mints, dies and die-output, the weights and fabric of coins and their methods of production, the analysis of hoards, the behaviour of coins in currency, and so on. In 1975 all of these topics were covered in the very concise but perceptive exposition of numismatic method in his little book entitled *Numismatics* which, despite its small scale, also incidentally includes the best general account of oriental coinage in the English language.

It was no accident that the title of the festschrift presented to Philip in 1983 was *Studies in Numismatic Method*. Topics covered in his Presidential addresses had included weight and coinage, coin wear and finds, and his own gradually developing thoughts on these and other questions may be found in many of his subsequent articles. In the 1960s and 1970s he was planning a general book on the techniques of medieval numismatics with Ian Stewart, and drafts of several chapters were written; but time and opportunity for completing this, in the face of competing priorities, did not prove to be available. Much of the material did however find its way into print in other forms. Grierson was particularly interested in the weights, values and contemporary names of coins; in their fineness and metallic composition; and in volumes of mint output and ways of estimating them that involved counting the dies used (an area in which his familiarity with Greek numismatics was useful). He was of course only one of many scholars working in these areas but one of the reasons why his influence was so great was the breadth of his knowledge of coinages of other times and places. This universal view was reflected in the *Numismatic Bibliography* which he compiled for the Historical Association as early as 1954; twenty-five years later a successor edition in French was more than four times its size, reflecting the huge expansion in numismatic activity in the intervening period. This growth was accompanied by great improvements in understanding between historians and numismatists, to which Grierson made a pre-eminent contribution. Quite apart from all his other writings, to have played the major role in the Dumbarton Oaks work on Byzantine coinage, to have planned and launched the first comprehensive account of western medieval coinages, and to have created the collections on which each of these is built, constitute a phenomenal and unique achievement.

PARTS I AND II   CHRISTOPHER BROOKE
Fellow of the Academy

PART III   LORD STEWARTBY
Fellow of the Academy

Note. The chief source has been personal knowledge. In Parts I and II C.B. gratefully acknowledges the kind help of friends, Ian, Lord Stewartby, Peter Spufford, Neil McKendrick, Lucia Travaini, and most of all Mark Blackburn. For Philip Grierson's early career his reminiscences, 'A numismatic career' recorded in Helsinki in December 1987 by Knud Wallenstierna and Panu Saukkonen, re-edited as 'A numismatic career', *Spink's Numismatic Circular*, 99 (1991), 223–4, 259–60, 291–2, 334–6, and 100 (1992), 3–4, 43, and Edward Timms, 'An interview with Professor Philip Grierson', *The Caian* 1977–8, pp. 33–55, have been especially useful (though occasionally needing minor correction from other sources). A perceptive appreciation is L. Travaini, 'Philip Grierson, storico della moneta, economica monetaria, barbe russe e origini della moneta', *Rivista di Storia Economica*, 22 (2006), 267–79. Philip's personal papers have been divided between the Fitzwilliam Museum and the Gonville and Caius College Archives—including more than 300 pages of biographical notes, mostly compiled in the 1990s. Details of his college and university career have been checked by the Gonville and Caius College Archives, by the *Biographical History of Gonville and Caius College*, VIII (ed. J. Whaley and C. N. L. Brooke, Cambridge, 1998), pp. 53–4, and the *Cambridge University Reporter*. I am very grateful to

James Cox, College Archivist, and Jacqueline Cox, Deputy Keeper of the University Archives, for their help with the sources; to Peter Brown, Amrit Bangard, Peter Marshall and Colin Baldwin for help in the editorial process; and to Grant Tapsell and Mark Blackburn for permission to print the extracts on pp. 84–6.

C. B.

Supplementary Bibliography

This supplements the bibliography covering 1934–81 by J. G. Pollard which was printed in *Studies in Numismatic Method presented to Philip Grierson*, ed. C. N. L. Brooke, B. H. I. H. Stewart, J. G. Pollard and T. R. Volk (Cambridge, 1983), pp. xv–xxv, and is partly based on the bibliography provided by the author himself to the British Academy. In completing it we are especially indebted to the bibliography published by Lucia Travaini in the *Rivista italiana di numismatica*, 107 (2006), 581–94. The following abbreviations have been used:

BNJ   *British Numismatic Journal*
BSFN   *Bulletin de la Société française de numismatique*
CISAM *Centro Italiano di Studi sull'Alto Medioevo*, Spoleto
NC   *Numismatic Chronicle*
RIN   *Rivista italiana di numismatica*

Books and pamphlets

1982:
Byzantine Coins, London and Berkeley.
Byzantine Coinage, Dumbarton Oaks, Byzantine Collection, Publication no. 4, Washington DC.
1984:
Introduzione alla numismatica, Società editoriale Jouvence, Guide 15, Rome [Italian translation of *Numismatics*, Oxford, 1975].
1986:
(With Mark Blackburn) *Medieval European Coinage, with a Catalogue of the Coins in the Fitzwilliam Museum, Cambridge*, I, *The Early Middle Ages (5th–10th Centuries)*, Cambridge.
1990:
Byzantine Coinage in its International Setting, Fitzwilliam Museum, Cambridge.
1991:
(Ed., with Ulla Westermark) Otto Mørkholm, *Early Hellenistic Coinage, from the Accession of Alexander to the Peace of Apamea (336–188 B.C.)*, Cambridge.
Coins of Medieval Europe, London.
(Edited and translated by G. Libero Mangieri) *Tari, Follari e Denari. La numismatica medievale nell'Italia Meridionale*, Salerno.

1992:

(With Melinda Mays) *Catalogue of the Late Roman Coins in the Dumbarton Oaks Collection and in the Whittemore Collection. From Arcadius and Honorius to the Accession of Anastasius.* Dumbarton Oaks Research Library and Collection, Washington DC.

1998:

(With Lucia Travaini) *Medieval European Coinage, with a Catalogue of the Coins in the Fitzwilliam Museum, Cambridge*, XIV, *Italy (III) South Italy, Sicily, Sardinia*, Cambridge.

1999:

Catalogue of the Byzantine Coins in the Dumbarton Oaks Collection and in the Whittemore Collection, V, Parts 1 and 2, *Michael VIII to Constantine XI (1258–1453)*, Dumbarton Oaks Research Library and Collection, Washington DC.

Byzantine Coinage, 2nd edn., Washington DC.

2001:

E. A. Arslan and L. Travaini (eds.), *Scritti storici e numismatici* [reprinted articles], CISAM Collectanea 15, Spoleto.

Articles

An asterisk indicates an article reprinted in *Scritti storici e numismatici*, Spoleto, 2001.

1981:

*'Thirty years of numismatics', in *Histoire et méthode, Acta Historica Bruxellensia* IV (Brussels, 1981), pp. 503–19.

'The "Gratia Dei Rex" coinage of Charles the Bald', in M. T. Gibson and J. L. Nelson (eds.), *Charles the Bald: Court and Kingdom* (British Archaeological Reports, International Series 101, Oxford, 1981), pp. 39–51. [See also under 1990.]

'A dandyprat reference of 1511', *BNJ*, 51, 197.

1982:

*'Computational fractions of the grain: mites, droits, periods and blanks', *BNJ*, 52, 181–6.

1983:

'A re-discovered siliqua of Valentinian III (425–55)', *NC*, 163, 217–18.

1985:

*'The Date of Theoderic's gold medallion', *Hikuin*, 11, 19–26.

'The dates of Patriarch Sophronius II of Jerusalem (post 1048–1076/83)', *Revue des études Byzantines*, 43, 231–5.

1986:

(With A. Shaw) 'A new follis type of Constans II', *Spink's Numismatic Circular*, 104, 10.

'Early Middle Ages' in *A Survey of Numismatic Research 1978–1984*, I, 314–31.

'A denier of Pepin the Short (751–68)', in 'Coins of the Anglo-Saxon period from Repton, Derbyshire', in M. A. S. Blackburn (ed.), *Anglo-Saxon Monetary History: Essays in Memory of Michael Dolley* (Leicester, 1986), pp. 127–30.

'Iconografia, circolazione monetaria e tesaurizzazione', in *La Cultura bizantina: oggetti e messaggio. Moneta ed economia*, Corsi di Studi V (1979) (Rome, 1986), pp. 29–57.

'Domesday Book, the geld *de moneta* and *monetagium*: a forgotten minting reform', *BNJ*, 55, 84–94.

'A semissis of Mezezius (668–9)', *NC*, 146, 231–2.

1987:

'A Syracusan follis of the second reign of Justinian II (705–11)', *Spink's Numismatic Circular*, 95, 324.

'The monetary system under William I', and 'Weights and measures' in *Domesday Book: Studies*, Alecto Historical Editions, 75–9, 80–5.

1988:

'Ein unedierte Grosspfennig Heinrichs II. von Virneburg, Erzbischofs von Köln (1306–1332), aus der Münzstätte Bonn', in *Commentationes Numismaticae 1988: Festgabe für Gert und Vera Hatz zum 4. Januar dargebracht* (Hamburg, 1988), pp. 247–50.

'The fineness of the Venetian ducat and its imitations', in W. A. Oddy (ed.), *Metallurgy in Numismatics*, Royal Numismatic Society Special Publication 19, pp. 95–104.

'Numismatic history', in J. Cannon *et al.* (eds.), *The Blackwell Dictionary of Historians* (Oxford, 1988), pp. 304–5.

'Foreword' (pp. vi–vii) to D. R. Cooper, *The Art and Craft of Coin-Making: A History of Minting Technology* (London, 1988).

'An enigmatic coin legend: IMP XXXII on solidi of Theodosius II', in P. Kos and Ž. Demo (eds.), *Studia Numismatica Labacensia Alexandro Jeločnik oblata*, Situla 26 (Ljubljana, 1988), pp. 279–84.

1989:

'An early reference to sterlings (Guibert of Nogent 1115)', *BNJ*, 58, 129–30.

1990:

'Un follis inédit d'Alexis Ier Comnène (1081–1119)', *BSFN*, 45, 740–2, 797.

'The "Gratia Dei Rex" coinage of Charles the Bald', in M. T. Gibson and J. L. Nelson (eds.), *Charles the Bald: Court and Kingdom*, 2nd edn (Aldershot, Variorum), pp. 52–64 [revised article of 1981].

'Eric A. Blackall' [a memoir], *The Caian* 1990, pp. 150–4.

1991:

*'A numismatic career: Philip Grierson (1910–)', *Spink's Numismatic Circular*, 99 (1991), 223–4, 259–60, 291–2, 334–6; 100 (1992), 3–4, 43.

34 articles in *The Oxford Dictionary of Byzantium*, 3 vols. (Oxford, 1991).

(With M. Blackburn) 'England: Medieval' in *A Survey of Numismatic Research 1985–1990* (Brussels, 1991), pp. 546–70.

'Presentazione' in L. Travaini, *Storia di un passione: Vittorio Emanuele III e le monete* (Salerno, 1991), pp. 5–11 (with English version at the end of the book); repr. in 2nd edn. (Rome, 2005), pp. 5–11 (English version, pp. 23–9).

1992:

'Keisari Bysantin rahoissa (Imperial Byzantine representation)', *Numismaatlinen Aikakauslehti*, 2, pp. 36–43.

*'Numismatics', in J. M. Powell, (ed.), *Medieval Studies: an Introduction*, 2nd edn. (Siracuse, NY, 1992), pp. 114–61.

'Spink's in 1945', *Spink's Numismatic Circular*, 100, 336–7.

'The coinages of Norman Apulia and Sicily in their international setting', *Anglo-Norman Studies*, 15, 117–32.

'Ercole d'Este e la statua equestre di Francesco Sforza, di Leonardo da Vinci', *RIN*, 94, 202–12 [trans. by F. Saetti of the article in *Italian Studies*, 14 (1959), 40–8].

1993:

*'The role of silver in the early Byzantine economy', in S. A. Boyd and M. M. Mango (eds.), *Ecclesiastical Silver Plate in Sixth-Century Byzantium* (Washington DC, 1993), pp. 137–46.

'Un denier de Toul inconnu: Otton Ier avec Otton II', *BSFN*, 48, 675–6.

'A new Visigothic mint: Carmona', in *Homenetge al Dr. Leandre Villaronga, Acta Numismatica*, 21–3 (Barcelona, 1993), 329–30.

'The Dumbarton Oaks Coin Collection', *International Numismatic Commission, Compte rendu*, 40 (1993), 55–60.

'Prolusione', and 'La moneta di conto nel medioevo', *Atti del convegno internazionale di studi numismatici in occasione del Centenario della Società Numismatica Italiana (1892–1992)*, *RIN*, 95, 49–51, 605–14.

'Frank Charles Powell, 1905–1993' [a memoir], *The Caian* 1993, pp. 100–9.

1994:

'Préface', in F. Delamare, *Le frai et les lois* (Paris, 1994), p. 11.

1995:

'Les grandes collections mondiales: The Dumbarton Oaks Coin Collection', *La Vie Numismatique*, 45, 167–73 [translation of the article of 1993].

'Les premiers *stavrata*: pièces byzantines ou pièces provençales?', *BSFN*, 50, 1060–3.

1996:

*'Six late Roman medallions in the Dumbarton Oaks Collecton', *Dumbarton Oaks Papers*, 50, 139–45.

1998:

*'Le dernier siècle du monnayage byzantin: problème et nouveautés', *Académie Royale de Belgique: Bulletin de la Classe de Lettres*, 9, 99–123.

2000:

'Coinage in the feudal era', in *Il Feudalismo nell'alto medioevo*, XLVII Settimana CISAM, 8–12 April 1999 (Spoleto, 2000), pp. 949–59 [with discussion, pp. 961–3].

2001:

'Le origini della moneta', *RIN*, 102, 13–48 [trans. of *The Origins of Money* (London, 1977)].

2002:

'The earliest coin portraits of the Italian Renaissance', *RIN*, 103, 385–93.

2006:

'Il fiorino d'oro: La grande novità dell'Occidente medievale', in *RIN*, 107, 415–19.

STUART HAMPSHIRE   *Orren Jack Turner*

Stuart Newton Hampshire
1914–2004

STUART HAMPSHIRE WAS ONE OF the most interesting philosophers of the last half-century. He wrote extensively on ethics and politics during the second half of his career, but everything he wrote reflected the concerns that drew him to Aristotle, Spinoza and Freud at the beginning of his career; and although he was never a Marxist, he never lost his respect for Marx's analysis of the conflicts and tensions inherent in any economically complex society. The last book he published in his lifetime was called, characteristically, *Justice is Conflict*, having begun with the title, *Justice is Strife*. To the very end of his life, he wrote with an extraordinary fresh-ness and lightness of touch, and preserved an open-minded curiosity about the human condition in all its aspects that would have been remark-able in someone fifty years younger. If it was sometimes less than clear at what destination an argument had arrived, the journey was always worthwhile.

Hampshire made a less visible impact than several contemporaries; he was less of a public figure than Isaiah Berlin, less of a celebrity than A. J. Ayer, and less influential in setting the philosophical agenda of the day than John Austin, Peter Strawson, or Donald Davidson. Conversely, he had a strikingly wide range of close friends in the worlds of literature, art, and politics. His work was never less than engrossing, perhaps because he tackled philosophy with an outsider's perspective as much as an insider's; he saw philosophy in its cultural and historical context as one of many ways in which a culture and the individuals who embody it come to terms both with their own cultural and intellectual artefacts and with the non-human world in which culture is embedded. Philosophy neither could be nor should be insulated from the ethical and political concerns of the

Proceedings of the British Academy, **150**, 107–123. © The British Academy 2007.

surrounding culture nor from that culture's scientific and non-scientific understanding of human and non-human nature. A measure of indecisiveness was a small price to pay for the resulting richness of perspective. Nor was this richness all; his treatment of ethics and political morality was unforcedly radical. If morality is a cultural artefact, one should not expect a comfortable answer to the question of how deeply rooted in underlying human nature any particular set of values is, and Hampshire never offered comfortable answers.

Stuart Hampshire was born in Healing, Lincolnshire on 1 October 1914. Healing is a village on the outskirts of Grimsby where his father had a fish merchant's business. The family was prosperous, and Hampshire was duly sent to Repton School, a school that specialised in the production of eminent cricketers and Archbishops of Canterbury. One future Archbishop, Geoffrey Fisher, was headmaster at the time, though Hampshire remembered him as more interested in the stock market reports than in the Bible. At Repton Hampshire overlapped with Roald Dahl without either of them mentioning the fact thereafter. In 1933 Hampshire gained a scholarship in Modern History to Balliol. His time at Repton coincided with what Hampshire later saw as his social and political awakening. As he describes it in *Innocence and Experience*, early in the Depression he and his family were holidaying in North Wales and went to Liverpool's Adelphi Hotel for lunch; outside, old women begged in the street and proffered sprigs of lucky white heather to passers-by, and the journey to and from North Wales took them past the silent and deserted shipyards of Birkenhead and clusters of unemployed men hanging about on street corners. The sharpness of the contrast between upper-middle-class comfort and grinding poverty was intolerable. *Innocence and Experience* also records his distress at the sight of ragged children in Oxford going barefoot even in the middle of winter. It did not produce an immediate conversion to any particular form of political activism, but it did produce a deep contempt for the sort of conservatism that set the protection of private property ahead of the welfare of the most vulnerable. The Second World War had a greater impact on his politics, but Hampshire never deviated from his hostility to conservatism or from the egalitarianism of his youth.

Hampshire had gained his scholarship in Modern History, but he switched to Greats. Like many students whose tastes ran to philosophy and history rather than to ancient languages, he by-passed Honour Moderations in favour of the three-year Greats course, graduated with a First in 1936 and that autumn was elected to an All Souls Fellowship. He was already a friend of Isaiah Berlin, who gave Elizabeth Bowen a thumb-nail sketch in the summer of 1936: Hampshire was 'approved by Maurice [Bowra] who declares that he has a keen sense of enjoyment, and is a good loyal boy, thought silly by Goronwy [Rees], unfascinating by B.J. [Maire Lynd], is much admired by Freddie Ayer; I feel both respect and affection, the former because of Cambridgy qualities, intelligence, integrity, purity of character, awkwardness, donnishness etc., the latter for the same reasons again, &, I suppose, because I seem to be able to talk about my subjects to him more successfully than to most people, also he likes music and bullies me politically. He is and looks a gentle, antelopelike, herbivorous character.' 'Antelopelike' was replaced with 'the Gazelle,' soon afterwards. Hampshire recalled at the time of Berlin's death that they had first met in 1934 to talk about Kafka; the conversation continued for the next sixty-four years.

On arriving at All Souls, Hampshire became a member of the philosophical group that Berlin and J. L. Austin had just established. Of their meetings, Berlin later said that 'in retrospect they seem to me to be the most fruitful discussions of philosophy at which I was ever present'. They went on until the outbreak of war in 1939. Their object was simply the pursuit of the truth about whatever the term's topic happened to be, with no thought of publishing whatever conclusions they might come to or of disseminating them more widely than among the group of Austin, Berlin, Hampshire, Ayer, Macnabb, MacKinnon and Woozley. Berlin later deplored their uninterest in the wider philosophical world, but the habit of attending carefully to what was being said at the moment and by the particular persons in the room was itself a valuable one, and Hampshire's attentiveness to his students when he subsequently taught in the United States struck his colleagues both in Princeton and in Stanford.

Hampshire gave a brief but engrossing account of his frame of mind at the time in the autobiographical introduction to *Innocence and Experience*. Since All Souls was deeply implicated in the policy of appeasement pursued by the Conservative government of the day, Hampshire could there observe at first hand the 'servility of Conservatives in the face of Fascism'. Unlike many of his contemporaries, his distaste for conservatism did not lead to an enthusiasm for its communist opposite; to the extent that he succumbed to any doctrinal position, it was to the positivism of the Vienna Circle; and in the cold light of logical positivism, all theories of history, whether Hegelianism, Marxism, Comtean positivism, or liberal doctrines of progress, looked like the decayed remnants of metaphysical systems that had been erected to console their adherents for the death of Christianity. The Nazi government of Germany was vile and appeasement disgusting, but one needed no theory of history to confirm that.

In 1937 Hampshire began the long relationship with Renée Ayer that ended only with her death in 1980. Today, nobody would flinch at a wife abandoning her husband for one of his colleagues after five years of a marriage that had been ricketty from the beginning; but for a decade after 1937 the attachment threatened to destroy Hampshire's chances of an established career, either in academic life or in the civil service. Most of Hampshire's friends disapproved of the relationship, not because they had moral objections but because they thought it rash, and some of them had never much liked Renée, whose indifference to the world's expectations they mistook for selfishness. It did not inhibit Queen's College from appointing Hampshire to a college lecturership. The person apparently least put out by it was Ayer himself; he finally divorced Renée in 1941, citing Hampshire as co-respondent, but so far from bearing a grudge, acknowledged the child born to his friend and his wife in 1939 as his own. Julian Ayer was inevitably known as Julian Ayrshire. Julian's younger sister, Belinda, was acknowledged as Hampshire's from the first.

On the outbreak of war, Hampshire joined the army; he was sent, briefly, to Sierra Leone. He was not a natural infantryman and was rapidly transferred into military intelligence. He spent much of the war analysing the activities of the *Reichssicherheitshauptamt*, the central command of Himmler's SS; unlike some of his colleagues, he did not afterwards talk much about what he had done there, but like almost everyone else in military intelligence he came across an assortment of characters whose loyalty lay to the Soviet Union rather than their own country. One story told by his obituarists was that Hampshire had in late 1942 drawn up a plan for encouraging the hostility to the Nazi regime on the part of senior military officers that later gave rise to the Stauffenberg Plot; the proposal gained general support but was shot down by Kim Philby. Nobody could understand why, but retrospectively, it seemed plausible that Philby had been acting on the Soviet line that it was better to prolong the war until the Red Army was firmly on German soil. At the end of the war, Hampshire himself was interviewed at length about his ties to Guy Burgess, during the first of several failed attempts by MI5 to uncover the full extent of the spy ring that Burgess had established. Many years later Goronwy Rees sought to blacken Hampshire's name by accusing him of having been, as it might be, the Sixth, Seventh or Eighth Man; he was duly investigated, questioned by Peter Wright, and cleared. The occasion was somewhat awkward for everyone because Hampshire had been appointed in 1965–6 to conduct a review of the intelligence gathering activities of GCHQ at Cheltenham.

By the end of the war, Hampshire was fully acquainted with the atrocious history of the SS in occupied Europe and Russia. It made him realise that 'unmitigated evil and nastiness' are as natural to human beings as kindness, a thought that as he said he might have gleaned from Shakespeare but previously had not. The feeling was sharpened when he had to interrogate Ernst Kaltenbrunner, the successor to Heydrich as head of the SS, and a man who was thought by his fellow SS officers to be a particularly ruthless and unpleasant piece of work. He took what even they thought a disgusting interest in the various methods of execution practised by the SS, and was eventually executed for the long list of war crimes for which he was tried at Nuremberg in 1946. The war over, Hampshire's future was uncertain. Ayer was appointed to a vacant philosophy fellowship at Wadham; the Master of Balliol, Lord Lindsay, blocked Hampshire's appointment to a fellowship, and Herbert Hart was appointed at New College. A permanent post in the Foreign Office was unlikely in view of Hampshire's marital status, and for over two years, Hampshire occupied a variety of slightly obscure positions in the Foreign Office that must sometimes have been a cover for continuing to work for MI5. They took him to San Francisco for the opening session of the United Nations and to Paris for some hard work on setting up the Marshall Plan.

Hampshire's return to academic life was brought about by Ayer. He had left Wadham for University College London when he became Grote Professor in 1947; determined to create a philosophy department to outshine Oxford, he immediately appointed Hampshire to a lecturership. In 1950, a long drawn-out game of musical chairs began, as Berlin left New College for All Souls, and Hampshire became a philosophy fellow at New College. In 1955 Hampshire was elected to a Senior Research Fellowship and the Domestic Bursarship at All Souls; in 1960, Ayer left University College London for New College as Wykeham Professor of Logic, and Hampshire succeeded him as Grote Professor. Berlin advised him not to move to London, and the fact that he remained there for only three years before moving to Princeton suggests that Berlin may have been right to warn him against the job. On the other hand, he was a very successful head of department, and graduate seminars in his large L-shaped office overlooking Gordon Square were wonderfully interesting occasions, not least for the variety of personal and intellectual styles on display.

By this time, Hampshire had written the two books for which he is best known, *Spinoza* in 1951 and *Thought and Action* in 1959. In 1960 he was elected to the British Academy. But America beckoned, and in 1963 Hampshire joined the Department of Philosophy at Princeton. At this time, it was the best philosophy department in the world, and it remained so during Hampshire's years there. He became chairman of the department the year after he arrived, and was a very successful chair. He had a sharp eye for talented young people and was instrumental in bringing David Lewis to Princeton among others. Hampshire's teaching style was—and remained—at odds with the conviction of his more analytically minded colleagues that philosophy should aim to achieve as sharp, brisk, and non-complex an account of the world as reality would accommodate; Hampshire invariably conducted seminars in a more circumambulatory fashion than that. Paul Benacerraf later recalled Hampshire's pleasure at the savagings he received from then Young Turks such as Gil Harman and Robert Nozick; they in turn later recalled Hampshire taking the same pleasure in the savagings he received from Benacerraf. To Hampshire, who had experienced much worse at the hands of J. L. Austin both before and after the war, it was more exhilarating than painful.

Hampshire's years at Princeton coincided with the increasing hostility to the Vietnam War, and by extension to modern capitalism and its political manifestations that convulsed American campuses. He played an important role in defusing conflicts at Princeton that could all too easily have led to real bloodshed. Princeton students were determined to have the Institute for Defense Analysis evicted from the campus, and on at least one occasion the local police faced protesting students with their weapons at the ready. Hampshire chaired the crucial meeting of the entire academic community in the enormous Jadwin Gym at which they hammered out not only enough of a compromise to keep the campus from erupting into the sort of violence experienced in Berkeley and elsewhere, but the beginnings of a much more open and democratic administration for the university as a whole. Hampshire tended to play down the whole business, and self-deprecatingly referred to himself as having joined 'the stage army of the good', whose house journal was *The New York Review of Books*, or—as George Will had it, *The English Review of Vietnam*. He enjoyed Princeton even though he found its pastiche Gothic painful; but he had no difficulty deciding to return to Oxford as Warden of Wadham when the chance came.

In 1970, Maurice Bowra retired from the position as Warden of Wadham that he had occupied since 1938. He had been elected a Fellow in 1922. The college had flourished under Bowra, and although Bowra was a markedly twenties-ish figure, Wadham was the most left-leaning, radical and 'modern' of the traditional colleges. Bowra was something of a *monstre sacré*, however, and dining in his company could be mildly terrifying as one waited for the next loud, and not infrequently gross, observation about a fellow diner. The college was not of one mind about how different it wished the next Warden to be, and initially there was little support for Hampshire's candidacy. Wardens had always been chosen from among fellows and former fellows; and Hampshire was very much not one. Details of the election were widely leaked, as often as not by Bowra, who was supposed to be wholly in the dark about events. The older fellows thought Ayer should become Warden, the younger fellows preferred Hampshire, once his name was in contention; when Ayer backed out on discovering that it was not to be a shoo-in, other fellows threw their hats in the ring. What clinched things for Hampshire was the issue of co-education. He was unequivocally in favour of Wadham admitting women undergraduates, Ayer was mildly hostile; in the eyes of young fellows, it was a litmus test of one's attitude to all aspects of university and college life.

Hampshire later said that he thought the fourteen years of his wardenship were the best thing he ever did. By the end of his time, that would have been the consensus among both students and fellows. Initially, things were awkward. Renée was not cut out for the role of 'Head of House spouse' as it was then understood, and was considered eccentric by the more conservative fellows. She never dined on high table, and if the Warden was forced to give a dinner party for people who bored her, she would cook dinner and retire to the kitchen. But she was unfailingly kind to the unhappy and the bewildered; she was much liked by the undergraduates, for whom she evidently felt a great deal of affection, and whom she happily invited to lunch; and she was seen as a role model by the new generation of women undergraduates. She had her own enthusiasms, of which the annual children's party complete with donkey rides is the best remembered, not least for the sight of Hampshire trying to coax the donkey—in one version—or manhandle it—in another—into the back of a small car. Hampshire had more trouble with the two fellows who thought they should have had the job rather than he; they sulked ostentatiously. Nor was he assisted by the continued presence of Bowra. Bowra was loudly in favour of Hampshire, and did his best to be unobtrusive, but unobtrusiveness was not in his repertoire. Having decided to die where he had lived for so long, Bowra established himself in rooms above the main gate; the porters continued to refer to him as 'the Real Warden' in contradistinction to 'the New Warden,' and it was only when Bowra died (suitably enough on Independence Day 1971) that Hampshire could get on with the job.

Because Wadham had become a thriving modern institution, Hampshire's task was essentially to keep it true to itself and to ensure that it could weather the assorted financial and emotional storms to which all such institutions are exposed. He maintained that he disliked administration, but sometimes pulled rank by reminding his colleagues that he had been a very efficient domestic bursar some twenty years before. Comparisons with Bowra inevitably lingered; Bowra had dominated a small governing body, most of whose members he had—or said he had—been instrumental in appointing. Hampshire faced a more numerous body and was less concerned to get his own way on all occasions. He had none of Bowra's passion for string-pulling either in the college or in the wider university and none of his taste for sliding unlikely candidates into not wholly suitable posts. His authority over the college was that of someone who was seen to be a considerable figure in the culural and intellectual life of the country as a whole, but he neither sank into college life nor became irritated by it.

In 1979 Hampshire was knighted for services to philosophy; the following year, Renée died. Initially, Hampshire withdrew into himself, but then turned more often to colleagues and the college for companionship. Students from the early 1980s remember Hampshire with affection, as someone whose conversation ranged over everything from the quality of the beer in the college beer cellar to the particular form of moral enlightenment to be gained from a careful reading of Henry James. In 1984, Hampshire reached the age of seventy and had to retire from the wardenship. He was appointed to a chair in philosophy at Stanford University, and remained there until 1990, when he returned to Oxford. He purchased a small house in Headington within a few yards of the Berlins. In 1985, he had married Nancy Cartwright who was at the time a professor of philosophy at Stanford; they immediately adopted their first daughter, Emily, and the following year had a daughter of their own, Sophie. Nancy Cartwright became professor of philosophy and scientific method at the London School of Economics, and Hampshire very happily—though somewhat to the alarm of some of his old friends—settled into the role of househusband, while continuing to write on Spinoza and much else until the very end of his life. On 13 June 2004 he died of cancer of the pancreas after a short illness.

Hampshire was part of a very remarkable philosophical generation. In the first decade after the war, what was generally called 'Oxford philosophy' was not only felt by philosophers to be fresh and exciting, but was thought by a much wider audience to mark a new, unstuffy, unpretentious approach to philosophy. For that decade, it was the cutting edge of anglophone philosophy, though despised then as later by anyone who craved the excitement of the latest Parisian fashion, and disliked by the fiercer sort of logical empiricist. Of course, many distinct varieties of philosophy were practised under that capacious umbrella; not everyone wanted to follow J. L. Austin down the path of mapping the ways of ordinary language, and an antipathy to the excesses of Heideggerian existentialism did not exclude an acknowledgement of the merits of Maurice Merleau-Ponty, the one French philosopher of the day for whom Hampshire had a lot of time.

The distinctiveness of Hampshire's own view of the analysis of mind was announced forcibly enough in a review of Gilbert Ryle's *Concept of Mind* that was notably unsparing in its criticism of what Hampshire saw as an overly simple behaviourism. Hampshire began by demolishing Ryle's identification of the 'Ghost in the Machine' model with Cartesianism by pointing out that the model was built into the natural languages of Europe and the Middle East, and rubbed salt into the wound by going on to argue that Ryle had essentially resiled from his avowed intention to stick to what was revealed by the way we ordinarily and actually speak by resorting to a vulgar verificationism. It is easy to suspect that what had got under Hampshire's skin was Ryle's claim that human beings are 'relatively tractable and relatively easy to understand'. War service in MI5 had no doubt made Hampshire more keenly aware that human beings are genuinely 'Occult' not 'Obvious': that 'just because they alone of natural objects are language-users and therefore are potential reporters, they are (unlike stones and dogs) liars, hypocrites, and suppressors of the truth about themselves'. He was no kinder about Ryle's claim that what novels record is essentially and overwhelmingly what their characters *do*. It was, after all, implausible as a claim even about the novels of Ryle's beloved Jane Austen, and as a claim about Proust, it was jaw-droppingly unlikely.

Spinoza was the first book that brought Hampshire to public notice; it sold 45,000 copies in a few months, and is sometimes said even now to have been Hampshire's best book. It appeared in a Penguin philosophy series in 1951 with a friendly preface from the series editor, Freddie Ayer, who confessed that he did not wholly understand what Spinoza had been up to, and was not sure that he wholly understood Hampshire's explan-ation. It remains a book worth worth reading fifty-five years later, espe-cially in *Spinoza and Spinozism,* which reprints the revised edition of 1987 accompanied by Hampshire's last thoughts on Spinoza and a wonderful short essay on Spinoza's conception of freedom from 1962.

It is not quite true that *Spinoza* is the essence of Hampshire; for one thing, Hampshire simply refused to follow Spinoza more than a very short way in his theological concerns. Perhaps more importantly, Hampshire was quite certain that Spinoza's hankering for a social and political harmony that was to be instituted by the educated elite's dexter-ous but paternalistic manipulation of untutored opinion, was not an option for a modern society, however much of an improvement it was on the violent and fanatical politics of the era of the wars of religion in Holland and the rest of Europe. For another, Hampshire himself was deeply sceptical of the role of reason in ethical and political matters, and did not entertain Spinoza's rationalist conception of knowledge that provided the foundation of his political rationalism.

The affinity lay elsewhere. Hampshire always thought of Spinoza as a philosopher who displayed the openness to the findings of science in whose absence philosophy would simply wither. He did not quite think of Spinoza as engaging in a Collingwoodian search for the presuppositions of the scientific world-view of his day—though there are elements of that thought in Hampshire's account—so much as someone sketching a pro-gramme for an absolute world-view consistent with the advances to be expected of science as it developed. The master science of Spinoza's day was physics, but Hampshire thought that Spinoza provided even greater illumination in a world where biology and psychology had been put on a scientific basis. Like Spinoza, Hampshire thought that these sciences had ethical implications. Berlin would occasionally tease Hampshire by telling him that he saw Spinoza, Marx, and Freud as the three Jewish prophets of freedom and himself as their Aryan interpreter. There was a small grain of truth in the joke. The grain of truth was not that they were Jewish, but that in different ways they put forward the seemingly paradoxical thought that freedom—autonomy—was the rational determination of the will.

Hampshire's understanding of Spinoza's conception of freedom con-trasts quite sharply with Berlin's in 'From Hope and Fear Set Free'. The latter was part of Berlin's broad-brush assault on all and every 'positive' conception of liberty; Berlin's anxiety was always that, *pace* the intentions of the originator of these ideas, some form of totalitarian state attached to an ideal of 'compulsory rational freedom' will be the end point. Hampshire treads more delicately, seeing Spinoza's insistence that we can liberate ourselves from self-destructive and unhelpful reactions as interestingly anticipating twentieth-century writers such as Freud, and not looking backwards to the Stoic doctrine of *apatheia*. Almost more interestingly, Hampshire argued something he did not subsequently make much of, which was that just as Spinoza thought the science of his day would liberate us in all areas of life, so we should now deepen our understanding of the forms of freedom available to us by using all the resources of the sciences of our own day. It was absurd to defend the liberalism of John Stuart Mill as though we had learned nothing more about human nature than Mill had known.

The crucial feature of Spinoza's metaphysics, of course, and the thing that Hampshire found most fruitful for his own work was Spinoza's insistence that Nature was one substance, not as in Descartes, Mind and Matter interacting unintelligibly, but one substance viewed under its active aspect as *natura naturans* and under its passive aspect as *natura naturata*. Man was not a union of Mind and Matter, but part of the natural order, containing in Spinoza's view, more reality than lesser creatures, but separated by no sharp gulf from them—not that Spinoza was any more concerned than Descartes with the interests of the inferior animals. The 'double aspect' theory that Spinoza provided was in its own time an answer to questions that Descartes's interpretation of the new mechanics had posed, but it was also the basis of a research programme for the future. Hampshire was much taken with an interpretation of Spinoza's concept of the *conatus* that every entity possessed that identified it with what sustained any entity as an individual of that particular kind.

For many students of philosophy 1959 was an *annus mirabilis*. It was the year Peter Strawson published *Individuals* and Hampshire published *Thought and Action*. Fifty years later, one can see what they had in common: an ambition to do philosophy in a more constructive vein than had been the case for the previous fifteen years, a greater friendliness towards the metaphysical ambitions of the past, and an emphasis on the centrality to our understanding of the world of the fact that we are embodied individuals who act on the world. The 'spectatorial' vision that had characterised traditional empiricism was replaced with a starting point that emphasised the role of individuals acting in and on the world. What made *Thought and Action* unusual at the time was the way in which Hampshire linked epistemology, the theory of action and moral philosophy; some of the contemporary reviews were mildly uncomprehending of what was going on; reading *Thought and Action* forty years later, some of Hampshire's *obiter dicta* retain a power to shock, but the project that animates the book has long since become part of the mainstream.

At the time of the publication of *Thought and Action*, Mary Warnock described Hampshire as an 'Aristotelian existentialist', an evocative phrase that catches the flavour of his writing, if not much of the detail. Hampshire's later account of Aristotle's contribution to ethics picks up the theme. On Hampshire's reading, Aristotle was right on one crucial issue—what 'good' means. A great deal of time could have been saved if this had been better understood. This was a rebuke to those who had profferred emotivist and imperativist analyses of 'good'. The larger point was enshrined in Hampshire's argument that what was needed was an analysis of the particular virtues, with due attention to the social and epistemological conditions that made sense of them. He has therefore sometimes been regarded as a communitarian ahead of his times. This slights the other striking feature of Hampshire's work, which was the emphasis, much influenced by his reading of psychoanalytic theory, on what he described as the 'unsocialized' mind.

While Hampshire had sided with Aristotle's view that the task of ethics was—in large part—to explicate the nature of the virtues, he was far from endorsing very many of Aristotle's substantive views, and over the years distanced himself still further from Aristotle. One of the pleasures of Hampshire's work was that he himself had a strong sense of how far he had travelled intellectually and perhaps more importantly morally. At the beginning of *Two Theories of Morality*, he reflects on the fact that we all have something like fifty years in which to make moral sense out of the world and our lives within it; children, as Aristotle said, were too busy being formed by others to embark on the process, but childhood over, we had, if we cared to undertake it, a project before us, in which we can draw on the assistance of other people, of imaginative literature, and of philosophy.

It usually appeared that Hampshire thought that most moral philosophy in the immediate post-war years had dropped below the level of interest or sophistication that was needed, though he always praised the insights of such authors as Ross and Prichard even when agreeing that they might have done well to choose more interesting examples. The standard he thought we should live up to was set, as it was in *Two Theories*, by the writers to whom Hampshire always returned for inspiration: Aristotle and Spinoza. This was not because one or other of them claimed his allegiance, let alone both. The idea that both might do so was absurd, since they represented the opposite poles of ethical thinking; the idea that one or other might was not at all absurd, but Hampshire had in fact come to think that there was little room for theory in ethics.

There was room for scrupulous and exact argument, and where argument was in place, nothing less than scrupulous and exact argument would do. But the ambition to systematise ethics was, he came to think, fundamentally mistaken. Morality was not 'about' one thing but many, and certainly about two very discordant things. On the one hand, there was the search for first principles that could claim universal validity and might plausibly be seen as the dictates of reason; on the other was the elaboration of ways of life, culturally grounded ways of dealing with the exigencies of existence that were quite obviously local in their reach. The tension was not always sharp, at least according to many philosophers, because it seemed to them that the local, culturally grounded ways of life and the attitudes and affections associated with them were also grounded in nature, and to that extent were the dictates of reason. But once it was claimed that the dictates of a local culture were also the dictates of nature, the door was open to unsettling questions about what it was that nature really demanded.

There is an interesting paragraph in *Two Theories* which justifies Mary Warnock's description of Hampshire as an Aristotelian existentialist. Looking back to the arguments of *Thought and Action*, Hampshire recalled that he had there emphasised that actions and intentions were susceptible to multiple descriptions, if not infinitely many, at any rate indefinitely many; 'I stressed the inexhaustibility of features that may be discriminated within situations requiring action and that may be morally interesting, and of the confinement within a morality left to itself, not to be further developed imaginatively, as a giving up of much of practical thinking.' Any one moral perspective, adopted once and for all, irrationally dictates only one set of acceptable reasons for action. When the argument, as it in this context, is directed against utilitarianism, it very elegantly illuminates the many tensions in J. S. Mill's attempt to make morality systematic and yet endlessly open to experiments in living.

It also illuminates Hampshire's criticisms of Aristotle's vision of the good life; in part, they are conventional, emphasising the narrowness of Aristotle's view of what sorts of good lives there were and the implausibility of his belief that there could be ultimate and unresolvable conflicts of obligation. But characteristically, Hampshire went beyond those observations to argue that what most thoroughly undermined Aristotle's ethics was the arrival of the modern world; a new sense of time and a new conception of freedom could not be accommodated within Aristotle's metaphysics and theory of action. Spinoza's theory of morality provided Hampshire with the foil he needed. This was not because Hampshire was himself much attracted to Spinoza's view that the good life culminated in a transcendence of time and space in thinking the thoughts of God, or at any rate, thinking with the freedom with which God thinks. Aspects of that view were attractive; liberation from irrational desire was certainly to be wished for and worked at. But Hampshire's exploration of the nature of ethical conviction led him to the view that in the last resort people had to choose between one way of life and another, and neither Aristotle nor Spinoza could show that one ideal was uniquely required by reason.

This became a more prominent theme of Hampshire's later thoughts on ethics and politics. Both in *Justice is Conflict* and *Innocence and Experience*, he pursued a line of thought that done in a less deft fashion might have seemed simply nihilistic or irrationalist. Hampshire subscribed to much of the ethically pluralist view of the world that Herbert Hart, Isaiah Berlin, and Bernard Williams shared, but he added nuances of his own. One was a focus on the difference between private and public virtue that followed, though it did not seem to do so quite exactly, a parallel distinction between the virtues of innocence and the virtues of experience; the sense in which it did so was, largely, that the virtues of innocence could be pursued in ways that guaranteed clean hands, while the virtues of experience were those proper to leaders, the visualisers of great projects, and the takers of risks. It was, and was intended as, a restatement of Machiavelli, but Machiavelli with a stronger sense of the costs of effectiveness in the public realm, and without any of Machiavelli's relish for dirty tricks as an art form. Nor was there any of Machiavelli's brusqueness about the relative attractions of different kinds of life; the virtues of innocence were not 'monkish,' nor suited only to those without the nerve to risk their necks in the political realm.

The most striking part of the argument, perhaps, was the analysis of justice. It was not quite true that Hampshire set himself against the dominant trend in political philosophy since John Rawls first sketched his account of the two principles of justice in the 1950s, but it was certainly true that where Rawls had set out to find constitutional and allocative principles that could command the conscientious allegiance of any rational person, Hampshire emphasised the role of justice in allowing us to live with conflict rather than trying to eliminate it. With some pulling and pushing, one could assimilate Hampshire's contrast between the realm of ultimate ideals where no convergence of view is to be expected—

any more than a convergence of tastes in music and art—and the realm of those rules that allow us to live with each other in spite of our disagreements to Rawls's contrast between our metaphysical convictions and our commitment to the 'political' conception of justice. But the entire tone and purpose of *Justice is Conflict* and *Innocence and Experience* are too different to make any such enterprise worthwhile.

Hampshire was defending just what Rawls repudiated: the institutionalisation of compromise. He ended the lecture that was expanded into *Justice is Conflict* with a rousing defence of 'smart' (as distinct from 'shabby') compromise: 'To speak of a smart compromise, as opposed to the usual shabby one, is half serious. A smart compromise is one where the tension between contrary forces and impulses, pulling against each other, is perceptible and vivid and both forces and impulses have been kept at full strength: the tension of the Heraclitean bow.' The analogy that springs to mind is with an artistic performance, but Hampshire repudiates it, as he did elsewhere in discussion with Elaine Scarry. It is rather that we must not expect too much of reason, must expect to change our minds and must not expect to convince everyone else of our own unique wisdom. 'Let there be no philosopher-kings, and no substantial principles of justice which are to be permanently acceptable to all rational agents, seeking harmony and unanimous agreement. Rather political prudence, recognized as a high virtue, must expect a perpetual contest between hostile conceptions of justice and must develop acceptable procedures for regulating and refereeing the contest.'

To the end of his life, Hampshire was reworking his view of Spinoza. The posthumous volume, *Spinoza and Spinozism*, that reprints his *Spinoza* and his essay on Spinoza's view of freedom, begins with his last essay on Spinoza. The book provided what it was supposed to do: an account of Spinoza that stuck quite closely to Spinoza's own exposition of his views in the *Ethics* and *The Correction of the Understanding*. In this last essay, Hampshire allowed himself to reflect more freely on what one might do with Spinoza's insights in a world quite unlike the world he had lived in, and against a scientific background unlike that against which he was writing. The main thread is familiar; it is once again the 'double aspect' picture of human beings as embodied intelligences and all that flows from it; and as before, Hampshire defended one kind of materialism against all others. That is, he was utterly unconvinced by any form of reductive materialism, but happy to accept the Spinozistic view that the mental and the material were two aspects of the same single Nature, as it were the concave and convex faces of a sphere. This was not to subscribe to the panpsychism that some critics have thought Spinoza's system implied, though Hampshire found room for the thought that the question of how an individual entity of any degree of complexity maintained itself as such was something towards which Spinoza had pointed the way.

Nonetheless, Spinoza omitted too much from his picture of the freedom that was for him the only unequivocal and unqualified value. 'Spinoza wrote that we know and we feel that we are eternal. But we also know and we feel that we have moments of ecstasy, and momentary aspirations that go beyond reason, and we have obsessions that lead to the making of music, poetry, sculpture, architecture and dance. The uses of imagination are also paths to freedom, alongside the uses of reason.' Many philosophers have gestured at the importance of the imagination, but few have written as though they really meant it. Hampshire was one of those few.

Indeed, if one were looking for a passage of deeply felt argument to press on an intelligent person who wished to understand why philosophers were obsessed with the issues that in fact engross them, one very good place to look would be the Introduction to Hampshire's collected literary criticism, *Modern Writers and Other Essays*, published in 1969. Everyone who read Hampshire in *Encounter* or the *New York Review*— perhaps above all, everyone who read him in the *New Statesman*—was entranced by his reviews; he had an uncanny ability to depict the inner workings of an author's mind and to hold in balance an attention to the deeply individual features of a writer and to the culture in which he or she worked, and the universal features of human life that he or she illuminated. Hampshire discounted these essays as contributions to criticism properly speaking; this was not affectation but the reflection of a sense of the different tasks proper to the critic and the philosopher.

The critic ought, on this view, to tackle single works, one at a time, and evaluate them by the standards of the genre and the aspirations of those who worked in that genre. Hampshire, on the other hand, was doing what the remark quoted above suggested; he was trying to show the philosophically minded how they might nourish their imaginations, and was uncovering for the benefit of anyone interested the intellectual and theoretical allegiances that animated much modern literature. The account of *Dr Zhivago* that he wrote for *Encounter* was thought by Pasternak himself to be the most insightful of any; it is hard to believe that Pasternak did not flinch momentarily when Hampshire contrasted the chaotic and coincidence-driven narrative of *Zhivago* with the swift, decisive beginning of *Anna Karenina*, and hard to believe that he did not relax two pages later when Hampshire said that the book's deepest and most moving theme was 'the overwhelming need to communicate one's own individual experience, to add something distinctive to the always growing sum of the evidences of life', and that the inconsolable characters in the work were those who had never 'succeeded in communicating perfectly with one other person, giving the testimony of their own experience, either in love or in a work of art'. It is not surprising that the author of that sentence was so engaging, both in himself and on the page.

ALAN RYAN
Fellow of the Academy

WILLIAM McKANE   *Peter Adamson*

William McKane
1921–2004

THERE WAS LITTLE IN WILLIE MCKANE'S background and upbringing to
herald the distinguished career as Semitist and Old Testament scholar
that would follow. Nor was his path into academia one that would be
usual in these days, when the track from Bachelors to Masters and a doctorate seems almost to be a *sine qua non*. Rather, the fact that he arrived
where he did by the route that he took is itself testimony to the single-
minded, even ascetic, dedication to the rigorous pursuit of excellence
which was such a hallmark of his scholarship.

Born on 18 February 1921, Willie was brought up with his two sisters in Dundee. His father was a mechanic in the local jute mill of H. & A.
Scott and his mother, to whom he was especially close, cared for the children of some of the other mothers who worked at the mill. Although he
obviously did well during his years at Stobswell School, where he was
dux, it was therefore probably more by assumption than forethought
that he left at 15 in order to become a clerk in the same firm, apparently
intending to pursue a business career.

There was another influence besides his family which began to make
itself felt at this time, however, namely that of the church which his family attended. It was a congregation of the Original Secession Church, a
fiercely independent-minded denomination whose origins reached back
to a split in the Church of Scotland in 1733 over the issue of patronage—
whether or not the congregation retained the right to choose its own minister by accepting or rejecting a candidate proposed by the church's
patron. The path to ordination was long, and in Willie's case prolonged
by the intervention of the Second World War. Whether or not it was
the case from the outset, certainly by the time of ordination itself a

Proceedings of the British Academy, **150**, 127–146. © The British Academy 2007.

significant motivating factor in proceeding was the desire to work more effectively for the reunion of the denomination with the Church of Scotland. When this was successfully concluded in 1956, Willie was among the first to accede to the Church of Scotland (though to no one's surprise there were individual congregations, including the one of which Willie had himself been the minister, which remained apart).

Ordination required first a university degree, and for an arts subject, at least, that meant Latin. At an early stage, however, his studies at night school were interrupted by the war, and Willie saw service in the RAF from 1941–5. Of what that involved in detail little enough is known, but it is a firm part of family tradition and pride that he succeeded in passing the final hurdle for university entrance, including Higher Greek, in a special examination held at an RAF station in Holland in 1945; evidently, he had sufficient time and strength of resolve to continue his studies even while on active service.

Thus it was that as what would nowadays be called a mature student Willie embarked upon an honours degree at St Andrews in English and Philosophy in January 1946. Although he did not ultimately pursue either subject professionally, it is not difficult to detect their impact on some of his later writing, both in his choice of the so-called Wisdom literature of the Old Testament as a major field of research and perhaps even more, as we shall see later in connection with his last published book, in his handling of some of the wider theological issues arising from a scholarly approach to the biblical text.

Two other undergraduate activities were perhaps more indicative of things to come. On the one hand, he attended Hebrew classes with Professor A. M. Honeyman, presumably purely out of interest in the first instance, and this, of course, was to set him on his life's career. Only marginally less important, one is tempted to suggest, he collected a blue in association football. His interest in several different sports remained with him till the end. To regular participation in football on Saturdays during his years in Glasgow should be added his abiding love of cricket, which he continued playing as a member of the St Andrews University Staff team until well into his sixties. He was also a keen follower of rugby, supporting the University XV and not infrequently travelling to Edinburgh for the internationals at Murrayfield, and a member of the Royal and Ancient Golf Club at St Andrews. The editors of his festschrift saw fit in the course of a very brief introductory appreciation to make mention of the fact that 'Monday morning coffee in St. Mary's usually centres on a discussion of the weekend's soccer or rugby or, depending on the season, cricket'.[1]

During the three long vacations of his undergraduate years he attended summer schools at the Bible Training Institute in Glasgow[2] in order specifically to prepare for ordination under the guidance of Principal Francis Davidson. Thus as early as 1949 he was ordained to serve in the church at Kilwinning. He was conscientious as a minister, preaching twice on Sundays and again once on Wednesdays as well as editing the denomination's magazine. But according to one member of the congregation, he was not really cut out for the pastoral ministry because he was not sufficiently social—and she should know, for this was none other than Agnes, who was nursing in Glasgow at the time. They were to be married in 1952 and it is difficult to imagine how he could have succeeded without her devoted and steadfast support over some fifty-two years. But that is to anticipate.

In addition to fulfilling his church duties, Willie travelled daily during those years into the centre of Glasgow in order to study Semitic languages (principally Hebrew, Aramaic and Arabic), eventually graduating with first-class honours. This led to the offer of an assistant lectureship in 1953, and from that point he never looked back. The first three years were marked by the uncertainty which attends all untenured junior positions, but he worked for his Ph.D. at the same time and promotion to a full lecturership (and later senior lecturership) duly followed.

As Willie's doctoral thesis was never published, he was already 35 before his first article appeared and over 40 before his first book was published. Both were in the field of Arabic studies, expertise in which is noteworthy in much of his later work on the cognate language of Hebrew but which he did not pursue in research terms after these opening forays (indeed, it is of interest to note that his election to a Fellowship of the British Academy later on was by the Oriental and African Studies Section, not Theology, as might have been supposed). The book is a translation with a brief introduction and minimal annotations of one of the four volumes of al-Ghazali's major work, *The Revival of the Religious Sciences* (*c*. AD 1096).[3] His Preface gives no indication as to why he should

---

[1] J. D. Martin and P. R. Davies (eds.), *A Word in Season: Essays in Honour of William McKane* (Sheffield, 1986), p. vii.

[2] The Institute was later transformed into the Glasgow Bible College, and in 1998 it merged with the Northumbria Bible College to become the International Christian College of today.

[3] W. McKane, *Al-Ghazali's Book of Fear and Hope* (Leiden, 1962). The text itself is not reproduced and the work is based on a modern edition (1939) rather than on manuscript sources.

have undertaken this particular task other than acknowledging that it was suggested to him by his former teacher, the Revd E. F. F. Bishop—so perhaps there was an element of understandable concern to keep in favour with a senior colleague. He claims this to be a pioneer translation into English and accepts that there are passages where he does not think that he has penetrated through to the full meaning of the Arabic: 'It will be a task for future translators to clear up these obscurities.' A recent informed opinion is that 'it looks competent, on the whole. A bit short on annotation . . . a reference to the relevant Qur'anic passages would have been helpful . . . some strange transliteration mistakes of very common words', and so on.[4] At all events, this was not a direction that Willie pursued in any further publications, which thereafter were firmly in the areas of Hebrew and Old Testament studies.

From the Glasgow years came a number of articles and three further books. Several of the articles were published in the *Transactions of the Glasgow University Oriental Society*. Willie himself edited the journal for a number of years (1965–72), and its demise some years later has been frequently lamented. Not a few scholars who were subsequently to make a mark in the field published there early if not, indeed, first.

Unlike all his later publications, the next two books to appear were at the more accessible end of the market, intended especially for students and ministers, but also for others interested in the Bible from a lay perspective. *I and II Samuel* (London, 1963) has long been noted for the fact that it is nevertheless based upon deeper scholarship than some others in the series to which it belongs (Torch Bible Commentaries), and this is no doubt in part because it will have drawn on insights gained while writing his unpublished Ph.D. on 'The Old Israelite Community and the Rise of the Monarchy'. The other book in this category will have served its purpose at the time, but today it is hardly remembered at all.[5]

---

[4] Private communication from Professor Geert Jan van Gelder, FBA, of St John's College, Oxford. He adds, 'I came across one funny translation error: "youths passed by in skiffs, beating with the oars and drinking" (24); this sounds like punting English undergraduates. It should be "youths passed by in a boat [singular], playing the tambourine and drinking".' It is unlikely that at this stage of his career Willie would have had much experience of punting, however!

[5] W. McKane, *Tracts for the Times: Ruth, Esther, Lamentations, Song of Songs* (Bible Guides 12; London, 1965). The series was edited by W. Barclay (a Glasgow colleague) and F. F. Bruce, and was intended to introduce biblical literature to a lay readership. Characteristically, Willie was concerned to allow these ancient texts to speak in their own voice, not constrained by ulterior agendas: 'they will not speak to us if we submit them to constraint or torture [*sic*], but, if we allow to each the truth of its own nature, they will speak to our times with fluency and weight'.

Quite different, however, were both the content and the reception of the final book from the Glasgow years, *Prophets and Wise Men*, a little book of which Willie is said always to have been particularly fond. In it he advanced an analysis of the two great institutions of the title in Ancient Israel which was not wholly new but which had not previously, perhaps, been seen in such starkly differentiated colours. On the one hand, careful exegesis of selected passages leads to the conclusion that what he calls old wisdom was 'a disciplined empiricism engaged with the problems of government and administration' (p. 53). These politicians were not necessarily godless, but professionally they had to engage in hard-headed decision-making based on accumulated experience and practical politics. On the other hand, the prophets (and it is principally with Isaiah and Jeremiah that he is concerned) stood in the tradition of those who viewed the whole of history on the international as well as the local level as being under God's control and they knew his will in current circumstances through their access to his Word. In normal circumstances, these two could co-exist because they were applied to separate spheres of national life. But with the rise of the Assyrian empire with its impact on the Levantine states, there arose situations of crisis where both addressed the same situation—a clash of *Realpolitik* and *Heilsgeschichte* which was simply irreconcilable. Writing in the 1960s, Willie was able to hint in his conclusion that such conflicts of authority were still very much in evidence.

In retrospect, it is helpful to appreciate something of the prevailing movements, both in narrowly Old Testament and in wider theological discussions, in order to understand why this slim volume had the impact it did, given that, albeit in modified form, there are some aspects of its thesis that seem rather commonplace today. Within the circles of Old Testament scholarship, this period was the heyday of the so-called Biblical Theology movement, in which a significant stress was placed upon the interpretation of the past in terms of God's mighty acts. A consequence of this was that little place was found for the Wisdom literature (Proverbs, Job and Ecclesiastes, for instance), though in compensation a major drive was initiated to seek to find wisdom influence on other parts of the canon. Though not framed as such, Willie's book must be seen as in part a reaction against this one-sided view, and while in his Preface he rightly states that he has no intention of taking sides with either statesman or prophet, since partisanship 'will not do justice to this conflict nor show its contemporary relevance', nevertheless anyone who knew Willie's own personality is unlikely to overlook the fact that he would have felt that the importance and value of rational decision making should not be underestimated, as it was tending to be in contemporary debate. More widely, these were also the years when the theology of Karl Barth, with its emphasis on the Word, was dominant, not least in Scotland, and of course this was entirely congenial to the work of the biblical theologians, as exemplified especially in the writings of the great German Old Testament theologian, Gerhard von Rad, with whom the book interacts closely. I should stress that neither Barth nor the Biblical Theology movement as such are named in the book, so that it is speculative to assert that Willie had either explicitly in his sights as he wrote. Nevertheless, it is legitimate to read his work historically against that background and to see how in a modest fashion it contributed to the crisis which beset the movement not so many years after.

By the time the book was published, Willie and Agnes already had four children, and a fifth was to follow soon. A dilemma now faced him in terms of his career: should he wait for a vacancy to occur in the Glasgow chair, and so hope to continue to work and raise his family in familiar and congenial surroundings, or should he respond to the advertisement for the chair of Hebrew and Oriental Languages back at his Alma Mater of St Andrews? His choice of the latter course is not one that he subsequently regretted. Although for the first year of his tenure he had to travel to St Andrews for two days a week, the family was able to move to join him in the summer of 1968, buying a pleasant house in an area which the University itself developed for staff housing. Friends have written appreciatively about the generous hospitality of the McKane home both in Glasgow and then in St Andrews.

In the department he found Peter Coxon already in post. He soon brought over Jim Martin, a former colleague, from Glasgow, and within three years they were joined by a former pupil, Robin Salters. These four remained together in harmonious relationship for some twenty years, a remarkable, and one ventures to say unique, example of academic collegiality which reflects well on them all, but not least on Willie, who was the acknowledged academic leader. It will have helped too that Jim was happy to undertake the lion's share of routine administration. Though he took his expected turn as Dean of the Faculty of Divinity in 1973–7, Willie was mostly content to be left alone with his books, and no doubt this was one of the reasons why he resented government interference in universities. He was a conscientious teacher (mostly at the undergraduate level, with only a few graduate students over the years), and it must have pained him to see how a department of Hebrew and Old Testament was changed to Hebrew and Biblical Studies and then ultimately to Divinity. He made no secret of the fact that in his opinion this was symptomatic of what he regarded as a decline in standards, and it goes along with this that he fought hard at the General Assembly of the Church of Scotland for the retention of Hebrew as a compulsory element in ministerial training. His comments in private on Old Testament scholars who did not get fully to grips with the problems of the Hebrew text at first hand were outspokenly trenchant.

Life in St Andrews seems quickly to have settled into a comfortable routine, which suited Willie's unpretentious style. The University was within twenty minutes walk from home, and he would go in on such days as he was teaching, generally taking morning coffee with students as well as colleagues. But it was at home that he wrote, and so he would return there as soon as possible. As we shall see, these were immensely productive years, and it was to this side of his duties that he gave his main attention. He seldom spent any prolonged periods away from home. The one major exception was a year spent as Andrew Mellon Senior Fellow of the National Humanities Center, North Carolina (1987–8), where he was engaged on the second volume of his Jeremiah commentary. Even there, however, Agnes recalls how he quickly reduced life to a routine that suited research, taking the minibus to the NHC in Research Triangle Park each day between the hours of eight and five. He speaks warmly in the Preface to his volume of the generous hospitality of the Center and of the intellectual stimulus from contacts with its fellows. Among them were Professors S. Talmon of the Hebrew University and John Van Seters of Chapel Hill. It is likely that Willie will have appreciated this sustained contact with a small group of colleagues; he was never comfortable in large social gatherings but he was excellent company in small groups of like-minded people. And this was evidently appreciated in Chapel Hill, for Van Seters has recently dedicated a book to his memory,[6] writing positively of Willie's scholarship and also mentioning how they became 'good friends' during that year.

Apart from that year, there was a spell of three months spent in the Lebanon under Foreign Office auspices (1959) and a separate trip to Israel (April/May 1975). Otherwise, he preferred to remain reclusively at home.

---

[6] John Van Seters, *The Edited Bible: The Curious History of the "Editor" in Biblical Criticism* (Winona Lake, 2006).

Willie was not overmuch interested in reactions to his writings, nor did
he actively court the various honours which came his way. Accordingly,
he kept no correspondence which might be revealing of his thinking, and
for most matters we have to rely on the memories of others and deduc-
tions from his publications. There is one exception, however, the very isolated nature of which underlines how strongly he felt on the subject. St
Mary's College was founded in 1539 on the Continental trilingual model
with an emphasis on the knowledge of Latin, Greek and Hebrew. Within
forty years, following the Reformation, it was reconstituted as the
Theological Faculty of the University and this in particular, it must be
remembered, within a system where a University education in Theology
may itself serve as a preparation for ordination. The College is still
housed in part in its original buildings, and it has a distinguished and justifiably proud history. When Willie arrived at St Andrews the Principal
was Professor Matthew Black, who held the post, as was customary, until
his retirement. Whether the two following facts are related is not clear, but
after Black's retirement in 1978 the University authorities decreed that
the role of Principal should become a four-year, fixed-term appointment,
and Willie was evidently disappointed, not to say hurt, to be passed over
in favour of Jim White. Willie then succeeded him (1982–6). Willie wrote
to Professor George Anderson of Edinburgh relating this saga and giving
his side of the story, uncharacteristically giving Agnes a copy of his letter
for safe-keeping. It is clear that he thought that the affair had not been
handled with the sense of integrity which was the hallmark of his own
dealings, and it seems to have been the one really painful episode during
his otherwise happy tenure.

Six major works, one in two volumes, mark the St Andrews years,
and retirement in 1990 was if anything merely a spur to greater productivity. The first, much of the work on which must have already been
completed in Glasgow, was his massive commentary on the book of
Proverbs.[7] It is not difficult to see how naturally one of its major theses
develops an aspect of *Prophets and Wise Men*, already discussed, but it
goes further than just this. Indeed, a case can be made for the judgement
that those aspects which seem most indebted to the former work have
been largely discarded in more recent work whereas the other, and really
new, departure has been generally adopted.

So far as the commentary proper is concerned—roughly two-thirds of
the whole—it is typical of the style of commentary work that was to fol-

---

[7] W. McKane, *Proverbs: A New Approach* (Old Testament Library; London, 1970).

low in subsequent years: careful attention on a verse-by-verse basis to the problems of the Hebrew text, on which light may be shed either by the translations in the ancient versions (Greek, Latin, Aramaic and Syriac) or by consideration of the meaning of the word in cognate Semitic languages (Arabic, Aramaic, Akkadian, Ugaritic, and so on). At the time Willie was writing, this latter method was extremely popular in some circles as an approach to the Hebrew text of the Old Testament, and it may be said to have reached its height (if that is the right term) in the translation of the Old Testament in the *New English Bible*, which coincidentally appeared the same year (1970).[8] While open to the method in principle, Willie shows himself more cautious in its application than some, and it is interesting to note that later on he was to be a member of the group which worked on the preparation of the *Revised English Bible* (1989), a major purpose of which was to purge the *NEB* of some of its more speculative translations based upon this principle. When this sober text-critical work is allied to Willie's thoughtful observations on many of the proverbs themselves, it makes the commentary a standard resource for the study of this book.

The long introduction is largely given over to an important survey of comparable Wisdom literature elsewhere in the ancient Near East in order to establish that two separate types of composition have been combined in the biblical book, so-called sentence literature on the one hand (i.e. something closer to our modern use of the term proverb) and instruction literature on the other (i.e. more extended discourses, of which there are a number in Proverbs 1–9 in particular). According to an important view which dominated in the middle of the twentieth century, there was to be traced an evolutionary development from the former to the latter, and a consequence of this was that the opening chapters of the book were to be dated last, and certainly not before the so-called post-exilic period. Willie was not alone in protesting against this consensus, though he was certainly among the most influential. By the simple expedient of working through many examples of instruction texts, especially though not exclusively from Egypt—that is to say, extended compositions of wisdom material that was often used for the training of the royal and scribal classes—he was able to show that this was quite simply a different genre

---

[8] For an account of this method and discussion of some methodological issues which were all too frequently ignored by its more enthusiastic practitioners, see James Barr, *Comparative Philology and the Text of the Old Testament* (Oxford, 1968). It should nevertheless be emphasised, in view of the way some later writers have referred to this book, that Barr does not regard the method as inherently invalid.

of writing from the sentence literature and that historically it was quite as old (in Egypt both genres existed for well over a thousand years before any possible date for Proverbs). No evolutionary development of this sort should therefore be traced in Proverbs, and the whole issue of dating the relevant material needed to be tackled from a different angle. This was one of Willie's all-too-rare forays into the biblical analytical method known as form criticism, and it was brilliantly successful.

The same cannot be said of the other major thesis which he sought to defend in the commentary. He arranges the sentence literature into three groups, in the first of which the 'sentences are set in the framework of old wisdom' while in the third the sentences 'are identified by the presence of God-language or by other items of vocabulary expressive of a moralism which derives from Yahwistic piety' (p. 11). Very much in line with the argument of *Prophets and Wise Men*, this third group represents a rein-terpretation of the first and is therefore to be dated later. The theory pre-supposes that old wisdom operated without any religious underpinning and that the later collectors of the proverbs acted somewhat automati-cally, bringing together every saying that they had received without con-sideration for its present context. The theory is clearly open to the charge of circular reasoning, and it has been criticised on other more technical grounds as well.[9] Unlike the work elsewhere in the commentary, this particular theory has not withstood the test of time.

The next book to appear is very different in character and in substance from anything else that Willie wrote, and it may be that for that reason he appears to have had some difficulty in getting it published: in the Preface he is unusually effusive in his expression of thanks to Professor Black 'for his energetic efforts to have the book published . . . I cannot adequately express my thanks to him for his concern, persistence and expertise which have brought the book to the point of publication'.[10] Moreover he refers to a book published two years before his own as having appeared after he had completed it.

It is not that the book is not learned or based upon sound scholarship. Rather, the subject matter is likely to have been such as to cause publish-ers to wonder about an adequate market. Although entitled *Studies in the Patriarchal Narratives* (Edinburgh, 1979), which sounds attractive enough, it is really a reaction to what is perceived as being a mistaken

---

[9] For a particularly incisive critique, see Stuart Weeks, *Early Israelite Wisdom* (Oxford, 1994), ch. 4.

[10] We may note that Willie wrote the obituary notice of Matthew Black in the 1995 *Proceedings*. It is warmly appreciative, but offers honest criticism in places where that is called for.

trend in (then) recent study of the Genesis narratives to use archaeology in an attempt to salvage historicity, a quest not only dubious in itself but distracting from other and, in Willie's opinion, more important aspects of these narratives. From the point of view of method, questions of literary genre should be settled before historicity can be addressed, and with this in mind he tracks back to an earlier phase of scholarship and seeks to recover its importance with chapters on genre, tribal history, tradition-history and so on. Unfortunately, its publication coincided with two important monographs which negatively went a long way to destroying the archaeological approach from within, with an expertise in that field that Willie would never have claimed to have, and secondly with an alternative movement towards literary readings of these same texts which captured the imagination in a way that left Willie's work floundering high and very dry. His work retains its value in terms of the history of scholarship in the earlier part of the twentieth century, but as a programme on which to move forward it sank almost without trace. It is perhaps significant that at the point where he left off detailed textual and exegetical work he seems to have lost his voice. Fortunately, he was to find it again in his next major publication, the first volume of his *magnum opus* on the book of Jeremiah.

The 'International Critical Commentary' (ICC), for which Willie was invited to write on Jeremiah, has long had a special place in English-language biblical scholarship. The original series started to appear in the late nineteenth century, and although most of the volumes appeared before the First World War, one or two appeared later, the latest being in fact in 1951. Some books were never completed, however, and by the 1970s some of the older volumes were in urgent need of replacement. New editors therefore began to commission some new volumes, and Willie's on Jeremiah was the first Old Testament volume of the new series to appear (1986 and 1996). While the series aims at comprehensive coverage of critical issues concerned with the Old Testament, one of its particular strengths (and in the nature of the case one that is only occasionally paralleled in other series) is its detailed attention to the problems specifically of the Hebrew text—text-critical and philological in particular. Not surprisingly in the light of what we have already seen, the choice of Willie proved to be an inspired one.

The book of Jeremiah raises several major problems which are peculiar to itself. At the textual level, it is striking that the Greek translation, the Septuagint, is some 20 per cent shorter than the Hebrew on which it is supposedly based (mostly by numerous small minuses rather than the omission of large blocks of material) and, what is more, at one point it presents the chapters in a radically different order. One uncertainty about this situation was clarified by some small fragments among the Dead Sea Scrolls which include a Hebrew text comparable with the Greek; it is therefore certain that the Greek is based on a Hebrew *Vorlage* and is not the result of the translator's work. There must therefore have been two versions of the Hebrew text of Jeremiah in circulation in antiquity, but why? And which was earlier?

Secondly, there are three types of writing in the book, the origins of the third of which, at least, is uncertain. First, there are poetic oracles, as in many other prophetic books; in the opinion of most moderate scholars, most of this material probably derives from Jeremiah himself. Then secondly there is prose biographical material about Jeremiah. Traditionally, this has been ascribed to the prophet's secretary, Baruch. Even if this seems unduly optimistic, the probability that these stories were written and ordered in order to present a theological message of their own by some who stood in the Jeremiah tradition is widely believed. Thirdly, however, there are speeches or sermons purportedly by Jeremiah, but in prose, and prose which closely resembles Deuteronomy at that. On the origins of this third class of material opinions are sharply divided.

Willie's commentary makes a distinguished and influential contribution to the study of these and related issues. That is not to say that the work is above all criticism, and fairness dictates that these should be mentioned first in order to clear the ground. It is a weakness that he chooses to interact with a very limited range of secondary literature; he tends to interact with only the major commentators and a limited range of other studies. This may be defended in terms of space saved (the two volumes are already about 1,500 pages long), but it reduces the work's value for certain purposes. Secondly, and more seriously, it does not deal in much detail with some important critical methods, such as form criticism. Whether he felt out of sympathy with some of the modern trends in exegetical research or simply wanted to concentrate on his strengths is not clear, but certainly one learns quickly that there are topics on which it is not worth bothering to consult him. Finally, the book is not presented in the most helpful manner. Whereas most volumes in the series distinguished clearly between text-critical and linguistic discussion, general exegesis and wider considerations on each section as a whole, Willie tends just to plough through on a more or less verse-by-verse basis (though without actually highlighting which verse is being dealt with at any given point), with discussion of whatever he considered important all jumbled together. It is true that he justifies his approach with the observation that the versions are not only of text-critical importance, but are also the fountainhead for all subsequent exegesis (p. xv), but however accurate that may be, the result is a book which is quite hard to consult (not helped by its demanding English style) when wanting an answer to a specific question of a verse, as is often the case with commentaries.

That said, however, there are areas of commentary work where Willie is without peer, and he handles many issues in detail and with reference to sources that very few others are competent to tackle. In addition, he has made an influential contribution to some of the major issues which the book raises.

First, his attention to the ancient versions of the Old Testament as well as to the work of the great medieval Jewish commentators (who wrote in both Hebrew and Arabic) is detailed and judicious.[11] These sources are important both as textual witnesses and as giving an indication of the possibilities for the interpretation of obscurities from antiquity on. Not surprisingly, many of these alternatives remain live options to this day, as may be seen by a comparison of the different English translations. The book of Jeremiah had not been treated with this kind of analysis for a long time, if ever, and it is work which will endure for several generations.

Secondly, his conclusions about the manner of composition of the book are turned in a novel way to explain his understanding of both the major critical issues which were introduced earlier. The name of McKane will be for ever associated with the expression 'rolling corpus', by which he meant that the book was never subjected to the kind of tidy editing (redaction) which many scholars now seek to find, but rather that it grew in a somewhat random manner as several generations of scribes added to it in different ways. At the micro-level, this is evident from many of the small pluses in the longer Hebrew as against the shorter Greek text, where titles are added to named individuals and so on. This is not evidence (as some have supposed) for a systematic work of expansion according to a major conceptual programme, such as might characterise a complete redaction of the work; the whole process was far more haphazard in Willie's opinion.

---

[11] According to Professor J. A. Emerton, FBA, who was the Old Testament editor of the series, in his own preparatory study of any given passage, Willie would in fact consult the medieval commentators first, even though in his written presentation he usually presents the material roughly in chronological order.

But the same observation may be taken to the higher level of some
of the prose additions to the underlying poetry of the book, so that here
the 'rolling corpus' idea is supplemented with the saying that some of
the poetry has 'triggered' the prose. This proposal (which comes close
to the more recent fashionable development of the notion of
Fortschreibung) is thus able to explain how it comes about that some of
the prose includes phrases or other features which are thought to be characteristic of the poetry (and which have therefore been used by more conservative scholars to argue that Jeremiah could himself have been the
author of the prose). On the other hand, it excludes the more comprehensive theories of Deuteronomic redaction—the theory that the whole
book had been systematically worked over by a single editor who was
much influenced by both the linguistic style and the ideological notions
which are characteristic of the book of Deuteronomy. Willie seems at
this point to have had an almost pathological aversion to any theory
which tried to reduce what he saw as the untidy nature of the book to any
kind of externally imposed order. It is in the nature of scholarship that
people will keep trying to find some single key that will unlock this most
confusing of books. Willie was content rather to allow the confusion to
speak for itself; all subsequent writers have had to come to terms with his
presentation of the evidence, and it is not clear at the present time that
any have succeeded in getting any further.

In what they choose to present, these two volumes are a remarkable
achievement of sustained erudition, and they are unlikely to be surpassed, or even equalled, for many decades. But with his characteristic
modesty Willie was not willing to rest on his laurels. Indeed, one very different book appeared between the two volumes of the commentary.
Though it is based on earlier lectures, it almost looks as though he sought
recreation from the main task of the mid-seventies to the mid-nineties by
turning aside to a somewhat different field of research, albeit one that
informed much of his other writing.

Selected Christian Hebraists (Cambridge, 1989) 'arose', Willie tells us,
'out of public lectures which were offered in St Mary's College, St
Andrews, as "The St Mary's College Lectures" in the Candlemas Term
during the years 1982–5'.[12] These were the years, it will be recalled, when

---

[12] His general interest in the history of Christian Hebraists surfaces elsewhere too, not only in
the book cited in the following footnote, but also in such articles as 'Benjamin Kennicott: an
Eighteenth Century Researcher', *Journal of Theological Studies*, NS 28 (1977), 445–64, and
'Calvin as an Old Testament Commentator', *Nederduits Gereformeerd Teologese Tydskrift*, 25
(1984), 250–9.

Willie was Principal of the college, and he is quite self-conscious in having chosen his topic 'as one which should give scope for the exercise of trilingual scholarship'. He links this concern with a few words about the origins and subsequent history of the college, and given his strength of feeling over the way in which he was initially passed over for the role of Principal once the new arrangements for tenure came into force, it is hard to resist the temptation to see here (whether consciously or unconsciously) a playing out of some of his earlier hurt and frustration. Several of the Christian Hebraists whose work he analyses were themselves either rejected or at the least marginalised in their day because their scholarship put them at odds with one or another aspect of Church authority. This in itself was not, of course, a problem that befell Willie, but there are indications elsewhere in his writing that in many respects he felt that his approach to scholarship by way of the old-fashioned virtues of textual and philological analysis as well as his intensely humane rationalism meant 'that I have tended to resist the fashions of Old Testament scholarship and that I have usually been swimming against the current'.[13] It is likely that he felt a strong affinity in purpose, if not in circumstance or opinion, with the likes of Origen, Richard Simon and Alexander Geddes among those to whom he devotes a chapter. A remark in the introductory chapter is surely autobiographical as well as historical:[14] 'The critical study of the Hebrew Bible does not co-exist easily with powerful theological preoccupations, and it lies in the nature of their scholarly interests and the mental habits which these encourage that Hebraists do not usually set themselves up as great theological innovators' (p. 10). Willie was to return to some of these concerns in his next book.

Before turning to that, however, we should take note of the remarkable fact that, whereas most people would have had enough of such work after the completion of a task the size of his Jeremiah commentary, Willie seems just to have carried on in similar vein with the preparation of a commentary on the very much shorter book of Micah.[15] This was the last of his books to appear, though at the time of his death he had made some considerable progress with a commentary on the book of Job. Although this latter was not yet in a fit state for publication, it is planned that its substance should be put at the disposal of the future ICC commentator on Job so that its insights will not be entirely lost.

[13] W. McKane, *A Late Harvest: Reflections on the Old Testament* (Edinburgh, 1995), p. vii.
[14] Reassuringly, Willie's daughter Ursula quite independently hit upon this same sentence as one where 'he could have been talking of himself'.
[15] W. McKane, *The Book of Micah: Introduction and Commentary* (Edinburgh, 1998).

Neither of these commentaries was specifically commissioned; it seems Willie chose to work on them out of his own interest. In the case of Job, this is readily intelligible. Its formidable philological obscurities would have drawn him like a magnet. The case of Micah is not so clear, and he gives us no hint as to why he chose it. Perhaps after Jeremiah he just wanted something shorter! At any rate there are parts of the Hebrew text of this book which are notoriously difficult, if not corrupt. Willie's commentary follows exactly the same style and approach as that on Jeremiah, with all its strengths and drawbacks, and once again it will serve future generations at the level of the study of the text and versions while perhaps leaving problems at the level of composition and history to be taken up afresh in the light of the firmer foundations which he has laid.[16]

In 1995 there appeared what is in some respects the most personal of Willie's many publications; indeed, he introduces it as 'a concatenated description of my own Odyssey' (p. vii). *A Late Harvest: Reflections on the Old Testament* is said to be the fruit of the Honours Seminar on Old Testament Theology which he conducted at St Mary's throughout his tenure there, though quite in what way is not clear.

The main concern of the book seems to be an exploration of the nature of prophecy and how, if at all, it relates to revelation. As we have seen to be his practice sometimes elsewhere, he does not approach this topic head on but rather by way of a (selective) history of scholarship on the subject from the time of Maimonides on. Maimonides was a twelfth-century Jewish philosopher, aspects of whose great work *The Guide of the Perplexed* were clearly congenial to Willie's own position; indeed, it will be recalled that part of his first degree was in philosophy. However, in order to reach that, we are taken carefully through the relevant works of some of the greats of Old Testament scholarship not only from the Reformation period (Zwingli, Calvin, and so on) but also from the nine-teenth century (A. Kuenen, J. Wellhausen and William Robertson Smith) and on down to the present with particular attention to such diverse scholars as J. Pedersen, I. Engnell, J. Lindblom, A. Farrer, L. Alonso Schökel and G. von Rad.

---

[16] Willie himself would not have talked so much of foundations as of the 'basement where linguists do their work' in contrast with the 'penthouse of hermeneutics' (*A Late Harvest*, p. 163). Ursula comments that 'basement dwellers are not well known to the public and so they never really go in or out of fashion. Penthouse dwellers are fashionable for a season until the next trend arrives.'

For the most part, Willie does not spell out his reaction to each scholar, but leaves us to infer his agreement or disapproval. Sometimes this is not altogether apparent, though at other times it is not difficult. For instance, when he says of Farrer that his understanding of prophetic inspiration 'diminishes their humanity to vanishing point and makes them into puppets controlled by God' (p. 119), we may legitimately infer that he does not approve. Indeed, in the Preface he speaks of the 'spookiness of Farrar's portrayal',[17] just as he also states forthrightly that he 'could not stomach von Rad's contention that New Testament meanings should be found in Old Testament texts by an exegesis done in the freedom of the Holy Spirit' (though whether this is an entirely fair characterisation of von Rad's position as a whole is another question). At any rate, guided by such clear statements we may reconstruct Willie's approach to the issue of prophetic inspiration somewhat as follows.

As he states several times both in this book and elsewhere, he is convinced that 'God does not speak Hebrew'. By this he means that such expressions as 'the word of God' and that 'God speaks' should not be over-interpreted, as he finds they often are, as though the prophets 'supplied their vocal chords to enable the Almighty to speak'. The prophets were fully human at all times, and they spoke in a language which is accessible to other humans by way of the normal study of grammar and lexicography. They were not Jekyll and Hyde characters—inspired one minute and 'normal' the next—and any suggestion to the contrary is open to the charge of docetism. The 'humanity of the canonical prophets should be preserved and . . . any diminishment of that humanity, associated with a dichotomy of man and prophet, or a normal state of consciousness and a "revelatory state" should be avoided' (p. 144). Indeed, in an uncharacteristically personal moment, he concludes that:

> If they entertained such magical views about the words which they spoke and the symbolic acts which they performed as is alleged, they have been significantly disengaged from the pattern of humane thinking which some of us supposed that we shared with them, and resort to them, for a contribution to theistic truth and ethical elevation has been, more or less, put out of court. (p. 127)

Note that there is no problem here with referring to 'theistic truth'; this is not a totally secular rationalism which is being advocated, but rather an

---

[17] It may be noted that here as consistently elsewhere Willie misspelt Farrer's name. This is so uncharacteristic that one is tempted to speculate that it is unconsciously related somehow to his obvious aversion to Farrer's work.

urgent plea that 'a literary description should not be transposed into a doctrine of revelation and be thought to supply transparent theological conclusions. This is a disastrous confusion of categories' (p. 103). He does not deny that the prophets may have had visionary or other similar experiences,[18] nor that they had a conviction that they were speaking the truth about and from God. What matters is the affirmation that they remained fully human all of the time, and so do their words.

The consequence of this line of reasoning is that biblical, and in particular prophetic, literature should be studied like any other, and as we have seen repeatedly, this is just what Willie did throughout his career. He may have felt that some modern trends as well as some forms of more theological exegesis were casting him into the mould of an old-fashioned positivist for whom traditional historical-critical research was the only worthwhile approach, but if so he was more than prepared to take the brickbats if that was the cost of his intellectual integrity. Anything more would have to be cast into the realm of spooks.

The appeal to the dangers of docetism indicates that he is casting his understanding of scripture as being in some way analogous with an orthodox christological doctrine—the affirmation of the full humanity as well as the full divinity of Christ. His insistence on the humanity of scripture, with all the consequences that flow from it in terms of appropriate scholarly methods, is well made and urged with a degree of passion on occasions which might seem surprising. Of the other side of the coin, however, little is said either in this book or elsewhere. There are those who would criticise him for this, but it should be appreciated that he was not attempting to formulate a doctrine of scripture in the manner of a systematic theologian. His purpose was to discuss the issue in a way that should lead to the framing of an appropriate academic method for study and research. For this, the human side of the text was all important, and he would have had no truck with those who in very recent years have tried to suggest that because scripture was written from within a standpoint of faith it can therefore only be expounded from within that selfsame standpoint. His rigour and discipline in writing were such that he rarely indicated what other considerations influenced his personal understanding of scripture. He is prepared to talk sometimes of the mystery of divine encounter, but he would not have considered it the role of an academic

---

[18] See, for instance, p. 145, 'I shall assume, without argument, that there is a transcendental dimension, an encounter of the prophet with God, though I am aware of the logical disadvantage of producing such an ultimate—an unanalysable—mystery out of the hat.'

exegete to tease out the implications of what that involved.[19] Humanity and rationalism should accept their limitations and be content.

As I have mentioned, retirement in 1990 meant no slackening of effort. He was regularly in his study until the day before his death on 4 September 2004, when for the first time in his life he had to be taken into hospital. Agnes, on whom he relied for so much (not least guidance when going to meetings outside of his normal circuit, for he had a terrible sense of direction), expressed relief that the end was swift and that he was able to continue working more or less to the last. 'He would have made a terrible patient.' None who knew him would disagree.

Willie received a number of honours during the course of his career, including a Glasgow D.Litt. (1980), an honorary DD from Edinburgh (1984), Fellowship of the British Academy (1980) and the award of its Burkitt Medal for Biblical Studies (1985), a Fellowship of the Royal Society of Edinburgh (1984), a Fellowship of the National Humanities Center, North Carolina (1987–8) and a Corresponding Membership of the Göttingen Akademie der Wissenschaften (1997). He was elected President of the (British) Society for Old Testament Study in 1978, acted as Chairman of the Peshitta Committee of the International Organization for the Study of the Old Testament from 1980 onwards and served on the advisory board of *Zeitschrift für die alttestamentliche Wissenschaft*.

But though these honours brought him satisfaction, they were as nothing compared to the pleasure he derived from music, literature and sport and above all the pride that he took in his large and expanding family. His daughter Ursula has written perceptively of his 'sense of belonging to a cultural tradition. His rootedness in his heritage was not uncritical, but it gave his life shape. He never missed a Sunday service of worship.' Indeed, throughout his tenure at St Andrews he would faithfully (if not always too comfortably) attend the University chapel, though it was only occasionally that he preached. As soon as he retired, however, he and Agnes moved their allegiance to Cameron Church in the small village on their side of St Andrews. There he found greater contentment, and it is fitting that he should have been buried there. The simple headstone has at its foot a reference to Micah 6:8, a verse which Ursula also

---

[19] As already mentioned, we have to be content with hints dropped almost in passing. To add to the words cited in the previous footnote, for instance, Ursula draws attention to a quotation from p. 132 in which Willie more or less repeats what he had previously written on p. 459 of his Jeremiah commentary: 'It is the quality and profundity of the prophetic utterance, its piercing theistic vision, its exceptional moral discernment and the anguish with which it is touched (for prophets do not arrive at the truth without suffering for it), which make it a word of God.'

mentions as a clue to the secret of his own deepest convictions. Those who visit are expected to know the reference, of course. In Willie's own translation, it reads:

> You have been told what is good
> and what is it that Yahweh asks of you:
> only to do what is just, to love mercy
> and to walk modestly with your God.

It is appropriate.

H. G. M. WILLIAMSON
Fellow of the Academy

Note. I am especially indebted for help in the preparation of this memoir to Mrs Agnes McKane, Dr Ursula Reader and Dr Robin Salters. I am also grateful for comments and corrections from the following Fellows of the Academy: J. A. Emerton, M. A. Knibb, E. W. Nicholson, E. Ullendorff and G.-J. van Gelder.

MALCOLM PASLEY

Ulrich Greiner

John Malcolm Sabine Pasley
1926–2004

MALCOLM PASLEY ACHIEVED A UNIQUE authority as a British scholar in a major area of German literary scholarship, the work of Franz Kafka (1883–1924). Good scholars are often blessed with serendipity, the tendency (it can hardly be called an ability) to chance upon what they need without actually looking for it or even knowing it was there. As with candidates for promotion to General, there is sense in Napoleon's question 'Is he lucky?' A chance encounter gave Pasley's work a new and unexpected direction; indeed, it turned what would always have been intellectually distinguished into something unquestionably central, and directed his meticulous mind to the most basic literary issues.

John Malcolm Sabine Pasley was born on 5 April 1926 in Rajkot, Kathiawar, India, where his father, Sir Rodney Pasley, was teaching history and cricketing at Rajkumar College (Ranjitsinhji's old school). Malcolm once said his birth was the grandest day of his life, celebrated in style by the local maharajas, palaces, elephants and all. He was educated at Sherborne School and Trinity College, Oxford. At 17 he volunteered for the Royal Navy and saw service at the end of the Second World War, using his German for radio traffic interception. (The rumour that he had some involvement with Enigma looks like a legendary back-formation from his later work on Kafka's enigmas.) After hostilities ended, he spent time with the occupation forces in Germany and came away with one useful item of booty, a German typewriter on which all his subsequent writing and editing was done. After graduating in 1949 he held a Laming Travelling Fellowship at the Queen's College, Oxford, which took him to Munich for a year. The college having not favoured his proposal to work on nineteenth-century lyrical poetry, Pasley began research into social

Proceedings of the British Academy, **150**, 149–157. © The British Academy 2007.

novelists of that period, initially Fontane, then the Low German dialect writer Fritz Reuter. In 1950 he was appointed a Lecturer at Magdalen and Brasenose Colleges. In 1958 he was elected a Fellow of Magdalen. In 1965 he married Virginia Wait. They had two sons. In 1982 he assumed the baronetcy bestowed on an eighteenth-century ancestor for gallantry at sea against the French.

Quite when Kafka began to fascinate Pasley is not clear. There are no early publications. At that time it was a respected, even revered, vocation to be a university teacher and there was no pressure to rush prematurely into print. Something substantial and considered might well ripen in its own time. That matched Pasley's essentially reserved and fastidious character. The turning point came in 1960, when a tutorial pupil made him aware that a great-nephew of Kafka's, Michael Steiner, was studying law at Lincoln College and, at an energetic remove from what we think of as Kafka's world, rowing in the college boat. The trail led back to Kafka's nieces, Michael's mother Marianne Steiner in London and Vera Saudková in Prague, and to the discovery that their generation (the rest of the family having been murdered in the Shoah) were the legal owners of the bulk of Kafka's manuscripts.

Until then scholars had loosely assumed that these were the property of Kafka's close friend Max Brod. He certainly held them and on one occasion used the manuscript of *The Trial* to disprove the revisionist speculations of a scholar whom he had not allowed to inspect it. Kafka had however three times asked Brod to collect and burn all his manuscripts after his death.[1] The failure to carry out that wish would have left Brod with a somewhat dubious legal title. To be fair, he never claimed ownership of the bulk of the manuscripts, recognising all along the claims of the survivors. Not destroying the papers was a service of unforeseeable magnitude to literature, and was only the start of Brod's positive role in his friend's literary fortunes. Brod was responsible for getting the principal works published in the 1920s, and for again rescuing the manuscripts at threatening moments in twentieth-century history. When the Nazis marched into Prague in 1939, he escaped with the papers via Rumania to Tel Aviv. In 1940 he deposited them in a special safe in the Schocken Library in Jerusalem, where Klaus Wagenbach, the biographer of Kafka's early life and later a collaborator of Pasley's in dating the manu-

---

[1] Once in conversation, as reported by Brod, 'Franz Kafkas Nachlaß', in *Die Weltbühne*, July 1924, reprinted in *Marbacher Magazin*, 52 (1990), 71; and twice in written form, on a slip Brod found in Kafka's desk after his death and in a never-sent draft letter of 29 Nov. [?1922], later similarly discovered. Both reprinted in *Brod-Kafka Briefwechsel* (see below, n. 4) pp. 365 and 422 f.

scripts,[2] was able to see them; some use was also made of them for the American edition of the works. Then, during the Suez crisis of 1956, Brod transferred them for safety to Switzerland. He still held on to the manuscript of *The Trial* which he claimed was a personal gift, inconsistent though that too was with Kafka's known instructions. At Pasley's suggestion, Mrs Steiner and Mrs Saudková in 1961 generously agreed to have the other manuscripts placed in the Bodleian Library on permanent revocable loan. It was up to Pasley to get them there.

His journey has become a legend among scholars of German: how he travelled across icy roads to Zurich in his exceedingly small car—in the light of Kafka's novella *Die Verwandlung* (*The Transformation*) it makes a good story that it was a Volkswagen Beetle, but alas it was an even smaller Fiat—and collected the manuscripts in person. Only slight adjustments to the story are needed in the interests of exactness. Pasley was in fact already abroad, skiing in Austria, when news reached him of a final agreement with the New York house of Salman Schocken, whose firm still today own the primary publication rights. Though Schocken had always recognised the legal claims of Kafka's remaining relatives, he could somehow never bring himself to loosen his *de facto* hold on the manuscripts. Things moved, however, after his death. Pasley drove to Zurich and matched the bank's elaborate security check of his identity with a rigorous scholarly check of the material they were handing over. The wintry arrival and the confrontation with officials have atmospheric echoes of Kafka's *Castle* and *Trial*. Pasley insured the manuscripts for what now seems the modest sum of £100,000, at which the clerk at Thomas Cook's did not bat an eyelid, packed them into a hurriedly purchased suitcase, and drove his haul back to Oxford. Bodley's then Keeper of Western Manuscripts seemed not unduly impressed by the author's name (it makes a difference having such originals as the *Chanson de Roland* in house) but the Bodleian made up for that later when in 1983, jointly with the Taylorian Library, it mounted a substantial exhibition to mark the centenary of Kafka's birth.

The arrival of the papers in the Bodleian made Oxford the centre of textual scholarship on Kafka, especially of the critical edition in the S. Fischer Verlag, Frankfurt, on which work now began. A scholarly edition had been expressly foreseen in the contract of March 1965 by which

[2] Malcolm Pasley und Klaus Wagenbach, 'Versuch einer Datierung sämtlicher Texte Franz Kafkas', *Deutsche Vierteljahrsschrift für Literaturwissenschaft und Geistesgeschichte*, 38 (1964), 2, 149–67.

Schocken granted the German rights to Fischer, and Brod too had expected there would eventually be one. The first volumes appeared in the late 1970s and the edition is now (December 2006) complete except for a volume of Kafka's Hebrew studies and the last two volumes of letters. Pasley became the leading figure in a small team of otherwise German editors, and himself took responsibility for the most important texts: *The Castle*, published in 1982, and *The Trial* in 1990. Where diplomacy was necessary among the team or between editors and publisher, he supplied it. The one major material element missing at first was the manuscript of *The Trial*, which Max Brod had meanwhile bequeathed to his partner, Frau Ilse Ester Hoffe. The effort to secure access and edit this text became the centre of a further mini-plot. The manuscript was still entombed in Zurich and only a photocopy was available to work from—wholly inadequate for the kind of minute genetic reconstruction which Pasley was practising. In 1987 and again in 1988 he was allowed to work on the original 'in the ill-lit bowels of a Zurich bank, under the eye of its owner', each time for no more than three or four days.[3] Even to get this far involved prolonged diplomacy on his part: not just personal meetings with and cajolings of Frau Hoffe in Israel, but an elaborate scholarly epicycle, the editing of Kafka's correspondence with Max Brod and their joint travel diaries in two volumes.[4] These, though, were not just a sprat to catch a mackerel. As the central figure in Kafka's life and the precarious preservation of his work, Brod and the record of his friendship with Kafka fully deserved the scrupulous editing that they too received.

Then, suddenly and unexpectedly, in September 1988 the manuscript of *The Trial* was sent for auction to the London branch of Sotheby's. Pasley was able to do some work on it there, but still with interruptions, since the priceless papers were constantly and irresponsibly being flown about the world—to Frankfurt, Vienna, Hong Kong, Tokyo, New York, 'to be dangled in front of potential buyers'.[5] Between underlit Zurich and sporadic access to Bond Street, there can rarely have been more unsettled circumstances in which to carry out a complex scholarly task on a major work. Finally and blessedly, the manuscript was bought at auction by the

---

[3] Malcolm Pasley, 'Kafka's *Der Process*: what the manuscript can tell us', *Oxford German Studies*, 18–19 (1989–90), 109.

[4] *Max Brod, Franz Kafka. Eine Freundschaft. Reiseaufzeichnungen.* Herausgegeben unter Mitarbeit von Hannelore Rodlauer von Malcolm Pasley (Frankfurt am Main, 1987); and *Max Brod, Franz Kafka. Eine Freundschaft. Briefwechsel.* Herausgegeben von Malcolm Pasley (Frankfurt am Main, 1989).

[5] Pasley, 'Kafka's *Der Process*', see above, n. 3.

Marbach Literaturarchiv, even then not without some last-minute drama: an unknown figure appeared to have outbid Marbach's visible representative, but turned out to be an agent also bidding on the Archive's behalf, for what tactical reason is not clear. The price was around a million pounds, and there had been a bit more in reserve. It was put together in exemplary fashion with the help of the German Federal government, the Kulturstiftung der Länder (Cultural Foundation of the German States), the government of Baden-Württemberg, and private donations, in particular from the publisher Klaus G. Saur. The Marbach Archive celebrated their coup appropriately with an exhibition in the spring and summer of 1990, in which Pasley played a major part.[6] It coincided with the appearance of his corresponding volume in the critical edition.

By harsh misfortune it also coincided with the early signs, ironically first felt at Marbach, of the multiple sclerosis that was to accompany and end his life on 8 March 2004. In 1986 he had taken early retirement from his college and university posts, to devote himself full-time to editing and writing on Kafka. He also confessed to unease at no longer having total recall of textual detail across the broad range of literature he taught, something that few tutors would claim and fewer still would regard as a necessary condition for continuing to teach. Pasley had, incidentally, been an admirable tutor: unshowy, not voluble, but with a concentrated attention that registered any flaw of argument or formulation, sometimes with a slight catch of the breath. A glance up from one's erring script would meet a famous pair of quizzically raised eyebrows. The scholarly precision did not conceal a cordial personal commitment.

The progress of his illness did not stop Pasley working. He edited a further volume of writings and fragments from Kafka's Nachlass, put together a collection of his own essays and produced new translations of some of the primary texts. It became increasingly hard for him to receive visits, but he went on responding with a prompt and supportive word to the work former pupils sent him: a tutor to the last.

Life was not made more comfortable by attacks on Pasley's integrity over a facsimile edition of Kafka planned by the Frankfurt Stroemfeld Verlag. This had been started with a volume reproducing the Marbach manuscript of *The Trial*, announced as the first in a complete historical-critical edition, although the publisher and editors had not yet even ascertained who owned the manuscripts, let alone sought their agreement. Mrs Steiner was understandably reluctant to grant instant permission.

---

[6] It is the subject of *Marbacher Magazin*, 52 (1990).

Pasley acted as her representative in correspondence. If his responses
were somewhat abrupt, that too is understandable. Having probed the
depths of Kafka's manuscript complexity, he was unimpressed by the
naïve presumption of the new would-be editors. Transatlantic protesters,
including a not unknown professorial grandee, rushed in, invoking the
principle of free scholarly access and appealing to the Academy. (In
response, a note stating the facts was at once circulated to the Fellowship.)
The protesters failed to consider that access to manuscripts, which the
Bodleian grants for legitimate scholarly use, does not automatically
include permission to reproduce and publish them wholesale.

If it had been more tactfully approached from the start, the project
need never have caused such friction, and once the dust had settled, the
Stroemfeld edition was able to proceed—rightly in the end, since there is
no questioning the vivid impression a good facsimile allows. Nor was
there essentially any 'conflict of interests', since the two kinds of edition
have different aims and in practice can complement each other. The
claims made for the facsimile edition to a 'higher authenticity'[7] were
tautological: a facsimile is self-evidently authentic in its own terms, but
stops short at the level of primary textual material. Historical, yes;
critical in this instance barely, since the edition sets its face against a stable text ('authoritarian text-constitution') and is aimed at an imagined
reader who prefers to be faced with raw manuscript material and its still
unresolved problems.[8]

As to the fate of the manuscripts, Mrs Steiner and Mrs Saudková have
since gifted them to the Bodleian, an astounding act of generosity when
one considers the profit private owners customarily make from the lucky
possession of important papers and works of art, and the immense sums
Kafka's manuscripts would have fetched. A third share is held by another
niece, Frau Gerti Kaufmann, but since the shares are notional, not identified, there is no possibility of selling it off separately. It too thus remains

[7] In a brief obituary of Malcolm Pasley in the *Frankfurter Allgemeine Zeitung* for 9 March 2004,
also suggesting that the Fischer edition was already 'too late'. My objections to both points
appear in a letter published by the *FAZ* on 27 March.
[8] 'Probleme [. . .] wollen nicht gelöst sein, sondern als solche herausgearbeitet und begriffen wer-
den'.—'Wer Kafka mag, hängt auch an den Zügen, der Graphik seiner Handschrift. Und wer
sich mit Kafka auseinandersetzt, will wissen, "was geschrieben steht." Hierzu benötigt er nicht
einen sogenannten "Lesetext", sondern neben dem Faksimile eine minutiöse Transkription der
Handschrift sowie detaillierte Beschreibungen der in Kafkas Nachlaß häufigen internen
Manuskriptwanderungen und der Überlieferung (Angaben über Fundorte, Besitzer).' Roland
Reuss, introductory volume of the *Historisch-kritische Ausgabe sämtlicher Handschriften, Drucke
und Typoskripte Franz Kafkas* (Basel/Frankfurt am Main, 1995), pp. 16 and 17.

in Bodley. In a touching letter of 2 May 1961 to Marianne Steiner, with whom he had been corresponding amicably since the Second World War, Max Brod expressed his pleasure that the manuscripts had found a home in the Bodleian. He called it an event of the highest historical importance ('höchste säkulare Bedeutung') and he recognised Pasley's enthusiasm and commitment to Kafka and his works. Whatever reservations Brod may later have had about new critical directions in the sphere which had been so intimately his own, he had handed on the torch in a generous spirit.

Pasley's place in Kafka scholarship is secure and *sui generis*. His reconstruction of the major texts is authoritative and of an order of intricacy that will surely never need repeating. It matches torn pages, analyses watermarks, measures the ebb and flow of Kafka's inspiration through changes in his (always impeccably clear) handwriting and in the word-density per page, and registers the way in which transition to a new notebook—Kafka used notebooks to give his writing a gently compelling frame—made composition harder, as is shown by the greater incidence of erasures and new starts. Later critics may draw further conclusions from these bibliographical findings, but the essential spadework is done.

Nor is it merely mechanical and external to the form and substance of the texts. For example, reinstating their original punctuation, where Brod had consistently replaced commas by full points, not only restored dramatically the rhythm of Kafka's prose but could be shown case by case to be crucial in constituting literary meaning. Punctuation, *pace* the bibliographer W. W. Greg, was anything but an 'accidental'; it was an integral part of the creative act.[9] Again, retracing Kafka's compositional process as he followed his pen into the labyrinth and improvised a narrative—it was even possible provocatively to say 'in the beginning was nothing'[10]—virtually undid the earlier view that he was a planner and executor of systematic religious allegory, the view popularised by Brod. Indeed, only one work, *The Trial*, can be conclusively shown to have been conceived from the first complete with its ending. Even titles were correspondingly a later addition: only after the accomplished birth (a favourite metaphor of Kafka's) could the child be given a name. Pasley achieved these insights by methods developed as he worked, without prior training in the editorial craft.

---

[9] Pasley, 'Zu Kafkas Interpunktion', in Malcolm Pasley, *Die Schrift ist unveränderlich* (Frankfurt am Main, 1995), p. 121.

[10] Pasley, 'Der Schreibakt und das Geschriebene. Zur Frage der Entstehung von Kafkas Texten', in Pasley, op. cit., p. 106.

'Not by Brod alone' was the witty heading to the *TLS* review of the
first volume in the historical-critical edition. Brod regarded this new
textual scholarship as dry positivism, yet in an anything but dry way
the account Pasley gives in his textual commentaries and essays takes
the reader close to Kafka's mind and hand as he explores his inner world
through a tentative pen. In a more precise and fruitful sense than the
wearisome cliché that all modern writing is 'really about writing', the
twists and turns of the fiction are shown to refer also to the ups and
downs of the writer's creative mood, the alternating phases of self-
confidence and self-doubt. At the humorous extreme, enigmatic figures
about whose meaning much ink had been spilled sometimes turned out,
as in the story *Eleven Sons*, to be references to other stories of Kafka's
own.[11] None of this gainsays the seriousness and profundity of Kafka's
explorations.

At first sight, author and critic were strangely paired. It was paradoxical that, as one obituary notice put it, 'this model English gentleman
understood the mind of one of the most idiosyncratic and radical writers
of the twentieth century better than anyone else in his time'.[12] He even
came to think of Kafka as a younger brother.

As an editor in a less stringent sense of the word, Pasley was also
responsible for a volume of essays on the crucial issue of Nietzsche's
imagery, and for a high-level introduction to German history and culture
by various hands.[13] He was also a founding co-editor of the yearbook
Oxford German Studies. But Kafka was the centre of his life's work, quietly symbolised by the Kafka manuscript—a simple postcard—on his
mantelpiece at home.

Pasley's distinction was early and variously recognised: by an
Honorary D.Phil. of the University of Giessen (1980), by membership of
the German Academy of Language and Literature (1983), by the award
of the Austrian Cross of Honour for Learning and the Arts (1987), and
by Fellowship of the British Academy (1991). As important to him as
these formal recognitions by the scholarly world was his connection with
Kafka's family and home city of Prague, where Pasley was very much
persona grata. In the Prague Spring of 1968 Kafka had become a central

---

[11] See J. M. S. Pasley, 'Two Kafka Enigmas: "Elf Söhne" and "Die Sorge des Hausvaters"',
Modern Language Review, 49 (1964), 1. 73–81; and J. M. S. Pasley, 'Franz Kafka: "Ein Besuch
im Bergwerk"', *German Life and Letters*, NS 18 (1964), 1. 40–6.
[12] Kevin Hilliard, in the *Daily Telegraph* for 25 March 2004.
[13] *Nietzsche, Imagery and Thought* (London, 1978); and *Germany, A Companion to German
Studies* (London, 1972).

feature of the city's culture and a focus of interest and pride to Czech scholars and intellectuals. Forced underground by the crackdown that followed, Kafka triumphantly resurfaced after the Velvet Revolution of 1989. It was at this point that Pasley paid his last visit to Prague, to be received with enthusiasm and orchids by members of the Franz Kafka Society, surely a day to equal the maharajas and elephants.

In 1995 Pasley published the slender volume, *Die Schrift ist unverän-derlich*, bringing together his Kafka essays—or most of them. Leaving out a couple meant there were just eleven.

T. J. REED
Fellow of the Academy

BEN PIMLOTT

Benjamin John Pimlott
1945–2004

BEN PIMLOTT WAS BORN ON 4 July 1945, the day before Britain swung strongly Labour in the general election which propelled the Attlee government to power, an administration of which he was to become a deft and sensitive chronicler. In fact, Ben's writings were to provide one of the most significant scholarly spinal cords of post-war contemporary British history from Attlee to Blair. The politics of the centre Left were central to both his scholarship, his personal convictions and his renown as a public intellectual. Yet he was never tainted by dogma or ideology and respect for him and his works straddled the political divides. Very tall, arresting, quietly spoken, courteous, attractive to women and intellectually fastidious, he dominated—but never domineered—his special scholarly patch and, in the 1980s and 1990s, raised the art of political biography to new heights. His early death in 2004, aged 58, left a very considerable gap in both the country's intellectual and public life.

Ben's formation was thoroughly Fabian. His father, John Pimlott, was an open scholarship boy from a west country grammar school to Oxford at a time when such an event was a rare example of a meritocrat rising. As Ben recounted in an affectionate memoir of his father, he came third in the formidable examination for the administrative class of the Civil Service in 1932 and rose fast in the Home Office. By 1937 he was an assistant private secretary to the Home Secretary, Sir Samuel Hoare. Pimlott senior's glory years were as principal private secretary to Herbert Morrison, the wartime Home Secretary and Minister for Home Security. Morrison came to depend greatly on him and Pimlott stayed with him in the Lord President's Office following Labour's victory from which

Proceedings of the British Academy, **150**, 161–179. © The British Academy 2007.

considerable swathes of the economic, industrial and social reconstruction of the UK were coordinated.

Improving the social condition of the country was Pimlott senior's motivation from his time at Toynbee Hall in East London (a history of which he published in 1935) right through until his last Whitehall posts in the Department of Education and Science before his early death in 1969. For example, John Pimlott played a pivotal role in the mid-sixties creation of the polytechnics (he chose the name to describe the new breed) in which he firmly believed as an instrument for bringing higher education to those whom the universities could not, or would not, reach. Pimlott senior was also the moving spirit behind the creation of the Police College at Bramshill. Ben's high public service charge and thoroughly Fabian instincts about the indispensability of rational, incremental social change were squarely in his father's tradition.

Pimlott senior was too intellectually curious a man to be satisfied with his weekday Whitehall life. The Pimlott household was not merely book-ish, it was book producing too. Before the war, J. A. R. Pimlott (as his reading public came to know him) had completed much of the work for his first piece of social history, *The Englishman's Holiday*, which was finally published in 1947. This was followed by the beautifully crafted *The Englishman's Christmas* written in the sixties but only published, thanks to Ben's efforts, in 1977. Ben's literary heritage from his father was not confined to Britain or to social history. In 1947–8, supported by a Commonwealth Fund Fellowship, John Pimlott took his American wife, Ellen, and young family (Ben had two sisters, Anne and Jane) to the United States to study how the Federal Government, from the New Deal on, had made use of public relations as an instrument of policy and per-suasion. Morrison was the most media-sensitive member of Attlee's Cabinet and it was a subject on which Ben and his wife, Jean Seaton, were to write in the 1980s. John Pimlott's *Public Relations and American Democracy* was published in 1951 and aroused considerable interest in the United States. Ben, in fact, had dual US/UK citizenship and only relinquished it when he received a letter, during the Vietnam War, summoning him for the draft.

Ben's 'biographical note' at the end of *The Englishman's Christmas* shows how much he savoured his childhood inheritance and the legacy of his tall, thoughtful public servant/private author father and the family home that had nurtured him and his sisters. Among its many bequests to him were a lifelong love of poetry, a fluent pen and a degree of literary precocity. Ben produced his first book at the remarkably young age of 18 when he collaborated with a small group of his fellow sixth-formers at Marlborough to write an institutional, social and political history of the college. In many ways, it was an affectionate collection of essays as its slightly over-rhetorical concluding paragraph showed.

> Only when his last term begins does he [the Marlburian] have the time or aloofness to sit back and examine his society critically; if his opinions are cold, much can be put down to the fact that he is a schoolboy now by definition only. His outlook is no longer that of one intricately bound up, unquestioningly, in the security of a stable, if somewhat isolated society. Perhaps, as he adjusts his Old Marlburian tie with apprehensive, excited fingers, he will realise this. Even if he does not, even if all he is outwardly grateful for is his impending freedom from petty restrictions, he has much he can be thankful for. For it was at Marlborough that the boy became a man.

As his co-author and lifelong friend, James Curran, recalled at Ben's funeral in St Mary-le-Strand on 23 April 2004, their headmaster, John Dancy (widely regarded as among the most progressive of the public school breed in the early 1960s) summoned them when *Marlborough* was published in 1963. He told them it was just the kind of book, should it fall into his hands, to provide aid and comfort to a Labour MP who might use it to frame questions in the House of Commons. Whereupon Ben replied that nothing would bring him more pleasure if the volume had precisely that effect. Dancy took particular offence at the book's survey of Marlburian sexual attitudes. In the book, Ben and James wrote: 'One topic of conversation, however, has not been mentioned. Samuel Johnson is supposed to have said that wherever two Englishmen meet they talk of the weather. It would probably be true to say that wherever two Marlburians, who know each other fairly well, meet they talk of sex.'

Part of the sociological survey which the future professors Pimlott and Curran had undertaken for the book, showed that in February 1962 (when Harold Macmillan was Prime Minister, Hugh Gaitskell led the Labour Party and Jo Grimond the Liberals), the voting intentions among the members of the college were Conservative 82 per cent, Liberal 10 per cent, Labour 4 per cent with a further 4 per cent saying they would not vote. Ben's interest in the Attlee governments was no doubt responsible for the questionnaire including 'Who won the 1945 general election?' The response? 'Some 32 per cent did not know. Of these, a third guessed it was the Conservatives, and there were two very emphatic Liberals.' What Ben's and James's poll did not seek to discover was CND affiliation. This is surprising because, as a 14-year-old, Ben had tramped and camped all the way from Berkshire to Trafalgar Square over Easter 1960 as a keen participant in the Aldermaston March. (Forty-three years later he would march with his sons in protest at the coming war in Iraq.) His unilateralist instincts did not survive into his maturity, though the thrill of political bonding, as he had experienced it on the road from Aldermaston, never left him. His later multilateralism may have cost him safe Labour seats during the 1980s, including Sedgefield, where he was beaten for the nomination by a certain Tony Blair. Maybe this was among the reasons why Ben did not have a place in the Blair administration. The dissenting side of Ben was undoubtedly appreciated by his two very different history teachers at Marlborough, the touch louche medievalist, Peter Carter, and the Quaker, Bill Speck. And Ben certainly appreciated them.

Ben followed his father as an open scholar in history to Worcester College, Oxford, where he changed to Philosophy, Politics and Economics. Perhaps surprisingly, Oxford was not Ben's salad days, though he made several good friends such as Mike Radford, the film producer to be, and Bill Bradley, the future mayor of Los Angeles. He found, however, a kindred spirit in his third year when he was sent to Nuffield for tutorials to the still young, but already formidable, Patricia Hollis. After his first degree, he took a B.Phil. in Politics. And politics were his spur. Though possessing the supplest and subtlest of political minds, the *party* political star Ben was steered by was simple and consistent throughout his life. Labour, he believed, existed above all else to do something about poverty and the poor. This profound, bone-bred conviction saw Ben through Labour's civil war in the 1980s and inoculated him against the slightest temptation to join Roy Jenkins, Shirley Williams and others in the Social Democratic Party breakaway. He had few illusions about the Labour Party, but, in his way Ben loved it as the first and best political instrument for improving the condition of the British people. He flourished as a scholar, but the academic life was never going to be enough for him and he tried three times to become an MP.

This political impulse was what took him to a lectureship in politics at Newcastle University in 1970, deep in Labour stronghold territory, and guided him into the research on what became his first major book, a study of Labour's locust years in the thirties. When published in 1977 as *Labour and the Left in the 1930s*, there was pain on almost every page about the futility of a party condemned to opposition in a decade when unemployment and the rise of fascism cried out for a British New Deal at home and collective resistance to the dictators abroad. For Ben, that so much of the sensible Left's energies were diverted in fighting off the Communist Party of Great Britain and the United Front efforts of that 'political goose', as Attlee called Sir Stafford Cripps, was a cause of retrospective fury. In the 1980s, the destructive self-indulgence of the Labour Left and the accusations of 'betrayal' against the Wilson and Callaghan governments would cause him great and real-time frustration as the centre Left tradition got no more of a look in during the Thatcher years than it had in the Baldwin–Chamberlain era.

His thirties book was written at a time when Ben Pimlott was a seriously active and aspiring young Labour politician. He stood twice for Parliament in 1974. In Ted Heath's snap election in February he was Labour candidate for the safe Conservative seat of Arundel; a long way, in every sense, from his north-east base. A friend called Jean Seaton, who had met him through James Curran (fellow scholars of the politics of press and media), canvassed for Ben in Sussex bringing a team of experienced doorsteppers with her. In the October election, when the Wilson government was returned with a majority of three, Ben came within 1,500 votes of unseating Leon Brittan, then a rising star in Conservative circles, in Cleveland and Whitby. He ran against Brittan again in May 1979 by which time the political tide was flowing firmly in a Tory direction.

Historians are meant to eschew the counterfactual. But suppose he had gained a couple of thousand more votes in October 1974 and served as a backbencher in the last Wilson government and the Callaghan administration. He would certainly have made a mark as one of the most cerebral young MPs with much to say—and to say well—on unemployment, poverty and the special problems of deindustrialisation in the north-east. It is highly unlikely that he would have achieved ministerial office before the winter of discontent and the lost confidence vote on devolution brought down the Callaghan government in March 1979. And, if through a strong personal vote, he had clung on to Cleveland and Whitby, the locust years of opposition would have seen him rise as a public figure but not one, I suspect, of the width and the lustre he became in the 1980s which were the decade of his take-off as a widely known and admired public intellectual. Books there would have been— but would they have been quite so plentiful and important? Roy Jenkins, who played a crucial part in Ben's take-off, as we shall see in a moment, showed that a fine mind and a fluent pen could still operate within a parliamentary career. But the demands of a constituency a long way from London and of the House of Commons itself would have sapped even Ben's formidable energies.

As it turned out, Ben acquired width and depth in the seventies way beyond his scholarship on Labour in the thirties. He took his Ph.D. while at Newcastle. As a young man, he had assisted Anthony Eden (by this time the Earl of Avon) on his memoirs and he helped Eden once more with his final and most elegiac work, *Another World*, which was published in 1976 about his experiences in the Great War. Richard Thorpe, Eden's second official biographer, wrote of Ben's 'successfully encouraging him to draw more fully on his personal memories in a detailed analysis of the first typescript. The fact that this book was generally considered Avon's finest owes much to Pimlott's sympathetic input.' In the sixties, while working on the Eden papers, he spent two months living with the Avons at Alvediston in Wiltshire. Ben was required to buy a dinner jacket and wear it every evening when, Noel Coward, for example, might just drop by: undoubtedly a strain for a somewhat austere young Fabian.

In 1974–5, Ben travelled to Portugal to witness first hand the revolution taking place in the wake of the demise of the long-standing fascist regime in Lisbon. For a time it looked as if the country might go communist, but, eventually, the social democrats led by Mario Soares emerged to lead Portugal into the community of western European open societies. The experience left a vivid and lasting impression on him. Portugal was important to Ben. He learned his journalism reporting for *Labour Weekly*. And he learned to trust his political judgement arguing with US embassy staff, for example, that the revolution was Left, but not communist. A grant from the Nuffield Foundation in 1978 enabled Ben to come to London to work on the rich collection of papers, letters and diaries deposited by Hugh Dalton's executors in the British Library of Political and Economic Science at the London School of Economics.

By this time one of the great human and scholarly partnerships of their generation had been officially formed. For in 1977 Ben and Jean were married in Cambo, Northumberland. Ben and Jean swiftly became a cynosure for a wide circle of political and intellectual friends that embraced Whitehall and parties other than Labour as well as the university and artistic worlds. First in Hackney and then in Islington, the well-stocked Pimlott table on a Saturday night became a place of flair and fable. If the British centre Left has such things as a political salon, the Pimlotts ran one. High seriousness mingled with laughter and the ripest of gossip, though Ben could never stand frivolous chit-chat. How future Ph.D. students, reconstructing the politics of the eighties and nineties will quite capture it I do not know. But they will certainly need to try. Jean and their three sons gave Ben the most marvellous home life and his devotion to them was palpable.

In the late seventies, Ben began the process of rescuing Hugh Dalton from the condescension of posterity. Once the biography and the two volumes of diaries were published, Ben talked and wrote of what it was like to have this extraordinary character move in to the Pimlott household for a very considerable time. Ben and Hugh were very different — Dalton malicious where Ben was generous, devious where Ben was straight and an arch plotter which Ben was not. Ben never lost sight, however, of how considerable a figure Dalton had been before the war in helping Labour face up to the threat of tyranny in Europe, suppressing its pacifist instincts and, at last, embracing rearmament; during the war at first the Ministry of Economic Warfare and then at the Board of Trade; as Attlee's first post-war Chancellor; and, following a gap after a foolish Budget Day indiscretion to a journalist brought him down, as Minister of Town and Country Planning. Above all, it was Dalton the serious policy-maker that fascinated. Dalton's antipathy to Keynesianism, because he (Dalton) so loathed the rich, particularly intrigued Ben.

It was Ben's combining of Dalton the high politician with Hugh the tortured human being (unhappy marriage; homosexual leanings; burgeoning ambition brigaded with a remarkable capacity to arouse mistrust and create enemies) which made the biography such a triumph when it was published in 1985. And Ben had taken quite a professional risk in devoting himself to its production. In 1979, he left his tenured lectureship at Newcastle for a two-year Nuffield-funded research appointment at the LSE. As it happened the permanent move to London paid off. He was appointed a Lecturer in the Department of Politics and Sociology at Birkbeck College, University of London, in 1981. From the start, Ben adored Birkbeck. As his friend and fellow Labour movement historian, Ken Morgan, put it, by coming to LSE and Birkbeck, Ben 'moved into a congenial new world of metropolitan intellectual sophistication'. He never acquired, however, the metropolitan chic that shades into arrogance. He was inoculated against that by his temperament, his social conscience and the R. H. Tawney tradition of Fabianism in which he breathed and wrote.

Such personal and scholarly ingredients kept his feet firmly on the ground when fame came in a rush in 1985. Rarely can the trigger for enduring renown be so easily identified as in Ben's case. Roy Jenkins pulled it in *The Observer*. Jenkins knew Dalton well. He had been among his protégés, like so many of the most promising Gaitskellites in the 1940s and 1950s. Jenkins's book reviews in *The Observer* were, in effect, the gold standard against which new works of political biography especially were judged, Jenkins himself being a master of the genre as well as a connoisseur of others' efforts. 'This', wrote Jenkins,

> is a masterly biography ... I do not think I shall ever read a more satisfying definitive biography, in which familiar events are recalled with accuracy, pace and style while a searchlight is shone into hitherto dark places. Mr Pimlott certainly does not avoid the dark places of Dalton's life, and he writes about them with an unsqueamish precision which occasionally takes one's breath away. I find Mr Pimlott's book not only the last word on Dalton but also a rather frightening commentary on the human condition.

As the cliché has it, you cannot buy publicity like that. *Labour and the Left in the 1930s* had won Ben his spurs within the scholarly profession, but *Hugh Dalton* projected him to wide and swift prominence as a literary-politico figure of the first order—no mean feat as Dalton was hardly a household name forty years after what he (Dalton) had called in his memoirs Labour's 'high tide'. And the zenith of the Thatcher era was hardly a propitious moment for a 750-page biography of a long-dead Left-wing figure. But, as Bernard Levin's review in *The Times* put it,

> Ben Pimlott's *Hugh Dalton* passes the ultimate test: those not at all interested in Dalton can still be enthralled by his story, so firm is the author's grip, so keen is his insight, so fascinating is the tale he has to tell.

Ben's fellow Fabian, Phillip Whitehead, himself no mean connoisseur of the Attlee–Dalton–Bevin–Cripps–Morrison–Bevan era, declared simply in the *New Statesman* that it was 'The best biography for years'.

Ben began his biography of Dalton in 1977 and it took him six years to write, a period, he recalled in the Preface to the 1995 edition, when 'contemporary images were, of course, much affected by Labour's fortunes, which were moving from fragile to catastrophic'.

In a characteristically eloquent passage, Ben delivered a kind of *apologia pro vita sua* in intellectual terms and a catharsis for the pain he and others had suffered during Labour's eighties civil war. After the 1979 defeat, he wrote,

> many well-informed people began to argue that Labour was finished, *kaput*, in terminal decline. In such conditions, the party's record became a happy-hunting ground for polemicists. Insiders alternatively denounced Labour's past for its compromises and sell-outs, or else romanticised it as a lost golden age. Non-Labour people saw no reason to be concerned about such an inward-looking organisation at all.

In this climate, writing about Dalton became a refuge from much that was sterile in the present. It also became a way of expressing my own defiant belief that—contrary to a right-wing view that serious history was about the Establishment, and a left-wing one that true 'labour history' looked only at the rank-and-file—Labour had a heritage in high politics, and high ideas, that needed examining. The point kept on forming itself from the material: despite recent appearances, the left-of-centre in Britain had often in the past been a complex, fecund tributary to the mainstream of the nation's intellectual and cultural life.

This was exactly what Ben wished the centre Left to be and to do again. It was certainly what he strove mightily to do himself. And, in that same 1995 reflection on anatomising Dalton, he was quite open about it. 'I cannot,' he explained,

entirely deny that the book had a missionary purpose. Though I strove to be non-partisan, critical and 'objective'—whatever such terms amounted to—I also found myself engaged in a kind of guerrilla warfare against current assumptions. In an ideological decade of political saints and villains, I remember hoping that the contradictions of Dalton's personality would puzzle and befuddle Labour's rival tribalists. At the same time, I wanted to remind defectors of the rich traditions they were deserting; and to suggest that expectations of Labour's imminent demise . . . did not take account of deep and multifarious roots.

All of Ben's books had a purpose way beyond his scholarly peer groups or totting up the required tally for the research assessment exercise. He was utterly convinced that telling the truth, however uncomfortable, was the key to proper biography—and that biography which was readable opened up large swathes of history to a substantial reading public.

With his friend David Marquand (who did 'defect' from Labour to the SDP), Ben, on the back of *Hugh Dalton*, became the leading fugeler and philosopher for serious political biography. It was Marquand, the biographer of Ramsay MacDonald, who had declared when that study appeared in 1977 (the year Ben embarked upon Dalton), that the 'historian is not a kind of celestial chief justice sentencing the guilty and setting free the innocent. He is part of the process he describes, and his judgements can never be more than provisional.'

Ben would have agreed with that and wrote something similar in the Preface to the first edition of Hugh Dalton. 'Biography', he declared,

may be distinguished from fiction by what Virginia Woolf called 'the creative fact; the fertile fact; the fact that suggests and engenders.' In biography, you strive to be accurate, and although you may speculate a little, you do not say what you know or suspect to be untrue.

On the other hand, it is wrong to see biography as a search for the 'whole truth' about a character. Some distinguished biographers have presented themselves as humble explorers, seeking only to discover and inform. This is misleading. Biography is not mere reportage. The form is literary, the method interpretative: it is significant that 'portrait' should be the common metaphor. The author attempts to build not a distillation of important facts, but an impression, rising a *pointillisme* of detail, quotation and comment. But it is not achieved by deductive reasoning; nor is it testable.

It would be foolish to claim that biographers are born, not built. But there is something in it—not least, as Ben liked to say, a willingness to let someone you have never met into your lives, from breakfast-time to bedtime, for five years or more.

Ben was fortunate to have found his métier in one go and to have produced a gold-standard work first time round. The early eighties had also seen him, in Labour historian mode, producing two edited volumes: *The Trade Unions in British Politics* with Chris Cook in 1982; and *Fabian Essays in Socialist Thought* in 1984. But, naturally enough, it was the art of biography that featured as the subject of his inaugural lecture in 1987 when Birkbeck appointed him Professor of Politics and Contemporary History (he had been promoted to Reader the year before).

By the time he rose before an immensely distinguished audience to deliver it (Jim and Audrey Callaghan at the front), Ben had won the Whitbread Prize for *Hugh Dalton* and published two skilfully edited volumes of his diaries (*The Second World War Diary of Hugh Dalton, 1940–45*, in 1986; and *The Political Diary of Hugh Dalton 1918–40, 1945–60*, in 1987). Couched in his development of the philosophy and methodology of biography, there came a gem of a moment of Pimlott honesty—what he called 'the problem of the widow'. And he gave the example of the difficulty that Hugh Gaitskell's official biographer, Philip Williams, had in dealing with Gaitskell's affair with Ann Fleming, wife of Ian of James Bond fame. Ben went on for quite a bit about this. The Callaghans were of a generation and a non-conformist background that rather disapproved of sex being spoken of in public, as, I suspect, Ben knew full well (Jim Callaghan, himself a Dalton protégé, had been very helpful to Ben writing the biography). Ben, quite rightly, had insisted that the emotional life of a subject was important to understanding them as political and public figures especially in an age when public opinion was still shockable about such matters. Though he sympathised with Williams having to write and publish while the formidable Dora Gaitskell was still alive. Over tea after the lecture, Jim Callaghan said to me 'Ben's wrong about old Hugh, you know.' Then, in his best Dixon of Dock Green manner, Jim explained: 'Hugh had a very tidy and well-organized mind. In one compartment he put the party; in the other compartment he put his ladies.' A very Jim remark.

In the late eighties, Ben was operational on a huge variety of fronts. The success of *Hugh Dalton* and his gifts as a columnist, a book reviewer and an essayist (some of the best examples of which he collected and published in *Frustrate Their Knavish Tricks* in 1994), meant that the features and books editors at the better end of what was still Fleet Street and Gray's Inn Road would turn quite naturally to him as their first choice. He was a political columnist for *Today*, 1986–7, *The Times*, 1987–8 and *The Sunday Times*, 1988–9 as well as serving a spell as the *New Statesman*'s Political Editor in 1987–8. His journalism carried his trademark of past knowledge and present analysis. Writing for the nationals meant that by the tenth anniversary of his arrival in London from Newcastle, Ben had reached a very wide public indeed if one includes his appearances on television and his radio broadcasts.

There was a distinct Pimlott style in the seminar room, too, especially at the regular Wednesday evening gathering of contemporary British political and administrative historians at the Institute of Historical Research in which he and Jean played a central role. Ben, as Jean said after his death, 'was the most peerlessly unfashionable man whose judgement about what was going on in the world was always absolutely uncompromised by anything other than clarity and evidence. He never had comfortable judgement but he always had an accurate judgement.' In the seminar room he gave the impression that he had really tussled with a subject, there was nothing quick, glib or facile about his process of ratiocination. And that once he *had* made up his mind, it was going to need something quite remarkable and compelling to shift it. Ben had referred to a similar trait in his father in the 'biographical note' appended to Pimlott senior's *The Englishman's Christmas*. In it Ben had quoted a 'close colleague' of John's in Whitehall who said of him that 'he could, when he thought fit, stick to his guns with a tenacity which his friends called determination and his opponents obstinacy'. This never meant that Ben belittled other people's interpretations if they were based on scholarly sweat and a care with the sources. In Ph.D. vivas, for example, he was very good with candidates who had constructed their theses and reached their conclusions in a different way to the route Ben would have taken had it been his own research project. Ben never used his formidable intellect as a weapon to demolish people.

The Pimlott of the newspaper column and the Pimlott of the seminar room came together in the late 1980s in a fascinating, if controversial, fashion. Like many others on the centre Left, Ben was cast down by Mrs Thatcher's 102-seat majority in the June 1987 general election. Neil Kinnock had fought a brave fight and energetically begun to syringe the sectarian poison out of Labour—but there was a very long way to go. Pimlott the intellectual and Pimlott the activist decided something must be done. Was this the time for a new popular front of the mind among the sensible centre Left that would stretch from the Labour mainstream to the Liberals and the Social Democrats? He thought it was and created *Samizdat* as a journal of ideas under his editorship. Ben saw *Samizdat* as a way of helping recapture intellectually the middle ground as an indispensable precursor to Labour's regaining power (as did the young John Rentoul who spent hours around the Pimlott kitchen table putting the magazine together). *Samizdat* had a short life between 1988 and 1990.

It was vigorously criticised from the Right by those who argued that its very title was an insult to those inside the Soviet Union and the Soviet bloc who had risked (and still were risking) a great deal in the preparation of underground literature. How could a group of comfortably off centre Leftists in an open society be so insensitive? More prosaically, Labour tribalists loathed the very idea as reeking of compromise, sell-out and coalitionism if not outright defeatism. *Samizdat* was well-written and thoughtful—and more than a mere gesture by frustrated centre Leftists of the more literary kind.

For those who sat on its board, there were special rewards. Michael Young, who had shared a room with John Pimlott at Toynbee Hall before the war, was an enthusiast for the project and the board met at the Institute of Community Studies in Bethnal Green which Michael directed. The discussions in the interstices of the business were wonderful (Michael Young and Eric Hobsbawm, for example, debating the degree to which Michael had foreseen the growth of the eighties 'underclass' in his *The Rise of the Meritocracy* thirty years earlier). *Samizdat* threw good parties, too. It was a tribute to Ben's stature and reach that so disparate a group relished those meetings under his chairmanship. Ben had a gift for bouncing back from electoral failure. For example, Tony Wright (later a Labour MP and highly influential chairman of Commons select committees) recalls Ben simply saying at a Fabian meeting shortly after the 1987 election, 'Right! What we need is a book called *The Alternative.*' Similarly after 1992 he staged a conference, with a tonic effect, on a Saturday in London, called *Whatever Next?* which brought Tony Blair and Shirley Williams together on the same platform.

Ben had written *Hugh Dalton* for Jonathan Cape. Its success meant that other publishers were sure to compete for his next blockbuster. Ben was a great believer in scholars breaking into the top end of the trade press circuit and the sales and the advances that came with it. His decision to write an official biography of the still living Harold Wilson brought him into fruitful and formidable partnership with the mercurially brilliant Giles Gordon as his agent at Sheil Land and Stuart Proffitt as his young and intellectually muscular publisher at HarperCollins.

Ben now had a project whose subject he knew, though Wilson was fast fading in health. It was the former Whitehall officials, Mary Wilson and Marcia Falkender, Harold's Personal and Political Secretary, who provided the richest ingredients for the life. He also had that special feel for Wilson's prime ministerial years having lived through the period and actually having fought under the banner of two Wilsonian election manifestos in 1974. Here, like Dalton, was another immensely controversial figure who, in the late eighties and early nineties, really did need rescuing from the enormous condescension of posterity—not least from the Labour Party for whose unity he had sacrificed very nearly all, during the *In Place of Strife* crisis in 1969, over Britain and Europe in the early seventies and for virtually every minute of his two twilight premierships between March 1974 and April 1976.

Harold Wilson was a monumental 800-pager which took four years from conception to birth. This was literary and scholarly productivity of a high order. Ben began with a great deal of knowledge which Jean supplemented and shaped as what he called his 'cleverest and most inspiring critic'. Though only one book, *The Media in British Politics*, which they co-edited in 1987, bears both their names, Jean's presence is evident throughout the Wilson biography and indeed in everything Ben published.

Ben warmed to Wilson as a human being, as many scholars did who came to know him. However, he had no illusions about Harold's delusions and absurdities (as he had none too about Dalton's), or about the hows and whys whereby Wilson became a by-word for political brilliance indistinguishable from deviousness. He understood the roots of Wilson's one strand of consistency—keeping Labour together and electable. Here is Ben on Wilson's twists and turns on Europe in the difficult opposition years between June 1970 when he lost power, to his shock, and his equally surprising resumption of office in March 1974:

> Wilson went to great pains to defend himself against the charge of being incon-
> sistent, although there is no clear reason why—in politics or in life—people
> should not vary their remarks and opinions according to the circumstances. In
> fact, he was inconsistent in the impression he gave about his Party's purpose—
> facing this way, and then that—but carefully consistent on the key point that
> he was not opposed to entry in principle, and favoured it if the terms were right.
>   It was true that, playing his cards one at a time, he always strove to keep as
> many options open as possible. It is also understandable that those with strong
> opinions, especially the pro-Marketeers, should at times have been infuriated by
> his behaviour . . . whether a more partisan figure, like Jenkins, or an even more
> political one, like Callaghan, would have done better—taking a firmer line,
> while avoiding splits or purges—is debatable. By one measure, Wilson suc-
> ceeded. He remained Leader, and Labour stayed together, even forming
> another administration, though some would argue that the seeds of the Party's
> later division were sown by his handling of it at this time.

The Pimlott style blended personality, private lives, private demons, policy and historical context with a light touch that made even the potentially dreariest patches of intra-Labour history absorbable by the general reader.

Ben's wider interests and activities meant that *Harold Wilson* was written against an insistently ticking clock and the regular reminders about deadlines from his highly efficient publisher, Stuart Proffitt, who was determined it should be the flagship of HarperCollins' 1992 autumn season. As a result, a good part of the book was written in a pair of houses lent by friends in the very un-Wilsonian setting of the Ionian island of Paxos (Harold was a confirmed Scillies man and is indeed buried there). I can remember, too, a slightly desperate phone call from Ben on a September Sunday afternoon at the printers in Bury St Edmunds twenty minutes before the *final* final deadline checking a point with me about Harold's 'agreement to differ' with the anti-marketeers in his Cabinet in the run-up to the 1975 EEC Referendum and the 1932 precedent over free trade/protection during the National Government on which it was based.

Peace finally descended at the printers, the publishers and chez Pimlott in Milner Place, N1. The book was done and it did indeed dazzle through the autumn mists. Once more Ben received the gold medal from Roy Jenkins in *The Observer* ('Fascinating . . . Pimlott the X-ray has produced another work of formidable penetration'). For David Marquand in the *Times Literary Supplement* the key Pimlott skill had resulted in a 'mass of complex material . . . [being] . . . marshalled with the art that conceals art'. For Andrew Marr in *The Independent*, Ben was simply 'the best political biographer now writing'.

Ben finished writing before Wilson's No. 10 papers for 1964–70 reached what is now The National Archives. His life of Harold relied heavily, therefore, on the extended interviews with his subject and Wilson's contemporaries at which he was adept. Only in January 2007 did the last of Wilson's prime ministerial files reach Kew and it will be a successor generation of younger historians who produce the studies within which the primary sources are fully blended. Yet future scholars, wanting to acquire an indispensable feel for Harold the man and the politician and for the times in which he operated, will always have to start with Pimlott on Wilson.

By the end of the 1992 book-reviewing season, the name Pimlott was firmly associated in the reading public's mind with top-flight political biography of the Left. It was a shock to many, therefore, when the news broke that Ben's next subject was the Queen. Indeed, it caused a touch of incomprehension verging on outrage in those circles of the Pimlott friendship penumbra where republicanism lurked. Though some, like Raphael Samuel, saw the point instantly, telling Ben, when told of his plan, 'What a marvellous way of looking at the history of Britain.' Others, as Ben recalled tactfully in his Preface to the first edition,

> expressed surprise, wondering whether a study of the Head of State and Head of the Commonwealth could be a serious or worthwhile enterprise. Whether or not they are right, it certainly has been an extraordinary and fascinating adventure; partly because of the fresh perspective on familiar events it has given me, after years of writing about Labour politicians; partly because of the human drama of a life so exceptionally privileged, and so exceptionally constrained; and partly because of the obsession with royalty of the British public, of which I am a member.

There were those, of whom I was one, who were certain it would be another triumph, intellectually and commercially, for the Pimlott–Gordon–Proffitt trio. And so it proved.

The point about Pimlott on the Queen is that it *was* another *political* biography and it was about a woman (which interested Ben). It was fascinating on personality and circumstance, but the special value it added was the Queen as Head of Government, the conductor of constitutional functions of which few among the absorbed consumers of royal literature knew hardly anything at all. Ben, however, did not shrink from criticism where he thought it merited. He thought she had mishandled the succession to Macmillan in October 1963 when the Earl of Home took the prize and not the Deputy Prime Minister, R. A. Butler. 'Her decision', Ben wrote, 'to opt for passivity and in effect to collude with Macmillan's scheme for blocking the deputy premier, must be counted the biggest political misjudgement of her reign.'

In reaching this judgement, Ben stood apart from most other constitutional historians who have, before or since, sought to reconstruct the events of October 1963. His friend Professor Vernon Bogdanor, for example, in his *The Monarchy and the Constitution* (1995), had written that

> the criticisms made of the queen with regard to the 1963 succession crisis lack substance. It is implausible to believe that Macmillan was able to misrepresent the opinion of the Conservative Party in the memorandum which he handed to the queen. Faced with the preponderant judgement in favour of Home, based, the memorandum apparently declared, on a canvass of the Cabinet, the Conservative Party in both Houses of Parliament, and in the country, it was not for the queen to conduct her own separate canvass and involve herself in the internal politics of the Conservative Party ... The queen took the straightforward course, and it was for the Conservative Party, if it so wished, to make it clear it would not accept Home as prime minister.

(The Queen acting on a mid-nineteenth-century precedent, had given him time to see if he could form an administration.) Nevertheless, the experience of the Macmillan–Home succession quickly led to the Conservatives abandoning the consultative 'customary processes' for leadership selections in favour of votes by the Conservative Parliamentary Party, the first of which, in 1965, saw Sir Alec Douglas-Home (as he had become on renouncing his peerage in 1963) replaced by Ted Heath.

Ben dined with the Queen at Windsor after the biography appeared but he did not discover what she had thought of it. Protocol prevented him from asking and her from saying. Writing about the Queen affected Ben profoundly. Those who heard him speak about her at Whitsuntide 2002 in Christ Church Cathedral in Oxford, to mark her jubilee, will never forget it. Ben captured how dreadful it must be to be *born* into a function that you have not sought or worked for—and what a remarkable character this had made her. The stolid if highly distinguished audience succumbed to genuine emotion when Ben ended with 'God Bless the Queen!' 'God Bless the Queen!' they cried in return. The Chancellor of Oxford University, Roy Jenkins, was seen to dab his eyes. (Five years earlier, on the day after Princess Diana died, No. 10 rang up Ben for advice. It was the biographer of the 'people's Queen' who gave Downing Street the phrase the 'people's Princess.')

His first edition of *The Queen: Elizabeth II and the Monarchy* was published in 1996 (he published an updated edition in 2001—it now weighed in at 780 pages—to mark her golden jubilee). In the same year Ben was elected FBA and joined S5, the Academy's section embracing political studies, political theory, government and international relations. Senior figures in Whitehall came to associate Ben with the Academy because 10 Carlton House Terrace became the venue for a remarkable Friday afternoon seminar he would alternatively chair with the Cabinet Secretary of the day. This was a legacy of the Economic and Social Research Council's Whitehall Programme Commissioning Panel which Ben had chaired in 1993–4 and whose steering committee he led for a further five years. The subjects ranged widely from devolution and immigration through the role of the Treasury to civil contingency planning for emergencies and terrorist attack and public service reform. These occasions were relished by the group of scholars invited and especially by Sir Robin Butler and Sir Richard Wilson during their time as Secretary of the Cabinet. Wilson's successor, Sir Andrew Turnbull, to Ben's great regret, brought them to an end, thus breaking probably the most fruitful link between the scholarly and the Whitehall communities of recent times, though Ben, in his last months, was on the point of agreeing a new format with Turnbull.

Baffling as that rupture was, it was as nothing compared to New Labour's failure to make use of Ben after the Blair election victory in 1997. No one in the university world had done more to help Labour reacquire electability. Ben's M.Sc. in Public Policy at Birkbeck had groomed numerous special advisers in the Labour government to come (and they, rightly, swore by their mentor). Maybe Ken Morgan, himself a Labour peer, had it right when he declared his astonishment 'that the Blair government saw no need to call on Ben, or some of his Fabian friends, for assistance or advice after the 1997 election. Perhaps this reflected the instinctive apprehension of New Labour towards academics, however distinguished, who were felt all too liable to stray unpredictably "off message" into the dangerous pastures of independent thought.' Certainly had Ben gone to the House of Lords and been appointed a minister, there would (to his credit) have been uncomfortable times ahead even before the Iraq War of 2003 to which he was strongly opposed. With a few exceptions, a knowledge of history (including that of the Labour Party itself) has not been among the strongest suits of those upon whom the Blair patronage has fallen and Ben would never have succumbed to what one of his Cabinet ministers called the 'Tony wants' syndrome.

A few months after Labour's return to power, Ben astonished some of his friends by becoming Warden of Goldsmiths College, University of London. He had served his time as Head of Department at Birkbeck. But he had never been a Dean or a Vice-Master. He got on with administration but never seemed to relish it. Some friends (of whom I was one) perhaps selfishly wanted him to keep writing as the chief absorber of the best hours of his working day. He was 53 and at the peak of his powers. He could be a touch short when such regrets were voiced, talking of the importance of well-run public institutions in general and of the glories of Goldsmiths in particular.

It soon became apparent, however, that he loved Goldsmiths and was hell bent on raising its profile generally and capitalising on its glowing artistic and media studies reputation. He set about being a campus builder too. His aim was to make a marvellous if gritty place a thing of glory. Yet he would always find time to examine a Ph.D. or to review a serious book. Ben the planner and shifter of business fell foul of the Association of University Teachers at Goldsmiths. But the College's Council backed him and he was into his second term as Warden when leukaemia was diagnosed in 2003. He bore his illness with immense fortitude and his laptop clicked until almost the end. He died in University College Hospital on 10 April, Easter Saturday, 2004, aged 58.

Ben was not a religious man in the formal sense though he and Jean were married in an Anglican ceremony; Dan, Nat and Seth were all christened in the Anglican Church. He rarely missed Sunday morning service at St Paul's Cathedral. 'He didn't believe in somebody on a white cloud', said Jean. But he had a spiritual side, he loved Anglican form and order and he was a connoisseur of beauty in words, sound and pictures. The gap he left was huge both in the scholarly and the political world. He gave the notion of the public intellectual a good name for there was nothing flash or meretricious about his fame or his public thinking. His learning was fastidious, his spirit generous. When a serious book dealing with some aspect of the Pimlott terrain has appeared since Easter 2004, the reaction has been 'I wonder what Ben would have made of it?'—but one among many measures of his enduring influence.

In the wider sweep of history, Ben will be remembered politically for standing firm in the age of centre Right Labour defections to the SDP in such a way that others rallied, took heart and stayed at a time when the great tradition, in which Ben had always believed, might have been lost for ever. Above all he will be remembered for the books that were written and, among his friends, for the great ones that might have been (a nearly completed novel may yet appear and there *were* Pimlott diaries, too), not least the big work on Clem Attlee, Harry Truman and the early post-war years that he was planning when illness struck. Ben, had he been a musical score, would have been marked *Nobilmente*—just like the opening bars of Elgar's First Symphony.

PETER HENNESSY
Fellow of the Academy

Note. The author is indebted to Professor Jean Seaton for her indispensable help in the preparation of this memoir.

ROBERT PRING-MILL

Robert Duguid Forrest Pring-Mill
1924–2005

ROBERT PRING-MILL WAS ONE of a generation of young men whose education was interrupted by the Second World War and who went to university as mature students after demobilisation. In Hispanic Studies, as in other subject areas, it was academics of that generation who laid the foundations of the modern discipline and Pring-Mill, an all-rounder who firmly believed that his various research activities were mutually enriching, had the distinction of making a significant contribution to several of its branches.

The First World War likewise played its part in shaping the course his life was to take. The only child of Scottish parents, he spent his early childhood in the Essex village of Stapleford Tawney where he was born on 11 September 1924. However, his father, a professional soldier who had been gassed in the trenches during the war, was advised by his doctors to seek the beneficial effects of a warmer climate and the family moved to the Continent, first to France and then Majorca, where they settled in 1931. Apart from a short period in Italy, where they were evacuated in the early months of the Spanish Civil War, they were to remain there until the outbreak of the Second World War in 1939. In Majorca the young Pring-Mill learned Catalan and developed a love of Catalonia and its culture that was to stay with him all his life. He also received a Catholic education at the Jesuits' Montesión college in Palma, a training that was to leave its mark on his thinking and his academic writing.

Still a teenager when the family returned to Britain, he somehow contrived to enlist in the army in 1941, keeping alive his Scottish heritage by joining the Black Watch. He served with the 25th Indian Division in Burma before ending up in Malaya, where he celebrated his twenty-first

Proceedings of the British Academy, **150**, 183–198. © The British Academy 2007.

birthday shortly after the Japanese surrender. During his service he rose to the rank of captain, became an intelligence officer and was mentioned in dispatches. In Malaya in 1946 he produced his first publication in the form of a thirty-page cyclostyled pamphlet on Chinese Triad societies. Though he claimed to have written it mainly to alleviate tedium, its interest in ideology and metaphysics points forward to the preoccupations that underpin his later work.

In October 1947 he entered New College, Oxford, where he took the shortened ex-servicemen's honours course in Modern Languages. He read Spanish and French, and under a new dispensation he was also able to take Medieval Catalan as an optional subject, thereby becoming the first student to study it at Oxford. At university he demonstrated his talent by winning two undergraduate prizes—a Heath Harrison Travelling Scholarship in Spanish (1948), which he used to finance a pilgrimage to Santiago de Compostela, and the Arteaga Essay Prize (1949)—and confirmed it by obtaining a First in his Finals in December 1949. That success led to a scholarship at Magdalen College and in 1952 he was appointed to a university lectureship in Spanish. He held that post until his retirement in 1988, together with a tutorial fellowship at St Catherine's College (1965–88) and college lectureships at New College (1956–88) and Exeter College (1963–81).

During his time as an undergraduate Pring-Mill got to know fellow student Brigitte Heinsheimer and they married in 1950. The marriage, which produced a son and a daughter, Francis and Monica, was stable and lasting, largely because the couple had personalities which complemented each other and shared strongly held Catholic beliefs. Pring-Mill was a quiet and private man whose life was centred on home and family, but at the same time he and his wife were known as generous and affable hosts, frequently entertaining Oxford colleagues and visiting scholars and writers at their cottage in the Buckinghamshire village of Brill. Among those who enjoyed their hospitality was the celebrated Chilean poet Pablo Neruda. Some time later, he commemorated the occasion by concocting in their honour a cocktail which he named Brill's Smile: 1 soup-spoon raspberry juice; juice of 6 sweet oranges; 1 soup-spoon Cointreau; 2 soup-spoons cognac; ½ litre white wine; 1 bottle *brut* champagne.

One of Pring-Mill's earliest publications, a co-authored book of Spanish translation passages intended for use in the classroom, was a standard textbook in its day and ran into several editions.[1] As that book

---

[1] Cyril A. Jones and RPM, *Advanced Spanish Unseens* (London, 1958).

indicates, he took teaching as seriously as research. Not only did he enjoy interaction with students but he regarded it as a means of developing new angles of approach and of honing his ideas. His lectures were always rigorously prepared and invariably stimulating and informative, but at the same time he sought to draw undergraduates into a shared exploration of the issues concerned and in his tutorials he encouraged them to express their ideas and to learn through dialogue. As one obituarist aptly put it, 'He had the old-fashioned virtues of an Oxford academic: not only did he appear to have time for everyone, but he always sought to bring out the best in them rather than display his own vast knowledge.'[2] He was also a kind and conscientious man who went to great pains to care for his students' welfare.

Notoriously Pring-Mill drove himself hard. He started the day early and was wont to reach college when most of his colleagues were still abed, joking that for him breakfast was his mid-morning break. He had, too, a remarkable capacity for long hours of sustained labour which enabled him to produce a substantial corpus of books and articles. Nor did he limit his endeavours to teaching and research, but engaged in a range of activities designed to promote his subject and take it to a wider public. He delivered countless public talks to bodies prestigious and humble. He made hundreds of radio broadcasts, including over a hundred on the BBC's Spanish and Latin American services. He contributed fifteen review articles to the *Times Literary Supplement* on assorted Spanish and Spanish American writers and movements. He also made numerous contributions to reference works such as *The Caxton World of Knowledge* and *The Fontana Biographical Companion to Modern Thought*, the first of which contains no less than thirty entries on Hispanic literary topics and the latter seventeen.[3]

Pring-Mill's enthusiasm for things Catalan led to an acquaintance with the Catalan publisher and bookseller Joan Gili, who had settled in England in the early 1930s and acquired British citizenship and who was to publish some of his early writings. In 1953 Gili, who was keen to promote Catalan culture in the United Kingdom, recruited him to translate literary critic Joan Triadú's introduction to an anthology of Catalan poetry and, in addition, he contributed a 'Biographical and

[2] Nick Caistor, in *The Guardian*, 17 Oct. 2005, p. 33.
[3] See *The Caxton World of Knowledge*, vol. II (London, 1960); *The Fontana Biographical Companion to Modern Thought* (London, 1983).

Bibliographical Index'.[4] With Gili and the likes of Frank Pierce, Geoffrey Ribbans and Arthur Terry, he was a founding member of the Anglo-Catalan Society—an organisation set up in 1954 to promote the study and understanding of Catalan culture in the United Kingdom and which during the Franco era was a symbol of solidarity with a region whose language and culture were denied public expression by the dictatorship—and he served as its President between 1973 and 1978. Given his childhood experience, it is hardly surprising that Majorca should have occupied a special place in his affections and one of his early publications was effectively a piece of PR intended to confer on it something of the romanticism associated with the liaison between Chopin and George Sand, being a translation of a Catalan account of the couple's sojourn on the island.[5] Likewise the first writer to be the focus of his research was a Majorcan, the medieval poet, mystic, philosopher and theologian Ramon Llull, sometimes Anglicised as Raymond Lully. Llull is famed as the originator of a complex 'art of finding truth', which he developed in successive revised versions known collectively as the *Ars Magna* (The Great Art). The primary aim of his Art was to assist in the conversion of non-Christians to the Christian faith, but it was also designed to bring about the integration of all branches of knowledge into a single theocentric system. In the course of his career, but primarily in the early stages, Pring-Mill produced a body of studies which earned him recognition as one of the world's foremost authorities on Llull's work.

The majority of these were subsequently collected and published in Barcelona as a 336-page book, which won the 1992 Serra d'Or prize for research on a Catalan topic.[6] The first part of the volume is devoted to 'El microcosmos lul.lià', a long essay that was originally published as an opuscule in 1961. Its overview of Llull's vision of the world is generally held to be the clearest exposition of the writer's thinking and has been

[4] Joan Gili (ed.), selected by Joan Triadú, *Anthology of Catalan Lyric Poetry* (Oxford, 1953), pp. 371–86.

[5] Bartomeu Ferrà, *Chopin and George Sand in Majorca* (Palma de Mallorca, 1961).

[6] Lola Badia and Albert Soler (eds.), *Estudis sobre Ramon Llull (1956–1978)* (Barcelona, 1991). See also 'Grundzüge von Lulls *Ars inveniendi veritatem*', *Archiv für Geschichte der Philosophie*, 43 (1961), 239–66; 'Ramon Llull's Four *Libri Principiorum*: An Introductory Note', in Raymundus Lullus, *Quattuor Libri Principiorum (Liber Principiorum Theologiae, Liber Principiorum Philosophiae, Liber Principiorum Juris, et Liber Principiorum Medicinae)* (Wakefield/Paris-The Hague, 1969), pp. vi–xxvi; 'The Lullian *Art of Finding Truth*: A Medieval System of Enquiry', *Catalan Review: International Journal of Catalan Culture*, 4 (1990), 55–74; 'The Role of Numbers in the Structure of the *Arbor scientiae*', in Fernando Domínguez Reboiras *et al.* (eds.), *Arbor scientiae, Der Baum des Wissens von Ramon Lull* (Turnhout, 2002), pp. 35–63.

extremely influential both in making Llull accessible to non-specialist readers and in shaping approaches to his work. It situates Llull's writings within the context of the ideas of his time, showing that he was operating within the parameters of a broadly Neoplatonic exemplarist world-picture accepted by Christians, Jews and Muslims alike. It also explains at some length the main features of medieval thinking: the common belief in a hierarchy or ladder of being, the theories of the four elements and of the heavenly spheres, the organisation of reality by numerical–geometrical symbolism, the idea of man as a microcosm. The basis of Llull's thought is shown to be the doctrines of the Dignities, God's divine attributes, and of the Correlatives, their manifestation in the created universe, all things being connected to them by sets of 'principles of relation' whose combinations constitute the sum of all possible relationships. Pring-Mill defines his Art as a system of enquiry and verification which makes use of logical methods to refer all truth back to the Godhead, adopting the combinatory methods employed by the science of the day to argue analogically about God and every aspect of the universe. As well as elucidating the Art, he skilfully deciphers the combinatory diagrams and symbolic notations which accompany the written text, though he is at pains to point out that these are ancillary to the system rather than intrinsic to it, being mere devices for speeding up its operations.

The essays in the second and third parts of the book respectively explore more fully key aspects of Llull's thought and offer readings of different literary texts. Two focus on the symbolism of numbers, addressing the question of why in early versions of the Art the Dignities are sixteen in number but are reduced to nine in later versions. Another discusses the analogical structure of the Art, arguing that the four elements of medieval science furnished Llull with the model which he used to structure his analysis of higher things. Yet despite the outstanding scholarship and perceptiveness that Pring-Mill brings to the exegesis of Llull's philosophy, he thought of himself primarily as a literary critic and as such he was concerned not just with the meaning of the work but with the interaction between it and the complex of signifiers that communicate it to the reader. A major element in his contribution to our appreciation of Llull was precisely the attention he gave to the literary aspects of his writing. Thus, for example, his magnificent analysis of the *Llibre d'amic e Amat* (The Book of the Lover and the Beloved), a series of reflections on the path to mystic union with God, convincingly demonstrates that beneath its apparent formlessness the book has an underlying structural unity in that all

of the various motifs and literary resources of its 365 versicles are
geared towards the same conceptual end.

Some of the features which characterise Pring-Mill's work on Llull—
most notably an interest in how the writers of a particular historical
period viewed the world and in the literary conventions they used to communicate their vision of reality—were carried over into his second area
of research activity, Spanish literature of the sixteenth and seventeeth
centuries, the so-called Golden Age.[7] Among his publications in that field
are two essays on the theatre of Lope de Vega, one a general introduction,
the other an examination of the role of maxims in *Fuente Ovejuna*, in
which he argues that they are a key to explain the relationship between the
general and the particular, between an abstract universal principle and
the specific concrete situations faced by the characters. Another two focus
on the way prose writers of the period depict reality and, in particular, on
their preoccupation with the conflict between earthly appearances and
eternal truth. Others explore how mystical experience is conveyed in
literature and analyse the ramifications of a conceit recurrent in writing
of the period.

However, his most substantial and most important work in the area of
Golden Age literature was his writings on Spain's greatest dramatist,
Pedro Calderón de la Barca. In the 1960s and 1970s he was one of a
group of British Hispanists who shared a common enthusiasm for the
theatre of Calderón and who, in a spirit of post-war conciliation, collaborated with German colleagues specialising in the same field and he
played an active part in the organisation of a series of Anglo-German
symposia which served as forum and focus for that collaboration, the first
of them held in Exeter in 1969. His studies of Calderón, written over a
period of thirty years, were collected in a 223-page volume published in
2001.[8] In the book's opening essay, a survey of the Anglo-Saxon contribution to Calderón studies, he acknowledges himself to be the heir of

---

[7] See 'Two Spanish Mystics and their Methods of Describing Mystical Experience', *The Aryan Path*, 26 (1955), 489–92, 536–40; 'Spanish Golden-Age Prose and the Depiction of Reality', *Anglo-Spanish Society Quarterly Review*, 32/33 (1959), 20–31; 'Introduction', in Lope de Vega: *Five Plays*, trans. Jill Booty (New York, 1961), pp. vii–xli; 'Sententiousness in *Fuente Ovejuna*', *Tulane Drama Review*, 7 (1962), 5–37; 'Escalígero y Herrera: citas y plagios de los *Poetices Libri Septem* en las *Anotaciones*', in Jaime Sánchez Romeralo and Norbert Poulussen (eds.), *Actas del Segundo Congreso Internacional de Hispanistas* (Nijmegen, 1967), pp. 489–98; 'Some Techniques of Representation in the *Sueños* and the *Criticón*', *Bulletin of Hispanic Studies*, 45 (1968), 270–84; '"Porque yo cerca muriese": An Occasional Meditation on a *Conceptista* Theme', *Bulletin of Hispanic Studies*, 61 (1984), 369–78.

[8] Nigel Griffin (ed.), *Calderón: estructura y ejemplaridad* (London, 2001).

such eminent scholars as W. J. Entwistle, E. M. Wilson and A. A. Parker and of an academic tradition whose approach to Calderón he labels 'análisis temático-estructural', a term he coined to distinguish it from French structuralism.[9] Put simply, that approach is the study of the way in which the action of a play is structured to convey a theme, a universal human truth expressed metaphorically by the stage fiction.

Much of the book is taken up with arguments of a theoretical nature, which are repeated, developed and refined from one article to another. The starting premise is that the ideological framework of Calderón's plays—and indeed of all Golden Age theatre—is an inherited theocentric world-view in which the monarch was perceived as God's earthly representative and a hierarchical society reflected the structure of the cosmos, where each element occupied a rung in a ladder of being. It is argued that Calderón makes use of the theologians' schematic abstractions as keys for the understanding of the everyday experience of human beings, presenting a system of universal principles whose operation is studied in particular situations which are conceived as exemplary illustrations of those principles. That being the case, the effectiveness of a play derives not from the verisimilitude of its action as measured against everyday life but from its validity as a concrete example of a general truth and can be judged only by examining the extent to which it has been constructed to satisfy the conceptual demands of the theme in a logically convincing manner. That is precisely what Pring-Mill does in the various essays, whether by analysing the structure of a specific play or the exemplary significance of a key episode in a play, or by comparing and contrasting the functioning of the different theatrical genres cultivated by Calderón or by examining the dramatist's use of the techniques of rhetoric and casuistry. In the way of things, Hispanic Studies have evolved and new approaches have emerged with regard both to seventeenth-century thought and the theatre of the Golden Age. Even so, Pring-Mill's essays remain a major contribution to Calderón studies, not just as an outstanding example of a particular school of criticism, but because they continue to offer important insights into the plays.

A key experience in Pring-Mill's academic development was two months spent in South America in 1949 as one of a small group of budding Hispanists sponsored by the British diplomat and Hispanophile Sir

---

[9] In a footnote he warns of the inappropriateness of a literal translation of the term into English ('thematic-structural analysis') and suggests that it is best rendered as 'the thematic approach to structural analysis'.

Eugen Millington Drake, who sought to foster Anglo-Argentine and Anglo-Uruguayan relations by financing such group-visits in both directions. The party visited Buenos Aires, Montevideo and other cities in the River Plate, taking turns to address local literary or cultural societies, but Pring-Mill and John Street, the future historian of Latin America, managed to fit in a week in Chile. There he was introduced to the poetry of Pablo Neruda and to the ugly face of Spanish American political life. The young Englishman, who had never heard of Neruda until then, was informed that not only was he the continent's foremost poet but he was a prominent political figure, a communist who had been elected to the Senate in 1947 but at that time was on the run, fleeing from a government crack-down on its leftist opponents. He was also presented with copies of a couple of Neruda's books, including part of the *Canto general* (General Song), a monumental poetic exploration of Latin America's history and destiny which he had completed while in hiding and which circulated in clandestine editions. That gift marked the beginning of a lifelong love affair with Neruda's poetry and, more generally, sparked off an interest in the phenomenon of socially committed poetry.

Pring-Mill never regarded himself as being primarly a Latin Americanist and Latin American subjects never took up more than half of his student contact hours. Nonetheless, he ranks alongside Jean Franco and Donald Shaw as one of the pioneers of the study of Latin American literature in the United Kingdom. Initially the Spanish American authors included in the Oxford programme were figures from the past, in keeping with the then widely held view that historical perspective was necessary before a writer could be deemed worthy of study, but in 1960 he succeeded in overcoming the resistance of the traditionalists to have Neruda introduced as the first living author on the Modern Languages syllabus. Five years later he was instrumental in having Neruda invited to Oxford to receive the honorary degree of Doctor of Letters. This was the first time the two men had met but they quickly hit it off and during the last eight years of the poet's life they met on a number of occasions as well as exchanging corrrespondence. Later, in the difficult times that followed Neruda's death in 1973, a few days after the military coup that brought Pinochet to power, Pring-Mill maintained contact with his widow, visiting her in Paris when she went into exile, and he was entrusted with the responsibility of travelling to Chile to archive the poet's estate. For Pring-Mill the honorary doctorate awarded to Neruda meant public recognition in Britain of a poet whom he regarded as one of the half-dozen greatest poets in the Spanish language. At the same time, the honouring of the distinguished Chilean writer helped to raise the profile of Latin American literature and was symptomatic of the trend that brought about the growth of Latin American Studies in the 1960s and 1970s.[10] Though he found the ceremony rather quaint and was greatly amused that it was conducted in Latin, Neruda later acknowledged on several occasions that the honour conferred on him by Oxford initiated the process that brought him the Nobel Prize for Literature in 1971, for it was the first time his standing had been officially recognised in a country outside the Spanish-speaking world and the communist bloc. Indeed, so grateful was he to Pring-Mill that he invited him to Stockholm to attend the prize-giving ceremony. It is an indication of the latter's sense of priorities that he declined because the event took place in the middle of term and he did not feel that he could take time off from his teaching.

In 1967–8 Pring-Mill managed to fund a sabbatical year in Latin America. Obtaining various minor grants by way of pump-priming, he equipped a short-wheelbase Land Rover in 1967, shipped it over to Montreal and spent six weeks lecturing his way through the United States to raise more money before spending almost a whole academic year travelling from Mexico to Chile and back again. Between November 1967 and September 1968 he covered 25,000 miles and visited fifteen Spanish-speaking countries. Travelling overland was time-consuming and out of the 309 days he spent in Spanish America 105 were spent mainly driving. For large parts of the journey there were no road maps available and thirty-two frontier-crossings tested his patience, for many crossings involved passing through the hands of six sets of officials and he sometimes spent four hours getting his Land Rover from one country into the next. However, for a considerable part of the journey he was not alone, for during the school holidays he was joined by his wife and two children. Not only did their presence turn the expedition into a family adventure but, since his wife had served as an aircraft mechanic during the war, he was freed from worries about the vehicle breaking down.

Two main purposes lay behind this journey. The first was to pursue his research on Neruda, particularly on the *Canto general*. In Mexico, for example, his priority was to study the muralist art of Diego Rivera, José Clemente Orozco and David Alfaro Siqueiros and to assess how it had influenced the semi-epic historical vision of the *Canto general*. Likewise,

---

[10] In the same year the Parry Report made a series of recommendations to promote the development of Latin American Studies in the United Kingdom. See *Report of the Committee on Latin American Studies* (London, 1965).

out of the four months he was in Chile, he spent a total of five weeks at
Neruda's home in Isla Negra, where he interviewed the poet on his work
and examined the original manuscripts of his poems. Above all, however,
Pring-Mill had come to realise that he would never be competent to speak
or write about the *Canto general* until he was familiar with the social, cultural, political and geographical setting that was its referent. The trip gave
him first-hand experience of the awesome immensity of the Latin
American landscape and of the continent's diversity and by making the
journey in both directions he was able to see the same places at different
seasons of the year. He also had his eyes opened to the chronic under-
development in which most of the region languished and to the spectacle
of widespread social and economic inequality. He came into contact, too,
with a cross-section of the Latin American population, ranging from
politicians, academics and writers to miners, fishermen and peasants.
Pring-Mill always claimed that what he saw and heard on his travels supplied him with deeper insights into the nature of Latin America than he
could ever have acquired by sitting reading in a library. Like Neruda, he
found himself identifying with the continent's downtrodden and came to
understand why socialist and communist ideas found such ready acceptance in Latin America. Indeed, one of his idiosyncrasies was that while
he was essentially conservative in his beliefs and attitudes, he held strong
views with regard to the need for social change in Latin America and was
a fervent supporter of the Allende government in Chile and of the
Sandinista regime in Nicaragua. Yet he was far from sharing Neruda's
political ideas—and always refrained from discussing politics with him—
and his belief in social justice was rather that of a Catholic in tune with
the spirit of the Second Vatican Council.

Pring-Mill's exploration of the changes that had taken place in
Neruda's poetry as a consequence of his politicisation in the 1930s led
him to interest himself in socially committed poetry as a genre and the
second main purpose of his travels around Spanish America was to examine the nature, origins and current state of that genre. That project
involved meeting poets and critics and collecting texts. Letters of introduction from Neruda and the Guatemalan novelist Miguel Ángel
Asturias opened many doors and as a means of establishing contacts he
gave forty-three lectures arranged for him by the British Council and
British embassies.[11] Over the year he acquired 1,332 books, booklets,

---

[11] An old friend of Neruda's, Asturias was at that time Guatemalan ambassador in Paris. He
was awarded the Nobel prize that same year.

periodicals, leaflets and unpublished texts, including some 500 volumes containing committed poetry, material which he further supplemented on later journeys to Mexico and Central America. He also extended his interest to embrace popular music and protest song and he amassed a collection of LPs as well as making his own taped recordings. This was to be an abiding interest and he built up his collection over several years. He later donated his committed poetry collection to Oxford's Taylorian Library, together with his collections of material on Pablo Neruda and Ernesto Cardenal. His collection of recordings of and publications about Spanish American committed song was donated to the University of Liverpool's Institute of Popular Music.

No one did more than Pring-Mill to make Neruda's work known in the English-speaking world. His introduction to the translation of *Alturas de Macchu Picchu* remains a superb guide to the text.[12] Concise but highly informative, learned but clearly expressed, it sets the poem in the context of Neruda's life and career and elucidates its themes and imagery for the reader, arguing that the journey to the ancient Inca citadel that was the inspiration for the work becomes a metaphor for the exploration of the poet's personal world and of the past of Latin American man. He also published an anthology of Neruda's verse that was intended both for the general reader and for use as a university textbook.[13] The selection spans the whole corpus of Neruda's work, from his earliest books to those written in the last years of his life and published posthumously. It is also a representative sample, in the sense that it presents a spectrum of the major tendencies in the poet's work at different periods, each represented in sufficient depth for individual poems to be appreciated in their context. The sixty-four-page introduction is conceived, not as an independent critical study, but as a tool to be used in conjunction with the body of poetry which makes up the anthology. It provides essential biographical information, traces the different stages in the development of the poet's work and describes the themes and style of each phase, thereby furnishing a context in which individual poems can be read. The first two volumes of *Residencia en la tierra* (Residence on Earth), published respectively in 1933 and 1935, are shown to mirror the collapse of the inherited world-picture in a studied disintegration of poetic form. The pages on the *Canto general* examine the thematic and stylistic features

---

[12] 'Preface', in Pablo Neruda, *The Heights of Macchu Picchu*, trans. Nathaniel Tarn (London, 1966), pp. 7–13.
[13] *Pablo Neruda: A Basic Anthology*, ed. RPM (Oxford, 1975).

that characterise Neruda's socially committed poetry, while those on the *Odas elementales* (Elemental Odes) of 1954 demonstrate that Neruda went on to develop a different kind of social poetry which celebrates the experiencing of the simple things of life, whose intrinsic beauty is enhanced through their relationship with others in a social context. Above all, the introduction reveals Pring-Mill's knack for explaining complex ideas in clear and simple language.

Though he never produced the major book that one might have expected of him, his essays put him in the front rank of Neruda scholarship.[14] These include one which explores at length and in depth the poetics of the *Odas elementales*, but the area where he most distinguished himself was the analysis of the originals. By virtue of his friendship with Neruda and his wife he had privileged access to draft versions of many of the poet's works. By relating these to the finished products, he throws fresh light on the latter by exploring the evolution that took place in the course of the creative process. This applies not just to individual poems but also to books, for by examining how the ordering of the poems in a collection changed he is able to highlight the set of intertextual relations that came to prevail.

Meanwhile, Pring-Mill had developed an interest in the leading Spanish American committed poet of the generation that came after Neruda, the Nicaraguan priest and champion of liberation theology, Ernesto Cardenal, whose work had first come to his attention during his 1967 trip. In 1972 he spent a month with Cardenal in the commune which the latter had established on the island of Solentiname in Lake Nicaragua and was able to discuss his work and thought with him. He also worked on translations of Cardenal's verse and three years later he introduced the Nicaraguan to the British reading public with an anthology in English presenting representative poems from different phases of his writing.[15] Following a pattern similar to that of the Neruda anthology, the introduction situates the poetry in the context of Cardenal's life and thinking

---

[14] See 'La elaboración de la cebolla', in Ángel Flores (ed.), *Aproximaciones a Pablo Neruda* (Barcelona, 1974), pp. 227–41; 'El Neruda de las *Odas elementales*', in Alain Sicard (ed.), *Coloquio Internacional sobre Pablo Neruda* (Poitiers, 1979), pp. 261–300; 'Neruda y los originales de *Los libertadores*', in *Actas del Sexto Congreso Internacional de Hispanistas* (Toronto, 1980), pp. 587–9; 'La composición de *Los versos del capitán*: el testimonio de los borradores', in Hernán Loyola (ed.), *Neruda en la Sassari* (Sassari, 1987), pp. 173–204; 'La evolución de *Los versos del capitán*: su composición y su reorganización', *Ibero-Amerikanisches Archiv*, 13 (1987), 175–89; 'The Building of Neruda's "Oda al edificio"', in Gisela Beutler (ed.), '*Sieh den Fluss der Sterne strömen': Hispanoamerikanische Lyrik der Gegenwart* (Darmstadt, 1990), pp. 198–222.

[15] Ernesto Cardenal, *Marilyn Monroe and Other Poems* (London, 1975).

and shows how he evolved a poetic style which eschews subjective elements and conveys its message through understatement, whether through
the poetic reworking of documentary material, the cultivation of epi-
grams modelled on and referring back to those of the great Latin poets,
or 'up-dated' versions of the Psalms. Pring-Mill also coedited an
American anthology of Cardenal's verse in translation, writing the introduction and reproducing sixteen of his own translations from the earlier
book.[16] In addition, he published four articles on diverse aspects of
Cardenal's work, of which one examines his use of documentary material
such as chronicles, anthropological reports and newspaper articles, two
analyse poetic techniques as illustrated by specific texts, and the fourth
discusses his treatment of America's Indian cultures as a means of making an implicit critique of the values of modern capitalist society.[17] He
also veered into cultural history by producing another two articles on
the popular writing workshops which Cardenal set up to promote
literary activity when he became Minister of Culture in the Sandinista
government.[18]

Pring-Mill also authored a number of general articles on the subject
of Spanish American committed poetry, as well as introducing a university course on that phenomenon.[19] Regrettably, this is the area of his

[16] Ernesto Cardenal, *Apocalypse and Other Poems*, ed. Robert Pring-Mill and Donald D. Walsh,
trans. Thomas Merton, Kenneth Rexroth, Mireya Jaimes Freyre and the editors (New York,
1977).

[17] 'The Redemption of Reality through Documentary Poetry', in Ernesto Cardenal, *Zero Hour
and Other Documentary Poems*, ed. Donald D. Walsh (New York, 1980), pp. ix–xxi;
'Comunicación explícita e implícita en dos poemas de Ernesto Cardenal ("Las ciudades perdi-
das" y "Katún 11 Ahau")', in Giuseppe Bellini (ed.), *Actas del Séptimo Congreso de la Asociación
Internacional de Hispanistas* (Rome, 1982), pp. 825–35; 'Acciones paralelas y montaje acelerado
en el segundo episodio de *Hora 0*', *Revista Iberoamericana*, 118–19 (1982), 217–40; 'Cardenal's
Treatment of Amerindian Cultures in *Homenaje a los indios americanos*', *Renaissance and
Modern Studies*, 35 (1992), 52–74.

[18] 'Ernesto Cardenal and the *talleres de poesía*', in Rob Rix (ed.), *Nicaragua: Pueblo y cultura*
(Leeds, 1985), pp. 18–39; 'Mayra Jiménez and the Rise of Nicaraguan *poesía de taller*', in Lloyd
King (ed.), *La mujer en la literatura caribeña: Sexta Conferencia de Hispanistas, 1983* (St
Augustine, Trinidad, 1987), pp. 1–39.

[19] 'Both in Sorrow and in Anger: Spanish American Protest Poetry', *Cambridge Review*, 91
(1970), 112–17; 'The Poetry of Protest', *Times Literary Supplement*, no. 3882, 6 Aug. 1976,
994–5; 'The Scope of Spanish-American Committed Poetry', in Sabine Horl *et al.* (eds.),
Homenaje a Rodolfo Grossman (Frankfurt, Berne and Las Vegas, 1977), pp. 259–333, reissued as
a pamphlet (Oxford: St Catherine's College, 1978); 'The Nature and Functions of Spanish-
American *Poesía de compromiso*', *Bulletin of the Society for Latin-American Studies*, 31 (1979),
4–21; 'Spanish America: The Social Role of the Committed Poet', in Ann Thompson and
Antony Beck (eds.), *Social Roles for the Artist* (Liverpool, 1979), pp. 81–8; 'La toma de

academic output that has least stood the test of time, for the essays project a somewhat one-dimensional image of Spanish American literature that reflects the simplistic assumptions and limited knowledge of the period when Latin American studies were still in their infancy. Nonetheless, they advance an argument that it was important to make in the early days of the discipline, namely, that since most modern Latin American literature displays some kind of social concern, it is necessary to eschew traditional European concepts of what constitutes literary studies and to consider that literature at least partially in terms of the socio-political context from which it has emerged. They also identify a particular type of literature which flourished in Latin America for the greater part of the twentieth century, explain it as a response to prevailing social, political and economic conditions and as inspired by a desire to promote social change, and analyse its characteristic features. Moreover, Pring-Mill is able to draw on his work in other fields to bring important insights to the study of committed poetry. Thus he establishes a parallel between the medieval world-picture and the various forms of Marxist ideology that inform much committed poetry in that both provide a coherent frame of reference to which everything can be related. Likewise, he demonstrates that, just as Calderón used the techniques of rhetoric and casuistry to convey a theocentric world-view, so too the committed poets were operating within a literary-cum-rhetorical tradition and followed the conventions of what he calls 'a familiar grammar of dissent'.

Furthermore, one of his most significant contributions to Latin American Studies grew out of his research in this area. Deciding that the study of committed poetry should embrace the oral as well as the written, he set about investigating the field of popular song and thereby foreshadowed the later emergence of cultural studies.[20] While stressing that the origins of Spanish American popular song go back to colonial times, Pring-Mill focuses on its modern manifestation, identifying two stages in its evolution as a vehicle for voicing social grievances and promoting class solidarity. The first began with the collection of existing folksongs by poet-singers like the Chilean Violeta Parra, the Argentinian Atahualpa Yupanqui and the Afro-Peruvian Nicomedes Santa Cruz, who then went

---

conciencia en la poesía de compromiso hispanoamericana', in Antonio Vilanova (ed.), *Actas del X Congreso de la Asociación Internacional de Hispanistas* (Barcelona, 1992), pp. 33–53.

[20] See '*Cantas—Canto—Cantemos*: las canciones de lucha y esperanza como signos de reunión e identidad', *Romanistisches Jahrbuch*, 34 (1983), 318–54, reissued as a pamphlet (Oxford, 1983); '*Gracias a la vida': The Power of Poetry and Song* (London, 1990); *The Uses of Spanish-American So-Called Protest Song*, IPM Occasional Paper 4 (Liverpool, 1993).

on to write original songs in traditional forms. The second, that of the so-called 'new song', shows the influence of foreign protest song, with singers such as the Chileans Víctor Jara and Patricio Manns and the Uruguayan Daniel Viglietti seeking to emulate in the Latin American context figures such as Bob Dylan and Pete Seeger. The articles on the subject explore how song involves the audience and how its music impacts on the listener, as well as examing recurrent themes and artistic conventions. The artists studied in greatest depth are Violeta Parra and Víctor Jara.

The most striking thing about Pring-Mill's scholarship is its range, since it not only covers three areas—Catalonia, Spain and Latin America—but spans three historical periods—the Middle Ages, the sixteenth and seventeenth centuries and the twentieth century. What is also striking is that he was not a scholar who produced 'big books', for the books that he published are either anthologies or collections of essays brought out after his retirement and he himself modestly described his longest study—*El microcosmos lul.lià* (1961)—as an opuscule rather than a book. Yet the impact made by his research output confirms the old saying that size does not matter. His preferred medium, in fact, was the essay, in the form of articles, conference papers and opuscules where he reworked and refined his ideas on the work of his favourite authors and it is a sign of the esteem in which his scholarship was held that others were willing to assume the role of editor to make his essays on Llull and Calderón available in book form. At the same time a substantial part of his publications played a significant role in the dissemination of the work of major Hispanic authors, whether in the form of anthologies or of introductions to selections of their writings edited by himself or by others or, in the case of his elucidation of Llull's world-picture, by making difficult texts accessible to non-specialists.

Many honours were bestowed on him in recognition of his scholarship. His contribution to Catalan studies led to his election as Corresponding Member of the Institut d'Estudis Catalans (1966) and of the Reial Academia de Bones Lletres (2002) and in 1990 the Generalitat de Catalunya awarded him the Cross of St George. In that same year the Spanish government acknowledged his work in the field of its country's literature by naming him Commander of the Order of Isabel la Católica. Chile honoured him by making him an Officer of the Order of Bernardo O'Higgins in 1992 and in 2004, Neruda's centenary year, awarded him the Presidential Medal of Honour. At home he was given a Doctorate of Letters by Oxford in 1986 and was elected a Fellow of the British

Academy in 1988. He was also the recipient of two festschrifts. To mark his seventieth birthday colleagues compiled a collection of essays covering the three areas of Hispanic literature which he had graced over the years.[21] For its part the University of Liverpool's Institute of Popular Music paid tribute to his pioneering endeavours in that area by organising a symposium whose proceedings were subsequently published as a book.[22]

Pring-Mill remained active for a decade and more after his retirement. He was regularly invited back to the university to give talks. He continued to research, write and deliver papers and, in particular, completed the first draft of a book on the songs of the Nicaraguan revolution which, unfortunately, never progressed beyond that stage. He also continued to travel and made return trips to Malaysia and Chile, where he had the satisfaction of being present when Salvador Allende was finally rehabilitated with the erection of a statue to him outside the presidential palace. However, his latter years were plagued by ill health, first in the shape of a heart condition and then of cancer of the oesophagus, which eventually killed him. He died on 6 October 2005. To the end, though, he bore his sufferings with the same serenity with which he had lived his life and which so impressed all those who had the privilege of knowing him.

JAMES HIGGINS
Fellow of the Academy

---

[21] Nigel Griffin *et al.* (eds.), *The Discerning Eye: Studies presented to Robert Pring-Mill on his Seventieth Birthday* (Llangrannog, 1994).
[22] Jan Fairley and David Horn (eds.), *'I Sing the Difference': Identity and Commitment in Latin American Song (A Symposium in Honour of Robert Pring-Mill)* (Liverpool, 2002).

JOHN STEVENS   *Eaden Lilley, Cambridge*

John Edgar Stevens
1921–2002

IN THE SUMMER OF 2002, John Stevens's personal copy of *Music at the Court of Henry VIII* came into my possession. Originally published in 1962 as volume XVIII of the monumental series *Musica Britannica*, initiated in the wake of the Festival of Britain, it remains the standard edition of some beguiling songs and instrumental pieces of early-Tudor England, many of them now fairly well known and often performed by both professional and amateur ensembles. To turn the pages of the editor's own copy is to discover a light dusting of annotations and corrections in pencil, written in his discreet and elegant hand, and in one place he has thoroughly revised one of the editions by taping staves of neatly handwritten music over the printed original, changing his solution to the tenor part in the intricate puzzle canon by Robert Fayrfax. In this and some other respects, this copy is a unique scholarly resource in its own right, just as it is a poignant reminder of scholarly tools and methods long relinquished by all save the most determined. Yet perhaps the most revealing part of John Stevens's personal copy of this edition lies elsewhere. At the back are two documents, left loose between the flyleaf and the cover. One is a letter from Thurston ('Bob') Dart, and the other a brief postcard from a young graduate student, named David Fallows, who respectfully questions (one might say politely challenges) Stevens on a particular point in one of his editions after a long day with the manuscripts in the British Museum.[1]

---

[1] The best conspectus of John Stevens's career, albeit with a necessary emphasis upon his musical research, is the article by Iain Fenlon in *New Grove* II, *sv* 'Stevens, John (Edgar)'. This also includes a substantial bibliography of Stevens's publications, omitting no major item. I am most

Proceedings of the British Academy, **150**, 201–217. © The British Academy 2007.

These two communications reveal much about John Stevens's benign and constructive presence among British musical and literary scholars for several generations, beginning in the late 1940s, when he was made a Bye-Fellow of Magdalene College, Cambridge, and extending virtually to the day of his demise on 14 February 2002. (A keen Chaucerian, he would have appreciated the melancholy irony of the date.) Of the two correspondents represented in the letters, Thurston Dart was the supervisor of Stevens's Ph.D. and a leading figure in British musicology for many years. While at Cambridge, Dart lived 'an immensely energetic triple life of teaching, writing and editing and concert giving'.[2] The author of the postcard, David Fallows, is now Professor David Fallows, FBA, a musicologist of distinction and a scholar who has often acknowledged the influence of Stevens's work upon his own.[3] As those two brief communications suggest, Stevens was always in touch with a wide range of scholars from those at the height of their careers to those just making a beginning.

John Stevens was born in East Dulwich, South London, on 8 October 1921, to talented parents who gave him a start in life that Boethius would have admired, for his father was a keen violinist and his mother a graduate in mathematics. They thus married together the two arts that the ill-fated senator, in the tradition of the Greeks, regarded as indissolubly wed. Stevens won a scholarship to Christ's Hospital where he acquired the statutory gratis copy of Lewis and Short's *Latin Dictionary* that he treasured (and used) all his life. He then went on to become a scholar at Magdalene College, Cambridge, first reading Classics (1940–1) and then, after war service, English (1946–8). He was never to leave Magdalene during his long and productive career except for a period, which he much

---

grateful to the following Fellows of the British Academy who shared their reminiscences of Professor Stevens with me, who loaned materials or who read an earlier draft of this memoir: Professor Dame Gillian Beer, Professor John Beer, Dr Margaret Bent, Professor Helen Cooper and Professor David Fallows. I am solely responsible for any inaccuracies or infelicities that remain.

[2] *The New Grove* II, *sv* 'Dart, Thurston'.

[3] See especially David Fallows, 'English Song-Repertories of the Mid-Fifteenth Century', *Proceedings of the Royal Musical Association*, 103 (1976–7), 61–79, at 78, n: 'I must express my gratitude ... particularly to John Stevens whose work obviously lies at the root of almost everything presented here, and who improved this paper by offering some extremely pertinent questions and observations at a time when he was heavily committed with other obligations.' For another tribute from a leading musicologist, see the dedication to M. Bent, *Dunstaple* (Oxford, 1981). Dr Bent dedicated this book on the most important English composer of the fifteenth century to Stevens in memory of his friendship and influence during her Cambridge days, and indeed long after.

enjoyed, as Visiting Professor at the University of California at Berkeley. In his Inaugural Lecture as Professor of Medieval and Renaissance English at Cambridge, *The Old Sound and the New*,[4] Stevens recalls how each student of Magdalene was called, twice a week, into the presence of the Master, A. B. Ramsay, a distinguished Latin poet and close friend of the great medievalist M. R. James; once inside the lodge, the students were required to recite a portion of verse in one of the classical languages. Stevens, who remembered these visits to Ramsay as elocution lessons under another name, recalled the question that the Master was fond of putting to the students: 'What are the three things I require of my boys?' The well-rehearsed and expected answer was 'Accuracy, Eloquence and Deportment, Master'. One might be tempted to pass quickly over this quaint story of Victorian values brought into the age of Philip Larkin and (almost) into the decade of the Chatterley ban, were it not for the fact that John Stevens derived so much more from those lessons in accuracy, eloquence and deportment than a picturesque anecdote.

The Second World War interrupted Stevens's studies at Magdalene. He served on a minesweeper, as many did who were gifted with sharp and sensitive hearing (this was also an acceptable task for a conscientious objector). When he returned to Cambridge he was eventually offered a Bye-Fellowship at his old college (1948), then a Research Fellowship (1950) and finally a full Fellowship in 1953. He married Charlotte Somner in 1946. From his house in Chesterton Road he was accustomed to row along the Cam to the English Faculty offices, using the water route to his place of business like a Tudor official taking the Thames to the Westminster steps. Stevens spent most of his Magdalene years in a magnificent fifteenth-century chamber in the first court, with a small cubby to one side that had once served, as he loved to relate, for a privy. At a small and crowded desk, he often worked at an appropriately monastic hour before dawn (Magdalene was founded for Benedictine monks to study at the university) while the rest of academic Cambridge was asleep. This was a habit he acquired in the early years of fatherhood of his two sons and two daughters, and he never relinquished it. Many generations of students and graduates passed through these rooms, reading their weekly essays and benefiting as much from hospitality as from criticism that could be firm but was never uncharitable, and which was given in a soft

[4] *The Old Sound and the New* (Cambridge, 1982), p. 12 n.

voice with a stammer that Stevens battled to overcome.[5] Graduates and academic colleagues from other faculties in Cambridge also came to these rooms for the Medieval Graduate Seminars that always began with a large and angry kettle boiling, remarkably quickly, for tea. Stevens had read Jerome K. Jerome's *Three Men in a Boat* (a book he much admired) and knew that the best way to make a kettle sing is ostentatiously to ignore it, which he invariably did. Academic visitors from overseas contemplated this British tea ceremony with almost anthropological interest.

In those rooms, or in the small and book-lined crow's nest at the top of his later Cambridge house in Bell's Court, situated halfway up Castle Hill, Stevens wrote his books and articles in a painstaking longhand with a fountain pen. (Only later in his life did he acquire a computer, but he regarded it as a most untrustworthy friend.) His studies were often laid aside when friends came to play viols or to sing Renaissance part-songs, often from his own editions. The element of conviviality in music was essential to him. Despite the undoubted breadth of his musical interests, Stevens's many writings do not suggest he wished to engage at all extensively with the notion that music should sometimes disturb or unsettle the listener, although he emphatically believed that there was something unfathomable, and therefore potentially disconcerting, in all musical effects. In his Inaugural Lecture of 1981 he may reveal more than a gift for apt use of quotation when he invokes 'sounds that give delight and hurt not', from *The Tempest*. In the manner of a consort assembled in a Jacobean house from musically gifted friends—and some very challenging music was played in such houses—Stevens associated music especially with the 'Elian spirit of friendliness and humour' that animates the Charles Lamb Society of which he was a member and at one time the President. Yet his standards of performance were always high, indeed professional, as some of his fellow players will remember. He was fond of quoting the passage in William Byrd's last publication, *Psalmes, Songs and Sonnets* (1611), which calls musicians to rehearse with care, since the excellence of a piece 'is seldom or never well performed at the first singing or playing'. Stevens associated music further with all the higher things of the spirit, in the manner of John Milton and especially of George Herbert, two poets whom he especially favoured among the many that

---

[5] It is no surprise to read the following in the preface to a recently published book by one of his pupils: '[I] sat around the fire in John's wonderful rooms at Magdalene College, discussing the vital questions of medieval monophony over a glass of wine' (M. O'Neill, *Courtly Love Songs of Medieval France: Transmission and Style in the Trouvère repertory* (Oxford, 2006), p. ii).

sustained him throughout his life. He sometimes spoke with feeling of the passage in Izaak Walton's *The Life of Mr. George Herbert* that describes how the poet would gather twice a week with friends in Salisbury for 'an appointed private music meeting', playing his part on lute or viol.

Stevens was also a skilled leader of musicians. For a number of years he directed The English Singers, a chamber choir that was based in the English Faculty (wondrous to relate, in these days of the RAE). The ensemble recruited its members from graduates and undergraduates by audition, as well as from Faculty members, and there are many in Cambridge who still remember a performance of the twelfth-century *Play of Daniel* in the crisp acoustic of the chapel in Jesus College, a perfect setting since the chapel was once the conventual church of the twelfth-century nunnery of Saint Radegund. Stevens had a light tenor voice that he used to good effect as a leader of singers (for a director must be able to sing wisely, but not too well), and he often sang to great effect in his lectures. As an instrumentalist, he played the piano and the harpsichord in an accomplished manner, but his greatest love was perhaps for playing the viol in consort (he listed 'viol-playing' as his recreation in *Who's Who*). The viol is arguably the supreme resource, after the human voice, for the performance of intricate counterpoint by English masters such as Byrd or Jenkins, and Stevens valued it highly. The viol ensemble he joined included amongst its distinguished members the instrument-maker John Isaacs and the musicologist Richard Maunder, and the performances were often adorned with readings by one of John's dearest friends and colleagues, Professor Dame Gillian Beer, FBA.

The eminence of Stevens as a musicologist, and the exalted reputation he left behind amongst his musicological colleagues, seem all the more remarkable when one considers that he passed his life as a university teacher of English literature. From 1954 until 1974 he was University Lecturer in English in the University of Cambridge, then Reader in English and Musical History from 1974–8. In 1978 he was appointed Professor of Medieval and Renaissance English in the University. (He was Chairman of his Faculty at this time and is remembered as a kindly but firm chairman.) Despite Stevens's profound and sympathetic musicianship, it was the critical traditions of English literary studies that shaped his intellectual temper. Among Cambridge medievalists, his principal models were his predecessor in the chair of Medieval and Renaissance English, J. A. W. Bennett, from whom he borrowed the term 'humane medievalist' that he chose for himself in his Inaugural Lecture of 1981,[6] and his predecessor but one in the Chair, C. S. Lewis, whom Stevens thanks in that same Inaugural for 'kindness and illumination'. Like Bennett and Lewis, Stevens was committed to the view that 'certain kinds of historical study are valuable and liberating', a view he expressed in an essay of 1981 for the *Cambridge Review* (on which more below) and a principle he believed to be enshrined in the period papers of the Cambridge English Tripos 'over the last fifty years', which meant a period reaching back to the early 1930s when he wrote those words. There is no doubt that Stevens would have been happy to defend, albeit with due circumspection, the founding and historical principles of the English Tripos as the enduring core of its intellectual and social value through the generations, giving the course the power to absorb and eventually to outlive other approaches. Yet it would be misleading to suggest that Stevens took no interest in new ways of reading and interpreting literature; he had far too much intellectual curiosity to be so quiescent. He attended the seminars on narratology led by Gillian Beer and Frank Kermode and was by all accounts an enthusiastic participant in the discussions that took place. He regarded feminist approaches, which first became prominent at a time when his own intellectual career was well advanced, with some reserve, but he could be very helpful to those who were then exploring them, often by passing on references to relevant essays or to other materials that he had encountered in his reading.

Stevens judiciously relinquished a chance to make a more exposed and theoretical statement of his position when he wrote the essay for *The Cambridge Review*, mentioned above, in the thick of what has become known as the MacCabe affair.[7] This began in late 1980 when a young Assistant Lecturer identified with structuralist methods in his research and teaching failed to win promotion from his untenured position to the post of full Lecturer. In the judgement of some, including Professor Raymond Williams who had lately given an address to an open meeting entitled 'The Crisis in the English Faculty' when Stevens wrote his essay, the situation was grave. A leading daily newspaper even spoke of Cambridge University being 'plunged into turmoil'. Stevens, in a measured and taut response that shows a skilled university politician and a highly conscientious Faculty officer at work, declined to be drawn into

---

[6] 'The Humane Medievalist' was the title of J. A. W. Bennett's Inaugural Lecture as Professor of Medieval and Renaissance English in the University of Cambridge, published under that title by Cambridge University Press in 1965.

[7] 'The state of the English Faculty and the Discussion in the Senate', *The Cambridge Review*, 102 (1981), 188–93.

making any developed statement of his own position as a critic, no doubt because he recognised that, in the climate then prevailing, it would only appear more personal and *ad hominem* the more he appealed to general intellectual principles and a supposed consensus. Yet in a revealing passage of the essay Stevens does openly condone the view of a colleague, expressed in a debate of the Senate and quoted in the essay, that structuralism and other -isms are 'in some sense irredeemably unimportant . . . in comparison with literature itself'. Even in his Inaugural of 1981, delivered at the height of the MacCabe affair, there is only a discreet reference to 'those linguists who regard language as an essentially arbitrary set of signs'.[8] It would be easy to say that Stevens, in common with many other literary scholars of his day, would have regarded a statement of intellectual principles couched in theoretical terms as an ungracious presumption upon the reader's patience, much as Classical Roman authors might decline to use specialised or technical terms in their prose on the grounds that they breached the decorum of letters. It would be even easier, in the critical climate of the early twenty-first century, to maintain that literary scholars of Stevens's generation in Cambridge (to look no further) believed they read their literary texts as common sense and humane principles demanded, grounded upon a good knowledge of Classical literature and a sound grasp of rhetorical and metrical terminology. Yet it would be nearer the truth to argue instead that Stevens was simply not dogmatic by nature. Tolerant of pluralism in others, he was in that sense a pluralist himself.

What is more, Stevens's books do make his intellectual position and heritage clear. One has only to read any page of his *Music and Poetry in the Early Tudor Court* (1961) to hear the echoes of the Tolkien and Lewis generation that succeeded in giving a sharp critical edge to the companionable (but now almost unbearably precious) manner of many early-twentieth-century critics. Stevens believed that it was possible to make an apt remark about a piece of writing because there was something stable, but not necessarily bounded, on the page for the critic to share with an imagined company of sympathetic interlocutors. The task of the critic was to entice and persuade the reader with a humane (even a genial) critical language that extended and developed the resources of civil conversation. Hence it is no surprise to discover that Stevens, both as a literary historian and as a musicologist, believed in the Common Reader as a constituency in British cultural life, and he would probably have endorsed

[8] *The Old Sound and the New*, p. 9.

Frank Kermode's remark that academics who regard their reviewing for daily papers or literary magazines as 'an interference with graver matters need to give some thought to the whole question of the wider literary public on whose existence their own, with its mandarin privileges, must depend'.[9] Stevens maintained this generous position with some tenacity, notably when he became Chairman of the Plainsong and Mediaeval Music Society in 1987, an office in which I had the honour to follow him. This is perhaps the least known and yet in some ways the most revealing of his many undertakings. The Society was founded in 1888, and Stevens respected its founding mission statement of that year, which was to advance 'public education in the art and science of music and in particular plainsong and medieval music'. He deftly steered the Society's journal to the safe haven of Cambridge University Press—which still publishes two numbers a year—and in 1993 a special issue was prepared in his honour and presented to him.

Stevens's commitment to the needs of the Common Reader owed much to his musical interests and activities. Of all the work that can bring the erudite and critical skills of a musicological scholar into sustained and stimulating contact with intelligent but non-academic minds, the editing of music for performance, followed by the experience of performance, is one of the most engaging. It also represents one of the traditions most deeply engrained in British musicology, reaching back to the pioneering work of scholars such as Edmund H. Fellowes (1870–1951), editor of Elizabethan madrigals and lute songs, or Sir Richard Runciman Terry (1868–1938) at Westminster Cathedral, who made the first modern editions of masses by John Taverner, among other Tudor composers, and performed them in the liturgy. The tradition continued into Stevens's lifetime when it touched virtually everything ever accomplished by his thesis supervisor and latterly his friend, Thurston Dart.

At the core of Stevens's scholarly legacy lie the three volumes of late-medieval and early-Tudor music that he edited, always with 'a singing acquaintance' in mind, for the series *Musica Britannica*. In these three handsome and indeed sumptuous volumes, he single-handedly put the greater part of English song before 1550 into print, only passing over the small and in many ways eccentric thirteenth-century corpus (which he hoped all his life to edit afresh) and a body of fifteenth-century polyphonic songs, in scattered sources, that still await an editor. The first of Stevens's editions to be published in *Musica Britannica*, volume IV of the

---

[9] Frank Kermode, *An Appetite for Poetry: Essays in Literary Interpretation* (London, 1989), p. 3.

series, is entitled *Mediaeval Carols* and is arguably the most revealing of all his three contributions to the series. The edition was originally conceived as a musical complement to the text-only edition of the carol repertory, published by Richard Leighton Greene as far back as 1935,[10] and seemingly the first publication in modern times to identify the carol as a poetic form in which a refrain or burden comes first, comes last, and appears between every stanza. Carol poetry encompasses a great range of themes and subjects, including some major feasts of the liturgical year (Christmas included), love and social satire. The tone is often convivial, for many of the carols appear to be poetry for the hall where the guests, having been admitted by the marshal, enjoy the pleasures of wine and food. The repertory of carols with musical settings is somewhat narrower in tone, ranging from simple (yet ingratiating) monophonic songs up to elaborate four-part settings with intricate counterpoint probably intended for chaplains and boys to sing in aristocratic or collegiate halls, yet usually retaining what Stevens calls a 'vigorous rhythmic drive ... warmth and sonority ... signs of a moral directness that might almost be called didactic' (p. xv). That, as one would expect, is a very apt characterisation.

Mediaeval Carols was first published in 1952, showing that Stevens must have been working on the material almost immediately after the end of his undergraduate years and during his time as a Bye-Fellow and Research Fellow at Magdalene. The book represents the dawn of his academic career, yet one should not underestimate the impression he must already have made upon Dart, among others, revealed by the invitation to contribute a volume to *Musica Britannica*, an 'authoritative national collection of the classics of British music' dedicated to the Sovereign. (It is easy to forget that Dart was actually Stevens's contemporary.) One only need scan the Preface to the edition, or indeed the earliest reviews, to be transported back to the world of musicological research that Stevens was just entering, one where experience of performance was considered necessary for any serious musical scholar. In the Preface to *Mediaeval Carols*, Stevens offers warm thanks (sounding a characteristic note in the process) to 'my friends, the Cambridge Singers', with whom he had evidently been exploring the music of the carols in performance. He also expresses his gratitude to Dart. The Introduction, in turn, advocates the unique value of a 'singing' acquaintance with the carols for anyone who wishes to appreciate their variety. Similar sentiments are expressed in the very extensive and collaborative review of the edition, published in the

---

[10] R. L. Greene, *The Early English Carols* (Oxford, 1935).

Journal of the American Musicological Society for 1953 and written by Manfed F. Bukofzer and Richard Leighton Greene. (One notes, in passing, that two scholars of great eminence in different fields were required to do justice to Stevens's first edition of music.) In this review, which Stevens rightly called 'scrupulous and constructive', but which must nonetheless have been an alarming sight to a scholar publishing his first edition, Bukofzer praised the 'happy combination of scholarly and practical considerations' that the editor had achieved, while Greene expressed the hope that 'all students of the carol . . . will seek out this work and call in the help of musical friends for the performance of the polyphonic pieces'. Both had their reservations about the editions, as was only to be expected, and Stevens published a revised edition of *Mediaeval Carols* in 1958 to take account of far-reaching suggestions that Bukofzer had made, complete with a remarkably candid admission that the older scholar had drawn his attention to some fundamental misconceptions. Not every user of the revised edition will necessarily be convinced that this *mea culpa*, emphatic but not ostentatious, was entirely necessary, or even that the changes in the revised edition of *Mediaeval Carols*, especially in the matter of barring, were for the better.[11] On balance, however, the joint authors of the *Journal of the American Musicological Society* review, which eclipses all others in its scope and extent, were warm in their praise of Stevens's work. Bukofzer found most of the musical editions impeccable; Greene thought the work on the carol texts first rate.[12]

The second and third of Stevens's monumental editions, *Music at the Court of Henry VIII* and *Early Tudor Songs and Carols* appeared in 1962 and 1975 as *Musica Britannica*, XVIII and XXXVI respectively. Both are dedicated to the contents of single manuscripts, the former presenting the contents of British Library Additional MS 31922, commonly known as 'Henry VIII's manuscript', and the latter giving the songs of the slightly earlier Fayrfax manuscript, now British Library Additional MS 5465. To compare the two is to learn much about the tastes and sympathies that shaped the curve of Stevens's academic career. As a literary scholar, he

---

[11] Some of the energy required might have been devoted to producing literary texts for the underlay that look more like fifteenth-century English and which preserve rhymes, even at the cost of the accessibility that Stevens valued so highly. Stevens retains the Middle English words of the carols but modernises their form, so that rhymes are sometimes obliterated as in *Christianity/thee . . . man/then . . . pity/me* in the underlay for *Christianité/thee . . . man/than(ne) . . . pité/me*, and many more. It remains unknown whether this policy was one of his own devising; it certainly violates a number of principles that he held dear.

[12] Bukofzer had a *Musica Britannica* volume of his own going through the press at the time, his edition of the works of Dunstaple.

responded warmly to the entire range of medieval English writing from at least Chaucer onwards (his published work gives little sign of engagement with Old English). Yet as a musical scholar, he was primarily interested in Western monophonic music from its ninth-century 'beginnings' in Gregorian chant until the later fifteenth century; his interests in medieval polyphony did not really begin until the course of musical history reached the 1440s and the earliest English carols.

It will be worth pausing over what this means. Stevens rarely chose to engage with the large repertory of thirteenth-century French motets, perhaps because the literary scholar in him did not relish the experience of hearing two or three texts, sometimes in two languages, sung simultaneously; he also found the high level of dissonance in these motets less than alluring. The same objections kept him away from the polyphonic conductus. Polytextual motets of the fourteenth century did not detain him much, partly because he had only moderate enthusiasm (I believe that is a fair comment) for the essentially cerebral technique of isorhythm.[13] The large and often exotic repertory of the French Ars Nova chanson, with Guillaume de Machaut (d. 1377) as the chief figure, or the extensive polyphonic repertoire of the Italian Trecento, did not excite any consistent interest in him, and he once evoked, perhaps without much true admiration, the 'hard brilliance of certain *ars nova* songs' (xvi).[14] In place of these, Stevens's chosen domain was the immense field of medieval monophonic song in Latin, Middle English, Middle High German, Galician-Portuguese, Old Occitan, Old French and Middle 'Italian'. He achieved a degree of control, and a breadth of coverage, in this vast area to rival or even exceed the old masters like Friedrich Gennrich.

Of the two editions under discussion here, it is *Music at the Court of Henry VIII* that also reveals most about Stevens's extraordinary industry and achievement. The manuscript was probably compiled during the early years of the reign when Henry was, in Stevens's view, 'a young and happily married king' preoccupied with his sports. As one turns the leaves of the manuscript, intricate pieces of Franco-Flemish polyphony, including some adapted versions of the most widely circulated songs of the later

[13] One should add here that much of the surviving English polyphonic music from Chaucer's lifetime, whether in the form of motet, cantilena or any other, was not available in adequate scholarly editions during the greater part of his academic career.

[14] Stevens's most sustained engagement with the music of Guillaume de Machaut appears in his essay 'The "Music" of the Lyric: Machaut, Deschamps, Chaucer', published in P. Boitani and A. Torti (eds.), *Medieval and Pseudo-Medieval Literature* (D. S. Brewer, Cambridge, 1984), pp. 109–29. Two musical items are discussed, but it is very telling that they are both monophonic.

fifteenth century, appear side by side with native consort pieces for instruments, some of them very brief and perhaps originally designed for use in pageants, chivalric disguisings or interludes, others showing a much greater intricacy, including the immense instrumental fantasia *Fa la sol* by Cornysh that evokes the extraordinary filigree work of the Eton Choirbook composers. The English music in the manuscript includes a substantial number of songs by composers now forgotten (such as Farthing, Lloyd, Daggere, Kempe), but best represented of all is the composer who is very well remembered for other things: King Henry VIII.

The project required Stevens to transcribe and edit a substantial corpus of pieces (109 items in all) representing some seventy years of art music as it was cultivated in England, or received there from the Continent, and to present the entire repertory in print for the first time. There was little to build upon except a few pieces in anthologies or studies from the 1930s and 1940s; Stevens even had to look back to William Chappell's work of 1865–7 for transcriptions of some items. Once again, the Preface to this edition records warm thanks to Thurston Dart 'who first introduced me to the arts of transcribing and editing old music', but now gratitude is also expressed to a wider range of scholars beyond Cambridge who had already achieved eminence, or were destined for it, including Daniel Heartz, Gustave Reese and Brian Trowell. Yet what is truly impressive about *Music at the Court of Henry VIII* is the richness of the introduction, which draws deeply on Stevens's first monograph, *Music and Poetry in the Early Tudor Court*, published the previous year in 1961. This most elegant and companionable book, arguably the best thing that Stevens ever accomplished outside of his editions, reconstructs the social milieu of the music and poetry in Henry VIII's manuscript, and to lay the monograph and the edition side by side is not only to sense the extraordinary industry of this busy university lecturer throughout the later 1950s, it is also to appreciate the enormous strides in the study of Early-Tudor song that Stevens had been able to make in a field of musical history that was wide open and now mostly his own. To produce his richly textured account of music and poetry under the early Tudors, Stevens drew deeply upon his reading of English poetry and prose from Chaucer onwards, using it to reconstruct the imaginative and social experience of courtiers in a milieu that he rightly perceived to be essentially 'medieval' and 'French' up to and including the years when the manuscript was compiled (p. xxi). Consider, for example, Stevens's brief sketch, in the Introduction to the edition, of the changes in English court music and court culture during the later sixteenth century:

The influence of Italian culture, which culminated in the Elizabethan madrigal and sonnet, superseded an 'international' French culture signified by the basse-danse, the 'castle-of-love' disguising, courts of love, chivalric ceremonies and pastimes of all kinds, the 'Chaucer tradition' in amorous verse, an esoteric professionalism amongst musicians, widespread techniques of improvisation used both by itinerant minstrels and by amateurs, the traditional pre-eminence of the harp, the use of fixed forms for composition (*rondeau*, *virelai*, carol) and so on.

More than forty years on, it would be difficult to improve on this masterly synthesis that reaches out beyond the musical sources to a richly imagined social context of entertainment, drama, dance and ceremony. It is underwritten by Stevens's profound appreciation of what it means to evoke a 'chivalric' culture where tournaments and disguisings might be loud with resonances from Chaucer, Malory and the great French prose romances. One also notes the author's characteristic vigilance towards musical traditions (such as the use of the harp at court during the fifteenth century rather than the lute, whose fortunes rose from the 1480s onwards) that can only be recovered from literary or archival sources because they have left no readily identifiable trace in the musical manuscripts.

In 1973, Stevens published his only book of purely literary criticism, entitled *Medieval Romance*, acknowledging the generous help of two Cambridge colleagues, Dr Richard Axton[15] and Professor Derek Brewer. Here Stevens sounds his characteristic and welcome note of sympathy for the Common Reader who may be inclined to suppose that he or she cannot expect to be beguiled, moved or even diverted by medieval literature. 'Medieval romance', Stevens comments, 'has for too long, like other branches of medieval writing, been regarded as the property of specialists' (p. 9). The book is an urbane and elegant justification of a claim that Stevens had polished during years of lecturing to undergraduates who were inclined to suppose that medieval romance must be something very strange and remote indeed. He argues that the themes of medieval romance are essentially those of narrative fiction in all times. Its concerns with love, death, test and vindication are 'fundamental and permanent' (p. 17). Stevens deploys an extraordinary range of reading to illustrate this claim, and it is always aptly done as when he proposes, for example,

---

[15] With Dr Axton, Stevens produced a noted translation of some medieval French drama, entitled *Medieval French Plays* (Oxford, 1971).

that the amorous conversation or *luf-talkyng* in *Sir Gawain and the Green Knight* reflects, *mutatis mutandis*, a social reality comparable to the world evoked in Elizabethan court comedy, in the social comedy of the Restoration wits, in Jane Austen's *Emma* (the exchanges with Frank Churchill) or in the drawing room comedies of Oscar Wilde (pp. 188–9).

Stevens's third and last monograph, *Words and Music in the Middle Ages: Song, Narrative, Dance and Drama 1050–1350*, was published by Cambridge University Press in 1986. Much inspired by the literary work of another distinguished colleague in Cambridge, Professor Peter Dronke, FBA, this large book offers the first comprehensive discussion of medieval song repertoires surviving with music in all the European languages. Its recurrent concern, already announced in the Inaugural Lecture of 1981 and in a sense present from the very beginning of Stevens's scholarly career—even from his birth to a violinist and a mathematician—is that the fundamental aesthetic of medieval song was numerical: a profound accord between the number of syllables in a poem, the number of notes, the pattern of the rhymes, and more besides.[16] On this interpretation, the pleasure that these songs offered their original listeners was one of deep and pervasive accord. This notion, which owes a great deal to medieval theories of *musica* as the art of sounding number, to say nothing of the Greek tradition upon which medieval ideas were based, was of special importance to Stevens because he believed that it revealed the way text and music came together in an expressive manner in medieval song. The composer's task, he argued, was to set the form of the poem, not the meaning, and if the task were correctly accomplished, then both the words and the music would bring their own, complementary *harmonia* to the experience of the song for both performer and listener. The relation between words and music was therefore not expressive, in later senses of the term, because the composers did not seek metaphorical equivalents in sound for the meaning of the text.[17]

It is difficult to assess the impact of this large and rich book, now more than twenty years old. The reviews, all commissioned from scholars of the front rank, were often very admiring. Professor Richard Crocker,

[16] These had long been major concerns of Stevens's work; see especially '*La Grande Chanson Courtoise*: the Songs of Adam de la Halle', *Proceedings of the Royal Musical Association*, 101 (1974–5), 11–30.

[17] Stevens used the term 'metaphorical' in this context to mean, for example, the 'expression' of sadness or melancholy by falling melodic lines, rather than the use of a mimetic vocal effect to mark a word like *Hélas*, a technique that he regarded as a form of onomatopoeia. The usage is discussed at length in his Inaugural Lecture, *The Old Sound and the New*.

of the University of California at Berkeley, and as distinguished a reviewer as any editor could hope to secure for such a study, called it 'one of the most fruitful contributions to a general understanding of medieval music in recent times'.[18] One notes the reservation implied by Crocker's allusion to a *general* understanding of medieval music. *Words and Music in the Middle Ages* perhaps tries to do too much, and there is substance in the remark of another distinguished reviewer, Professor David G. Hughes, that a survey so broad must inevitably be based upon scholarship of very uneven depth, and that there is therefore a sense in which 'no one is yet in a position to write this book'.[19] One might add that few were in a position to review it, whence even the most eminent reviewers can be seen moving quickly to the parts of Stevens's broad picture that they know well and leaving the rest aside or mentioning it only in passing.

Words and Music in the Middle Ages was not the last of Stevens's monographs. There was another, but one that he was never to see in print. For most of his career, he nurtured plans to explore the tri-lingual song culture of medieval England by editing all the songs with Latin, English and Anglo-Norman texts surviving from before *c*.1300. He called the projected book by the mischievously unlovely acronym *SLEME*, or 'Songs and Lyrics of Early-Medieval England'. In the last six years of his life he began to recognise that he would never complete these labours, and some of the fruits began to appear as journal articles, notably a detailed study of the widely disseminated song *Samson dux fortissime* and a checklist of Anglo-Norman lyrics surviving with music.[20] Then he resolved—for there are some kinds of optimism that even age cannot cure—that he would produce an edition of the most remarkable of all the sources that *SLEME* would have encompassed: the grim and untidy little booklet of songs, mostly in Latin, that is now Cambridge University Library MS Ff. 1. 17 (1). He was by now well into his seventies, and had long since retired from his Professorship. He estimated that the edition would take about two years, but it remained unfinished at his death in 2002.

It is easy to see why. The manuscript presents a great many difficulties. For the most part, it is poorly written, and the leaves are stained in some places or otherwise damaged. There are many textual corruptions in the

---

[18] *Music and Letters*, 68 (1987), 364–6.

[19] *Journal of the American Musicological Society*, 42 (1989), 407.

[20] '*Samson dux fortissime*: an International Latin Song', *Plainsong and Medieval Music*, 1 (1992), 1–40; 'Alphabetical Checklist of Anglo-Norman Songs *c*.1150– *c*.1350', *Plainsong and Medieval Music*, 3 (1994), 1–22.

poems, while the notation of the music raises numerous problems of detail and editorial principle that touch upon some of the most controversial issues in medieval musicology. Nonetheless, Stevens made substantial progress with the project during the last years of his life. He was able to consult the original virtually every day, for it was housed just down the road from his Cambridge home, and he gave the work his undivided attention. A grant from the British Academy allowed him to employ a team of graduates who brought fresh and sharp eyes to many aspects of the project under his supervision. At the time of his death, he had established the Latin texts and written very substantial parts of an introduction and commentary. He also finalised the translations with the help of Dr Leofranc Holford-Strevens of Oxford University Press, and at about this time I was able to place in his hands a complete recording of the music in the manuscript on a two-CD set, eventually edited down to a single CD and released on the Hyperion label.[21]

After Stevens's death on 14 February 2002, Dr Margaret Bent, with the help of Dr Richard Axton, established a first textual basis for the final stages of the edition, and it is due to Dr Bent's initiative and co-ordination that the work on Stevens's unfinished manuscript could be brought to completion. In accordance with his wishes, Professor Karl Reichl of the University of Bonn accepted the task of sorting and editing the materials; he also completed the list of manuscripts and the bibliography, which was a very substantial labour. In much of this work he was greatly helped by Dr Bonnie J. Blackburn. The final version of the Foreword to the book, which I had the privilege to write, names some fifteen people who worked on the project, and even so is far from exhaustive. It is now in print, a tribute to the author and to the continuing devotion of those whom he mentored and inspired.[22]

Stevens became a Fellow of the British Academy in 1975. He was awarded a CBE for services to musicology in 1980. From 1983 until his retirement in 1988 he was President of Magdalene.

Turning the pages of John's personal copy of *Music at the Court of Henry VIII*, which he wished me to have, I am reminded of some words written by another distinguished pupil from Christ's Hospital whom I have had cause to mention once before: Samuel Taylor Coleridge. John

---

[21] *The Earliest Songbook in England*, Gothic Voices, Hyperion CDA 67177.
[22] *The Later Cambridge Songs: An English Song Collection of the Twelfth Century* (Oxford, 2005).

Stevens 'continued my friend with a fidelity unconquered by time or even by my own apparent neglect, a friend from whom I never received an advice that was not wise, nor a remonstrance that was not gentle and affectionate'.

CHRISTOPHER PAGE
Sidney Sussex College,
Cambridge

PETER STRAWSON   *Gillman and Soame, Oxford*

Peter Frederick Strawson
1919–2006

Introduction

PETER FREDERICK STRAWSON WAS BORN in Ealing, London, on 23 November 1919, and died in Oxford on 13 February 2006. His life as a philosopher was spent mostly in positions at Oxford, first as a Fellow at University College, and then, after 1968, as Ryle's successor as Waynflete Professor of Metaphysical Philosophy, at Magdalen College. Writing primarily about the philosophy of language, metaphysics, epistemology and the history of philosophy, he succeeded in redirecting Oxford philosophy away from the limitations which had to some extent been accepted under the influence of J. L. Austin, towards a re-engagement with some traditional and also some new abstract philosophical issues. He established from the early 1950s onwards a pre-eminence within Oxford philosophy, both through his publications but also by his quite exceptional, although never brutal, critical abilities. Simultaneously, he established himself as one of the leading philosophers in the world.

His achievements were recognised by election in 1960, at a remarkably early age, to the British Academy, the conferring of a knighthood in 1977, and by many other honours and invitations from universities throughout the world. He lectured widely in North America, Europe and India. In 1998 he became the twenty-sixth philosopher to have a volume devoted to him in the famous, and famously exclusive, Library of Living Philosophers series. Earlier British recipients of this honour were Whitehead, Russell, Moore, Broad and Ayer. He carried on working after his retirement in 1987, and a volume of essays, of which he was co-editor

Proceedings of the British Academy, **150**, 221–244. © The British Academy 2007.

and which includes two essays of his own, came out after his death.[1]
Unlike some other recent British philosophers of distinction, notably A. J.
Ayer and Bernard Williams, Strawson did not, and had no desire to,
become a figure in popular culture or the world of the 'great and the
good'. He was, however, probably the most famous and most discussed
British philosopher within the academic world of philosophy from the
1950s until the late 1980s. His status is evidenced by the fact that his
writings attracted the attention of, and were discussed by, the world's leading philosophers, including, Russell, Sellars, Putnam, Quine, Davidson
and Kripke.

Life and works

Strawson was brought up in Finchley, and educated at Christ's College.
His parents were both school teachers, and his mother had, like Strawson
himself, an excellent memory for verse. Strawson was the second child,
between two brothers, and he also had a younger sister.[2] One of his passions then (and, indeed, throughout his life) was English literature and he
was awarded an open scholarship at St John's College, Oxford, to study
English. However, in part because he had already developed an interest in
philosophy, and in part because he wanted to study subjects which he felt
to be relevant to the threatening political climate in Europe, on arrival at
the college in 1937 he immediately changed subjects to Philosophy,
Politics and Economics. His tutors in philosophy were J. D. Mabbott,
later to become Master of the college, and H. P. Grice, whom Strawson
himself described as 'one of the cleverest and most ingenious thinkers of
our time'.[3] Tutorials with Grice clearly inspired Strawson, and the two
continued as colleagues and collaborators (and also rivals) after the war.
Strawson famously gained a second in finals, the reason being that by

---

[1] P. F. Strawson and Arindam Chakrabarti (eds.), *Universals, Concepts and Qualities* (Aldershot, 2006).

[2] Strawson's younger brother John had a military career of considerable distinction. He attained the rank of Major-General, was for three years Chief of Staff United Kingdom Land Forces, and was awarded a CB and OBE. He is also a military historian of note and author of a dozen books. Between them they have written over twenty books!

[3] This quotation comes from Strawson's own 'Intellectual Autobiography' contained in the volume about him in the Library of Living Philosophers. Strawson's description of his own life also provides much of the information upon which my account of it is based. It is also a marvellous document which conveys or reveals, as well as much about his life and thought, a lot about his character and passions.

1940 finals marking heavily involved older dons, many of the younger ones being away promoting the war effort, and Strawson's novel views about philosophy did not win favour with an older marker. Rumour also has it that efforts by a younger don, who shall be nameless, to argue in favour of Strawson were not helped by his having lost Strawson's scripts in the proverbial taxi.[4]

Strawson was then called up for military service, and so belongs to that generation of British philosophers, including Ayer, Hare, and Hampshire, who saw service in the Second World War. Strawson described his own military career as in 'no way distinguished'. It began in the Royal Artillery, when his training in Sussex allowed him to watch the aerial activity of the Battle of Britain and to observe the night sky over London as it was bombed by the Luftwaffe. He was then selected by the Army to master the intricacies of radar, leading to the command of a radar station, and, in 1942, to a commission in the corps of the Royal Electrical and Mechanical Engineers. His eloquence and quick wit made Strawson highly effective in the role of defending officer at courts martial, helping many to receive punishments far more lenient than perhaps they deserved. After postings to Italy and Austria, Strawson left the army in 1946 with the rank of captain.

Shortly before that, in 1945, Strawson married Ann Martin, having bestowed the name Ann upon her in preference to her original first name of 'Grace'. He said that his decision to marry Ann was 'probably the most judicious action' of his life and described her as 'a perfect wife'. They had four children of whose different talents and achievements he was very proud. One of his sons, Galen Strawson, is himself an eminent philosopher, and his other son and two daughters are gifted musicians. John, Strawson's younger brother, described their marriage in these words; 'He shared a very happy marriage with his charming, intelligent, accomplished and loving wife, Ann, and they were fortunate indeed to have four comely and talented children, all of whom had a bent for music. Not every man after all could reflect that he had his own family quartet, capable of doing justice to Beethoven or Bach or Haydn.'[5]

Strawson returned from the war wanting to become a philosopher but handicapped by his aberrant finals result. Thanks to Mabbott's influence he secured an Assistant Lecturership in the subject at Bangor, but returned

---

[4] I am grateful to Bill Child, of University College, Oxford, for that information (or, perhaps, misinformation).

[5] This quotation comes from John Strawson's address at the memorial service for Strawson held in Magdalen College, Oxford, in 2006.

to Oxford to sit for and come first in the John Locke Examination. His success eased his financial position and also caused Ryle to ensure that he received an appointment at University College, Oxford, which made him a full Fellow in 1948. Strawson's Oxford career had by then properly started, and two years later, in 1950, the publication of 'On Referring' in *Mind* and his debate at the Aristotelian Society Joint Session with, and the publication of his reply to, Austin about truth, brought him instantaneous national and international fame.

(i) Reference[6]

Strawson exploded onto the scene of world philosophy when he published 'On Referring' in 1950. (Like Frege, Russell and, later, Kripke, Strawson ensured his philosophical immortality by writing about reference.) He subsequently modified and developed his views on reference, but the central claim of 'On Referring' is something he always defended. Strawson's title contains, of course, an allusion to Russell's famous article 'On Denoting', the central idea of which Strawson is criticising. Strawson's conception of the debate is that Russell offered his theory of descriptions as a complete account of the role of definite descriptions in English (such expressions as 'the queen of England') whereas the truth is that the role of the word 'the' when embedded in definite descriptions cannot be captured in a single account. There are uses which Russell's theory does not fit because the phenomenon is simply more complex than Russell allowed. It is not, therefore, that Strawson is offering his own complete theory; it is, rather, that he is picking out uses for which, according to him, Russell's theory fails, and characterising them. That this is the way to understand Strawson's contribution to the debate has the important consequence that it is no objection to his approach to point to uses of 'the' about which, arguably, Russell (or something close to Russell's view) might be correct. Such points do not touch Strawson's central claim. Strawson's paper initiated a debate about definite descriptions that has run ever since its publication, and in which his views have remained central.

   Russell claimed that a sentence of the form 'The F is G' says; "There is one and only one F and it is G." ' The difference from 'An F is G' is that the latter merely claims that there is *a* (G) F, whereas the use of the defin-

---

[6] All the papers by Strawson which are referred to in this section and the next are included in P. F. Strawson, *Logico-Linguistic Papers* (London, 1971).

ite article imports the extra claim of uniqueness. Both are alike in making an existential claim about Fs, namely, there is an F, and hence, according to Russell, at least part of the role of 'the' is to be (or to introduce) what is called an existential quantifier. This, in a crude presentation, is Russell's famous Theory of Definite Descriptions. Against this Strawson argued, first, that it is unsupported. He claimed that Russell's main support for his theory is that a sentence such as 'The king of France is bald' remains meaningful even though there is no king of France. Its having meaning cannot, therefore, depend on there being a referent for the apparent subject expression. According to Strawson, Russell infers from that to the conclusion that the semantic role of the apparent subject expression in such sentences (i.e. 'the F') cannot be to refer to or designate an object, and must, rather, function as a quantifier. Against this Strawson suggested that the meaningfulness of 'The F is G' should be thought of as, roughly, there being rules as to what a use of the sentence in different circumstances will amount to. If the circumstances are right then it can be used in a referring way; if they are not then the use might not succeed in being an act of reference. Strawson's distinction between a sentence's having a meaning and the speech act performed by its use on an occasion is clearly sound and important. One question that was debated is whether Russell's reasons for his theory are all disarmed by the introduction of that distinction.

However, against the Russellian theory itself Strawson made the important point that the theory implies that a sentence of the form 'The F is G' must count as false when used in circumstances where there is no F. (These cases are often described as ones involving 'reference failure'.) It must do so because, according to the theory, part of the role of 'The F' (at least in such declarative sentences) is to say that there is an F. Contrary to this, Strawson claims that we would not always regard a saying of 'The F is G' as false in such circumstances. We would not react by saying 'That is false' but would rather say something like 'What do you mean?' or 'You must be under a misapprehension'. He suggested that in such circumstances the use amounts neither to saying something true nor to saying something false. It exhibits what came to be called a 'truth-value gap'. In discussion it became clear, not that this criticism is definitely mistaken, but that it is difficult to determine what the truth value of sentences involving referential failure actually is. Strawson's main objection to Russell's account is, though, that it is simply obvious that sometimes we use 'The F' to refer to or pick out an object, and we do not then use it to *say* that there is an F.

Strawson's attitude is well presented in a later important paper where he says:

> The distinction between identifying reference and uniquely existential assertion is something quite undeniable. The sense in which the existence of something answering to a definite description used for the purpose of identifying reference, and its distinguishability by an audience from anything else, is presupposed and not asserted in an utterance containing such an expression, so used, stands absolutely firm, whether or not one opts for the view that radical failure of the presupposition would deprive the statement of a truth-value. It remains a decisive objection to the theory of Descriptions . . . That . . . it amounts to a denial of these undeniable distinctions.[7]

This passage reveals three important aspects of Strawson's approach to definite descriptions. The first is that his fundamental objection to Russell is that it is simply obvious to him (as it should be to us), as a sensitive and self-reflective user of language, that the use of the word 'the' does not conform to the theory. Whatever puzzles there may be about language and reference, their solution cannot require us to deny such obvious facts. It is a recurring theme in, or perhaps a recurring part of the method of, Strawson's philosophical discussion of language that some aspects of language are more or less obvious to us. Second, one central concept in Strawson's developed description of the role of such an expression as 'The F' is that it can be a device for what he calls identifying reference. Roughly, Strawson's idea is that the definite description is sometimes chosen to enable the audience to fix on or pick out as the subject matter of the claim an item of which they already know. In this role it cannot be that 'The F' tells them of the existence of such an F, since its role rests on the prior existence of such knowledge. Strawson provides a detailed analysis of this function in the first chapter of *Individuals*, as well as in the article from which the quotation above comes. Third, a notion that Strawson introduced in his own description of the nature of definite descriptions and which surfaces in the quotation is that of *presupposition*. Strawson said that the use of a definite description standardly presupposes the existence of an object fitting the description even though it does not say, nor therefore entail, that there is such an object. This concept met with considerable resistance amongst philosophers but has had a colossal influence on linguists, who have tended to see it as a useful concept in the description of language. This paradox encourages us to ask whether it is more likely that linguists or philosophers have the better insight into language.

---

[7] P. F. Strawson, 'Identifying Reference and Truth-Values' in *Logico-Linguistic Papers*, p. 85.

(ii) Truth

Just as Strawson's target in the theory of reference was Russell, when discussing truth he developed his views with Austin as the target. Austin was perhaps a target in two ways. First, through his critical brilliance, vehement personality and an apparently revolutionary conception of philosophy, which gave its believers a sense that they were for the first time approaching philosophy correctly, Austin had become the intellectual leader of an outstandingly strong group of philosophers that gathered in Oxford after the Second World War. Strawson himself was part of that group and he attended Austin's Saturday morning meetings where discussion was carried on in line with the recipe approved by Austin's conception. It would not be strictly accurate to say so, but it would convey something close to the truth, if one were to remark that Austin had begun to seem almost infallible. It was therefore important to reveal the non-divinity of the leader. So, Austin himself was a target. Second, Strawson took exception to Austin's attempt to formulate a reconstructed version of the correspondence theory of truth. His theory of truth was also the target. Austin's account is complex, but, roughly, he held that in saying that a statement is true one is saying that the state of affairs which the referential conventions target the statement on to satisfy the conditions which the descriptive conventions target the rest of the sentence on to. To illustrate this with an example. The sentence 'The television is broken' conforms to certain referential conventions which target it on to some state of affairs in the world involving a particular television set and there are also certain descriptive conventions built into the sentence linking it to a type of state of affairs (the containing-a-broken-television type) and the former state of affairs conforms to, or falls under, the descriptively correlated type. Strawson, in criticism, principally alleges that Austin had no clear conception of what the supposed referential conventions link sentences with. Is it objects—say the television? But if it is an object then that is not a state of affairs, and certainly not a fact. Having very thoroughly shaken the ontology of Austin's account, Strawson, somewhat surprisingly seems prepared to allow that the conditions that Austin's account incorporates do, in effect, correlate with when a sentence is true, but, he says, the fulfilment of these conditions is not what we are *claiming* to obtain when we say that it is true. It is simply obvious that remarks about truth are not remarks *about* linguistic conventions. This criticism, I believe, has a similar status to the central criticism of Russell. Strawson's point against Austin is that it is simply obvious that the theory cannot be correct because it is obvious to us as language users that when we speak of truth we are not speaking of such things as referential (or descriptive) conventions. Finally, Strawson pointed out that Austin's account could only apply to a limited range of statements. If I say 'There are no unicorns' what are the referential targets of my remark?

Strawson's criticisms effectively buried Austin's account. The subsequent discussion occasioned by their debate primarily concerned some issues about the degree to which Strawson's criticisms as a whole were fair to Austin, and also whether the approach to truth that Strawson himself favoured was adequate. Strawson's, rather than Austin's account, became the focus of debate. Strawson himself returned to the former question in later articles, arguing persuasively that even on the most charitable interpretation Austin's idea of two sorts of conventions cannot be made sense of. Strawson himself favoured a view which took as the central insight about truth (deriving from F. P. Ramsey) that to say that P is true is equivalent to saying that P. Strawson's own main contribution to working out this idea was to stress, even though changing his mind about how strongly to stress, the linguistic acts that the word 'true' enables us to perform. This leaves Strawson free to point out that even if Ramsey's equivalence is the fundamental core of the notion of truth, it would not follow that the expression 'true' is a redundant expression. The presence in our language of the term 'true' might be of great, indeed, indispensable, utility.

(iii) Logical Theory

Strawson published his first book *An Introduction to Logical Theory* in 1952. In it he attempted to explain the nature, and the scope and limits, of formal logic. The eminence he had already achieved was reflected in the fact that it received a review by Quine in *Mind*. Strawson's aim, generated, in part, by his reflections on the correct treatment of definite descriptions, is to say what formal logic is. Strawson tries to explain or elucidate the central concepts of formal logic. One of these is the notion of entailment. Strawson favours explaining 'P entails Q' as ' "P and not Q" is self contradictory', and explains or elucidates the notion of self contradiction in terms of sentences saying nothing; in effect, they give and then take back simultaneously. Strawson then looks at the notion of form and of proof systems. He applies his ideas to traditional syllogistic logic as well as to modern propositional and predicate logic. It can be wondered how far his elucidation of the central notions is adequate, and it can also be wondered whether he attends to all the notions that need explanation in relation to formal logic (e.g., consistency and complete-ness). The main part of his book did not have a large influence on philosophers or logicians. However, three elements in his discussion had and continue to have considerable influence. He gave a fuller explanation of the notion of presupposition than he had previously provided. Second, Strawson asked how far the meaning of ordinary language connectives, such as 'and', 'or' and 'if . . . then . . .', can be equated with those of the truth functional connectives, such as '&', 'V', and '→', that logicians employ. Strawson argued that there are significant differences. His con-clusion is that these expressions do not have what might be called a pre-cise logic. The question that Strawson asked has continued to be central in the philosophy of language, and there has been no resolution of it. Grice took an opposite view to Strawson and part of the point of his account of implication, as opposed to meaning or saying, was to gener-ate an explanation for the data that Strawson appealed to in arguing for a semantic difference between ordinary language and formal logic, with-out having to postulate a semantic difference. Strawson himself later crit-icised Grice's theory, at least in relation to conditionals. This debate is still very active. The third element was the approach to the problem of induc-tion that Strawson proposed in the final chapter. I shall describe that later when looking at Strawson's contribution to epistemology.

(iv) *Individuals*

In 1959 Strawson published his second book *Individuals*.[8] It was ambi-tious, abstract, wide-ranging and original, and it attracted immediate attention. It has continued to be read and discussed, especially the first half. Strawson classified his task as 'descriptive metaphysics', as opposed to 'revisionary metaphysics'. By calling it 'metaphysics' Strawson was pri-marily emphasising the abstractness and generality of the questions. A consequence of this generality, Strawson suggests, is that the methods needed for settling the questions are different in kind from those employed in debating less abstract conceptual or philosophical questions. One such method, employed in chapter 2, involves imagining creatures with quite different experiences to our own, and trying to determine their capacities for thinking about objects. By calling it 'descriptive' Strawson means, in part, that he is not recommending revisions or additions to how we think, but I think the term also signals Strawson's conviction that

---

[8] P. F. Strawson, *Individuals* (London, 1959).

there is a shared and universal conceptual scheme which we human beings have, and know that we have, and which cannot be given, and which requires no such thing as a justification in terms of more fundamental concepts or claims. All, or almost all, we can do, therefore, is to describe and analyse it (or parts of it). As Strawson notes, his aim is to engage with *one* part of that total structure, namely our ability to direct our thoughts, and speech, on to items in the world. It is possible therefore to see *Individuals* as, in part, a development of Strawson's interest in reference.

Individuals is very much a book of two halves. In the first four chapters Strawson's focus is on our ability to refer to and think about items in our environment, including ourselves. In the second part, again of four chapters, the aim is to elucidate the distinction between subject expressions and predicate expressions. This latter task belongs more to philosophical logic than metaphysics, but the link is, according to Strawson, that the central cases of subject expressions are those picking out the entities to which we basically refer, the character of which it has been the task of the first half to determine. Since, in fact, the book's colossal and immediate impact was due primarily to the brilliance and originality of its first three chapters, I shall describe them in somewhat more detail than the rest of the book. The truth is that reading the argument developed in those chapters generates a continuous intellectual excitement, which the later chapters do not quite match. It is also true that issues to do with the subject–predicate distinction appeal to fewer people than do the issues focused on in the early part.

The question to which chapter 1 is devoted is whether there is a category of entities which we can think about without depending on thought about entities of other categories. The focus initially is not so much on thought as on talking to an audience, and Strawson clarifies the relevant idea of talking about an item by invoking the notion of identifying reference which emerged in his theory of reference. Strawson proposes the following model of latching on to an identifying reference. One case is where the referent is picked out as a currently perceived item—say, *this* page. The other is where it is picked out as falling under a description. Strawson's idea is that ultimately such descriptions need to relate the item in some way to currently perceived items—say, as the painter of *this* picture. (Such a two-fold structure of thought was also accepted by Russell, but arguments in the theory of perception persuaded him that the perceived scene was private rather than, as Strawson holds, public.) Strawson's further idea is that the descriptive relations are fundamentally spatio-temporal. Thus my ability to think of James I rests on thinking of him as the person ascending the throne in 1603, the present time being 2007. Ultimately I fix on him via his place in a spatio-temporal framework related to my currently perceived environment. Strawson further points out that since we need to update this relational framework over time as we move around, we need to be able to re-identify objects and also places encountered at different times. Strawson draws an important epistemological conclusion from this. Since our ability to maintain a grasp on the spatio-temporal framework depends on acceptance of such identifications, it is incoherent to be sceptical about the procedures we rely on to confirm them while still thinking in terms of the spatio-temporal framework itself. Strawson is then in a position to answer his fundamental question as to whether there is a basic category of items of reference. Obviously reference to theoretical entities is dependent, as is reference to experiences, which rests on reference to their subjects—for example, the pain in *Mary's leg*. Strawson's assumption seems to be that that leaves two candidates; material bodies (in a broad sense) and occurrences. Occurrences, however, cannot be basic since, standardly, they are picked out dependently—e.g., the fire in *that house*—and, moreover, they do not form a structured framework allowing the spatio-temporal framework to be grounded. Bodies emerge as referentially basic.

Strawson next asks, in chapter 2, whether it is possible to think of objective entities in a conceptual scheme in which the basic entities are not bodies. Since, according to the initial argument, if referential thought rests on a spatio-temporal framework then it rests on thought about bodies, this question becomes: can there be thought about objective entities which is non-spatial? Strawson introduces the idea of a creature with only auditory experience, the assumption being that auditory experience on its own is non-spatial. Just what objective notions would be available to such a creature? He imaginatively enters into the sound world to see how far ideas analogous to those that space makes available can be found. The best option relies on relating individual sounds to a continuous 'master sound' which, as it were, defines something analogous to space. Strawson himself appears to think this might work.[9] Strawson's view seems to be

---

[9] This brilliant chapter, quite unlike anything anyone else was thinking about, eventually occasioned an equally brilliant commentary by Gareth Evans, Strawson's most talented pupil and a successor of his as a Fellow at University College. Evans's paper is 'Things Without the Mind' in Z. Van Straaten (ed.), *Philosophical Subjects* (Oxford, 1980.) The volume also contains a subtle and illuminating response to Evans by Strawson himself.

that although spatio-temporal thinking rests on bodies, objective thinking cannot be shown to require spatio-temporal thinking.

In the next chapter, entitled 'Persons', Strawson leaves behind speculation about concepts based on attenuated experiences, and focuses on our rich thought about ourselves. His argument involves a comparison between three conceptions of such thought. The first is what he calls the no-ownership view. It is the idea that we do not really refer to ourselves when we use the first person pronoun, even though we seem to. There is nothing that owns or has the experiences to which to refer. Strawson's response is to argue that once this view is developed genuine self reference emerges as involved in its explanation of the illusion of ownership of experiences. The second conception is that deriving from Descartes, according to which, the item that 'I' picks out is something distinct from the physical body. Strawson argues that this conception collides with a basic principle about psychological thought; it says that one can ascribe experiences to oneself only if one is prepared to ascribe them to others. To fulfil this one must be able to pick out other subjects, and that means they cannot be, as Descartes claimed, non-spatial. Strawson concludes that when we self-refer we refer to an entity which has two sides or aspects, the physical and the mental, and not to a thing which possesses only the mental sort of feature, something else having the physical features. He famously describes this as the idea that the concept of a person is a *primitive concept*. Second, since we can self-ascribe we must be able to other-ascribe, and that means that our methods for doing so must be adequate. As Strawson puts it, the criteria we employ for psychological ascription to others must be 'logically adequate'. There cannot, therefore, be a *genuine* problem of other minds. Again, as in the first chapter, Strawson derives a significant epistemological consequence from his conceptual investigations. This famous chapter has exercised a fascination on philosophers thinking about ourselves and has been, perhaps, as much discussed as any piece of philosophical argument that Strawson wrote.

Finally, Strawson takes Leibniz as an opponent of some of his major theses and considers whether Leibniz might be able to avoid his conclusions. He argues, displaying considerable ingenuity in suggesting different interpretations of Leibniz, that Leibniz does not escape the problems.

Individuals then shifts focus onto the subject–predicate distinction. Strawson's initial aim is, in effect, to show that a novel theory is so much needed here. The reason is two-sided. First, we lack a proper explanation as to why absolutely anything can be the reference of a subject expression but only universals can be what predicates express. Second, he classifies the different accounts on offer and argues that they are either open to objection, or open to the demand for further explanation. The contrast between subjects and predicates that Strawson himself proposes for the central cases is that understanding a subject expression depends on the possession of empirical information whereas the understanding of predicates does not. For example, to understand the name 'James I' I need to know something like: there was a king who ascended the throne in 1603. But to understand the predicate '. . . is triangular' there is no empirical information about the world that I need to grasp. There need not be, or have been, any triangles at all. I have, rather, to grasp the principle of classification linked to the term. Strawson then attempts to explain some other elucidations of the subject–predicate distinction as deriving from his own suggestion, and to develop a more general criterion on the basis of his own account having captured the core cases. In the next chapter Strawson asks the very interesting and novel question whether, just as the employment of (the core type of) subject expressions presupposes empirical information, there is a type of proposition the truth of which is presupposed by subject–predicate propositions in general. He picks out what he calls *feature-placing sentences*, such as 'It is raining'. Such a sentence does not designate an object and describe it, rather the sentence affirms the presence of a feature. Strawson argues that where there are true subject–predicate propositions there must also be true feature-placing sentences. That answers his question.

Indivduals is far richer in argument than I have been able to convey. It occasioned, more or less immediately, considerable debate, and has continued to do so ever since. The epistemological conclusions that Strawson advanced, both about bodies and about other minds, were closely scrutinised. The overall arguments of the chapter on persons and the chapter on bodies were endlessly analysed. The contrast between descriptive and revisionary metaphysics, although briefly presented by Strawson, entered into the folk taxonomy of philosophy. As well as occasioning disagreement, Strawson's book stimulated, over time, a series of books all of which could be described as essays in descriptive metaphysics with a similar focus to, though not with identical conclusions to, *Individuals*. These include Gareth Evans's *The Varieties of Reference*, John Campbell's *Past, Space and Self*, and David Wiggins, *Sameness and Substance*. Within a year of its publication, Strawson was elected to the British Academy.

(v) *The Bounds of Sense*[10]

In 1966, seven years after the publication of *Individuals*, Strawson published his third book, *The Bounds of Sense*.[11] The theme is his attempt to sort the valuable and worth preserving from what he saw as the dubious in Kant's *Critique of Pure Reason*. Strawson abandons Kant's description of his task as the explanation of the possibility of synthetic a priori judgements, the notions that Kant uses not being properly explained, and substitutes for it the idea of determining what modifications of and combinations within conceptual schemes we can make sense of. He abandons too Kant's Transcendental Idealism, though he explores its interpretation with great care and considers why Kant might have adopted it. Any account true to Kant must at least credit his view with acceptance of the thesis that real objects are unknowable and beyond our experience. But there seems no coherent way to fit ourselves into such a picture. If we do receive appearances, as Kant claims, is that not actually a truth about ourselves that we know? Or is it only an appearance that we receive appearances? That is barely intelligible. The rejection of Transcendental Idealism requires Strawson to scrutinise Kant's arguments for it, and he very carefully and sympathetically analyses, and of course rejects, Kant's views on space and time, and geometry, and also the argument, presented in the Antinomies, that transcendental realism generates contradictions. Strawson also abandons much of Kant's talk of mechanisms of synthesis in the generation of proper experience. There seems no coherent way to explain what the materials are that such mechanisms work on, nor really how they work.

This leaves Strawson free to explore and evaluate the constructive and the destructive elements of the *Critique*. In his constructive phase Kant argues that our experience must be of recognisably independent objective items, which are spatial, temporal, and must satisfy some strong principles of permanence and causation. Strawson argues, with both care and brilliance, that Kant's arguments are, in various ways, weak, but that somewhat weaker, but nonetheless important, conclusions along similar lines can be defended. The most interesting part of Strawson's own argument is his defence of the claim that the experience of a self conscious creature must involve and be recognised as involving perception of objects. Strawson's reconstruction of the argument relies on the idea that

---

[10] P. F. Strawson, *The Bounds of Sense* (London, 1966).
[11] As Michael Woods once pointed out to me, Strawson's title, with its deliberate and rich ambiguities, fits perfectly the complexities of his reading of Kant.

the experiences of a self conscious creature must provide room for the thought of experience itself. But one can apply that notion only in the context of the application of categories of things which are *not* experiences. However, such categories can be available to a subject only if its experiences provide it with the grounds for applying them, which involves the idea that its experiences relate it to non-experiences, that is to say, independent things. Strawson then develops further requirements analogous to, but weaker than, those Kant advances in the Analogies. Kant's Dialectic also supplies Strawson with elements to develop as well as elements to reject. Strawson brings out the insights in the Paralogisms which undermine arguments for dualistic theories of the self. The chief problem for Kant is, according to Strawson, that his transcendental idealism prevents him from proposing a plausible and realistic account of ourselves.

The Bounds of Sense had an immediate impact and continues to be extremely influential. It altered the face of Kantian scholarship by suggesting novel and very well-supported interpretations and criticisms of Kant. It represents a sympathetic reading of Kant that any account of him must now come to terms with. But it also, as Putnam remarks, 'opened the way to a reception of Kant's philosophy by analytic philosophers'.[12] In one way *The Bounds of Sense* represents a general and continuous essay in epistemology. Strawson's idea is that a traditional form of philosophical scepticism can be opposed by a style of argument that Kant himself developed, in which the claims about which the sceptic is sceptical can be shown to be involved in the sceptics' own understanding of his position and view. Thus, the sceptics say that their experiences afford no knowledge of the objective world, but the ascription to themselves of experiences rests on and requires acceptance of the judgements they are sceptical of. The arguments which reveal the dependence are called Transcendental Arguments. As we saw, Strawson presented this same (or a related) style of argument in *Individuals*. In the years following its publication this anti-sceptical response was closely investigated, a large literature on it was generated, including notably a number of powerful contributions by the American philosopher Barry Stroud. One problem is that it is extraordinarily difficult to show that there are the conceptual dependencies which such transcendental arguments rely on. Interestingly, Strawson himself soon devised a different response to scepticism, but it

---

[12] H. Putnam, 'Strawson and Skepticism', in L. E. Hahn (ed.), *The Philosophy of P. F. Strawson* (Chicago and Lasalle, Illinois, 1998), p. 273.

is also true that the anti-sceptical approach that Strawson developed
here remains appealing to a range of epistemologists, and this debate
continues.

(vi) Later Books

Strawson published three more books (other than collections of essays) in
English (plus another in French which overlaps with one of those in
English). In 1974 *Subject and Predicate in Logic and Grammar* appeared.[13]
Strawson himself described this book as 'probably the most ambitious
and certainly the one that has received the least attention'.[14] He is right
about the second point but not, I suspect, about the first. It is an ambitious book, but can hardly be ranked above either *Individuals* or *The
Bounds of Sense* in that respect! In the first part of it Strawson presents a
revised version of his account of the normal subject–predicate distinction, and also presents a partial theory of one particular case of subject
expressions, namely proper names. In this he was responding to the emergence of direct referential accounts of the kind that Kripke had made
popular. The discussion of the subject–predicate distinction is clearer and
more direct than the one achieved in *Individuals*. What Strawson particularly brings out is that in ordinary language predicates have a complex
role, involving the indication of universals, the expression of exemplifica-
tion, plus expression also of temporal aspects. This functional complexity explains the correctness of certain other accounts of the distinction.
No consensus about the assessment of Strawson's proposal has emerged,
the reason being that there has still been no very general interest in the
subject–predicate distinction. In the second part, Strawson develops an
approach to the understanding of grammar in which he attempts to
relate grammar, in the sense of syntax, to much more basic functional
specifications of the elements of a language. It becomes possible to see
actual grammars as different ways to achieve these functional roles.
Again, no consensus has emerged about this highly original way to think
about grammar.

In 1985 Strawson published *Skepticism and Naturalism: Some
Varieties*.[15] The book grew out of Strawson's Woodbridge Lectures at
Columbia University in 1983. It is a book of philosophy *about* philoso-

---

[13] P. F. Strawson, *Subject and Predicate in Logic and Grammar* (London, 1974).
[14] From p. ix of Strawson's Introduction to a reprint of the book in 2004 by Ashgate Press.
[15] P. F. Strawson, *Skepticism and Naturalism: Some Varieties* (London, 1985).

phy. In each chapter Strawson focuses on a philosophical dispute in which there is a strong tendency to deny the reality or existence of an aspect which common sense affirms. One case is that of knowledge itself, denied by the philosophical sceptic. Another case is the denial by scientifically inspired philosophers of the reality of, for example, colour. A third example is the denial of the reality of thought and experience by a certain sort of materialist. In each case, Strawson's aim is to deny the denial, and to explain, as one might say, how philosophers can have their cake and eat it. The book is about philosophy in another sense, namely it employs and illuminates some ideas from earlier philosophers, especially Hume and Wittgenstein, and reveals Strawson's very deep understanding of them. The book marks, also, a further development in Strawson's engagement with scepticism. Strawson confesses to a lack of enchantment with transcendental arguments as anti-sceptical devices, and suggests instead that scepticism can be set aside because no one is persuaded by sceptical arguments. Philosophical sceptical doubts are not *serious* doubts, and so are not to be taken *seriously*. This further twist in Strawson's epistemology has, again, inspired considerable debate, and no consensus has yet emerged. As well as being an original contribution to epistemology the book presents what I am inclined to think of as an especially Oxonian approach to ontology. The idea is that there is no good reason not to be realists about most aspects of the world, including colour, mentality, and meaning (and perhaps value) but that does not require the defence of a reduction of such features to some fundamental realm. It is, therefore, the defence of the idea of *relaxed pluralism*. As subsequent debate has revealed, such relaxation is not to everyone's taste.

Finally, there was, in 1992, *Analysis and Metaphysics: an Introduction to Philosophy*.[16] Strawson had given introductory lectures once he became a professor, and so he published them. It is, again, a book about philosophy, contrasting different conceptions of the subject, and defending Strawson's own conception of analysis. Strawson's attitude is that the aim of analysis is to reveal conceptual links and connections, thereby illuminating some features, but that there is no favoured basic level of thought to which it is the goal to reduce everything else. One might call that a conception of *relaxed analysis*. Strawson in fact repeatedly wrote about the nature of philosophy, and the views in this book are his final conclusions. It is also a book in which he practises what he preaches in relation to certain chosen areas, including, for example, the topics of

---

[16] P. F. Strawson, *Analysis and Metaphysics* (Oxford, 1992).

causation and explanation, experience, meaning, and freedom. Whether it is a good introductory book or not, it is certainly a deep and interesting book for the non-beginner! Strawson himself prepares the reader by remarking that the book 'though introductory ... is not elementary. There is no such thing as elementary philosophy. There is no shallow end to the philosophical pool.'

(vii) Some Themes

I have devoted most of this memoir to a description of Strawson's books and of some of the debates to which he made a major contribution. But the picture is still very incomplete, and I wish to describe in a brief way some other aspects of his writings.

Strawson made a major contribution to the theory of perception. His conception is articulated to some extent in *The Bounds of Sense*, but also in a series of articles, of which the most famous (and most reprinted) is 'Perception and Its Objects' (1979). He suggests that the concept of perception should be analysed as a causal concept but that Grice, who famously argued for the same claim, went wrong when saying what sort of causal chain perception requires. But more important, he emphasised that there is no way to describe perceptual experience in terms which are not physical-object concept involving. The attempt to do so he takes to be the crucial mistake of the traditional empiricist model, as represented, for example, in the thought of A. J. Ayer. We are not reading in or interpreting our experiences when we make objective judgements. We are simply endorsing their content. Strawson therefore holds that it is myth to suppose that we can locate a level of claim on the basis of which we can defend the validity of our application of physical-object concepts. Rather, our experience is 'saturated' by those concepts themselves. Although he does not use the same terminology as some who endorse it, this model, in part under his influence, has become the main one in current philosophy.

Strawson's contribution to the philosophy of language is also far more extensive and important than so far indicated. He developed his views in relation to the leading ideas of others about language. One conception that he opposed is that of Quine. Writing with Grice, he argued that Quine's criticisms of the idea of analyticity rest on a commitment to a kind of reduction that itself is simply a dogma.[17] Moreover, repeatedly

---

[17] H. P. Grice and P. F. Strawson, 'In Defense of a Dogma', *Philosophical Review*, 65 (1956), 141–58.

over the next twenty years he argued that Quine's frankly sceptical approach to meaning, and related notions, is both unfounded and also wrong in that it deprives us of notions that we cannot do without in the study of logic and language. Strawson also engaged with Davidson's account of meaning, famously in his inaugural lecture 'Meaning and Truth' (1969), but also elsewhere. Strawson argued that truth is itself a notion secondary to saying (and communication) and cannot play the role in an account of meaning that Davidson proposed. His other reaction to the Davidsonian programme, which accepted a notion of logical form for natural language sentences specified in the complex formulae of predicate logic, was that there is no requirement to map ordinary language on to artificial logical structures, nor does that capture ordinary meaning anyway. This attitude of Strawson's placed him in opposition to a movement of thought that swept through Oxford's younger philosophers during the time he was a professor, and on this issue he struck many as behind the times. From the present perspective, however, it looks as if he may have been before the times. Strawson also made important contributions, on a number of occasions, to the assessment of Austin's theory of speech acts, and also in relation to Grice's own model of meaning. Finally, he responded to the anti-realist approach developed by Dummett, which also gained its adherents, in 'Scruton and Wright on Anti-Realism' (1976), a brief but brilliant critique which exposed, or so it seems to me, the fact that there are no obvious reasons to adopt the anti-realist account of truth, and moreover that it is hard to make it consistent with what appear to be obvious facts about the knowability (or unknowability) of our psychological lives and also the past.

Another theme that needs stressing is Strawson's engagement with the history of philosophy. *The Bounds of Sense* deals with Kant, but Strawson also wrote many articles about him. In other places he wrote about Descartes, Hume, Leibniz, Spinoza, and, from the last century, Wittgenstein and Moore. These writings reveal both a deep knowledge and a deep understanding of these thinkers, never unsympathetic and always able to see the wood as well as the trees. Strawson had a sense of the age of philosophical problems and of the insights from the great dead philosophers that need preserving and renewing.

I have plotted to some extent the development of Strawson's epistemological views, but have not described his earliest proposal in relation to the problem of induction. In *An Introduction to Logical Theory* he pioneered what came to be called the 'analytical solution', according to which there cannot be any question as to the rationality of the employment of induction, since by being rational we *mean*, amongst other things, using induction. The question whether induction is rational resembles the question whether the law is legal. This remains a discussed approach. The unity amongst Strawson's proposals is that the response to scepticism is never the production of a proof or demonstration based on a level of thought external and prior to the discourse in question. Each solution aims to turn aside scepticism in some other way. Strawson's ingenuity in devising such responses is very impressive and he is the source of at least three major currently investigated anti-sceptical approaches.

Strawson always joked that he would turn to moral philosophy only when his powers were waning. He wrote very little about that, but his main contribution 'Freedom and Resentment' is perhaps now his most famous and widely discussed paper. It is quite staggering, and a quite unique achievement, that on the more or less only occasion he wrote about morals he should have produced a classic. Strawson's aim is to dissolve the so-called problem of determinism and responsibility. His argument is that our 'reactive attitudes' towards others and ourselves, such attitudes as gratitude, anger, sympathy and resentment, are natural and irrevocable. Their presence, therefore, needs no abstract entitlement from philosophy, which is simply irrelevant to their existence. There cannot be abstract a priori principles locating general metaphysical conditions for such attitudes. Between determinism and responsibility there can be no conflict. One might see in this an application of some ideas of a Humean character to a domain to which Hume himself was not inclined to apply them.

There are many more topics about which Strawson wrote. The most outstanding quality of his writing is that in relation to every problem he wrote about he made a significant contribution.

(viii) Teacher, Writer and Person

I have charted Strawson's life primarily in terms of his writings and the development of his philosophical ideas. This has left out many aspects and I want to make the picture fuller by describing both him and some of his other achievements.[18]

---

[18] In the introduction I cited some of the outstanding honours that Strawson received. Amongst other honours, he was a Foreign Honorary Member of the American Academy of Arts and Sciences, 1971, an honorary Fellow of three Oxford colleges, (St John's, University, and Magdalen), the Woodbridge Lecturer at Columbia University, 1983, and a Member of the Academia Europaea, 1992. Strawson was invited to deliver the prestigious Willliam James Lectures

Much of Strawson's time as a philosopher was spent as a teacher, of both undergraduates and graduates. I was lucky enough to be taught by him at both levels in the 1960s and I can, therefore, testify to his unrivalled quality in both roles. Strawson was amazingly quick at understanding what he read and heard, and so throughout his career maintained contact with the developments in the subject. As a consequence his reading lists were helpful, up to date, and balanced. When he heard an undergraduate essay the same speed of comprehension enabled him to analyse it without apparent effort. He then pointed out the important lacunas or mistakes in the argument, suggested ways that it could be improved, and indicated approaches to the difficult problems that always struck me as persuasive and profound. In this way he encouraged us to think more effectively and self critically, and I always left with an uplifting sense that if only I had thought harder even the most difficult problems could be cracked. Sometimes we managed to ask a question that caused him to think, and then before our very eyes after some moments of intense concentration he answered it.

Professor John Searle brilliantly conveys the character of the experience of a Strawson tutorial, though in his case from ten years earlier than mine.

> After the usual greetings we would sit down and he would begin, typically with something like the following.
>
> 'Now it does seem to me, Searle, (we were not yet upon first name terms) that you are essentially arguing as follows.' Whereupon he would present an elegant, lucidly clear and powerful expression of what I had, in my fumbling way, been trying to say. 'Yes. Yes!' I would cry out. 'That is exactly it. Those are exactly my points.' 'Well, if that is so, it does seem to me that the argument is subject to the following four objections.' Whereupon he would proceed to demolish the entire argument step by elegant step. And the odd thing was, that though none of my points was left standing, I did not feel in any way diminished or defeated. On the contrary, I was positively elated because it seemed to me then, as it does now, that Peter and I were engaged in a common intellectual enterprise, the most wonderful enterprise of all: philosophical analysis . . .'[19]

---

at Harvard, but declined, feeling when he received the invitation that he did not have quite enough to say. Another mark of his recognition is the number of books and journal volumes devoted to him, usually including replies by Strawson to the discussion. Amongst the best known are Zak Van Straaten (ed.), *Philosophical Subjects* (Oxford, 1980), the journal *Philosophia*, 10 (1981), Carlos E. Caorsi, *Ensayos sobre Strawson* (Montevideo: Universidad de la Republica, 1992), P. K. Sen and R. R. Verma (eds.), *The Philosophy of P. F. Strawson* (New Delhi, Indian Council of Philosophical Research, 1995), and H.-J. Glock (ed.), *Strawson and Kant* (Oxford, 2003).

[19] This quotation comes from Searle's address at Strawson's memorial service, referred to earlier.

The awe that Strawson inspired in us is accurately conveyed by our description of such encounters as 'interviews with God'. I have absolutely no doubt that having Strawson as a tutor was the best possible introduction to philosophy. He was, of course, similarly effective as a graduate tutor, and he took enormous care to analyse our papers in detail. My sense, though, is that he enjoyed undergraduate teaching more. I conjecture that since his own views were those that graduates frequently wanted to write about, and, in the nature of graduates, to be critical about, in many graduate supervisions he had to spend time warding off attacks on himself, which is hardly an enjoyable occupation. Strawson himself mentions undergraduate tutorials as one group activity in philosophy which he found especially helpful. As he puts it, in such encounters 'one finds oneself obliged to clarify one's own half-formed thoughts in order to make things clear to one's pupils. Seeking a way past, or through, his or her mistakes and confusions, one may find a path past, or through, one's own.'[20] Strawson was, I believe, the outstanding teacher of philosophy of his generation in Oxford.

Strawson was also excellent in the role of Waynflete Professor. He worked hard with graduates and continued the tradition of professors offering informal instructions in which he led class discussion of selected papers. For a number of years he held what became rather famous graduate classes on Kant, in which graduates presented papers. The readers of the papers were invited to Magdalen before the class and over tea there Strawson would forewarn them of the objections he had to their claims. This double courtesy no doubt helped them bear the gentle but inescapable execution they were about to endure. He performed the many administrative duties tied to the chair with wisdom and patience, and without any manifest desire for power or an overwhelming desire to stamp his own image on the university. He valued Oxford's variety and its tolerance of different philosophical programmes. Above all, he saw his role as being, first and foremost, to produce, and to contribute to the production of, philosophical work of high quality.

Strawson, as I have said, had no wish to play the role of famous philosopher. However, in the 1950s and 1960s his voice was a central one in the discussions and talks about philosophy that were broadcast on the Third Programme. His role tended to be that of the profound and

---

[20] P. F. Strawson, 'Intellectual Autobiography', p. 22 in Hahn (ed.), *The Philosophy of P. F. Strawson*, p. 22. The way Strawson puts it makes one hope that one contributed to the development of his thinking by offering the confusions he needed to remove!

infallible metaphysician, just as Mary Warnock's tended to be that of the female looking for illumination from the men. She has recently revealed that the discussions were completely scripted and unspontaneous, written beforehand at hilarious preparatory meetings.[21] Despite that, these series led on the whole to publications invariably containing very good contributions from Strawson.

I have described the central writings of Strawson, but it needs to be stressed that Strawson wrote much else besides. An outstanding feature of his career was the quantity, breadth and quality of his publications. Three of his books are collections of his papers, and they by no means contain most of his papers.[22] Although he was not alone in thinking this, he realised that it was not enough for Oxford philosophers simply to talk amongst themselves. They needed to publish, which he did, and he also encouraged others to do so. He was helped by the fact that he wrote with facility and ease. He wrote in a style which is manifestly elegant, his vocabulary being rich and untechnical, and his sentences and paragraphs having a rhythm and structure that makes them a pleasure to read. I cannot *describe* the style but, I believe, it would be easy to recognise any extended passage by him as his. His writings are a contribution to English letters. Strawson used to say that he did not mind people criticising his opinions but resented any criticism of his style.

The elegance of his literary style leads me to remark on what one might call the general elegance of the surface he revealed to the world. His conversation, manners, appearance and behaviour were also elegant, imperturbable, urbane and such as are only possible in someone of exquisite intelligence.[23] Strawson himself describes the special pleasures of his life at the end of his 'Intellectual Autobiography'. 'Philosophy, friends, and family apart, my life has been enriched by the enjoyment of literature, landscape, architecture, and the company of clever and beautiful women.'

---

[21] In Mary Warnock, *A Memoir: People and Places* (London, 2000).

[22] They are: *Logico-Linguistic Papers* (London, 1971), *Freedom and Resentment and Other Essays* (London, 1974), and *Entity and Identity* (Oxford, 1997). Strawson once said to me that the title he would have preferred for the first collection was *Language, Truth and Logic*, but it was no longer available!

[23] Strawson's imperturbability can be illustrated by a story that I owe to Galen Strawson. Strawson and his friend John Carswell were engaged in conversation with others in Paris. The conversation was animated and in the course of it Carswell stubbed out his cigarette on Strawson's head who responded by simply carrying on speaking! It was also with John Carswell that Strawson would play, in their respective gardens, a military game they had invented, which involved lead soldiers and artillery, and extraordinarily complicated rules. It is rumoured that Strawson never lost! His brother John refrained from challenging Strawson in case he, a man of considerable military distinction, should lose!

Strawson's knowledge of literature was extensive, and his very accurate memory of it was phenomenal. He particularly enjoyed poetry and wished, or said that he wished, he had had the talent to be a poet. He did have the talent to produce mock verse in many styles. I feel that I cannot do better to convey the character of Strawson than to quote the description of him by his brother John.

> When today I contemplate Peter's character and achievements, I see a man of absolute integrity, brimming over with good nature and with magnanimity, with the gift of true friendship, a sense of humour spiced with benevolent wit, and I observe an intellect of prodigious power, a contribution to philosophy of enduring importance, indeed in the world of philosophy a legend in his own lifetime, a wholly likeable, clubbable man, full of the milk of human kindness, enriched by family ties and a host of friends and admirers, a well loved brother who commanded my whole-hearted admiration.

Conclusion

It is too early to say what enduring influence and importance Strawson will have, and about that I do not want to speculate. His life as a philosopher, though, resulted in an unequalled contribution to all the central areas of theoretical philosophy. The outstanding qualities of Strawson's thought are, it seems to me, its depth, originality, the very broad sweep of its subject matter, and its consistently level-headed rationality. If as Strawson suggested, the concept of a person merits being described as primitive, it can be said of Strawson himself that he merits being described as the least primitive of persons.

PAUL SNOWDON
University College, London

Note. I wish to express my gratitude to Quassim Cassam, Galen Strawson and Martha Klein for the help, guidance and information they have given me in writing this memoir. I am also grateful to Peter Marshall for helpful suggestions.

HUGH TREVOR-ROPER

Hugh Redwald Trevor-Roper
1914–2003

HOW TO RECALL, within the scope of this memoir, a life so crowded and varied, and writings so abundant and diverse? If my account is necessarily selective, and gives but brief attention to some well-known accomplishments and episodes, it may also have its unexpected sides. For he did not allow the world to know him well. Even his friends rarely if ever glimpsed some of the complexities and inner springs of character that emerge from private reflections in his voluminous papers, which are now in Christ Church, Oxford. In spite of his public profile, he lived, more than most men, predominantly within himself, through the inspiration, and under the burden, of his mind and temperament.

There are few signs of intellectual or literary interests in his family's past. The name Trevor-Roper (which he found an ungainly construction) derives from the eighteenth century, when the Ropers of Kent, the formerly recusant family that had produced the son-in-law of Sir Thomas More, inherited lands of the Trevors in North Wales and transplanted themselves there. Hugh's father Bertie, the youngest of thirteen children, grew up in a house close to the family's crumbling Jacobean mansion. He trained as a doctor and intended to work in India, but was told that his health would not survive there. Instead he moved to Northumberland, where he lived to the age of 94. His medical practice began in the village of Glanton, and sustained its rural base after his move, in Hugh's childhood, to the nearby town of Alnwick. It was at Glanton that Hugh was born, the second of three children, on 15 January 1914, to parents both in their late twenties. He and his brother Pat, the distinguished ophthalmologist who was two years Hugh's junior, remembered a grim household, where the expression of warmth or emotion was proscribed. There

Proceedings of the British Academy, **150**, 247–284. © The British Academy 2007.

may have been a streak of impishness in his father, who had a fondness for the turf, and whom a friend of Hugh remembers as having vaguely the appearance of a bookie. If so, marriage to Hugh's mother, Kathleen Davison, the censorious daughter of a Belfast businessman, repressed that trait. Hugh recalled bleakly silent car-journeys at his father's side as the doctor did his rural rounds.

His own early impishness revealed itself in exuberantly rhymed poems and playlets. Yet he remembered his childhood as unhappy. It was largely solitary. He was close neither to his mother nor to his sister Sheila, and was not particularly close to Pat. It was in his own company that he developed his love of the natural world, collected butterflies and moths, kept hedgehogs, tadpoles and caterpillars, and came to know 'all the wild flowers that grew in Northumberland, all the kinds of crustaceans, molluscs, sea-mice, marine spiders, etc. that crept along the coast', though his extreme short-sightedness precluded the same familiarity with birdlife. The other inner resource was reading. The family's was not a bookish home, but he devoured every encyclopaedia or work of human or natural history that he could find. He got through church services by studying the Prayer Book, the print held near to his eyes, and by calculating the dates of Easter down the ages. He came to know the Old Testament so well that, later, he could teach himself languages by reading it in them.

Having begun his education under an excellent governess he was sent first to a wretched preparatory school in Derbyshire, and then, for a longer period, to a better one at Dunbar. At thirteen he moved to Charterhouse, the public school in Surrey. There, though his intellectual capacity soon revealed itself, he was for long a withdrawn, even mousy figure. With time he emerged, 'like a chick from its shell' as he would remember, to become one of the school's conspicuous and respected personalities. Yet it was among books that he discovered himself. He had wanted to specialise in mathematics, but was told by the Headmaster that 'clever boys do classics'. Thus was he directed to the prime love of his mental life. 'How vividly', he wrote in adulthood, 'I remember each discovery' in Greek literature. First there was the day when, in his study at school, 'the vocabulary of Homer, as it were, broke in my hands'. Then came Theocritus, whom he first read 'amid the noise of grasshoppers and the smell of mown grass'. There was Pindar, 'whose majestic myths and magniloquent poetry transported me into a world so remote and elevated that one descended afterward with difficulty into the realm governed by the laws of gravity'. Greatest of all was Aeschylus, with his 'vivid, highly charged metaphors, swollen to bursting point by the presence of tormenting thoughts'. Homer he came to know by heart. Later he had his Virgil 'done up as a Prayer-Book' for company during chapel services. He would wake with classical poetry on his lips. In old age, when physical movement was impaired, he kept a Horace on both floors of his house, and with his failing eyes re-read his way through all of Cicero and Tacitus.

As a Classical Scholar at Christ Church from 1932 he won a series of prizes. A glittering career as a classicist awaited him. Yet in his second year he renounced that prospect and transferred to a degree in history, which had been an extracurricular addiction. The change was one of a series of repudiations that transformed him in the years of and immediately following his undergraduate career. Charterhouse, a worthy school pledged to Anglican piety and conventional virtue, had encouraged conformism of opinion and taste. At the time he conformed. The reaction came at Oxford. It can be explained partly by the confident worldliness of Christ Church—or rather of the secular half of the college, for the ecclesiastical presence was strong enough to nurture what became his fierce anticlericalism. Though none of his institutional allegiances was ever uncritical, he would always be a Christ Church man at heart, and it was there that he returned as a tutor after the war. On the two occasions when he was obliged to move to another Oxford college, first to a Research Fellowship at Merton in 1937 and then, twenty years later, to the Fellowship at Oriel that accompanied his appointment as Oxford's Regius Professor of Modern History, he did so with a heavy heart, though time would foster new affections.

In his first undergraduate year he ate at the Scholars' table, but cast envious glances at the jollier company of the Commoners, to which he thereafter gravitated. Hugh does not quite answer to the familiar caricature of the college's more boisterous undergraduates. He was not a window-smasher. Nonetheless he lived wildly and drank deeply. He also developed, with the income from his Classics prizes, the passion for fox-hunting that would consume a high proportion of his days until, in 1948, he broke his spine in the last of many falls from his horse. During the war, friends would urge him to renounce hunting and other frivolous intrusions upon a scholar's time. Yet he would hitch-hike in lorries in the icy dawn to get from London to the Bicester country, or use his military leave to hunt in Ireland, indeed would do anything to be among the sounds and smells of the chase, the changes of landscape and light in the fields and woods.

Alongside the social discoveries of his early twenties came intellectual and moral reappraisals. Having been taught, at Charterhouse, what to think and admire, he now began to develop his impregnable independence and individuality of viewpoint. A seminal influence was the Victorian writer Samuel Butler, whom for a time he idolised, and who 'saved my life', for under his example 'I turned my back on the prim, traditional paths of classical learning'. Hugh began to distinguish morality, about which he was always fastidious, from 'the systems people make out of their repressions', from 'social and sexual conventions, religion, and all the apparatus of God and Sin'. By 1937 his interest in theological abstractions, and 'my high-church leanings', had surrendered to a cool rationalism and a sharp insistence on the concrete and the material. In his rebellion he cultivated for a time a waggish scepticism, even a veneer of anti-intellectualism.

In his Finals in 1936, for which he had not worked hard, he completed his double First. He did work hard for the competitive exam, later in the year, for Prize Fellowships of All Souls, but failed to win election; which he minded at the time. He had hoped to use the position to prepare himself for the exam for the diplomatic service, a career to which he would have been fitted perfectly by intellect and disastrously by temperament. Instead, still at Christ Church and now under the exiguous supervision of Claude Jenkins, the Regius Professor of Ecclesiastical History, he embarked on the research that would produce his first book, *Archbishop Laud*, published in 1940. We do not know why, having taken undergraduate options on St Augustine and on very modern history, he settled on the seventeenth century for his research. Perhaps his choice reflects the influence of that leading historian of the period, Keith Feiling, who with J. C. Masterman was his principal undergraduate tutor in history, though Hugh respected him more in distant retrospect than at the time. Or perhaps the subject of Laud appealed to the 'high-church leanings' that he would surrender only in his third postgraduate term. He was awarded a University Studentship, taught for Christ Church and for Balliol College, and in his second year of research won his Merton Fellowship. During the war he remembered that 'golden period' of his graduate days, or one that seemed golden when 'viewed selectively from a colder, darker epoch', when he and his friends 'lived effortlessly', 'hunting foxes and hares, drinking and talking, reading new books and old books, walking hounds in the early summer mornings through Garsington and Cuddesdon and Coombe Wood, watching for the emergence of each new wild flower in those comfortable fields and hedgerows and water meadows, making new intellectual discoveries in those hours of infinite, astronomical leisure. How delightful to sit in a beautiful room' in Merton, 'south-facing through great bow-windows over the Christ Church Meadow, rook-racked, river-rounded, writing a book, after an early walk, amid pleasant interruptions . . .'

Archbishop Laud, though praised on its appearance for the industry behind it, is not, by later standards, a work of exhaustive research. Even so, it is startling to find that it was written, not only in less than three years from scratch, but with intermittent application and amid countless diversions. During the same period he spent months writing a novel on an anticlerical theme, which he tried to publish. He wrote a piece, which drew on archival work and appeared in *Country Life*, on the eighteenth-century foxhunting poet William Somerville, and a long unpublished paper on the authorship of *Prometheus Bound*. Or he would sit at a typewriter and compose 'wit, blasphemy and nonsense'. His talk was blasphemous too, imprudently so if he wanted a career at Oxford. Once Hugh's Anglican inclinations had been shed, it seems to have been only by discharging his new-found irreverence in other writings that he was able to preserve a measured tone in imparting what became the lesson of the book on Laud: that the conduct of the Church and churchmen is governed by the rules of this world, not of the next.

Even when we allow for the anti-intellectual posture, he does not look, in those years, like a major historian in the making. In the first year of his research he would easily 'weary of all this academic stuff'. 'I have been doing some work on my thesis lately', records the diary he kept in 1937–8, 'but have now given up through boredom of solitude and spend my time writing frivolities and reading Dostoevsky.' 'The Public Record Office', he decided after his first visit, paid between lunch and tea, to its reading-rooms in Chancery Lane, 'is no place for a gentleman. Dinge, incredible dinge, must, fust, and influenza germs.' In the absence of a postgraduate community, the habits of his undergraduate life persisted. The nocturnal peace of Oxford's quadrangles and back-streets would be shattered, on his return from the chase or from drinking expeditions, by his blasts on hunting-horns and bugles and trumpets. He lived restlessly, taking enormous walks, sleeping beneath open skies. He lived dangerously, too, swimming in choppy seas, driving too fast, charging at hedges on a horse as impetuous as he.

In September 1938 came the Munich crisis and its call to seriousness. Its shadow falls over his diary like the arrival of the messenger of death amid the festivities of *Love's Labours Lost*. Outrage at appeasement merged with despair for the future of Europe, of England, and of himself and his generation. He read *Mein Kampf*, as no one he knew did, and acquired his preoccupation with Hitler's character and purposes. After the outbreak of war he was drawn into Intelligence work by the accident of his acquaintance with the Bursar of Merton, Walter Gill, with whom he worked, in an office converted from a prison cell in Wormwood Scrubs, in what would become the Radio Security Service (RSS), and with whom he shared a flat in Ealing. Charged with identifying radio messages to Germany from (non-existent) spies in England, the two men, through Hugh's cryptographical skills and Gill's knowledge of wireless, made a discovery on a different front, outside their remit. In early 1940 they intercepted, and in the evenings at Ealing gradually learned to decipher, messages, some between Hamburg and a ship off Norway, others from Wiesbaden to Hamburg, which they identified as belonging to the radio network of the *Abwehr*, the German Secret Service. It was from that seed that the extensive penetration of *Abwehr* wireless by Bletchley Park would grow.

Despite that achievement, Hugh had a contentious wartime career ahead of him. He was embroiled in a series of vivid confrontations with a number of his superiors, and developed a furious and lacerating contempt for the professional capacities of cosily recruited *habitués* of London clubland. He despaired at the competitive feuding of Intelligence departments and at their failure to pool their knowledge. But by 1943, when he became Major, his standing had improved, with the help of two influential friends: Dick White (then in MI5, and later the head of SIS), who wrote of Hugh in that year that no single officer in MI5 or MI6 'possesses a more comprehensive knowledge of the *Abwehr* organisation, particularly on its communication side'; and Patrick Reilly, the future diplomat, who was personal assistant to the head of MI6. Amid complex departmental reorganisations Hugh was able to win a degree of independence for himself, within SIS, as head of a small section which produced an imposing collection of research papers on German intelligence. His colleagues in it, whom he had recruited over the previous two years, were Charles Stuart—another Christ Church man, who was brought to Hugh's notice by J. C. Masterman, and who after the war would be Hugh's fellow-historian at the college—and the philosophers Gilbert Ryle, a close friend of Hugh before and during the war, and Stuart Hampshire. Reilly described the four men as a 'team of a brilliance unparalleled anywhere in the Intelligence machine'. Forthcoming work by Ted Harrison, including an article in the *English Historical Review*, will bring out the extent and significance of Hugh's contribution to Intelligence.

After the Normandy landings he spent much time at Allied Headquarters, first in France, then in Germany. At a press conference in Berlin in November 1945 he announced the findings of his conclusive report, which he had assembled in less than two months, on the circumstances of Hitler's death, a document produced to counter mendacious Soviet claims that the Führer was still alive. From it Hugh's classic study *The Last Days of Hitler* would emerge sixteen months later. Here as in so much else, he felt his life to have been governed by the power of accident. 'The whole business', he recalled shortly after the book's publication, 'began in a bottle; for it was when I was drinking hock with Dick White', at that time head of the Counter-Intelligence Bureau in the British zone of occupation, and Herbert Hart, another Intelligence officer with an eminent future, 'that my researches were first instituted. I was interested in the subject, and from a variety of casual sources had picked up a good deal of unsystematic information, some right, some wrong; and over the third bottle of hock I was drawing on this reservoir of conversational raw-material'—for among his friends the young Hugh was an incessant talker—'and was telling rather a good story, as I thought (though I have since discovered that it was thoroughly inaccurate), about the last highly charged days in Hitler's bunker. "But this is most important!" exclaimed Dick, his eyes popping, as they sometimes do, out of universal eagerness of spirit. "No one has yet made any systematic study of the evidence, or even found any evidence, and we are going to have all kinds of difficulty unless something is done."' Hugh was commissioned by White to do it, and promptly began his pursuit and interrogation of the surviving former inhabitants of the bunker. It was a time of high intensity, of exultant discovery (some of it achieved in bibulous company in mirthfully improbable circumstances), and of 'delightful journeys, motoring through the deciduous golden groves of Schleswig-Holstein, and coming, on an evening, when the sun had just set but the light had not yet gone, and the wild duck were out for their last flight over the darkening waters, to the great Danish castle of Ploen . . .'

The Last Days subsumes the excitement of the chase into a narrative of perfect proportions and pace, and into an enduring epitaph on a hideous tyranny. It is that rare artefact, a work of contemporary history written not merely for the present but for posterity. Readers of Tacitus, another recorder of a recent tyranny, notice echoes of him in Hugh's book. Yet it may have been only afterwards that Hugh himself became conscious of them. The Roman writer whose name the book invokes is not the historian of imperial tyranny but its satirist, Juvenal, whose spirit lives in Hugh's portraits of Hitler's courtiers, of the 'parasites' and 'toadies' and 'flatulent clowns' of that 'monkey-house'. Even on that terrible subject it is the deflationary force of Hugh's comic instinct that pierces the awe of appearances.

*

Wartime deepened Hugh, but the war itself was not the only cause. After his carefree life of the later 1930s he discovered adult unhappiness, and came to appreciate the aphorism of the first Marquis of Halifax: 'Content to the mind is like moss to a tree; it bindeth up so as to stop its growth.' In the preceding years, and in *Archbishop Laud*, there had been, as he regretfully recalled in 1943, 'no introspection', 'no hesitancy or doubt'. Two events of 1940, their impact heightened by the nation's crisis, were formative. The first, following a botched operation for sinusitis, was illness, 'which teaches sympathy and humanity to those who have forgotten it'. Its legacy, for decades, was a 'private disease', which would suddenly incapacitate him for days on end. Nervous fatigue played its part in that as in other illnesses.

Secondly, he came to know the elderly writer Logan Pearsall Smith, 'the sage of Chelsea', and learned from him that only in a 'vocation', and in the pursuit of 'truth', could life acquire a 'meaning'. Smith's ideals were bound to an aestheticism that Hugh would later shed, but his influence would have enduring legacies. It fortified Hugh's courage, not only in holding solitary opinions, but in living by them. It inspired him to perfectionism of writing and, in its pursuit, to struggle, long hours, high aims. *Archbishop Laud* had been about the place of the concrete and the mundane in the supposedly spiritual world. In writing it, as he would (not without simplification) remember, he had 'neglected poetry and prose, read neither Gibbon nor Homer, but only studied, and studied only essential monographs and laborious theses'. He had 'consciously ignored' the 'temptation' of style. Now Smith 're-interested me' in 'style and the world of sensation', and taught him to venerate 'style of living, style of writing, born of disinterested thought and sweat to ennoble and preserve the thoughts and memory of an else insignificant existence'. With Smith he rejoiced in shared literary discoveries and in the exploration of the properties and resources of language. From Smith, too, whom he fondly remembered as 'a rather wicked old man', he gained confidence in two deviant convictions: the necessity of pleasure for the sustenance of thought and energy; and the value of mischief, even of malice, in penetrating the humbug of power and of conventional opinion. Hugh would never confuse seriousness with solemnity, or be susceptible to the notion, which he ascribed to 'censorious historians', that 'serious political ideals can only be sincerely held by public bores'. He knew that it is not earnestness that kills, but irony or ridicule—the spirit that informs *The Last Days*, a work written for Smith, though Smith did not live to read it.

But what form would Hugh's 'vocation' take? He was surely destined to be a writer, but was he bound to be a historian? During the war he compiled notebooks, indebted in form to those of Samuel Butler and to Smith's book *Trivia*, where he experimented with style and mood and subject-matter. They are the record of a vibrant, nervous, romantic sensibility, and of a young man as restless in mind as in body. There are reflections on religion, art, literature and the natural world, and descriptions of walking, fishing, hunting, of friends and companions. Gossip and frivolity mingle with existential meditation, high spirits with the melancholy he seeks to keep at bay. There are poems, in English and Latin. He made a specialism of the ballad form, where he achieved comedic lines that Hilaire Belloc or John Betjeman would not have disdained. In those years he was upheld by literature. Amid the 'fits of depression, dank, meaningless, infinite gloom' which 'increasingly overcome me', his notebook of 1945 records, he turned 'for relief to literature', where sometimes 'I find my own condition, elevated into a momentary sublimity by the magic art of Aeschylus, of Euripides, of Shakespeare, of Leopardi, of Housman, and of that brutal and lecherous old Psalmist-King'.

The notebooks pay less attention to his voracious historical reading during the war. They do, however, acknowledge his 'fond ambition' to 'write a book that someone, some day, will mention in the same breath as Gibbon'. Subjects for historical books piled in his mind and pressed on it, as they would through his life. At this stage he seems to have been as much attracted by the prospect of evoking the past as of analysing it. In 1943 he had his eye on the later seventeenth and early eighteenth centuries, and contemplated first a book on the Duke of Marlborough, then one on the France of Louis XIV. But there were two grander projects, neither of them bound to a period, both of them pointing to lasting preoccupations. One was about class, the other about religion. He envisaged a large work, to be called *A History of the English Ruling Classes*, where he would convey the shifts of atmosphere and values as the power and wealth of the aristocracy altered across the generations, from Tudor times to the present. As often, his intellectual concerns were bound with personal ones. He half-wanted to join the aristocracy, half-wanted to beat it. He disliked his own class, in the middle-to-upper layer of the middle class, with its narrow, even 'semi-fascist' prejudices. He enjoyed and envied aristocratic style and confidence, at least in their more eccentric forms. Even in later life he liked, as he self-mockingly confessed, to 'listen, with guilty pleasure, to the inane but comforting flattery of jewelled duchesses'. It is no accident that he married the daughter of an earl, though there was nothing calculating, and in professional and material terms there was every risk, in that ardent and initially adulterous encounter. Yet he censured aristocratic rule when it took oppressive forms or separated itself from public responsibility. During the war he noted with pleasure and a touch of animus that the British aristocracy was now 'dead as the mammoth and the mastodon'.

The second project was a study, across centuries and civilisations, of religious revivals. Generally respectful of inherited religious allegiances, he had less time for voluntarily acquired ones. He thought the historical and intellectual propositions of Christianity, to which, 'if words mean anything', its adherents commit themselves when they say the Creed, absurd. His blasphemous instincts persisted into the war, when he embarked on a fictional 'Vision of Judgement', in which God regrets dispatching his son to save humanity and even doubts his own existence. In the post-war years Hugh aimed salvo after salvo at Catholicism. His study of religious revivals contracted into an unfriendly study, undertaken in 1953–4, of the Catholic revival of the nineteenth century. Though he insisted on calling it a pamphlet, it runs, even in its unfinished form, to nearly 55,000 words. Yet hostility and disbelief are not the total of his perspective on religion. Atheism he thought an arrogant and banal position, an affront to the numinous. 'Cosmic *enigmata*' tortured him long after his rejection of Christian teaching in his early twenties. The mistake, he thought, was to confuse religion with ethics, or alternatively to transport its properties from the realm of myth to that of fact. 'If I had a religion', he reflected in 1944—

> and I sometimes feel that I behave as if I were in search of one—I would be a pagan. For it is among meadows and hills, clear streams and woodland rides, that I find serenity of mind; in deep forests and dark caverns, among lonely crags and howling tempests that I feel the inadequacy of man; in the starry night and by the desolate seashore that the triviality of temporal existence oppresses or comforts me. If satyrs were one day to pop up and pipe to me among the Cheviot Hills; if a troop of nymphs were suddenly to rise with

seductive gestures from a trout-pool in the Breamish; if dryads and hamadryads were to eye me furtively as I hunted the tangled thickets of Hell Copse or Waterperry Wood; I would not feel in the least surprised—I already half assume their presence there. But if God were to speak to me through the mouth of a clergyman, or to appear to me in any of the approved Christian attitudes, then indeed I would begin to ask questions.

Christianity, like any other religion, was deserving of respect 'as an allegory, or harmless poetic belief, into whose historically consecrated shell successive generations have poured a philosophical or moral content'. But clericalism, dogmatism and fanaticism were different matters. His writings plead the claims of humanity, and of the life of the mind, against them. He could mock them to Gibbonian effect. What he could not do was convey the substance of religious experience, even in forms of it that he judged reputable. Lacking an explanatory framework, the allusions in his work to 'spiritual' qualities, or to 'genuine' religious sentiment, lack resonance.

The project on class contracted too, again into an unfinished book. Later he would look back on his '*Marxisant* phase'. He was always averse to Marxist determinism and to Marxist prophecy. Yet in his reaction against metaphysical assertion, and against insubstantial high-mindedness, he welcomed the materialism of Marxist explanation. In his younger writings he accepted the Marxist interpretation of the early modern period as a clash between declining feudalism and emerging capitalism. His study of Laud rested on that premise. So did his essay, published (in the *Durham University Journal*) in 1946, 'The Bishopric of Durham and the Capitalist Reformation', which centred on Thomas Sutton, the founder of Charterhouse, whom he had begun to study before the outbreak of war. In the late 1940s he contemplated a book on four rich men, whose patterns of getting and spending would illustrate the social and economic changes of the sixteenth and seventeenth centuries: Sutton himself; the Duke of Northumberland of Edward VI's reign; Sir Thomas Bodley; and the Earl of Strafford's antagonist the first Earl of Cork. The project in turn was reduced into one on Sutton alone, on whom, by around 1950, he had written five chapters of a book. Perhaps there was an element of revenge in his demonstration that Sutton, who was embalmed in Charterhouse's memory as a paragon of Christian charity, had been a ruthless usurer, to whom a high proportion of the Elizabethan ruling order had been beholden. Hugh painstakingly and expertly reconstructed, in the dinge of the Public Record Office, Sutton's dealings with the nobility. The book was not finished, but from it there would emerge the broader subject that in 1953 he explored in his long essay (published as a supplement to the *Economic History Review*), *The Gentry 1540–1640*.

Under Pearsall Smith's influence Hugh had told himself that the 'solid, austere research' which he had attempted in *Archbishop Laud* was 'compatible with faith in literary style'. Yet now he had moved into the area of historical study least hospitable to style, economics. 'I have read no books', he told his elderly friend the art connoisseur Bernard Berenson in 1950, 'only dry and dusty leases and records of debts and bills and docquets of inconceivable philistinism. What a price one pays to write history! But I hope to get back to literature soon.' He declared *The Gentry* to be 'dry' and 'dusty' too, 'of some interest to historians and economists, but fundamentally a piece of specialization which can give no pleasure'. The fact to be recognised was that 'the truth is often dull'. With time, as he wearied of economic in favour of intellectual history, a theme friendlier to literary self-expression, and as the romantic agony of the wartime notebooks abated, the claims of the cerebral and of the aesthetic learned to coexist in his mind. Yet as late as 1968 he confessed that 'I find more pleasure in good literature than in dull (even if true) history', and five years afterwards he complained to Frances Yates of the 'prolix and ungrammatical documents' that had becalmed his work on the Huguenot physician Sir Theodore Mayerne.

*

The Last Days of Hitler, which has never been out of print, brought him instant fame. After its appearance, editors competed for his pen, hostesses for his company. He embarked on what amounted to a part-time career not only as an authority on modern Germany but as a book reviewer on a vast range of subjects and, for many years to come, as a visitor to foreign lands and a commentator on their politics. He had a secure job, as a scholar and teacher at Christ Church, his old college, in whose politics and administration he would soon become a leading force, though never in his career did he spend an unnecessary minute on bureaucracy. The world saw the confident part of him, and in convivial company he showed the effervescent one. He would surround his life, and its contentious episodes, with a wealth of anecdote, which, in indiscreet monologues and letters, he related and embroidered with exquisite artistry. He exulted in *la comédie humaine*, in his love of battle and of controversy, and in the zest of his writing and talk. His unsparing rationality seemed—as he liked it to do—to be in control of his life and circumstances, so much so that even his friends mistakenly doubted his inclination or capacity for the passions and intimacies that defy reason's reach. Outwardly he was an imposing, often intimidating figure, resolute, fearlessly and at times mercilessly articulate, and ever ready to pass epigrammatic judgements, intellectual, moral and social, that came near to meriting a Boswell. He could be cold and disdainful. It was sympathetic observers who remarked on his 'penetrating and disapproving stares'—perhaps a maternal inheritance—or noticed, when some trivial or unwelcome point was put to him, 'the Trevor-Roper gesture of dismissal, that flap of the right hand'. He drew back from displays of weakness or softness in others. Yet on the rare occasions when the mask slipped—as when he surprised his stepchildren by breaking down while reading Turgenev to them—he would be paralysed by tears.

Fearful of being a burden to others, and perhaps of attracting their pity, he mostly kept to himself the depressions to which he would always be vulnerable. None of his letters seem more buoyant than the ones, published in 2006 as *Letters from Oxford*, that he wrote to Berenson between 1947 and 1959. Yet mid-way through that correspondence, and around the time of his fortieth birthday, he revealed in other letters, written to Xandra Howard-Johnston, Earl Haig's daughter, who would soon be his wife, the unhappiness into which, from high spirits, his mood would swing. Plagued by a sense of his own oddness and awkwardness, he felt blighted by his difficulty in making emotional contacts and by his involuntary retreats from the expression or reception of private feeling. He endured the kind of loneliness that is most oppressive not in solitude but in company. Though as a rule he loved cultivated landscape and disliked barren wastes, he went three times in the post-war years to walk in the desolate wilds of Iceland, where for days he would not meet a soul. Yet from that remote land he would write, to his friends in England, letters bursting with *joie de vivre*.

He had no small talk. Alert to falsity of mood or sentiment, and impatient of the second-hand opinion on which society feeds, he had no aptitude for feigning interest in platitudinous civilities, a deficiency which he keenly felt and which inhibited his relations even with the wide range of people he admired. He was more at ease in his compulsive letter-writing, where sentences could be formed at his own pace and human contact be essayed within protective limits. He was ebullient in relaxed company, but on his own terms. If he ever found equality in friendships, it was in the earlier part of his life, among his companions in his student years and in the war, or, in the decade or so after the war, in his comradeship with the historians Robert Blake and Charles Stuart at Christ Church. Yet, spirited as those relationships were, he was more intensely drawn to inherently unequal relations with older men, especially Pearsall Smith and Berenson. Later he would be drawn to inherently unequal relations with younger ones. Even the people who knew him best experienced uncomfortable silences. A colleague compared talking to him at a party with putting money into one of those machines that occasionally disgorge a mass of coins to a lucky player: one conversational gambit after another would fail, until the interlocutor hit on a subject that would bring Hugh's face to life and prompt his gifts of anecdote and maxim. When he was Regius Professor, visitors to his office in Merton Street were placed in a chair facing the back of his desk while he slowly paced the room, hands behind his back, chin raised in lordly posture, invisibly craving, if he liked the visitor, the contact that his own manner deterred.

The difficulties of conversation were heightened by his distaste for slovenly or poorly enunciated speech. He disliked losing his syntactical way, for ideally, he believed, there should be no difference between the written and the spoken word. He hated the misuse of language, especially obscurity and murkiness of expression, which, in the ideological convulsions of his own time, had had such 'tremendous consequences'. Freddie Ayer's *Language, Truth and Logic*, published in 1936, made a profound impression on him, and he got his undergraduate pupils to read George Orwell's antidote to argumentative dishonesty, the essay 'Politics and the English Language'. Behind that concern lay Hugh's classical training. 'At the back of my mind', he wrote to a friend, 'I see every sentence as demanding to be put into Latin. If it cannot be put into Latin, I know that it is, at best, obscure, at worst, nonsense.' In his reading he had a special affection for the classical orderliness and transparency of Dryden, and was most at home in the most classical of centuries, the eighteenth, the age of his heroes Hume—the person from the past, he once suggested, whom he would most have liked to know—and Gibbon, Hugh's model historian. Yet here too there were depths and complications, for alongside his classical inclinations lay more individual, and sometimes still keener, literary preferences. They drew him to styles of wrought intensity and exoticism; to the baroque and metaphysical intricacies of the seventeenth century; to 'the trinity of my stylistic devotion', Sir Thomas Browne, C. M. Doughty and George Moore; to the wild or grotesque comic fantasies of Cervantes and Carroll and Gogol and Bulgakov.

There was no want of orderliness in his own working habits. No historian of his own century, at least in his own country, surpassed him in swiftness and sharpness of perception. He could grasp the essence of a document with lightning speed, his eyes shining with concentration. Yet he was the most meditative of readers. He patiently took notes even on books which, in periods of the truancy that he judged essential to vitality of mind and to a sense of intellectual perspective, took him far in time and place from the subjects and commitments that crowded upon him. To ponder the lessons of a book that interested him he would make an index of its suggestive matter, or write an essay for his own eyes. He wrote his own publications, as he would always lament, 'painfully slowly'. Since he seems to have composed most of *The Last Days of Hitler* in less than a month, 'in the evenings', during his first term as an Oxford tutor, we might wonder what he imagined fast writing to be. Yet his prose was never hurried, never snatched from its hinterland of rumination. If the command and polish of his writing suggest ease of composition, the appearance is misleading. It gives no hint of his struggles for lucidity, for the imposition of form, for assurance of judgement.

The inside of a writer's head at the moment of composition is beyond historical recovery. Whence came Hugh's distinctive blend of poise and nervous energy? By what processes did his habits of mental discipline bridle and channel his restlessness of soul? Sometimes the restlessness seems an evasion of stillness, even perhaps of the pain that might be confronted in it. He was always drawn to motion, and with it to evanescence: to the changes of season, and to dayspring and dusk rather than 'the obvious noonday'. Shakespeare's lines, 'everything that grows | Holds in perfection but a little moment', were ever in his head. Then there are Hugh's recurrent aquatic metaphors, which commend fluidity and condemn stagnation. In his innumerable battles—with the historians Lawrence Stone and A. J. P. Taylor and Arnold Toynbee and E. H. Carr over their use of evidence or of language or over their argumentative premises; with the Catholics and Communists who, between them, occupied a place in the intellectual landscape of the post-war decades that is now hard to recall; over the Warren Commission's report on the assassination of President Kennedy; with some of the Fellows of Peterhouse, the Cambridge college of which he became Master in 1980; and a legion more—there was always an intellectual or moral purpose. Yet there was also the impulse to stir. Many of his campaigns assailed the comfort and complacency of closed or static institutions or systems of ideas. Delighted to give provocation, he himself was dependent on the stimulus of it. The errors of

Lawrence Stone's article of 1948 on the economic condition of the Elizabethan aristocracy led not merely to Hugh's comprehensive and pitiless (though not, as is commonly said, vituperative) assault on its statistical foundations in the *Economic History Review* in 1951, but to the rival interpretation advanced in his longer essay on the gentry two years later. Without Eric Hobsbawm's Marxist analysis of the revolts of mid-seventeenth-century Europe there would not have been Hugh's essay in *Past and Present* in 1959 on the 'General Crisis of the Seventeenth Century'. Without his exasperation at the insular conception of the subject among Scottish historians he might have made no study of that country's Enlightenment.

Combat upheld his spirits. During the post-war era they needed upholding. In the damp Oxford climate, especially in the torpor of the vacations, he would be crushed by lassitude and exhaustion. Sapped of the energy and morale on which his writing depended, he would ponder his unwritten and unfinished books and his want of fulfilment. Nothing of his dismay entered his writing of that time. His essays of 1951–3 on the aristocracy and gentry seem to exude self-esteem. So do the sparklingly didactic book reviews, written from the late 1940s and taking all history for their province, from which he gathered his *Historical Essays* in 1957. Beneath their brief, swift surfaces there lies a bewildering range of reading and reflection. Yet they scarcely satisfied him. He wanted to write books.

*

By the late 1940s he had found a new theme for one, Oliver Cromwell and the Puritan Revolution. He gave courses of lectures on the subject, a medium he would often use to shape books or potential books in his mind. But the idea was sidelined for some years. First, in 1951–2, there were his duties as Senior Censor at Christ Church, which were enlarged by the absence of the Dean as the university's Vice-Chancellor. Then came a series of other literary projects. Together with the account of the Catholic revival there was a more ambitious undertaking, which had formed in his mind by mid-1953. It would, he told Berenson, be 'a major work', of which his essay on the gentry was 'in part a sample or prefiguration', on Robert Cecil, first Earl of Salisbury, the leading royal adviser of the late years of Elizabeth I and the early ones of James I, a study 'which (I believe) may explain a hitherto unexplained set of problems in English history'. The problems, it is safe to guess, were ones which he was to explore in other works, finished and unfinished, in the years to come: those of the tensions between the swelling and parasitic Renaissance state, 'the court', and the taxpayers, 'the country', who bore the burden of it. Yet the book seems not to have been begun. Its place was taken by a long work, which did get going, on Max Weber's thesis on capitalism and the Reformation. Displacement had become a habit. Even as he wrestled with Weber, writing and tearing up successive drafts, fresh subjects were bubbling in his mind. He planned to revisit, during a period of sabbatical leave, the era of the proposed book on the Earl of Salisbury and to write on the succession problem in late Elizabethan England. Then, in 1956, he applied to give the Ford's Lectures at Oxford (for at that time the position was advertised), taking as his subject Anglo-Spanish relations from 1604 to 1660. He was thwarted by the opposition of Vivian Galbraith, whom he would succeed as Regius Professor the following year. Hugh's reflections on Protestantism and capitalism were eventually condensed into the essay that gave the title to his volume of essays *Religion, The Reformation and Social Change*, but there was still no book.

That omission was much remarked on, not least during the months of public speculation about the succession to Galbraith. In the public mind the leading contenders for the Regius chair were Hugh and A. J. P. Taylor, though the Prime Minister, Harold Macmillan, first offered it to the eighteenth-century historian Lucy Sutherland. Hugh felt Taylor's claims to be stronger than his own. The two men had been allies, even fellow *enfants terribles*, against the establishment of Oxford's history faculty. For all their differences of character and principle, they shared a breadth and incisiveness of historical outlook, an eagerness to communicate it beyond the academic world, and, albeit in contrasting forms, a mastery of literary style. Taylor was aggrieved by Hugh's appointment to the Regius chair, and in 1961 the two men would do battle over Taylor's book *The Origins of the Second World War*, a work which offended Hugh's conception of the responsibility of historians to their evidence and which permanently dented his respect for its author. Yet with time Taylor showed great magnanimity. After the breach, as before it, there was no more generous an admirer of Hugh's writings.

Early in 1957, the year that would see his translation to the chair, Hugh returned to the Puritan Revolution. In 1954–5 he had written, with a facility he thought he had lost, his essay 'Oliver Cromwell and his Parliaments' (published in *Essays in honour of Sir Lewis Namier*, edited by Taylor and by Richard Pares in 1956), but only now was the larger project resumed. By December 1957, at the end of his first term as Regius, he was 'desperately trying to write what I know will be a very long book', which 'weighs heavily on my conscience'. Publishers, eyeing the tercentenary of Cromwell's death in 1958, had wanted him to write a biography of him, a financial opportunity to which Hugh, who often lived beyond his means, was not averse. Yet he found it easier to sign potentially lucrative contracts than, when it came to the writing, to set scholarly seriousness aside for them. The claims of 'this piddling anniversary' made way for a larger study, which would relate the course of the revolution to its social and political origins from the late sixteenth century. Again there was a great deal of rewriting. For a time he envisaged three volumes, to amount to about 300,000 words. The first of them, which was to trace the origins of the wars and to be called *The Crumbling of the Monarchy*, would be the longest. Initially he expected it to be about 100,000 words, but it gradually grew, for the work for that first volume was the heart of the project. In what he for a time expected to be more or less its final form, the account of the origins of the war, and of the events of 1640–2, amounts to around 200,000 words. By contrast his plans for the years after 1642 contracted. Drafts survive of his writing on that period, though it is hard to tell at what stage of the project they were written. In length they would have warranted a second volume but not a third. By early 1961 he had resolved to treat those years much more briefly, in about 30,000 words, which would constitute the last of six parts of what he now expected to appear as a single, long volume, provisionally to be called either *The Crisis of English Government 1640–1642* or *Reform or Revolution? 1640–1643*.

Yet no subject, even one on which he was so intensively engaged, could monopolise his attention or restrict his curiosity. Somehow, even as he struggled with the Puritan Revolution, he found time for other learned writing. In 1959 there appeared his essay 'The General Crisis of the Seventeenth Century', a work of dazzling range and startling interpretative ambition which at last gave Oxford a leading voice in the European historiography of the period. It appeared in *Past and Present*, where it stimulated an amicable and distinguished debate. The essay projected on to Continental history, to which he had not hitherto given prolonged attention, the thesis of a conflict between 'court and country' that also supplies the connecting argument of the attempted book on the Puritan Revolution. Together with his essay on the Weber thesis, which complemented it in his mind, the piece on 'The General Crisis' shifted attention away from the economic creativity which Weber and others had detected in Protestantism, towards the economically inhibiting bureaucracies of the Renaissance state. Royal courts, Hugh argued, had provoked not only material grievances but moral and political dissent and, eventually, the revolutions that swept through the Continent, as through Britain, in mid-century.

Thus in England, as he concluded in his projected book on the Puritan Revolution, 'the machinery of government . . . had become a social and economic burden both on the country and the crown: a burden so heavy that the country sought desperately to reduce it, so wasteful that the crown could no longer sustain it unchanged'. In February 1961 he sent the typescript of the book, in its single-volume form, to the young historian John Elliott, whose shrewd criticisms brought home to him the need for surgery. Hugh worked anxiously on the project again that summer and autumn, adding or restoring extensive material on the post-1642 period. That is the last we hear of the writing. Much of the book, as of his work on Weber, was condensed into fertile essays. There was the classic study 'Three Foreigners and the Puritan Revolution' (1961), which was followed by 'Scotland and the Puritan Revolution' (1963) and 'The Fast Sermons of the Long Parliament' (1964). His emphases, in the book or the essays or in both, on the circle of the social reformer Samuel Hartlib; on the British dimension of England's civil wars; on the role of the politics of the city of London; on the provincial horizons of the lesser gentry; on the parliamentary leadership supplied by the peerage: all those themes either influenced or foreshadowed research by others, that massive enterprise which had been set in motion by the gentry controversy and which would gradually devour the hypotheses that had generated it. Yet he was tormented for some years by his failure to publish the book. What had gone wrong?

The problem of which he was most conscious was one of form. There were, at that time, two ways of writing about the Puritan Revolution. There was the tradition of narrative, which was ably and engagingly represented by C. V. Wedgwood's books of 1954 and 1958, *The King's Peace* and *The King's War*, but which lacked the analytical and sociological dimensions for which Hugh strove; and there were the approaches of R. H. Tawney and Stone and Christopher Hill, which were indeed analytical and sociological, but which, treating events as the logical outcome of long-term social and economic developments, barely paused to describe them. Determinism—in either its hard or its soft forms—affronted Hugh morally, by eliminating the freedom of the will and the responsibilities it brings. It affronted him intellectually, by its insensitivity both to the dependence of the course of events on political decision-making and to those pressures of mood and circumstance under which the decisions are taken. For there was, he maintained, nothing inevitable about the revolution or about its course. The parliamentary leaders were not revolutionary in their aims, but conservative. In church, state and society they looked backward, to an idealised image of the reign of Queen Elizabeth. There was indeed a crisis in 1640–1, born of deep-seated social grievances, the grievances of 'the country', which had grown up over half a century and which Hugh's book explored. Yet the crisis, he maintained, could have been resolved by the reforms and projected reforms of the early phases of the Long Parliament. What happened after the summer of 1641—the drift to war, the struggle for victory, the destruction of the constitution, military and sectarian rule—was not a logical consequence of earlier long-term developments. It was the outcome of the decisions and qualities of politicians and of chance and personality. Revolution, once launched by those forces, bred its own momentum. A struggle for reform and settlement became one for sovereignty. Those claims, which to many historians would now seem barely contentious, boldly confronted an orthodoxy of the time. To substantiate them he needed to write a narrative that would reveal the separate stages of the movement towards civil war and convey the pressures under which the politicians acted. He had to find a way of doing what no one else was attempting: of bringing analysis and narrative together.

It looks as if Hugh, when he intended to carry the story into the post-war years, planned to take it up to the death of Oliver Cromwell in 1658. In drafting the later parts of that project, he confronted two problems, one of scale, the other of sympathy. Was he attempting a rounded narrative of the revolution, akin to those written on seventeenth-century history by Macaulay and S. R. Gardiner? Or was the material on the years after 1642 essentially an extended epilogue to the account of the earlier years, one intended to bear out, by an examination of the course of the revolution, his analysis of its causes? The drafts on the period 1642–58 fall between those stools. Besides, his heart was not quite in them. Other historians, making an equation, one to which he was always resistant, between revolution and progress, portrayed the civil wars as a cause or symptom of an advance towards the modern world. To Hugh they were mostly a series of 'blind ends and wearisome repetitions', the product not of enlightenment but of fanaticism. He sympathised with the aristocratic reformers of the early stages of the revolution. In the Earl of Bedford he found something like a hero. From his parliamentary base the earl had tried to address the structural and financial problems of the monarchy which, under James I, the Earl of Salisbury, the focus of Hugh's earlier project for a major work, had attempted to solve from his base in high office. But the essentially constructive movement of reform led by the nobility had thereafter yielded to 'the grim, repellent, joyless face of militant, middle-class English Puritanism' and to the hideous and needless destruction that it wrought.

In the form in which he sent it to John Elliott, the book was essentially on the causes, long-term and immediate, of the civil war. It could easily have been published more or less as it then stood. Had it been, it would have been likely to earn, alongside some professional hostility and scepticism, wide acclaim both inside and outside the academic world. Its combination of narrative power and analytical sophistication is what the study of the Puritan Revolution has lacked over the succeeding half century, when the story-tellers and the academic specialists have gone separate ways. Yet the text, full as it was of luminous insights, had limitations, which would have looked increasingly significant with time, and of which, we may guess, he was at least partly aware. The writing is over-rhetorical and has more brilliance than depth. The content, which might have worked as part of a grand, evenly paced narrative of the whole revolution, lacks a sense of roundedness. That is partly because the thesis of 'court and country' provides too restricted an explanatory foundation for both the constitutional and the religious demands of 1640–2; and partly because the narrative, which strains to catch the epic quality of the events of those years, commands too small a range both of evidence and of sympathy. From a more recent perspective, the text seems, in its inspection of the social and economic origins of the war, to have more in common with the works it opposed than with later writing on the period. It is no less distant from subsequent interpretation in the scale of its argument and the breadth of its vision.

*

There had now been at least five uncompleted books, and there would be at least five more. Yet the demise of the work on the Puritan upheaval, far from defeating him, was followed by a period of astounding productivity and versatility. There survives from 1963 a notebook in which we can sense him taking stock. In place of the self-consciousness and the stylistic experiments of the earlier, wartime notebooks we now find mature and deepening historical reflection. He gives the impression, after his long immersion in Puritan fanaticism, of coming up for air. He was also moving away from economic explanation to the history of ideas. In themselves, economic documents had ceased to have much interest for him by the time he published *The Gentry* in 1953. The book on the Puritan Revolution had itself rested on, rather than developed, the economic conclusions he had reached in that essay, and the same would have been true of the projected book on Salisbury. By 1963 it was intellectual history—a dimension of the past to which he now regretted having given too little space in his essay on 'The General Crisis'—that commanded his enthusiasm. A new subject was beckoning him, the Enlightenment of the eighteenth century. In 1965 he made the historiography of the Enlightenment the subject of his Trevelyan Lectures at Cambridge, which in the following year he tried unavailingly to find time to get into book form. Also in 1965 there appeared *The Rise of Christian Europe*, the televised lectures he had given at the University of Sussex two years earlier. They gave scope to his enthusiasm, which went back to his teenage years, for medieval history, to which he now brought the boldest, though to many medievalists not the most palatable, of his exercises in broad synthesis. After that diversion he returned to historiography, extending his enquiries back from the eighteenth century to the sixteenth, as, later, he would carry them into the nineteenth. In 1965 he worked on the Elizabethan historian William Camden, who would be the subject of his Neale Lecture six years later (which in turn would be reprinted in his *Renaissance Essays* of 1987). In 1966 came his long essay on Camden's Scottish contemporary George Buchanan (published as a supplement to the *English Historical Review*), and the reflections on Sir Walter Ralegh, and Ralegh's *History of the World*, that were contained in a long review (in *History and Theory*) of Christopher Hill's *The Intellectual Origins of the English Revolution*. 'A whole book', Hugh had ominously written in his work on the civil wars, 'could be written on the cult of Sir Walter Ralegh in the 1620s and 1630s', and he seems to have thought of writing it. In 1967 there followed (in the series of *Studies on Voltaire and the Eighteenth Century*) his seminal essay on the Scottish Enlightenment, which—as is emphasised in the shrewd assessment of its impact by Colin Kidd in the *Scottish Historical Review* for 2005—placed its subject on a map of European rather than merely native history.

Yet those manifold pursuits were not, in that period, his only or even his principal ones. Even among them he produced his account, the length of a short book, of the witch-craze of the sixteenth and seventeenth centuries, a work that pleased him more than any since *The Last Days of Hitler*. It was written to round out the collection of long essays of 1967, *Religion, The Reformation and Social Change* (in the wake of which he was elected in 1969, at the age of 55, a Fellow of the British Academy: a conspicuously late appointment, though he was not one to covet academic honours). In that book, too, there was published his essay 'The Religious Origins of the Enlightenment', perhaps the highest achievement of a volume that shows him at the peak of his powers. It applied to intellectual history the preoccupation with the relationship of Protestantism to progress that his work on the Weber thesis had brought to economic history. Developing a theme he had explored in an essay on Erasmus in 1954 (subsequently republished in his *Historical Essays*), he insisted that the intellectual advances of and after the Renaissance were to be traced, not to ideology or dogma, but to a tradition of tolerant scepticism that rose above them. He would return to that argument in a number of later essays, as he would in the Wiles Lectures that he gave at Belfast in 1975 on 'The Ecumenical Movement and the Church of England, 1598–1618'. It was a condition of the Wiles Lectures that the lecturer should make a book of them and be paid his fee only once the book was written. Yet that inducement could not extract a finished text from him.

The productivity which marks the years 1965–7 scarcely abated over the succeeding three years. If anything the fare becomes more varied still. He now wrote the most searching of his essays on Macaulay (published in 1968, and subsequently reprinted as the introduction to Penguin's abbreviated edition of Macaulay's *History of England*), a historian on whom, as on Gibbon, he often wrote; his published lecture *The Romantic Movement and the Study of History* (1968); a reflective piece *The Past and the Present*, delivered as a lecture in tense circumstances at the London School of Economics amid insurrectionary students whose principles it did not flatter (and republished in the journal *Past and Present* in 1969); his short book *The Philby Affair* (1969); the pseudonymous commentaries, modelled on the prose of John Aubrey, on Oxford life during the same disturbances, which appeared in brief book form as *The Letters of Mercurius* (1970); and another published lecture *The Plunder of the Arts in the Seventeenth Century* (1970). The last gave voice to a theme that, through the inspiration of Jacob Burckhardt and Émile Mâle and Bernard Berenson, had long attracted him, the relationship of the art of the Renaissance to the social and political circumstances of its production. The preoccupation runs from his essay on Rubens in 1954 to his book of 1976, again the product of lectures, *Princes and Artists*.

By 1970 yet another large project was under way: his study of Sir Theodore Mayerne. Mayerne brought many of Hugh's interests together: the Calvinist International, to which the physician belonged; the relationship between English and Continental history; art history; medical history; and, behind medicine, the cosmological systems within which its practitioners had placed it. The book also returned to a theme of his collected essays of 1967: the end of the Renaissance and the break-up, in the 1620s, of its intellectual assumptions. Even to conceive of the book was a feat of courageous originality. Mayerne had been known only to specialists. In the broader patterns of his life, which they had missed, Hugh saw a means to capture the spirit and experience of a whole age. The archival evidence, in numerous countries and languages, presented severe challenges. Only in 1994 would he give up hope of finding Mayerne's personal papers, which, had they turned up, might have transformed the subject he was having to undertake without them. Mayerne's medical papers, on the other hand, survive in abundance. Hugh worked through them in 1971–2 and found that 'the subject widens at every touch'. By early 1973, however, the book was 'at a standstill'. As usual, other commitments, this time the Wiles Lectures and *Princes and Artists* among them, crowded upon him. 'My general philosophy, the more you do, the more you do', he blackly reflected, had reached 'a point of self-cancellation'.

It was in that burdened state that he took on yet another fresh adventure, which he knew to be a diversion but could not resist. This was his study of Sir Edmund Backhouse, the fraud and fantasist of early twentieth-century Peking, whose unpublished memoirs came into his hands in 1973, and whose biography he would publish in 1976 as *A Hidden Life* (or, in another edition, *The Hermit of Peking*). Never were his spirits more elated than in his discovery of the farcical yet triumphant deceptions of Backhouse's life, and of his preference for fantasy over fact, a human trait more widespread, Hugh decided, than is generally recognised. In principle Hugh had doubts about biography as a form, for 'you have to do the flats'. Yet a high proportion of his writings, most conspicuously those on Laud, Hitler, Backhouse and Mayerne, centred on individual lives.

In 1977 he had a further project in mind. He gave a series of polished lectures in the United States on history and historical philosophy, from Chinese and classical writing through to modern times, and wanted to make a book of them. But by 1978, when 'I have so many books to finish', he had returned to Mayerne. Most of the book, which would be posthumously published with the title *Europe's Physician* (2006), had been written by the end of 1978. In its depth, and in the variegation of its texture, it is the most substantial of his works. A more equable tone, one that drew less attention to its author's cleverness, had entered his writing. Yet the book stalled for a second time. Even with the end in sight, 'gloomy thoughts rise in my mind as I contemplate this bulk of paper. Is it worth it?' His attention was turning, we cannot be surprised to learn, to still another subject. This one, too, grew out of a lecture-series. If the theme of the Backhouse book had been the power of fantasy, that of his new study was the power of myth, which, as he had observed in *The Last Days of Hitler*, 'is a far more common characteristic of the human race . . . than veracity'. Now he tackled the mythopoeic tendencies of the Scots, a nation he had always viewed with a certain Northumbrian disdain. His opinion had not been improved since his and Xandra's purchase in 1959 of an elegant early nineteenth-century house, once the residence of Sir Walter Scott, across the border at Melrose, where, until Hugh's retirement from Peterhouse in 1987, when they sold the property, they would spend the greater part of the university vacations. The theme of the book is the obstinate readiness of the Scots to prefer fictitious accounts of their past to true ones. The work explored first the Scots' invention, during the later Middle Ages and the Renaissance, of an ancient free constitution; then the manufacture of the poetry of Ossian in the eighteenth century; and finally the fabrication, in the nineteenth century, of the traditions of the kilt and the tartan.

Need one add that that project, too, was suspended? Two events diverted him. First came his elevation to the peerage, as Lord Dacre of Glanton, in 1979 and the comedy of an intricate heraldic contest, which he savoured to the full, over his choice of the 'ancient, musical, romantic' title of Dacre, which members of the Roper family had briefly held in earlier generations. Then, in 1980, he began his seven contentious years as Master of Peterhouse, Cambridge, a reign that is penetratingly recounted, with an interlinear delicacy that he would himself have relished, in the *Peterhouse Annual Record* for 2002–3. He challenged what he saw as an introverted oligarchy among the Fellows, which was accustomed to running the college while a weak Master and the rest of the dons looked on or away. He found supporters among the wider Fellowship—especially its distinguished scientists—who welcomed his efforts to bring more intellectual life and breadth to the college. But the tenacious resistance to him, though eventually it was worn down, produced acidic and widely reported trials of strength. His opponents had been his kingmakers, who in choosing him had hoped for a *roi fainéant*. Perhaps the commitment he brought to his reign surprised him too, for always a side of Hugh yearned for the imagined bliss of writing in undisturbed tranquillity. He could have acquired such leisure merely by seeing out his term as Regius Professor at Oxford and retiring in 1981. When problems mounted at Peterhouse he sighed to remember how, just after he had accepted the position, he had been offered a grand, undemanding, lucrative post at the European University in Florence. Yet we can be sure that that institution would have been no less vulnerable than Peterhouse to his reforming instincts.

The book on Scotland, which is due to be published in 2008 by Yale University Press as *The Invention of Scotland: Myth and History*, came as close as any of his unfinished works to completion. It has been wondered whether it was the affair of the Hitler diaries in 1983, the fabrication of which he failed to detect, that brought the project to a close. In reality he had already dropped the book by 1982, and was by then thinking in yet other directions. He was planning further volumes of collected essays, for which he intended to revise some writings and add fresh ones. Among the latter would have been a long piece (which is also to be published posthumously, in a volume of essays, due from Yale University Press in 2009 as *History and Enlightenment*, on eighteenth- and nineteenth-century historiography and its intellectual background) on Conyers Middleton and eighteenth-century deism, the subject of his Leslie Stephen lecture at Cambridge in 1982. Nonetheless the episode of the Hitler diaries shook and distressed him. He knew that, on that fateful afternoon in a Swiss bank vault when the forged documents were shown to him, he had yielded not only to the rational arguments for their authenticity, which, on the evidence then available to him, were reputable enough, but more decisively to an 'irrational' impulse which afterwards he could not comprehend. When, ten years earlier, he had been handed the manuscript memoirs of Sir Edmund Backhouse, he had at first taken the authenticity of their narrative, which at that time no one had cause to doubt, for granted. He penetrated the fraud only after weeks of thought and investigation. This time he allowed himself to be bounced into an instant verdict. He went to Zurich, on behalf of *The Times* of which he was an Independent Director, under-prepared and in a sceptical and grudging frame of mind which brought out the loftiness in him. Perhaps he relied too heavily on a sureness of instinct that, by his seventieth year, had begun to falter. He had been spending the Easter vacation at Melrose, distancing the cares of the world, and especially of Peterhouse, by truant reading, his mind far from Hitler. He returned to that seclusion after the journey to Switzerland, and seems to have thought little about the diaries during the ten days or so before his reluctant return south, when there began the rapid sequence of events that led to his public validation of the documents.

The episode, a media event, would occupy a grossly disproportionate place in public perceptions of him, as it would in the headlines that announced his death. Nonetheless it had a dimension of dramatic tragedy. 'Pride', he had observed in 1941, 'is my chief fault, and will be my undoing.' Now, with symmetrical irony, that flaw mocked his greatness. He had made his name by his detective-work on Hitler, and the exposure of fraud had been a *motif* of his life and writing. The public sensation over the diaries occurred at the exact time of year, in late April, of the decisive events in the Führer's bunker that he had magisterially reconstructed in *The Last Days*. The remorselessness of misfortune, which declared itself in accidents of circumstance and timing, reached its climax during a performance of *Don Carlos* at Covent Garden, when his conclusions about the diaries gradually dissolved in his mind. He remained trapped in his seat while his authenticating article rolled from the press.

He recovered from the episode, for he did not lack resilience. Soon the collected essays, which were intended to appear, in chronological sequence, in five volumes, were under way, though he would complete only three, which reached the early eighteenth century. Two were essentially collections of previously published essays, fuller and deeper than the *Historical Essays* of 1957, which had been mostly book reviews, but scarcely less remarkable in their range: *Renaissance Essays* (1985) and *From Counter-Reformation to Glorious Revolution* (1992). By contrast the third volume, *Catholics, Anglicans and Puritans* (1987), consisting of five fresh long essays, amounted to a new book. Having earlier moved from English to Continental history, he here concentrated on English intellectual and religious history between the accession of James I and the restoration of Charles II. The most striking contribution, on the intellectual circle that met at Lord Falkland's house at Great Tew in Oxfordshire in the 1630s, resumed his exploration of the Erasmian tradition.

In the year of the book's publication, the Dacres moved, on Hugh's retirement, to a Victorian rectory at Didcot, south of Oxford, a handsome house in an unhandsome town. At Cambridge, Xandra's aesthetic sense had brought interior elegance to the Master's Lodgings in Peterhouse, a fine Queen Anne house, and she had found a role for herself in the sponsorship and encouragement of music, a world in which she had high connections. She was less fond of Oxford, where Hugh would have liked to return. The convenience of access to London and Oxford by train persuaded them to settle on the apparently incongruous setting of Didcot, the Thebes of the Thames Valley as he called it after he had formed cultivated friendship in nearby Long Wittenham, which he correspondingly termed its Athens.

Old age brought him disproportionate wretchedness. Xandra, who was seven years his senior and to whom he was devoted, contracted Alzheimer's Disease and died with her mind lost to the world and to him. He himself developed cancer, which took distressing forms and would eventually claim his life. Depression, which over the years had become less frequent but which was never far away, returned. Yet he had impregnable stoicism. He brightened—now as always—when visited by friends, from whom he concealed the extent of his afflictions. He drew heart from the frequent company and the practical assistance of his stepchildren James—himself an Oxford historian—and Xenia (their younger brother Peter living far away). When Hugh succumbed to Charles Bonnet Syndrome, a rare eye condition that induces frightening hallucinations, he would describe its symptoms with the urbane humour that—now as always—seemed to put the difficulties of life in their place. His mental energy and discipline rose to the challenges of near-blindness, among them the increasing dependence of his writing and lecturing on his powers of memory. He had plans for new projects and worked on unfinished ones. Writing a short life of Thomas Sutton for the *Oxford Dictionary of National Biography*, he revisited his faded notes from half a century earlier and struggled, far beyond the demands of the commission, to reconstruct his subject's complex finances. In the last year of his life, aged 88, he published, in a collection edited by David Stafford on Rudolf Hess entitled *Flight from Reality*, a vintage essay on Hess's flight to England, a study he somehow brought together from drafts which had inevitably got muddled with each other and with the bills and circulars and letters that piled around him. Having defiantly remained at home until the last weeks, he died in the Sobell House hospice in Oxford on 26 January 2003.

*

Who would categorise his writing, or place it in a school of thought? He has, it is true, often been called both a Whig and a Tory historian, a distinction he shares, perhaps fittingly, with Hume. There is truth in both descriptions, provided we do not take the first to imply generous illusions about the motives of Whig politicians and writers, or the second a liking for the Establishment, with the complacent side of which he was often at odds. Not many Tories make donations to *Private Eye*, as he did when its survival was imperilled by a lawsuit. He was a Whig insofar as he believed in a plural, liberal society, in constitutional checks and balances, and in social counterweights to centres of power. He believed that there had been advances, however uneven, in civility and freedom between the seventeenth century and the nineteenth, and that they mattered. He disliked authoritarian or absolute power, and thought it had been a real threat in seventeenth-century England. The word Whig has acquired some wide meanings. He was a Whig if one means by Whiggism, as many now apparently do, a commitment to the study of developments over time. By the same token he was a Whig if it is Whiggish to deny that historical investigation can or should be value-free, or to reject the supposition that scholarship, to be objective, must be separated from the concerns of citizenship. He was a Tory insofar as he recognised the power of traditional institutions, if they are kept up to the mark, to channel constructive human characteristics and restrain destructive ones. His unfinished work on the Puritan Revolution is in the spirit of Clarendon's *History of the Rebellion*, but not of the uncritical and reactionary Toryism which has sometimes drawn support from that work. Hugh took the Tory whip in the House of Lords, but was ready to defy it, especially in the party's ideological moods (though he was neither a confident nor a frequent speaker in the upper house). Toryism, to his mind, had never had an ideology and did not need one.

Neither the Whig nor the Tory label, nor any other, captures his idiosyncratic essence. In everything he was his own man. The historians of his own time whom he most admired were not the panjandrums of the academic community but figures eccentric to it, whom he discovered for himself: above all Gerald Brenan and Frances Yates, neither of whom had been trained as a historian. On other fronts, too, he stood outside or against the movements of his time. 'I like a various world', he wrote in 1967, 'full of social, political, intellectual differences. . . . Must we have an identical pattern of thought and behaviour, of food, habits, speech, political totems, value-judgements, cant, from China to Peru?' Or as he remarked six years later, 'As institutions, free-trade areas, units of government, become larger, reform becomes ever more difficult because there is an ever-growing bureaucracy with a built-in tendency to inertia, mediocrity, conformism, dullness. Only small institutions can be turned round.'

His historical writing likewise rowed against the tide. He defied the advance of professional specialisation, which induces the progressive contraction of horizons, and which strips history of that comparative dimension without which it cannot yield general lessons. Prolonged concentration on a single era, he maintained, can accumulate knowledge but not wisdom, can refine understanding but not transform it. He was not drawn to the notion of mastering a field, or of pushing understanding to the very limits of the evidence. Yet there were tensions in his thinking, for scholarship itself he revered. He applauded it when he could, despised betrayals of it, and believed that the intensive practice of it in recent times had raised standards. He also saw, as in the work of Frances Yates, that fertile broad hypotheses can arise from the close and single-minded inspection of detail. A second argument against specialisation was that it cuts historians off from the laity, whose outlooks and choices it is the function of a humane subject to inform, and who, if deprived of that guidance, are liable to turn instead to historical writing, even to historical ideologies, which break free of scholarship and thus of truth. Historians, he enjoined, should study problems, not periods. To divide the past into regions of time, or to separate any branch of history—political, economic, intellectual, cultural—from the tree, was to court introspection, pedantry, antiquarianism. There was a further danger of specialisation of period. It isolated the past from the present, which—at least from the early 1940s, when he felt himself to be living through Europe's Peloponnesian War—he instinctively saw in historical terms. In analysing any contemporary problem his first instinct was to set it within a historical framework that took the reader beyond the narrow perspectives of the present. His mind lived at least as much outside his own time as within it.

He knew, of course, that historical parallels are always partial and imperfect and can be misleading. He never over-pressed them. Nonetheless his inclinations were with the sociologically minded 'philosophic historians' of the eighteenth century, whose premises met most of his own philosophical requirements. Like Gibbon he roamed the past for analogies, and for contrasts, that would illuminate one age by the light of others, the art which specialisation gainsays. In answering the claim of Tawney and Stone that the economic transformations of the sixteenth century had produced the rise of the gentry at the aristocracy's expense, he noticed in passing that the phenomenon, if true, would have been a historical exception. For 'who survived better the economic crisis of the Roman Empire, the great magnates or the small landowners? Who weathered the crisis of the fourteenth century better, the great landlords or the gentry? Whose economic condition proved stronger in sixteenth-century Spain, the nobles or the *hidalgos*?' A Gibbon, presented with the same phenomenon, would have asked such questions automatically: to Hugh's adversaries they had not occurred. Or, through a comparison between the political calculations that produced the renewal of European war in 1621 and the manoeuvres that provoked war in 1914, he would turn a study of the early seventeenth century into an investigation of the general question, 'Why do great wars break out?' Comparisons between the seventeenth century, which he had studied before the Second World War, and the twentieth, whose darkest period came during it, recur through his writing. His mind dwelled on parallels between the ferocity of Calvinism, or its appeal to the casualties of economic change, and corresponding features of present-day ideologies; between the seventeenth-century persecution of witches and the modern persecution of Jews; between the shattering experiences of the 1620s and those of the 1930s. The post-war struggle of Communism and capitalism likewise took his mind back to what is now called the early modern period. Dismayed, in 1950, by the confrontational anti-Communist stances at a congress, promoted by the CIA, which he attended in Berlin, he wrote on his return an essay on the productive co-existence, even amid fear and hostility, of the great power-blocs of the sixteenth century, Christendom and the Turkish Empire. His interest in Erasmus had its scholarly origin in his admiration for the work of Marc Bataillon, but it was also spurred by Hugh's own wish, amid the crude antagonisms of his own century, for a humane and sophisticated middle way.

His analogical instincts asserted themselves in his constant flow of metaphor. 'I can't understand anything', he observed in 1942, 'that I can't present to my imagination in a pictorial form; and when I comprehend anything vividly, it is always in the terms of some visual image.' The translation, often the playful translation, of concepts into images was an inherent feature of his speech and writing. Even inanimate objects acquired mobile personalities in his mind. In describing the doomed social vision of the secular technocrats whom he met on his visit to Iran in 1957, he

imagined 'pylon nodding to pylon in the Persian hills'; he observed of Sir
Theodore Mayerne's castle in Switzerland that 'the slit eyes of its great
cylindrical dome squint malevolently over a fresh and delightful landscape'; during the eleventh-hour revision of his study of Backhouse, when
a late discovery took over the centre of the book, he envisaged, in an
impromptu conversational aside, his other chapters 'turning on their footnotes' towards the new material. Watching, in a pub, a darts-player aiming at the outer rim, he thought instantly of the mind of the former
Warden of All Souls, John Sparrow, which 'unerringly finds the exact
periphery of any intellectual problem'. Metaphor carried two twined
temptations that ran through his intellectual and literary life: the impulse
to improve life into art; and the lure of caricature or satirical distortion,
which, while it gave force to general truths, could be unjust to his particular illustrations of them. Yet it served his purpose of bringing the past alive,
and of taking the reader's imagination into remote minds and settings.

For Hugh blended—as what other historian has done?—the generalising concerns of eighteenth-century philosophic history with the insistence of the Romantic movement, which reacted against them, on entry
into the feel and texture of each age. Acutely sensitive to mood and
atmosphere in the world around him, he brought the same antennae to
the past, where he was rapidly at home in fresh territory. The challenge to
a historian was to reconstruct, in any time or place, the distinctive experiences of the generations to be found there: experiences which constituted, he submitted, 'the real motor of history', but which the dry
dissections of both determinist and academic history pass over. He
often remarked on the formative impact, on his own generation, of the
1930s—of mass unemployment, the rise of fascism, the Spanish civil war,
above all of the 'electrical moral atmosphere' of Munich—and asked
how that memory could be conveyed, across the intervening 'great gulf',
to the succeeding age. Mental processes, he knew, could not reconstruct
the preoccupations of earlier times without the aid of feeling and
imagination.

The volume of his writing, both published and unpublished, is almost
exhausting to contemplate. The books, essays, reviews, letters and private
reflections amount to millions of words, very few of them lacking distinction of mind and style. Yet he had no interest in quantity of production, or in publication for its own sake. The courtesies of lucidity and
guidance that, he insisted, are owed to the reader exercise a sovereign
claim in his prose; and yet he wrote it as much for himself as for an audience, indeed took secret delight in interlinear allusions to which few if any

readers could be alive. When asked, in the later part of his life, why he had not published more long books, or a very long book, he would recall the comment of Burckhardt, whom he revered, on the heap of tomes erected by the Swiss historian's German contemporaries: 'they forget the shortness of life'. Who, Hugh asked, had time to read so many volumes, the essence of which, in any case, could often be reduced into essays?

Yet he had tried to write many more books than he had published. He had tried to write a very long one, and a side of him seems to have accepted, at least until his book on the civil wars had been abandoned, that that is what major historians do. There are, I think, three explanations of the pattern of non-completion. One was his literary perfectionism. Another was a hidden want of confidence. Though he cared nothing for the world's opinion, he did respect informed and intelligent judgement, to which a historian who spread himself so widely could easily be vulnerable. Thirdly, and perhaps most profoundly, there was the tug of temperament. Solitude, delicious at moments of intellectual animation and discovery, oppressed him at ones of tedium and inertia, of which the final preparation of a book, requiring as it does the checking of references and the resolution of small uncertainties, brings its full measure. Always he needed, and found, the stimulus of fresh engagement. In the 1960s his elderly friend the historian Wallace Notestein urged him, repeatedly and forcibly, to set all other commitments aside and produce a multi-volume work by which posterity would know him. 'The trouble is', replied Hugh, 'I am interested in too many things', and 'by the time I have written a chapter I have got interested in something else.'

His essays made a virtue of that predicament. The English historical essayist whom Hugh most resembles in eloquence of persuasion is Macaulay. Macaulay could not match Hugh's scholarly equipment: Hugh does not surpass, and does not always equal, the commanding force of Macaulay's mind. But Macaulay's hammering judgements, the over-insistence of his partisanship, and the complacency of his Englishness look crude beside the nuances of Hugh's arguments, the musicality of his prose, and the internationalism of his perspective. Macaulay's accumulating certainties overpower the reader: Hugh's nib prises apart what unobservant or conventional opinion conflates. Who that surveys the breadth and penetration of his essays would say that he would have given more stimulus and lasting insight to the world if he had written on fewer fronts? Now that the essay, which addresses a lay audience, has yielded in historical writing to the article, which does not, his union of argument with artistry seems to speak, with much of his historical philosophy, from a past world. Yet if the form has been lost, the mind and the reflective power behind it remain easy to meet and to learn from, even where time has overtaken his factual or interpretative premises. Of the writings of the first half of his life, the ones written long enough ago for some provisional assessment of their durability to be made, it is the long books and the studies intended as preliminaries to them—*Archbishop Laud*, and the published and unpublished work on the origins and course of the Puritan Revolution—that now seem largely confined, together with the rival interpretations of the mid-seventeenth century against which he contended, by the era in which they were written.

The essays, it is true, are inevitably uneven, not only in length but in depth. Many of them derived from invitations to mark centenaries or other commemorations. There was a pattern to his responses to those requests. First came pleasure at the prospect; then, when the work had to be done, irritation at having yielded to the timetables of other people, and so having interrupted his own; finally gratitude at having been made to re-read half-forgotten books and to explore their contexts. Even at the most congested times, when he was despairingly seeking to finish the writing of books, he would take on a breadth of commitments, literary and non-literary, outside them. During the most anxious time of all, the crisis in 1960–1 when he was 'fighting for every moment of time' to complete his book on the Puritan Revolution, he wrote the essay 'Spain and Europe 1598–1621' that would appear in Volume IV the *New Cambridge Modern History*; compiled a long, carefully prepared series of undergraduate lectures on sixteenth- and seventeenth-century Spanish history; conducted the colourful campaign by which, through mass mobilisation among the electorate of Oxford's MAs, he secured the choice of Harold Macmillan as Chancellor of Oxford University, an episode compared by Macmillan himself to an eighteenth-century parliamentary election; reported for *The Sunday Times* on the trial of the Nazi war criminal Adolf Eichmann in Israel; and fought with Taylor over *The Origins of the Second World War*. In 1965, when the subjects that had replaced the Puritan Revolution were competing urgently for his attention, we find him working, against the resistance of the Home Office, for a review of the case of James Hanratty, 'the A6 murderer', who had been convicted on what seemed doubtful evidence, and with whose life he had a distant and accidental connection.

If it is too easy to say that he should have written more books, so is it to suggest that his taste for controversy diverted him from more important activity. For beside the claims of posterity there were those of public spirit, which demand a historian's engagement with his own time and with the struggles for truth and opinion on which the course and health of public life depend. In the years of James Callaghan's premiership he suspended his own scholarly projects to combat, with historical arguments, the pressures to weaken the Anglo-Scottish Union, and to counter the initial defeatism of the Tory Opposition in the face of them. To him that seemed the right priority. He detested the evasion, whether in national or in academic affairs, of the responsibilities and realities of politics, where the choices and exertions of free actors shape the surrounding world. It is the failing that prompts the concluding passage of *The Last Days of Hitler*, where judgement is passed on Albert Speer, who, 'supposing politics to be irrelevant', went along with them and so became 'the real criminal of Nazi Germany'. Hugh delighted in demonstrating that the seemingly inevitable can be confounded: a serious point even in the sport of securing Macmillan's election at Oxford against the apparently unassailable wishes of the university's leaders. He contended against the 'cowardice dressed as virtue' that he saw stalking both the political and the academic world, for in invocations of liberal principles he detected 'an unhappily common confusion of thought' between 'a positive belief in certain basic principles (such as freedom of enquiry, belief and teaching) and a general willingness to make concessions and compromises—which may even be at the expense of such principles'. He was unimpressed by the pretence which enables fragmented academic communities, to the cost of their collective standards and their steadfastness, to live and let live: that all academic disciplines or subjects, or all subjects within a discipline, can be assumed to be of equal stature or significance. And he at least would not have left unresisted the carnage that is now wrought by the agencies of the state on the values and language of scholarly learning.

Another diversion from the writing of books was the reviewing of them, sometimes at length, sometimes briefly. Yet even his shortest reviews impart to a lay readership something of the reflective wisdom below their surface. Often he would detect in a book a significance to which its own author had not been alert, and place it on an intellectual map that might otherwise not have included it. Most of his reviewing was benign. Not all of it was. Here as elsewhere he courted controversy. Yet he knew that only platitudes command general assent, that the truth is often uncomfortable, and that debate is an essential instrument of its advance. Then there were the battles to fight within Oxford. He half-loved the Oxford of the 1950s, but half-despised it as a village. With a few honourable exceptions its historians knew little if anything of the historiographical revolution which, through Pirenne and Febvre and Braudel and others, had been achieved on the Continent, and to which he was drawn in the post-war years. He tried to raise funds for a research institute in Oxford that would import that trend, and conducted a long struggle to create a post in the university for a protégé of Braudel, the fiscal historian Frank Spooner, whose gifts Hugh, in his eagerness, idealised. Thwarted on that front, he had lost the taste for such initiatives by the time he became Regius Professor. Instead he would keep to the familiar paths, and the pleasures, of electoral intrigue, striving to bring in forces of vitality to college fellowships, and hoping to have, as his professorial colleagues, 'two historians of eccentric genius': Richard Cobb, whose appointment he helped to achieve, and Peter Brown, over whom he was outmanoeuvred.

Other distractions from his writing were less conspicuous. He took tireless, unobtrusive trouble in fulfilling a range of professional responsibilities, and often in going well beyond them. In his labours for the proper care of collections of manuscripts, or to secure the access of historians to them; in his careful and penetrating reports for editors and publishers (even if, amid the press of his commitments, he was often behind with them as with much else); in his patient advice to authors with books to write or rewrite; in his endeavours on behalf of scholars whom the sun of preferment had not touched or whose work lay off the beaten track; in his courtesy towards, and encouragement of, the writers of innumerable unsolicited letters and enquiries—in those exertions we see the most affecting and attractive side of his character. We see it too in his kindnesses to his graduate students. As a teacher of undergraduates he had been mindful of the perils of over-attention, to which, in any case, he was not much tempted. It was the general stamp and style of his mind, and the broadening of their own mental landscapes, that his undergraduates remembered. Some of them saw a lot of him outside tutorials, for he enjoyed youthful company. Something of the undergraduate always persisted in him, not least in his taste for spoofs and pranks. He liked the openness of youth to experience and discovery, and, remembering juvenile confusions of his own, was ever-tolerant of youthful failings. The youthfulness of graduate students refreshed him too. He loved to take refuge from committees and administrative papers to discuss their work. 'There is', he wrote in his affectionate preface to the published version of the thesis of his pupil Felix Raab, who had been killed in a climbing accident, 'no better way of learning about a subject' than through the enjoyable supervision of a graduate student.

I met Hugh, and became his pupil, in 1967. During my first term of research, a dismal period both personally and intellectually, a professor who was visiting Oxford, a leading authority in my chosen field, a man of great kindness but not always of light touch, gave me lunch in the Cadena Restaurant in the Cornmarket. As we consumed our salad and milk, his face lengthened and he became ever gloomier about the technical challenges of my chosen subject. Early that evening, heavy with melancholy in the autumn mist, I happened to meet Hugh in Broad Street. 'Oh', he said of the professor, 'he's a pessimistic man. I'm optimistic. Come and drink a bottle of wine with me.' He took me to his home in St Aldate's, gave me excellent Riesling, and talked, not about my thesis, but about books and ideas far removed from it. I emerged into the chill air, exhilarated and slightly tipsy, with a sense of fresh horizons and fresh hope. 'I'm going to China tomorrow', he said as I left, 'so you won't see me for a while. But you'll be all right.' After his return he sat by my side and went through the first work I had written for him. Three hours passed, and supper-time came and went, before I again emerged gladdened in heart and mind. Later, when, still a graduate student, I had left Oxford, I began to receive, to my puzzlement at the privilege, long letters from him, full of gorgeous and scandalous comedy but also of delicate intellectual guidance. How the sight of his writing on an envelope would lift my morale! I had no means of knowing that his own morale—a noun he used with telling frequency—could so need lifting, or how dependent he was on communication with people from whom he had so much less to learn than from himself.

*

'The trouble with controversies', Wallace Notestein warned him, 'is that they will take you far away from history. Historians need leisure and quiet almost as much as poets.' In reply Hugh gravely, but not too gravely, promised to follow 'your sage advice'. Yet just after receiving it, he went on, he had found himself reading another letter, this one composed three and a half centuries earlier, 'which reminded me (somewhat wryly) of our correspondence'. It too was written by an older to a younger scholar. In it, in 1615, Jacques-Auguste de Thou had offered paternal advice to Hugo Grotius, Hugh's 'new historical hero', through the seven volumes of whose correspondence he was working his way. 'There is one thing that grieves me', the venerable de Thou told Grotius, 'and that is that you spend too much of your time in controversy. I beg you leave that arena, and get on with that great *History*, to which we are all looking forward.' Grotius had replied with proper humility, defending his controversial writings, which had been written in truth's cause, but conceding the older man's point: 'persuaded by your authority . . . from now on I am resolved to shun all unnecessary controversies. I am going to finish my *History*.' Hugh's reply to Notestein continued: 'A fine moral tale, a noble example, I said to myself, as I put your letter into the volume to mark the place.'

But then, he added, his eye had been caught by Grotius's next letter, composed on the same day to a Dutch preacher. 'In spite of many preoccupations which distract me', the newly reformed Grotius had written, 'I could not resist the temptation to read' a recent treatise by the theologian Faustus Socinus; and 'when I saw that nobody had answered his rotten arguments, I thought it my duty to enter the fray. In great battles, even a skirmisher is of use. . . .' In accommodating the rival claims of scholarship and controversy, Hugh was true to himself. The contention between them was the source, not only of his permanent frustrations, but of the prodigious range of his achievement.

BLAIR WORDEN
Fellow of the Academy

BILL WADE

Henry William Rawson Wade
1918–2004

I

SIR WILLIAM WADE, known to his friends and colleagues as 'Bill', died on
12 March 2004 at the age of 86. His obituary in *The Times* stated that 'he
dominated two diverse areas of law, real property and administrative law,
by writing the textbooks that became a source of first reference for students, scholars, practitioners and judges'. While he was the leading academic land lawyer of his generation, he will principally be remembered as
one of the two scholars who did most to revitalise our administrative law
during the twentieth century. The other, Stanley de Smith, died at the
early age of 51 in 1974.[1] Wade's scholarly career lasted over sixty years,
and he remained active into his eighties. He wrote with penetrating clarity and an elegant and memorable turn of phrase, often expressing himself in trenchant terms. He did this both when grappling with the
technicalities of property law and, in the heady atmosphere of constitutional principles, with the respective roles of executive government and
the courts. Lord Denning said that Wade's 'felicitous presentation of
complex problems is beyond compare'.[2] This was in part the result of the
certainty of his intellectual vision.

Wade's work has meant that principles of judicial review, more or less
dormant in the common law, or seen as what he described as a
'Tennysonian wilderness of single instances', were rediscovered and reac-
tivated to address the questions thrown up by the role of the modern

---

[1] See H. W. R. Wade, 'S. A. de Smith', *Proceedings of the British Academy*, 60 (1974), 477, 478.
[2] Letter to HWRW, 1 Nov. 1988, on receipt of the 6th edition of *Administrative Law*.

Proceedings of the British Academy, **150**, 287–310. © The British Academy 2007.

administrative state. Wade was a believer in the common law and equity rather than in statute, thinking, for example, that it was for the courts to regenerate administrative law and that the old equitable doctrines achieved fairer results than the Land Charges Act.

Bill Wade was born in London on 16 January 1918, the son of Colonel H. O. Wade, a solicitor. He was educated at Shrewsbury School. In 1936 he was awarded a major Classics scholarship by Gonville and Caius College, Cambridge, the college in which he spent the last twenty-eight years of his life, as Master between 1976 and 1988, and thereafter as a Fellow. After obtaining a First in Part 1 of the Classics Tripos in 1937 after one year rather than the usual two, he switched to Law. He obtained a First in Part 1 of the Law Tripos in 1938, and a starred First in Part 2 in 1939. His success in the Tripos led to a Cholmeley Scholarship at Lincoln's Inn and a Tapp postgraduate scholarship at Caius. As an undergraduate he was a keen oarsman, and as Master he made a formidable sight urging on the Caius eights from his enormous bicycle on the towpath. His later passion for mountaineering may have had its origins when, in 1937, as a 19-year-old, he climbed the Wildspitze in the Otzal Alps.

Wade spent part of 1939 and 1940 as a Henry Fellow at Harvard. During the war he was a temporary officer at the Treasury, stationed for much of the time in Washington DC. It was in the United States that he met his first wife, Marie Osland-Hill, born in Beijing of British parents, who graduated from Swathmore College in 1940.[3] They married in 1943 and had two sons, Michael, who after post-doctoral work in experimental physics worked on technology exploitation and product development, and Edward, a metallurgist by training. Only one of his direct descendants, his granddaughter Marianne, a post-doctoral researcher in European criminal law at the Max Planck Institut in Freiburg, has a link with the law.

In 1946 Wade left the Treasury, was called to the Bar, and was elected to a Fellowship of Trinity College, Cambridge. Thereafter, his career fell into four roughly equal parts. The first was in Cambridge from 1946 to 1961, from 1947 as a lecturer in the Law Faculty and from 1959 as a Reader. Perhaps as a result of his experience working for the Treasury during the war, he became part-time assistant to Trinity's Bursar, T. C. Nicholas. A colleague has said that he was sure the college hoped Wade would succeed Nicholas. Wade, however, decided to stay with the law, and the college elected John Bradfield, an outstandingly successful Bursar.

---

[3] She had an American step-mother.

The second part of Wade's career was in Oxford. He moved there in 1961 at the age of 43 as the first holder of a new chair of English Law and a Fellow of St John's College. He told Francis Reynolds, a Faculty colleague, that this was his last move and he expected to play out his time in Oxford. While his return to Cambridge in 1976 as Master of Caius was not a surprise, his departure was regretted. In 1978 he succeeded Glanville Williams as Rouse Ball Professor of English Law. He retired from the chair in 1982 and from the Mastership in 1988. His retirement from the Mastership marked the beginning of the last part of his career, in which he was active and productive until not long before his death.

II

The foundations for Wade's later contribution to administrative law were laid during his time at Trinity. C. J. Hamson, then Director of Studies, persuaded him to teach it and constitutional law, and writing soon followed the teaching. In two important articles he argued for a broader approach to the principles of natural justice which required a fair hearing be given to those who were to be the subject of a decision by a public body.[4] He lamented the toleration by the courts in this period, which he described as 'the twilight of natural justice', of what he saw as unfair administrative procedures, and wrote about the defects in procedures at planning inquiries.[5] Almost two decades before the Law Commission recommended the simplification of the ancient prerogative remedies,[6] Wade argued for procedural reforms to enable them to continue to play a part in the control of administrative powers in the modern state.[7]

Wade must have largely completed his text on *Administrative Law* in Cambridge although it was not published until after he moved to Oxford in 1961. In Cambridge the family lived in Barrow Road. He constructed ingenious gadgets for the house and garden, made a working model of a railway engine for his sons, and was a keen gardener. Marie shared the

---

[4] '"Quasi-judicial" and its background', *Cambridge Law Journal*, 8 (1949), 216; 'The Twilight of Natural Justice', *Law Quarterly Review*, 67 (1951), 103. See also *Cambridge Law Journal*, 12 (1954), 154.

[5] *The Times*, 23 Dec. 1954; *Solicitors Journal*, 99 (1955), 19; 'Are Public Inquiries a Farce?' *The Listener*, 25 Aug. 1955.

[6] *Report on Remedies in Administrative Law* (1976) Law Com No. 73, implemented by SI 1977 No. 1955.

[7] 'The Future of Certiorari', *Cambridge Law Journal*, 16 (1958), 218.

latter interest and did much of the lighter work, as she did after their
move to Oxford at their house at East End, near North Leigh. Wade also
kept up his interest in rowing, going out regularly with Tony Jolowicz, a
younger Trinity colleague and former pupil.

Wade's growing reputation led to invitations to lecture abroad, including lecture tours for the British Council in Scandinavia in 1958 and in
Turkey in 1959. This period also saw conspicuous public service, from
1958 as one of the inaugural members of the Council on Tribunals (on
which he served until 1971) and as a member of the JUSTICE inquiry set
up in 1960 which proposed the establishment of a British Ombudsman.[8]
The proposal was largely enacted in the Parliamentary Commissioner
Act 1967.

It can, however, be argued that during this period Wade made his principal contribution in constitutional law and land law. His seminal article
'The Basis of Legal Sovereignty' was published in the November 1955
edition of the *Cambridge Law Journal*. This restated in a modern form
A. V. Dicey's concept of Parliamentary sovereignty, taking on Dicey's
many critics, in particular Jennings, Keir and Lawson, and Cowen. It was
controversial and some of its propositions were ultimately rejected by the
courts. But it has had a fundamental influence on the study of constitutional law. The arguments Wade first expressed in it have also been important components in wider debates about the concepts of sovereignty and
the source of legal power at times of constitutional change. This became
particularly evident in the debates about the legal implications of the
United Kingdom's membership since 1972 of what is now the European
Union. It was also seen in the discussion of the nature of legislation
passed without the assent of the House of Lords under the Parliament
Acts.

Wade argued that:

> The rule of judicial obedience [to Parliament] is in one sense a rule of common
> law, but in another sense . . . is the ultimate political fact upon which the whole
> system of legislation hangs. Legislation owes its authority to the rule: the rule
> does not owe its authority to legislation.[9]

For Wade 'the relationship between the courts of law and Parliament is
first and foremost a political reality': sovereignty is a political fact which
is acknowledged and recognised by the courts. The rule of common law
which says that the courts will enforce statutes is 'a rule which is unique

---

[8] JUSTICE, *The Citizen and the Administration, The Redress of Grievances* (1961).
[9] *Cambridge Law Journal*, 13 (1955), 172, at p. 188.

in being unchangeable by Parliament—it is changed by revolution, not by legislation; it lies in the keeping of the courts, and no Act of Parliament can take it from them'.[10] It is thus ultimately the courts which determine the seat of sovereignty. When faced with great changes, the courts have to decide for themselves what they will recognise as the proper expression of sovereign legal power.

The article attracted considerable attention and generated correspondence between him and leading scholars. Only the Canadian, D. M. Gordon, was convinced by it.[11] Wade's argument that laws made under the Parliament Act 1911 are to be classed as delegated legislation, was doubted by Arthur Goodhart, whose doubts were vindicated forty-eight years later in the context of the Hunting Act 2004.[12] Stanley de Smith and Herbert Hart described the article as the best defence of the classic conception of Parliamentary sovereignty, but did not agree that no statute can alter or abolish the rule.[13]

The correspondence between Wade and Hart, since 1952 the Professor of Jurisprudence at Oxford, is particularly interesting. In his first letter Hart said he agreed with what Wade said about the 'fundamental rules upon which the legal system depends' but that Wade then fell into a logical error in arguing that because fundamental rules are not created by legislation they cannot provide for their own transformation by legislation. This was like saying that because a man cannot create himself so he cannot kill himself. Wade accepted that the fundamental rule could provide for its own modification by statute but said he had probably not stated this because what he had in mind was the authority behind the rule rather than its content.[14] Wade later added that what interested him was how the legal system is to provide itself with a new basic rule after cutting itself off from its old basic rule and the source of the new rule.[15]

Wade considered Hart was taking the source for granted and assuming a complete and settled legal system in which all fundamental rules are already in existence, so that the task of ascertaining them was merely one of deduction or interpretation in the ordinary legal way. He considered that the *grundnorm* analysts were logically right in saying that a *basic rule* differs from legal rules generally in having a political, not a legal, source.

---

[10] Ibid., at p. 189.
[11] DMG to HWRW, 18 Jan. 1956.
[12] *R (Jackson) v Attorney-General* [2006] 1 AC 262.
[13] SAdeS to HWRW, 9 Dec. 1955; HLAH to HWRW, 15 Dec. 1955.
[14] HWRW to HLAH, 19 Dec. 1955.
[15] HWRW to HLAH, April 1956, in reply to a letter from Hart dated 30 Dec. 1955.

The last letter on this topic in Wade's correspondence file is a holding reply from Hart stating that he would defer replying fully until he had re-thought a bit. He considered careful description was needed of what it was for a *grundnorm* to change and also that there must be some criteria for distinguishing non-revolutionary changes from revolutions.[16] It is worth recalling that Hart's account of the 'rule of recognition' in his *Concept of Law*, published in 1961,[17] rests on a similar conception of 'political fact' to Wade's conception of legal sovereignty.[18]

In 1972 when the Bill that became the European Communities Act 1972 was before Parliament, Wade wrote an important article in *The Times* entitled 'The Judges' dilemma'.[19] He wanted to explain why the impending loss of sovereignty loomed large in the speeches of the oppo-nents of membership, but was played down by the government which argued that the proposed legislation involved nothing constitutionally out of the ordinary. Wade argued that while there would be a loss of *practi-cal* sovereignty there would be no loss of *legal* sovereignty. He stated that the government could justifiably claim that Parliament's ultimate author-ity would remain unimpaired: the attempt in the Bill to make Community law prevail over future Acts of Parliament was 'useless' because it fell 'foul of the classic principle of Parliamentary sovereignty'. Wade sug-gested that the technical problem could be avoided and we could 'show that we intend both to be good Europeans and, at the same time, to preserve Parliament's ultimate sovereignty' by altering the form of Acts of Parliament to provide that they were subject to Community law. His suggestion was not taken up.

At that time some lawyers argued that the judges might spontaneously accept Community law as paramount, even in opposition to later Acts of Parliament. Although Wade's 1955 article had recognised that the judges *could* choose to do this, he said if they did do so this would be 'a true rev-olution, a shift in the political basis of the legal system'. For this reason his *Times* article described the argument as 'a political prediction which no purely legal argument can justify, and which most lawyers would regard as somewhat fanciful, at present at any rate'. Qualifications such as that in the last phrase were not characteristics of Wade's writing, but this one was appropriate. Less than twenty years later, in 1991, the House

---

[16] HLAH to HWRW, 10 April 1956.
[17] Ch. 6. There are references to Wade's article in the endnotes at pp. 247 and 250.
[18] See T. R. S. Allan, 'Parliamentary Sovereignty: Law, Politics, and Revolution', *Law Quarterly Review*, 113 (1997), 443.
[19] 18 April 1972, p. 14.

of Lords, in the second *Factortame* case,[20] in effect held that Parliament had indeed bound its successors on European Community law so long as the United Kingdom remained in the EC. Their Lordships, and in particular Lord Bridge, stated that the situation was 'in no way novel'. Also, that by passing the 1972 Act Parliament voluntarily accepted a limitation of its sovereignty. They did not recognise in their speeches that there was any problem of a constitutional kind.

Some considered that what was done in the *Factortame* case was achieved by way of statutory construction under ordinary principles.[21] Wade disagreed. He retorted that if what was done was 'not revolutionary, constitutional lawyers are Dutchmen'[22] and that 'Parliament's powers had suffered a seismic change'.[23] Wade also said this was an example of the ability of the constitution to bend before the winds of change, which he considered 'in the last resort it will always succeed in doing'.[24] In saying this he appears closer to those scholars who consider that the *Factortame* case determined what the existing constitutional order required in novel circumstances.[25]

Wade's writing on land law in the late 1940s and early 1950s did much to develop it as a subject of academic discourse. His articles on licences and equitable mortgages, and on the effect of the land charges legislation[26] showed his view, expressed a decade later in a letter to Lord Denning, that 'the Land Charges Act was a bad piece of legislation and that the old doctrines of equity produced much fairer results'.[27] These were, however, the offshoots of what was his principal project during this period. That was to write a treatise on land law in collaboration with Sir Robert Megarry. *Megarry and Wade's Law of Real Property*, first published in 1957, was founded on a manuscript from which Megarry's

---

[20] *R v Secretary of State for Transport, ex p. Factortame Ltd.* (No. 2) [1991] 1 AC 603.

[21] P. P. Craig, 'Sovereignty of the United Kingdom Parliament after Factortame', *Yearbook of European Law*, 11 (1991), 221; Sir John Laws, 'Law and Democracy', *Public Law* (1995), 72.

[22] 'Sovereignty—Revolution or Evolution?' *Law Quarterly Review*, 112 (1996), 568, at p. 573. He had revisited it in 1980 in his Hamlyn Lectures, see below.

[23] Ibid., at 574.

[24] Ibid., at 575.

[25] T. R. S. Allan, 'Parliamentary Sovereignty: Law, Politics, and Revolution, *Law Quarterly Review*, 113 (1997), 443; J. M. Eekalaar, 'The Death of Parliamentary Sovereignty—A Comment', *Law Quarterly Review*, 113 (1997), 185.

[26] 'What is a Licence?' *Law Quarterly Review*, 64 (1948), 57; 'Licences and Third Parties', *Law Quarterly Review*, 68 (1952), 337; 'Effect of statutory notice of incumbrances', *Cambridge Law Journal*, 12 (1954), 89; 'An Equitable Mortgagee's Right to Possession', *Law Quarterly Review*, 71 (1955), 204; 'Land charge registration reviewed', *Cambridge Law Journal*, 14 (1956), 216.

[27] HWRW to Lord Denning, 20 Dec. 1966.

earlier *Manual of Real Property* had been drawn. It was, however, a larger and deeper work, and soon became acknowledged as the land lawyer's Bible. It remained under their distinguished joint authorship for four more editions. One of his law colleagues at Trinity states that at the beginning of the 1950s Wade was principally working on Megarry and Wade. He remembers two copies of the *Manual* were cannibalised and Wade's room filled with enormous sheets of paper, each with a page of the *Manual* pasted in the middle in the manner of *Coke on Littleton.*

III

With hindsight, Wade's move to Oxford in 1961 may appear to have had something inevitable about it. Even in those less specialised times, his combination of interests in public and private law was noteworthy. His expertise in land law and administrative law strengthened the Oxford Law Faculty. He had published extensively in the *Law Quarterly Review,* then edited by Arthur Goodhart, Master of University College, and his forthcoming book on *Administrative Law* had been commissioned for the influential *Clarendon Law Series* by Herbert Hart.

During his Oxford years the seeds he had planted in Cambridge bore fruit. There were two editions of the *Law of Real Property*, the classic third edition of 1966 and the fourth edition in 1975, and three editions of *Administrative Law*, in 1961, 1967 and 1971. There were also many articles and notes, the latter often in the *Law Quarterly Review*. At that time it was difficult to detect a preference on his part between real property and administrative law. Indeed the 1962 *Law Quarterly Review* contains an important article on each subject by him, his inaugural lecture, 'Law, Opinion and Administration',[28] and an article, 'Landlord, Tenant, and Squatter', on adverse possession.[29] The latter bore two of his fingerprints; it was a scathing critique of a decision of the House of Lords, and it was right. In 1968 and 1969 Wade gave a roughly equal number of lectures on each subject. Although he did not fill a room as David Daube and Otto Kahn-Freund did, he had what was by the standards of the Oxford Faculty at that time a very respectable audience. His lectures were precise, clear but rather dry.

[28] *Law Quarterly Review*, 78 (1962), 188.
[29] Ibid., at p. 541.

Wade did his fair share of administration including two years as chairman of the Faculty Board. He was a successful Secretary of the Law Club, a dining club of Oxford law dons and Oxford educated judges. He is reported to have said that the primary differences between Oxford and Cambridge were small, but the secondary differences great. Within the Faculty, some thought that although he was well-intentioned, he did not really grasp the secondary differences.

In St John's, Wade was well-liked and quite active. The College was pleased to have secured such a distinguished first holder of the Chair and was quick to elect him an Honorary Fellow in 1976 when he returned to Cambridge. Presidents found him a very good source of legal and practical wisdom. Perhaps as a result of his experience as assistant to Trinity's Bursar, he suggested changes in the College Statutes in the area of trusts and property holding which have stood the College in good stead. He was particularly supportive of the efforts of Mark Freedland, who became the Law Tutor in 1970, to revive St John's law from the sorry state in which the previous tutor had left it. In Freedland's early days, Wade gave some helpful and memorable revision classes to the finalists. Bill and Marie Wade were also prominent (without being obtrusive) on the Oxford social scene. They entertained in the old style, and Marie also organised coffee mornings and the like for faculty wives.

In 1964 Wade was elected an Honorary Bencher of Lincoln's Inn, an honour he attributed to Lord Denning.[30] His contacts there gave him enormous social pleasure and intellectual nourishment. He enjoyed the exchanges with judges and senior barristers. Many were also invited to dine with him in Oxford, and later in Cambridge. His files suggest that it was during the mid-1960s that he started to correspond with senior members of the judiciary and lawyers in this country and abroad. In these ways he built up a formidable network with whom he discussed the legal issues of the time. He remained a great feast-goer into his late seventies, with an iron constitution and greater stamina for these occasions than many considerably younger than himself.

Administrative Law was presented 'in the form of a general discussion rather than in the cut and dried form of a textbook'.[31] For Wade, administrative law is the law relating to the control of governmental power and largely consists of general principles of judicial review. The book puts the courts rather than administrative process at the centre of the subject and,

---

[30] HWRW to Lord Denning, 20 Dec. 1966.
[31] Preface to 1st edn., at p. v.

while alive to the wider constitutional context, and aware of the particular administrative context, is less sensitive to the latter. In part this was because Wade considered that the cause of the dismal state of British administrative law in the middle of the twentieth century was the dispersal and fragmentation of material. He gave administrative law a unity and an internal anatomy of its own. His concise statement of principle and clarity meant that the book was soon regarded as a classic. It has had an enormous influence on legal thinking, not only in this country and the Commonwealth, but in many other countries. It has been cited on innumerable occasions, and has been translated into Italian, Spanish and Chinese. What started as a 'slim volume of fewer than 300 pages'[32] is now, in its ninth edition, over 1000 pages and a major treatise. The 1977 edition at over 850 pages could no longer be part of the *Clarendon Law Series*. Wade described it as only 'nominally' a fourth edition of his present book on the same subject.[33]

In his inaugural lecture at Oxford Wade argued that it was possible for the courts to develop the principles of judicial review without improper judicial law-making. 'The materials handed down by previous generations of judges supply all the right raw material.'[34] The courts soon responded with landmark decisions extending the circumstances in which the principles of natural justice required an administrative body to give a person a hearing in 1963, the limits of executive discretion in 1967, and the power of courts to control errors of law by administrative bodies, even where statute appeared to exclude judicial review, in 1969. In January 1967 in a letter to Lord Denning Wade said:

> I feel that Administrative Law is now really getting going at last. But most important things still seem to hang by a hair. Five of the nine judges concerned with *Ridge* v. *Baldwin*[35] were against natural justice, but fortunately the three Lords decided in favour.

His public work continued with membership of the 1966 Royal Commission on Tribunals of Inquiry chaired by Lord Justice Salmon.[36]

---

[32] Preface to 7th edn., at p. v.

[33] HWRW to Secretary-General of Cambridge University, 1 March 1977.

[34] 'Law, Opinion and Administration', *Law Quarterly Review*, 78 (1962), 188, at p. 198.

[35] [1964] AC 40. Lord Reid's critical questioning of Desmond Ackner QC, counsel for the appellant, led Ackner to consult Wade on the distinction between 'judicial' and 'administrative' acts. Wade cancelled an outing to the theatre, worked on Lord Reid's questions overnight, and provided Ackner with the answers to them before the next day's hearing.

[36] HMSO Cmnd 3121, Nov. 1966.

He was appointed Queen's Counsel in 1968 and elected a Fellow of the British Academy in 1969.

Wade had his critics, in particular those who favoured a more contextual approach and those who favoured less judicial intervention. They sometimes expressed themselves in extravagant language, but he was tolerant in his dealings with them. While strongly supporting a wide judicial review jurisdiction, Wade always showed concern about its proper scope, for instance disapproving of the review of non-binding guidance and arguing that if the judges claim more than their due share of constitutional power, nemesis may be in store. A former research student, Professor Mark Aronson of the University of New South Wales, considers Wade was far more politically astute than many of his detractors ever began to acknowledge.

The success of *Administrative Law* ensured him a warm welcome in many countries but especially within the common law world of the Commonwealth and the United States. He lectured widely, particularly in India, in Delhi in 1971 and 1982 and in Madras in 1974, where his Chettyar lectures comparing the protection of fundamental rights in India and the United Kingdom, attracted a crowd of 2,600. In a letter to Lord Justice Salmon he observed that academic work 'reaches so few people in this country (it is otherwise in India, and even in Nepal, where I was surprised to discover how notorious I am).'[37]

Wade's 1961 Cooley Lectures at the University of Michigan, published in 1963 as *Towards Administrative Justice*, were an attempt to explain British administrative law and its potential in the absence of any constitutional safeguards to an American audience. In 1969 he was a member of the third Anglo-American Legal Exchange. Led by Lord Diplock and Judge Henry Friendly, of the US Court of Appeals, Second Circuit, the exchange was productive. It resulted in *Legal Control of Government* (1972), by Wade and Bernard Schwartz of New York University, which compared the systems of the two countries. In 1981 Wade wrote to Lord Diplock saying his approach to standing in the *Fleet Street Casuals* case, in what Wade described as a 'bold and enlightened speech', brought back memories of their discussions on the exchange.[38] The exchange also fostered friendships. Sir Nigel Bridge, then a High Court Judge but later a Lord of Appeal in Ordinary, became a close friend.

---

[37] 16 Jan. 1971.
[38] 13 April 1981. Lord Diplock replied on 14 April 1981.

Wade also made a significant contribution to comparative law by his editorship of the *Annual Survey of Commonwealth Law* between 1965 and 1976. Launched under Wade's leadership by the Oxford Law Faculty and the British Institute of International and Comparative Law, with financial assistance from the Ford Foundation and All Souls College, the *Annual Survey* reviewed developments in major areas of the law in every Commonwealth jurisdiction. It was aimed at 'lawyers who wish to discover how far the law of other countries can throw light on their own local problems', and reflected and sought to foster Wade's belief in the unity of the common law. Legislative developments were covered but the emphasis was on case law.

Wade and his assistant editor, first Barbara Lillywhite, then Fellow of St Anne's, and later to marry Stanley de Smith, and then Captain Harold Cryer, formerly Chief Naval Judge-Advocate, enlisted members of the Oxford Law Faculty and others to provide chapters or sections of chapters. Contributors were provided with the raw material for other countries but expected to know about developments in the UK jurisdictions and to give them less prominence. During the summer vacation contributors could be identified in the Bodleian Law Library by the slips of paper with the summary details of recent statutes and cases they carried as they did the research.

By 1975 the circulation was dropping and the Ford Foundation grant had not been renewed. After 1972 when the United Kingdom joined the European Community, it was perhaps understandable that there was a shift of interest from Commonwealth law to European law. The original publishers, Butterworths, gave up in 1975 and Oxford University Press took over. In 1976 Wade left Oxford and Captain Cryer was ready to retire (he died not long after he did so). The decision was made to cease publication and John Finnis, assisted by Charlotte Beatson, edited the last, 1977, volume of the *Survey*. The view that there was a unity to the common law of the Commonwealth at the level of principle was probably outdated even in 1965. It should not, however, be thought that the *Annual Survey* was no longer relevant in 1977. The early manifestations of what have since been identified as 'globalising' influences existed, and there was a role for comparative Commonwealth law. In 2001 the Oxford Law Faculty and University Press returned to the area with the *Oxford University Commonwealth Law Journal*.

Wade was also an early advocate of the incorporation of the European Convention on Human Rights. In 1974 he stated that it was 'lamentable that our domestic law of fundamental rights is not raised at least to the level of our international obligations' and that the gap between them should be closed by enabling the European Convention to be enforced in British courts.[39] He would later argue that rights under the Convention existed not only against the state, but against private citizens and companies.

IV

In 1976 Wade returned to Cambridge as Master of Caius. He firmly, but diplomatically, guided the College in its decision to admit women. Joseph Needham, his predecessor, had not persuaded a sufficient number of the Fellows to agree to the change of statute required and the matter was to come before the governing body soon after Wade assumed office. He judged that some action on his part was required and wrote to all Fellows saying that his personal instincts were against change but that as there was a clear, if not statutory, majority in favour of change, he intended to vote for the change. The dissenters and the doubters were apparently disarmed by this and the statute was changed.

Wade continued writing his books and articles, with the fourth and fifth editions of *Administrative Law* published in 1977 and 1982, and the fifth edition of *Megarry and Wade* in 1984. He left the College officers to manage its day-to-day business as they thought fit, but without leaving any doubt as to who was in charge. As well as his enthusiastic support of the College eight, he endowed travel scholarships to enable under-graduates to share his passion for travel. He and Marie brought their gardening skills to the Master's Garden. He had found it neglected and overgrown with bracken and, early on his first day as Master, was seen 'shifting the broken ground with sturdy stroke'.[40] He was strongly opposed to the suggestion, made after he retired, for a new building to be erected in the Master's Garden. The suggestion was not pursued.

In 1978 Wade succeeded Glanville Williams as Rouse Ball Professor of English Law. By this time Marie's health was failing. Her illness had only gradually become apparent after they had moved back to Cambridge, but her health continued to decline and she died in 1980. In that year Wade gave his Hamlyn Lectures, *Constitutional Fundamentals*. He touched on

---

[39] *The Times*, 27 May 1974.
[40] *Cambridge University Reporter*, 128 (1998), p. 827 (oration on the occasion of the conferment of Wade's honorary Litt.D. on 24 June 1998).

many issues including reform of the House of Lords, problems of entrenchment and sovereignty, the definition of the royal prerogative, and the role of the judiciary in the 'renaissance of administrative law'. He spoke of 'deep dissatisfaction with the constitution'. His mood is captured in a letter dated 16 March 1980 to Sir Patrick Browne, recently retired from the Court of Appeal. Wade expressed dissatisfaction with 'the present mood of the Lords', and a negative view of the speeches of Lord Wilberforce and Lord Scarman in *Inland Revenue Commissioners v Rossminster*[41] in which they had taken the view that interim relief cannot be given against the Crown under the Crown Proceedings Act. Wade considered that 'it is perfectly obvious that the Act intended to allow it'. He thought the House of Lords was pro-executive and out of step with the Court of Appeal, in a reversal of the roles of the two courts a decade earlier. He considered this to be a serious matter both for the public and the profession and 'particularly deplorable because it is bringing in so much politics and clouding the end of Tom Denning's great career'.

While *Constitutional Fundamentals* was warmly received by some, others were more critical. Writing in *The Listener*, David Pannick said that Wade offered little by way of novel argument or fresh interpretation of fact, and that he was prone to overplay his hand, for example in comparing the Home Secretary's attempt to revoke overlapping television licences and the Minister of Agriculture's abuse of powers under the milk marketing scheme with the way the Stuart kings strained the Royal prerogative.[42] Alan Watkins, in *The Spectator*, stated that Wade

> ... has a masterly analysis, in a wider context, of the sloppy misuse of 'the prerogative' to explain or justify various governmental powers. Yet the lectures are marred by a certain harshness of manner, a coldness of tone: there is something a little too cocksure about Professor Wade.[43]

Wade served as Vice-President of the British Academy between 1981 and 1983. He was fully involved in the protracted discussions about the decision to move to new premises in Cornwall Terrace and about taking over the postgraduate studentships scheme from the Department for Education and Science. He also chaired a review of the Academy's involvement in university research appointments including the Readership Scheme and the UGC's 'New Blood' scheme. The review supported both. It suggested how to get 'more for less' from the Readership scheme, by

---

[41] [1980] AC 952.
[42] *The Listener*, 31 July 1980. See also Anthony Lester, QC, in The *Daily Telegraph*, 15 July 1980.
[43] *The Spectator*, 19 July 1980.

reducing the tenure from three years to two, and meeting only the costs of the substitute appointment. He was knighted in 1985. He had retired from the Rouse Ball Chair in 1982, under a generous early-retirement scheme at Cambridge and married Marjorie Browne in the same year. She, the widow of B. C. Browne, the geophysicist, and a Trinity colleague of Wade's, was full of vitality, and like him enjoyed travelling and entertaining others. She died suddenly in 2001, by which time he was beginning to show signs of physical frailness.

The fifth edition of *Megarry and Wade* appeared in 1984. Stephen Tromans, then a Fellow of Selwyn and now an environmental law practitioner, helped and did much of the research. Sir Robert Megarry, had retired as Vice-Chancellor of the Chancery Division in 1981. He was 74 and Wade did most of the writing. By then, however, Wade's principal interest was constitutional and administrative law, areas in which there continued to be important court-led common law developments. In 1992 he asked Charles Harpum, then a Fellow of Downing, to prepare a new edition. Wade was then working on the seventh edition of *Administrative Law* and, for understandable reasons, said he did not have the time to do both books. *Megarry and Wade* was a work born in an era of non-compulsory land registration. The authors described the legislation as of exceptionally low quality and in need of a thorough overhaul.[44] By the beginning of the 1990s reform was in the air, and if *Megarry and Wade* was to survive, it was important to have a new edition with the registered land system occupying the central ground. Megarry and Wade recognised what needed to be done, although in some ways found it difficult to let go of the book. The sixth edition was delayed when Harpum was appointed a member of the Law Commission in 1994, with responsibility for the Commission's work on land registration. It was published in 2000 with a generous recognition in the preface over the initials of both authors, but in words bearing Wade's hallmarks, of the advantages of the book being in the hands of someone described as at the 'epicentre' of 'seismic upheavals'.

Wade continued to be fully engaged with *Administrative Law* until shortly before he died but, since the sixth edition in 1988, Professor Christopher Forsyth, Fellow of Robinson College, has been his co-author. The collaboration was a happy one. Forsyth states that they 'worked together easily'; their 'views on almost all aspects of administrative law meshed together perfectly'; and they 'wasted little time on

---

[44] 5th edn., p. 196, cited in *Clark v Chief Land Registrar* [1994] Ch. 370, 382 (*per* Nourse LJ).

disagreement'.[45] The success of the partnership is also seen by the fact that one cannot tell which of them wrote a particular section of the book.

In 1988 Wade retired from the Mastership to a house in Fulbourn which Marjorie and he had bought in anticipation of his retirement. He continued to work in his rooms in Caius and in the Squire Law Library, until 1995 in the Cockerel building, and thereafter in the new Law Faculty building on the Sidgwick site, producing the seventh and eighth editions of *Administrative Law* with Forsyth. They had completed most of the ninth edition before Wade died. He attended meetings of the European Group of Public Law on the island of Spetses, and travelled extensively with Marjorie. In 1991 he was elected to an Honorary Fellowship of Trinity. Cambridge University awarded him an honorary Litt.D. in 1998, the year of his eightieth birthday. His writing had earned him his Cambridge LL.D. and Oxford DCL many years earlier. The Cambridge Centre for Public Law celebrated the birthday at its inaugural conference on the constitutional reforms planned by the new Labour government. A collection of essays on public law was presented to him and it was at that conference that he first argued that the Human Rights Act would give citizens rights against each other as well as against public authorities, a view which led to a vigorous debate, not yet resolved by the courts. He developed his argument later that year in his Judicial Studies Board lecture. The meeting of the European Group of Public Law that September included a *laudatio* for him.

V

Wade's contribution extended well beyond the world of scholarship. Apart from his public service, he deployed his felicity with the written word in articles and letters in newspapers on matters such as sovereignty, the European Community, and the European Convention on Human Rights. With his reputation came an advisory practice on Commonwealth constitutional problems in which his clear and decisive opinions were appreciated by those who sought his advice.

Wade built strong links with judges and practising lawyers at a time when the gap between academic law and the world of practitioners and judges was wider in the United Kingdom than in almost any other part of the common law world and far wider than it is now. He consequently

---

[45] Preface to 9th edn., p. v.

exercised considerable influence over decisions of the courts and the work of law reformers. He fostered and maintained these links at academic and professional meetings, in correspondence with members of the judiciary, and at social occasions, whether at Lincolns Inn, in one of his Colleges, or at meetings of the Oxford Law Club.

Judges read his books, articles and notes (sometimes because he sent them to them) and his criticisms were often picked up. So, in 1973 Lord Justice Roskill wrote to tell Wade that his criticism in the *Law Quarterly Review* of the procedural requirements imposed on universities in a case involving Aston University was to be upheld in a later case. Wade hoped the case would be reported 'since it will be a great aid and comfort to the hard pressed Vice Chancellors and their colleagues'.[46] In 1980 Lord Lane, newly appointed Lord Chief Justice, and a contemporary at Shrewsbury, wrote thanking Wade for 'a kind if over optimistic' letter of congratulation, adding that 'as you already know, Administrative Law is not my strong point, and I shall be reading your book under the desk of the Divisional Court'.

The power of Wade's ideas is also shown in a letter from Lord Wilberforce dated 10 June 1974. Written after argument but before the House of Lords gave judgment in the *Hoffmann-La-Roche* case[47] on the effect of disputed orders pending judicial determination, Lord Wilberforce said that Wade's note in the April 1974 issue of the *Law Quarterly Review* about the decision of the Court of Appeal:

> . . . plunges me into some consternation since (confidentially) my own opinion in the case corresponds exactly with the note—to such an extent that I shall certainly be charged with pillaging your ideas. The purpose of this note is just to say I acknowledge with gratitude the influence of your writing and teaching over the years which has clearly produced this community of outlook, while also putting on record that on this particular matter my piece was my own work in an immediate sense. That we were both thinking along these lines was brought out at our recent conversation.

Wade replied saying he was touched by Lord Wilberforce's 'very generous' letter, that there was no one with whom he would be more honoured to be in agreement, and was delighted that this was so. He continued:

---

[46] 23 July 1973. The case is *Herring v Templeman* [1973] 3 All ER 569, 587. It refers to the 'trenchant criticism by Professor Wade' in *Law Quarterly Review*, 85 (1969) of *R v Aston University, ex p. Roffey* [1969] 2 QB 538.
[47] [1975] AC 295.

It is only rarely that one can detect any connection between academic work and concrete decisions, so I am all the more gratified by what you say—even though in this case the parallel lines did not actually meet.

Wade's ideas may have matched Lord Wilberforce's but they did not prevail in that case. Nor were they acknowledged. As was common then, and is still not unknown, Lord Wilberforce's dissenting speech does not refer to Wade's note. In the October issue of the *Law Quarterly Review* Wade observed that there was much to be said for Lord Wilberforce's view.[48]

After the decision in *O'Reilly v Mackman*[49] in 1982 Wade became very critical of Lord Diplock. In a single speech given by Lord Diplock the House of Lords articulated a procedural dichotomy between 'public' and 'private' law proceedings, holding that a litigant who seeks a remedy for an infringement of a right in public law, *must* as a general rule proceed by the application for judicial review with its short time limit. Wade expressed his doubts to Lord Diplock in a letter written five days after the decision.[50] While he agreed there should be a single uniform procedure and time limit, he hoped that the distinction which Lord Diplock made so fundamental 'will prove sufficiently clear in practice, so that litigants are not caught out by using the wrong avenue. Otherwise we would be in the same trouble as the French.' Lord Woolf's 1986 Harry Street lecture[51] was more sympathetic to the distinction, and Wade wrote to him stating that, while Lord Diplock 'had a genius for getting down to the bedrock', his desire to restate the law in his own terms, notwithstanding its brilliance, had left 'a legacy of rigid statements which [seemed to Wade] to contain the seeds of much future trouble'.[52] The sixth edition of *Administrative Law*, published in 1988, contained what Lord Denning referred to as 'your sly dig at Kenneth Diplock'.[53] Wade also considered sweeping remarks in another case[54] typical of Lord Diplock's fondness for generalising on the basis of a single case.[55] Wade's views on the dichotomy introduced in *O'Reilly*'s case ultimately prevailed. So too did his long-held view that a minister of the Crown was bound by an injunction ordered in

---

[48] *Law Quarterly Review*, 99 (1974), 436, 439. The earlier note is at p. 154.
[49] [1983] 2 AC 237.
[50] 30 Nov. 1982.
[51] 'Public Law—Private Law: Why the divide?' *Public Law* (1986), 220.
[52] HWRW to Lord Woolf, 22 Feb. 1986.
[53] Lord Denning to HWRW, 1 Nov. 1988.
[54] *Town Investments v Department of Environment* [1978] AC 359.
[55] HWRW to F. A. Mann, 7 April 1986.

judicial review proceedings. This issue, which was settled in *M v Home Office*,[56] was the subject of extensive correspondence between Wade and a number of judges.

For Wade the task of the academic was to search for and identify the fundamental principles upon which a coherent legal structure and system could rest. He remained faithful to this in his exchanges with the judiciary, principally with Lord Denning, but also with many of the key figures in the transformation of our administrative law in the last forty-five years. Reflecting on the difference between the judicial and the academic minds, he said:

> The academic wants everything clear and sharp and logical and in accordance with principle. The judge, on the other hand, always wants to have a way of escape, so that he cannot be driven into a corner by ruthless logic and compelled to decide contrary to what he wants. I am sure that this is a sound instinct for the administration of justice, but I am by my cloth obliged to protest when blurring becomes woolly thinking and blasphemy against basics.[57]

His correspondence with Lord Denning during 1967 and 1968 about the effect of an invalid administrative act is a wonderful example. Wade, with courteous persistence, maintained it had no legal effect at all. Lord Denning, shaken, but not stirred by the force of Wade's argument, with equally courteous resistance, considered it had some effect until set aside by a court.[58] It was no accident that Christopher Forsyth and Ivan Hare, the editors of the book of essays presented to him on his eightieth birthday, called it *The Golden Metwand and the Crooked Cord*. Bill Wade was not a fan of the flexible and possibly more nuanced approach which many with a less certain view of what the 'right' answer is prefer—or are forced into. For him, that was 'the crooked cord of discretion' and antithetical to law.

Lord Cooke of Thorndon put it well when he said that Wade's intellectual vision was 'emphatically not of a twilight world' and that he had 'the gift of seeing things in black and white', whereas judges whose 'daily work constantly reminding them of the infinite variety of facts, sometimes over-sensitive to the need to allow for the case round the corner, are usually cautious to qualify in some way their propositions of principle'.[59]

---

[56] [1994] 1 AC 377.
[57] HWRW to Sir Robin Cooke (now Lord Cooke of Thorndon), 6 Jan. 1988.
[58] The last letter on this is dated 4 March 1968. By 1978, however, Lord Denning had changed his position. In *Firman v Ellis* [1978] QB 886 he said 'after some vacillation' he would adopt the meanings of void and voidable given by Wade in the 4th edn. of *Administrative Law*.
[59] *The Golden Metwand and the Crooked Cord* (Oxford, 1998), p. 203.

Wade was, as he said in his inaugural lecture at Oxford, a legal positivist. It was the clarity of the rules and principles he identified by what
he described as 'a more lively appreciation of the materials lying readily
to hand in the law reports'[60] that enabled cautious and even conservative
courts to step beyond the twilight not only of natural justice but of the
whole of administrative law. His skill in presenting truly original and creative insights as no more than rule identification, removing his own foot-
prints from the trail, was particularly attractive to judges working in a
system of precedent. We can now, however, say this was more than mere
'lively appreciation of the materials lying readily to hand'.

In 1972 Wade gave evidence to the Franks Committee on section 2 of
the Official Secrets Act 1911. It was robust: he described the section as 'a
blot on the statute book which needs to be removed'.[61] In 1980 he gave
similarly robust evidence to the Foreign Affairs Committee of the House
of Commons when it was considering the 'patriation' of the Canadian
constitution and the severance of Canada's last statutory links with the
Westminster Parliament.[62] The Canadian Federal Government and
Parliament, and the United Kingdom Government considered that the
Canadian Parliament did not require the consent of the Provinces before
seeking constitutional amendments which affected their powers. Wade's
view was that the unanimous consent of the Provinces was required.
Although not accepted by the Committee, it may have assisted it in concluding, contrary to the position of the Canadian and United Kingdom
governments, and anticipating the decision of the Supreme Court of
Canada, that the consent of a substantial majority of Provinces for such
amendments was required.[63] In 1985 he played a significant part in the
famous Old Bailey trial of the civil servant Clive Ponting for breach of
the Official Secrets Act 1959. Ponting had passed information to Tam
Dayell, MP, and his defence was that this was in the public interest. In
his supplementary remarks to Sir David Williams's obituary in *The
Independent,* Tam Dayell states that in his opinion the decisive moment in
the trial occurred during Wade's evidence. He describes Wade as a tall
shambling figure quietly and most precisely answering the questions that
were put to him. Dayell states that when the trial judge, Mr Justice

---

[60] 'Law, Opinion and Administration', *Law Quarterly Review,* 78 (1962), 188, at p. 199.
[61] Cmnd. 5104 (1972); vol. 2 at p. 411; vol. 4 at pp. 159 ff.
[62] HC 42. I and II (21 Jan. 1981) at pp. 102–14: his was 'the most emphatic' evidence (see Q 127).
[63] *Reference re Resolution to amend the Constitution* [1981] 1 S.C.R. 753 held that while no legal
rule constrained the Canadian Parliament, constitutional convention required the consent of a
substantial majority of Provinces for such amendments.

McCowan, unhappy that such a defence could be raised 'barked aggressively, "Are you trying to teach me my law"', those in court thought that the judge had made up his mind on the verdict that he wanted. Dayell states that 'the meting out of such treatment to Wade crucially stiffened any resolve that the jury had entertained to defy the judge and acquit Ponting'.

VI

Engagement with the great and the good is only part of the story. Wade was a conscientious and demanding but supportive supervisor of undergraduates. He was by far the most intimidating of Tony Jolowicz's first year supervisors at Trinity. Jolowicz comments that as a consequence, most people worked hardest for Wade. While Wade did not suffer fools gladly, Jolowicz cannot remember an unkind word in supervision. Two of Wade's Trinity pupils, Lord Lloyd of Berwick and Lord Slynn of Hadley, became Lords of Appeal in Ordinary. Lord Lloyd has said that, while Wade did not have the same ebullience as Jack Hamson, in his own way he was just as inspiring about a subject. He virtually commanded Tony Weir to apply for a Harkness Fellowship and subsequently referred to Weir as 'a brand saved from the burning', which Weir took to refer to saving him from practice as an advocate in Edinburgh which he would not have enjoyed.

Wade also encouraged research students, many from Commonwealth countries, and younger scholars. His friendships with Robin Cooke (later President of the Court of Appeal of New Zealand and Lord Cooke of Thorndon) and Ramu Ramakrishna of Madras had their roots in their time in Cambridge in the 1950s as research students of E. C. S. Wade and C. J. Hamson. Cooke was later a research fellow of Caius. As well as their academic contacts with Bill Wade at that time, both remember his skill on the tennis court. Wade had clear views as to what work needed to be done. Robert Sharpe, later Dean of the Law School at the University of Toronto and now on the Ontario Court of Appeal, recalls that it was Wade who identified the need for work on habeas corpus which led to Sharpe's D.Phil. thesis and what for many years was the only significant book on the subject. Soon after I joined the Oxford Law Faculty he thought I should work on the Ombudsman and invited me to a very good dinner to discuss this. I did not take up the suggestion but I remember the kindness the rather grand Professor of English Law showed a 25-year-old fledgling academic.

In the late 1940s and 1950s most of the very few research students in law[64] worked on either international or comparative law, or (particularly in Oxford) on jurisprudence. In his first Cambridge period Wade did not formally supervise any research students. Professors E. C. S. Wade, S. J. Bailey, and C. J. Hamson, who were more senior to him, supervised the small number working on his areas.[65]

In Oxford the position was different. Mark Aronson remembers the table as always full when Wade and Marie entertained his doctoral and other graduate students to lunch at St John's. David Elliott of Carlton University in Ottawa remembers Wade as a formal but friendly person, and research supervision meetings as intimidating but inspiring events. Wade's preference was to have something in writing, however short, as a focus for discussion. While he could be a fairly hands-off supervisor, he rigorously scrutinised drafts for looseness of language or of logic. He urged Sharpe, whom he supervised for one term before going on leave, not to think of spending a year or two doing all the research and then writing it up but to select a key area and write a chapter as soon as practicable. Sharpe thought he was very fortunate to have had Wade at the start because he had such a clear and provocative view about the subject and about how to attack it, was quite fearless in questioning authority, and had a profound belief that his vision for judicial review was central to the rule of law. But this certainty of vision was not coupled with intolerance. Aronson says that, some years later when thinking about what he describes as his own somewhat declamatory thesis, he realised just how tolerant Wade really had been of some of his over-confident and brash students.

After Wade returned to Cambridge he supervised a number of students, all working on administrative law. Abhishek Singhvi and Francis Alexis have combined practising law with politics in respectively India and Grenada. Donald Gifford teaches at the University of Queensland, and Edwin Wylie is a New Zealand Queen's Counsel.

---

[64] Between 1946 and 1961, on average only about 3 per cent of Cambridge's research students were lawyers, and a proportion of those took one year diplomas in comparative or international law.
[65] The contents of this paragraph are derived from the Reports of the Board of Research Studies, published in the *Cambridge University Reporter*.

VII

In 1953 at the age of 35 Wade took up rock climbing in the Lake District and the North West Highlands. In his forties he became a serious alpinist. Between 1958 and 1964 he also climbed many of the major peaks of the Pyrenees, mainly with another Fellow of Trinity, A. M. Binnie, FRS, who was seventeen years older than him. Wade joined the Alpine Club in 1964, supported by Binnie and other Cambridge dons. Although Marie did not share his enthusiasm, she accompanied him and their two sons on the easier walks in the Lake District and Scotland and in 1964 accompanied them on their first and last full family holiday in the Alps. Wade, Michael and Edward (then aged 20 and 17) and two companions were caught in bad weather and spent a very uncomfortable night at about 12,000 feet. Marie had travelled with their luggage from Zinal to Zermatt and the next day they met her wandering up the lower slopes, anxiously wondering if she would see them again. She announced firmly that she would not accompany any more climbing expeditions since she preferred to remain in ignorance of the details of their activities.

When travelling for academic purposes or for his advisory practice, Wade often seized the opportunity to climb. He climbed in New Zealand and Japan as well as in many European countries. He described expeditions to the Moroccan High Altas, the Rockies, and Kenya in articles in *Country Life*,[66] illustrated by photographs he took. He continued climbing into his sixties. In 1978 he asked the archaeologist Anthony Snodgrass to join him as a younger climbing companion at Arolla. They climbed together in the Dolomites in 1979 and in the Pyrenees in 1980. In his seventy-second year he trekked in the Karakoram in north Pakistan.

VIII

Bill Wade was not an obviously informal man. For instance, he thought it inappropriate that Tony Blair, who was a member of his Oxford College and attended his lectures but whom he hardly knew, should greet him as 'Bill'. Some thought him dry and unapproachable. Underneath the surface, however, there was a wry sense of humour and kindness. It was particularly evident in formal speeches and the legal debates in which he

---

[66] 'From Marrakesh to High Barbary' (25 Feb. 1971); 'The Rockies, a Climber's Elysium' (4 Jan. 1973); 'On the Roof of East Africa' (9 Jan. 1975).

loved to engage. One got the feeling that some of the more provocative things said—with a twinkle in the eye or with his characteristic smile—were teases, designed to get others to sharpen their arguments.

Wade was, as Sir David Williams said in his obituary, blessed by two warm and affectionate marriages. All that he did as a scholar, was done at the same time as being a generous host to many, and avidly and skilfully pursuing his interests in gardening and mountaineering until prevented by age.

JACK BEATSON
Fellow of the Academy

Note.   Dr Michael Wade generously provided me with information about the family, access to HWRW's correspondence, and copies of his articles in *Country Life.* I have also been greatly assisted by Mark Aronson, HH Judge Findlay Baker QC, Jock Brookfield, Peter Brown, Sir Richard Buxton, Lord Cooke of Thorndon, Stephen Cretney, Dale Densem, David Elliott, John Finnis, Christopher Forsyth, Mark Freedland, Charles Harpum, Alison Hirst, David Ibbetson, Tony Jolowicz, Lord Lloyd of Berwick, Toby Milsom, Michael Prichard, Francis Reynolds, Stephen Scott, Robert Sharpe, Tony Smith, Stephen Tromans, Sir Guenter Treitel, Tony Weir and Sir David Williams. Many of these will find their words pillaged here, not always with proper acknowledgement. I have drawn on Sir David Williams's chapter in C. Forsyth and I. Hare (eds.), *The Golden Metwand and the Crooked Cord: Essays on Public Law in Honour of Sir William Wade* (1998), my obituary in *The Guardian,* and the obituaries in *The Times, The Independent,* the *Daily Telegraph,* and the *Alpine Journal.*

ALAN WILLIAMS

Alan Harold Williams
1927–2005

ALAN WILLIAMS WAS, by common consent, the leading health economist in Britain. Indeed, it is in large part due to him that there is a community of health economics for anyone to lead. He was renowned for the logical rigour of his thinking, for his passionate commitment to the principle of universal health care supplied according to need, for his determination to ensure that health-service resources are used to the best effect, and for his evangelical sense of mission in advocating the use of the quality-adjusted life year as a measure of health-service effectiveness. He was also famous for the notice on his desk—later moved to his door so that callers would be forewarned of what to expect—with the injunction: 'Be reasonable—do it my way.' That so many people remember this message shows that it was something more than an office joke.

Alan was born in the Ladywood district of Birmingham on 9 June 1927, and spent his childhood and teenage years there. The Williams family ran an off-licence shop in this working-class part of Birmingham, living on the premises. As the owners of a small business, they were a cut above their neighbours, distinguished by their early acquisition of an inside toilet, an Austin Seven car and a telephone. The young Alan was weedy and had a stammer, and was bullied at the local infants' and junior schools. However, he must have shown intellectual aptitude, as he won a scholarship to Five Ways Grammar School, a satellite of the prestigious and academic King Edward's School. The foregoing information comes from an autobiographical note which Alan began writing in later life, but which never got beyond the event of the scholarship—perhaps partly because, with characteristic attention to detail, he had devoted much of his authorial energies to reconstructing the complete rules of the

Ladywood version of the street game of 'tip-cat' that he had played as a boy.

Alan spent the war years as a pupil at Five Ways School and, after his School Certificate and with another scholarship, at King Edward's School itself. Half a century later, he recalled that, as a result of his experience of wartime Britain, the concept of rationing was for him 'benignly synonymous with distributing scarce resources equitably'.[1] Throughout his life, his social and political outlook retained some of the spirit of the 1940s—an ideal of social solidarity, a deep but not doctrinaire commitment to equality, a confidence in the ability of a well-advised government to improve life for everyone, and an almost instinctive affection and support for the National Health Service.

Alan left school in 1945 with Higher School Certificate qualifications (the predecessors of 'A' levels) in Spanish, French and English. He was then required to do a period of National Service. He spent almost three years in the RAF, mostly behind a desk in Algeria, leaving with the rank of corporal. It seems that this was a pleasurable interlude in his life. On demobilisation leave in Birmingham in 1948, he had a night out at the local Tower Ballroom and met his future wife June Porter, a grammar-school girl from another part of the city.

The RAF had an enlightened policy of trying to make up for the disruptive effect of National Service on the education of its conscripts. As a result of this policy, Alan was offered financial support to go to university, something he had not previously thought of doing. With an eye to future employment prospects, he opted for a degree course in commerce. Possibly for reasons of economy, possibly out of loyalty to his family, he chose to live at home and study at the University of Birmingham.

It was at Birmingham University that Alan discovered economics. He was particularly inspired by a young economics teacher called Frank Hahn, only two years older than Alan himself, who delivered brilliant lectures without notes, and with cliff-hanger endings to arouse his students' curiosity about what would come next. Alan was a successful student, graduating in 1951 with an upper second, having narrowly missed a first (in an era when a first was a very rare honour). He considered a career in the civil service, entering the difficult competition for the administrative class and emerging with a job offer. By this stage, however, he must have decided on an academic career, since he turned the offer down and took

---

[1] Alan Williams, 'Discovering the QALY—or how Rachel Rosser changed my life', in Adam Oliver (ed.), *Personal Histories in Health Research* (London, 2005).

a one-year research post at Birmingham University. With help and encouragement from Hahn, he spent this period preparing, and raising finance for, an ambitious plan which was intended to lead to a Ph.D.

The idea was that Alan would go to the University of Stockholm, put his language skills to use by learning Swedish, and then translate into English some of the work of the great Swedish economist Knut Wicksell. At this time, Stockholm was one of the world's most famous centres of economics. The 'Stockholm School' of economists had made major developments in macroeconomics in parallel with those of John Maynard Keynes in Britain. The exchange of ideas between the two countries had been disrupted by the war, and now there was a desire to reconnect. Wicksell's theory of capital and interest, which synthesised ideas from the Walrasian and Austrian traditions of neoclassical economics, was a point of reference for the Stockholm School, and gave a perspective on what was then one of the major theoretical problems of the discipline—reconciling Keynesian macroeconomics with neoclassical microeconomics. Wicksell was also one of the founding fathers of public finance. His theory of 'just taxation', later developed by another Swedish economist, Erik Lindahl, is based on the principle that, in order for the tax-financed supply of public goods to be just, every individual must be a net beneficiary from the combination of taxation and public-good consumption. Among the public-finance economists who were influenced by this idea were James Buchanan, later to become the leading figure in the economics of public choice, and Alan Peacock, who was to play an important role in Alan's later career.

Alan went to Sweden in 1952. Finding it difficult to immerse himself sufficiently in Swedish-speaking life at the cosmopolitan University of Stockholm, he transferred to the University of Uppsala. Starting his work on Wicksell, he began to make a few scholarly discoveries, such as a significant error in one of the standard German translations of Wicksell's writings. But then, a year into his project, he was struck by the disaster that all Ph.D. students fear: he discovered that another young British economist, Ralph Turvey, had been working for some time on the same translations. Realising that his own work no longer had a purpose, Alan abandoned his Ph.D. research, returning to England in the summer of 1953.

For the rest of his life, Alan retained a love of Sweden. This was more than a natural nostalgia for a country in which he had spent a happy year in his twenties. He saw Sweden's form of social democracy—in which a comprehensive welfare state coexisted with economic growth, and high

rates of taxation seemed to be accepted in a spirit of social solidarity—
as a model for the rest of the world. Until English became the unchal-
lenged world language for economics, Alan continued to use his
Swedish-language skills by making for the *International Economic Papers*
an annual series of English translations of major current papers in economics. He succeeded Turvey as the member of that journal's editorial
board with responsibility for trawling the Scandinavian literature. Much
later, he played an important part in the development of health economics in Sweden. Alan's contribution to Swedish economics was given fitting
recognition in 1977, when he was awarded an honorary D.Phil. by the
University of Lund.

Back in England, Alan applied for a lectureship in economics at the
University of Exeter, and was successful. In November 1953 he and June
were married, and they moved to Exeter together when Alan took up his
position in January 1954. The following years were busy ones for the
Williams family. Alan and June's three children were born (Mark in 1956,
Susan in 1959, Paul in 1961). Through the intermediation of a friend who
now worked at the Massachusetts Institute of Technology, Alan was a
visiting assistant professor at MIT in the academic year 1957–8. With
Mark only a baby, crossing the Atlantic by ship and then living for a year
in America was a huge family adventure. For Alan, it was also an intellectual adventure: he was able to walk into the office of Paul Samuelson,
arguably the greatest economist of the day, for casual discussions.

After this experience of MIT, it was difficult for Alan not to find
Exeter dull. In fairness to the University of Exeter, however, it should be
said that Alan's own research output in this period was hardly exciting.
His most significant work was *Public Finance and Budgetary Policy*, published in 1963 as one of a series of 'student handbooks'.[2] This is an introduction to public finance, intended for advanced undergraduate students.
The emphasis is on issues of tax incidence, and on the economically dis-
torting effects of different forms of taxation. The method of analysis is
firmly neoclassical, by means of geometrical proofs in what now seem
frighteningly complicated diagrams, often in three dimensions. The most
distinguished journal publication of Alan's Exeter years was a short,
workmanlike paper in *Economica* on the possible effects of a current proposal to abolish local government taxation of agricultural and industrial
property.[3]

[2] Alan Williams, *Public Finance and Budgetary Policy* (London, 1963).
[3] Alan Williams, 'The abolition of derating: an exercise in differential incidence', *Economica*, 90
(1956), 150–7.

Some time around 1960, Alan began to work on an intellectually more promising project, growing out of his previous work on local government finance in Britain. In what was then the received theory of public finance, 'government' was represented as a unitary agency, choosing tax rates and levels of public spending so as to maximise some index of social welfare. Around this time, however, there was a growth of interest among economists, particularly in the United States, in 'fiscal federalism'—that is, the inter-relationships between the fiscal activities of different tiers of government. Alan's idea was to adapt the 'pure' theory of public goods, recently developed by Samuelson, to the case of two-tier government. This opened up the prospect of making a contribution to economic theory which could engage an international audience.

Determined to make the most of this opportunity, Alan invested some of his family's very limited resources in travelling to Istanbul to present his work at an International Institute of Public Finance conference. (The University of Exeter had offered to pay only his third-class rail fare—a decision which rankled with Alan for the rest of his life.) The investment paid off. Alan made himself known to the international public finance community as someone doing important work on fiscal federalism. His work impressed Richard Musgrave, the leading figure in public finance at that time, and he received an open invitation to visit Musgrave's department at Princeton. Early drafts of his paper began to circulate among public finance specialists around the world.

Like many other British academics of his generation, Alan was a beneficiary of the Robbins expansion of the university system. The new University of York took its first intake of students in autumn 1963 and, well before then, its first professors were recruiting academic staff for their departments. Developments in economics were under the effective control of Alan Peacock and Jack Wiseman. Both had reputations in public finance, and naturally wanted this area of economics to be one of the specialisms of their department. Both were also known for their inclinations towards what, in the context of the time, was seen as right-wing, free-market economics. Sensibly, they recognised that their own style of public finance was a minority taste and wanted to build their departmental specialism on a broader base. As a relatively young but recognised public finance economist, with a tendency to favour an active role for government in the economy, Alan looked a promising prospect. In late 1962 or early 1963, Alan was tentatively approached by Wiseman with the opening remark: 'I suppose you're well settled in Exeter?' Alan, for whom this approach was a complete but entirely welcome surprise, indicated that he was not *so* well settled, and shortly afterwards he was being inter-viewed in York. According to Peacock, after the candidate had left the interview room, Wiseman said: 'We must have him with us—but he'll be a bloody nuisance.'

Alan was offered a senior lectureship, to start eighteen months later, and he accepted. He immediately handed in his notice at Exeter and took up the invitation from Musgrave, spending the academic year 1963–4 as a visiting professor at Princeton. This time there was a family of five to enjoy the experience of living in America, with the added excitement of driving across the continent to Berkeley, where Alan taught at a summer school in 1964. While in Princeton, Alan completed his theoretical paper on fiscal federalism, which was published in the *Journal of Political Economy* in 1966.[4] This was the high point of Alan's career as a public finance theorist. The paper is an elegant extension of Samuelson's theory of public goods in the form of a model in which central and local gov-ernment decisions interact. It uses Alan's preferred technique of compli-cated geometrical proofs and leads to a mildly surprising result, induced (as such results often are in neoclassical analysis) by the possibility that income effects can outweigh substitution effects. Reading the paper forty years later, one can still see why it established Alan's reputation as a ris-ing star in public finance. At the same time, one does not get the sense that the author is deeply engaged in this theoretical exercise: there is none of the passionate commitment of Alan's later work.

Alan moved to the University of York in the autumn of 1964, the second year of its existence. He remained there for the rest of his life, successively as senior lecturer, reader and (from 1968) professor. From the beginning, he enjoyed the stimulating atmosphere of the newly cre-ated economics department. Alan Peacock was proving an inspired appointment as head of department, his sense of direction and institution-building skill camouflaged by a deceptively easy-going style. Peacock encouraged creative diversity in approaches to economics. Ideologically speaking, Alan Williams's inclination to be a bloody nuisance was given free rein.

Nevertheless, the true turning-point in Alan's career was not the move to York; it was the two-year period between 1966 and 1968 which he spent on secondment to the Treasury. His job description was 'Director of Economic Studies' at the Treasury's Centre for Administrative Studies

---

[4] Alan Williams, 'The optimal provision of public goods in a system of local government', *Journal of Political Economy*, 74 (1966), 18–33.

(later the Civil Service College). In that capacity, he devised and taught courses in economics for senior civil servants. In addition, he was asked to undertake a series of one-off commissions for various government departments which did not have economists of their own. As Alan later described it, this work was partly that of an odd-job man in the Government Economic Service and partly that of a 'Treasury spy', making reconnaissance missions to discover how other departments were making their spending decisions.

As the designer of short economics courses for busy civil servants, Alan was forced to consider what were the absolute essentials of the discipline that decision-makers needed to understand. In his roving commissions, he gained experience of a wide range of decision problems that the government machine had to deal with, and had to think creatively about how economic analysis could contribute to their solution. As the combined result of these two elements of his work, he developed a distinctive conception of the role that microeconomics can and should play in public decision-making; he maintained this position, at least in broad outline, for the rest of his career.

He seems to have concluded that, for the purposes of public decision-making, the essential core of microeconomics is the analysis of constrained maximisation. First and foremost, rational decision-making requires well-specified objectives and constraints: one has to decide what one wants to maximise, subject to what constraints. The maximand must be a desired *output* of the relevant system, not a measure of input or throughput. Alternative policy options must be understood as different ways of using scarce inputs to produce the desired output. Microeconomic analysis is then concerned with achieving efficiency in transforming inputs into output.

On this understanding, microeconomics and operations research are closely related. Of the two main techniques that Alan recommended for use in government, one (output budgeting) came primarily from operations research, the other (cost–benefit analysis) from economics.[5] Output budgeting is a method of organising the accounts of an agency so that desired outputs are defined and then the agency's costs are attributed to the outputs which they produce. Cost–benefit analysis, as understood by Alan, appraises specific policy options in terms of their marginal costs and their marginal contributions to desired outputs, and makes inputs

---

[5] Alan Williams, 'Output budgeting and the contribution of micro-economics to efficiency in government', CAS [Centre for Administrative Studies] Occasional Paper no. 4 (1967).

and outputs commensurable by expressing both in money units, discounted to present values. Crucially, the money values placed on units of
output are expressions of the priorities of the decision-making agency,
not measures of anything external to that agency. The main function of
these 'postulated' money values is as shadow prices, that is, as signals
which assist the pursuit of efficiency in achieving given objectives. Alan
defended this account of cost–benefit analysis in a forceful paper in the
first volume of the *Journal of Public Economics*.[6] It also appears as what
is called the 'decision-making approach' in a textbook on cost–benefit
analysis that he and I later wrote together.[7]

This form of constrained maximisation is a ruthlessly edited-down
form of microeconomics, which abstracts from many issues that other
economists would have seen as relevant for public decision-making.
Cost–benefit analysis was a fashionable topic in economics in the 1960s
and 1970s, but much of the profession's effort was directed towards finding ways of inferring private individuals' valuations of public-sector
outputs from observations of those individuals' choices in relevant contexts (or, sometimes, from their responses to survey questions). Such a
preference-based approach is closer in spirit to the public finance of
Wicksell and Lindahl than is Alan's operations research. By the end of
the 1960s, economists were beginning to become interested in *social
choice*, understood as the problem of aggregating the separate preferences
of individual citizens into a single system of consistent 'social preferences'. Alan's methodology short-circuits these problems by treating the
valuation of the outputs of public policies simply as a matter for decision-
makers' own judgements. Another set of issues concerns the motivations
of public decision-makers. The economics of *public choice*, also getting
under way by the late 1960s, models government itself as a system of rules
within which politicians and bureaucrats pursue their private interests.
This leads to the idea that procedures of public decision-making should
be designed so as to provide incentives for decision-makers to act in the
public interest. In contrast, Alan's approach takes the viewpoint of the

---

[6] Alan Williams, 'Cost–benefit analysis: bastard science? and/or insidious poison in the body
politick?', *Journal of Public Economics*, 1 (1972), 199–225.
[7] Robert Sugden and Alan Williams, *The Principles of Practical Cost–Benefit Analysis* (Oxford,
1978). Although I was the main author of this book, its basic structure was laid down by
Alan; I think it derived from courses he had taught at the Centre for Administrative Studies. The
decision-making approach is presented alongside an alternative 'Paretian approach' which, by
the time we finished the book, I had come to favour.

decision-makers themselves, accepting as unproblematic their postulated valuations of public-sector outputs.

By abstracting from these other issues, Alan was able to isolate problems that were susceptible to rigorous analysis according to economic principles of constrained maximisation. On Alan's account, identifying a decision-maker's problem is not a straightforward task: 'any practitioner [of operations research or cost–benefit analysis] who accepts the client's initial formulation of the problem uncritically is heading for disaster'.[8] In particular, most public organisations find it easier to characterise what they do than to identify those effects of their activities that are ultimately valuable. But by pressing decision-makers to specify their problems within a framework of constrained maximisation, Alan was able to expose ambiguities and confusions in their thinking. His single-mindedness in insisting on this framework and the remorseless logic with which he organised arguments within it were indeed captured by the famous motto about being reasonable and doing it his way.

These features of Alan's approach are well illustrated by the story (as ruefully told by Alan himself) of his first involvement with health economics.[9] The Treasury had sent him to the Ministry of Health to look at the ongoing hospital-building programme and to estimate when, given the criteria being used to decide on the need for new hospitals, the programme could be expected to tail off. The results of Alan's first enquiries suggested that no obvious criteria *were* being used, except the general principle of replacing hospitals that were judged to be 'old' (a vague concept, as most hospital sites had buildings of many different ages) and a rough notion that different areas of the country should take turns in getting new hospitals. So the Treasury asked Alan to propose suitable criteria. As a well-trained economist, he started from the assumption that capital and other inputs are substitutes, with the implication that as buildings age, the capital stock deteriorates and running costs increase; eventually a time will be reached at which it is less costly to rebuild than to continue using old buildings. But then Alan discovered that new hospitals had *higher* running costs than old ones. So, he asked the officials in the Ministry of Health, were new hospitals more effective than old ones? They were unable to say. Asked whether the construction of a new hospital improved the health of the population in its catchment area, they

---

[8] 'Cost–benefit analysis: bastard science?', p. 204 (see above, n. 6).
[9] Alan Williams, 'All cost effective treatments should be free . . . or, how Archie Cochrane changed my life!', *Journal of Epidemiology and Community Health*, 51 (1997), 116–20.

knew of no evidence, but guessed any effect would be small. With his usual logic, Alan concluded that the hospital building programme was probably a bad investment, and reported this to the Treasury.

Alan's Treasury superiors then indicated to the Ministry of Health that this finding might have repercussions for the funding of its capital programme. The Ministry responded by bringing in figures from the medical and scientific establishment, who insisted that it was well-known to experts in the field that new hospitals *were* more effective than old ones; evidence would be superfluous, but if the Treasury really felt it was necessary, could they specify what evidence was needed and how it might be collected? Alan went away and started work on constructing a population-based measure of health status which could be used as the basis of an output measure for hospitals. His first ideas were rejected as impractical by the Ministry. Then, in the usual civil service way, the Treasury lost interest and sent Alan off on another job.

Alan returned to York in 1968. It was at this stage in his career that I first met him. I was an undergraduate student in history and economics. Among the economics students, Alan was generally regarded as their best lecturer. He was not a charismatic performer, as Hahn had been at Birmingham. For most students (I was an exception in this respect), the topics on which Alan lectured—welfare economics and investment appraisal—were not particularly exciting. He was just exceptionally lucid and well-organised, and tailored his lectures to the abilities of his audiences. Alan supervised my final-year project, a retrospective cost–benefit study of a railway branch-line closure. He went far beyond the requirements of duty in helping me to get started. I recall his accompanying me to a meeting with a senior railway official, at which Alan's reassuring bureaucrat-to-bureaucrat mode of operation gained me access to the data I needed. (He must have been a very effective Treasury spy.) When I claimed that I had found a theoretical error in the Ministry of Transport's cost–benefit methodology, Alan listened to me patiently; when he had been convinced, he encouraged me to write what became my first publication. It is hard to imagine any undergraduate student being given so much attention by a professor today, but even in the 1960s this was very unusual. However, it was typical of Alan. Later, the help he gave to successive cohorts of trainee health economists led to many continuing friendships and professional relationships, and is part of the explanation of his eventual role as what one obituary described as a 'grandfather' of health economics.

I have said that Alan was not charismatic; in terms of his style at this time, that is an understatement. This was the period in which universities were at their most fashionable, and new universities like York were the most fashionable of all. Alan did not look like anyone's idea of a sixties professor. He dressed in a way that would have merged with the background in a civil service office of the time. His style of dress—serviceable jackets and ties of indeterminate colour, neither smart nor casual—remained constant over the thirty-seven years I knew him. Other professors came to work by car, but Alan drove a large blue Bedford van, more suitable for a parcel delivery service. (Eventually, this was replaced by a series of much-loved Volvos, but this move up-market was made only because the newer designs of Bedford van would not fit into his garage.) When transferred to intellectual matters, Alan's lack of concern for appearances was one of his great strengths. He was immune to the forces of fashion which govern so many developments in economics: once he had found a problem that he thought important or a method that he thought would work, he pressed on regardless of its status among his fellow economists.

To return to the main story: it turned out that Alan's arguments at the Ministry of Health had had more effect than he had thought at the time. In 1970, two years after leaving the Treasury, Alan was phoned by Archie Cochrane, Director of the Medical Research Council's Epidemiology Research Unit. Cochrane had been one of the medical experts who had helped the Ministry of Health to repulse Alan's reconnaissance mission. He enquired about the progress of Alan's investigations of effectiveness measures for health care. In fact, nothing more had been done: at this time, Alan's efforts in cost–benefit analysis were mainly directed towards the water industry. Cochrane set about persuading him to return to his unfinished work on health care, as part of a research project funded by the Nuffield Provincial Hospitals Trust. Alan agreed. That marked the start of his transition from public finance to health economics.

The first main product of this work was a paper on 'social indicators' for health, co-authored by Alan and two of his York colleagues, Tony Culyer and Bob Lavers, and published in 1971.[10] This remarkable paper provides the outline of an 'index of ill-health' based on two dimensions, 'painfulness' and 'degree of restriction of activity'. For each dimension, there is a set of different qualitative descriptions, arrayed in order of pain

[10] Anthony Culyer, Robert Lavers and Alan Williams, 'Social indicators: health', *Social Trends*, 2 (1971), 31–42.

or restriction. This defines a two-dimensional space of health states. Any given medical condition can be located in this space. An index can then be created by using judgements of equivalence between different points in the space, and judgements about the relative badness of different points. These judgements provide the *weights* for the index. Significantly, they are treated as 'statements about *health policy* . . . to be made by whoever is entrusted with that responsibility—e.g. "the Minister"'. The authors then show how two alternative prognoses for a patient ('with treatment' and 'without treatment') can be plotted as graphs of ill-health (measured by the index) against time. The effectiveness of treatment is measured by the net gain in units of health × time. This, in its essentials, is a methodology for creating a measure of quality-adjusted life years (QALYs), although this term is not used.

It seems that, at some time after this work on social indicators, Alan began to think that health measures should take account of judgements about the relative values of different health states made by members of the general public. This marks a significant change from the position Alan developed in the Treasury, namely that valuations are to be postulated by public decision-makers as expressions of government policy. Perhaps this change of perspective was a delayed effect of moving from the heart of the government machine to the position of someone arguing for reform from the outside. However, Alan continued to maintain that the weights used in a health-state index should be understood as collective judgements about relative need, whether these are expressed by responsible decision-makers or by individuals as citizens. In all his work in health economics, he has resolutely rejected the idea that the distribution of health care should respond to differences in individuals' preferences or willingness to pay. Thus, when offering a 'guide through the ideological jungle' in relation to setting priorities in health care, he firmly declares his personal commitment to 'egalitarianism', characterised by the ethic of 'equal opportunity of access for those in equal need'.[11] In a discussion piece on age-based rationing, Alan poses the question: Whose values should count in a social insurance setting? He asks us to suppose that older people are willing to pay more than younger people for health improvements for themselves. Is that relevant for the setting of priorities in the NHS? Alan insists it is not:

---

[11] Alan Williams, 'Priority setting in public and private health care: a guide through the ideological jungle', *Journal of Health Economics*, 7 (1988), 173–83; quotation from p. 174.

> But did we not take the NHS out of that [private market] context precisely
> because as citizens (rather than as consumers of health care) we were pursuing
> a rather different ideal—namely, that health care should be provided according
> to people's needs, not according to what they were each willing and able to pay?
> A person's needs (constituting claims on social resources) have to be arbitrated
> by a third party, whose unenviable task it is to weigh different needs (and
> different people's needs) one against another. This is precisely what priority set-
> ting in health care is all about. So the values of the citizenry as a whole must
> override the values of a particular interest group within it.[12]

So Alan was looking for weights for a health-state index which could
express citizens' judgements about relative need. He recalled that, in his
work on output budgeting for the Home Office (another of the roving
commissions of his Treasury period), he had come across an American
index of crime seriousness which was based on ordinary people's judgements. He contacted an operations researcher, Vincent Watts (later to
become the Vice-Chancellor of the University of East Anglia), who had
helped him in his Home Office work, to try to find out more about this
index. Watts told Alan that his wife, the psychiatrist Rachel Rosser, was
currently developing an output measure for hospital treatment. Through
Rosser, Alan learned about the work of other researchers around the
world who were working on the design of health-status indices, based on
individuals' preferences between health states, elicited by survey methods.

From this point, the Williams and Rosser projects coalesced. The
'Rosser index' became the template for Alan's subsequent work. It was
based on two dimensions, 'disability' and 'distress'. Rosser had collected
responses from a small convenience sample of doctors, nurses, patients
and members of the general public, which could be used to construct an
index of the relative value of being in each state. Alan had the idea of
recalibrating these data to fit a scale on which 'dead' had a value of zero
and 'full health' a value of one. This work was done by Paul Kind, one of
Rosser's researchers who later moved to York, and published in 1982.[13]
This index was the prototype QALY.

This is not to say that either the theoretical ideas or the survey methods underlying the QALY concept can be credited to Alan or to Rachel
Rosser. The idea of a survey-based measure of health status had already

---

[12] Alan Williams, 'The rationing debate: rationing health care by age: the case for', *British Medical Journal*, 314 (1997), 820 (15 March).
[13] This was published as Paul Kind, Rachel Rosser and Alan Williams, 'Valuation of quality of life: some psychometric evidence', in Michael Jones-Lee (ed.), *The Value of Life and Safety* (Amsterdam, 1982).

been developed by researchers in the US and Canada.[14] Nevertheless, Alan was very early in recognising the potential for using such a measure to determine priorities in health policy, and he pursued this idea with his characteristic energy and single-mindedness. Much of the rest of his working life was devoted to making QALY measurement operational and transparent, and convincing policy-makers to use it. It is entirely just that, in the world of health policy, the QALY has come to be so inseparably linked with the name of Alan Williams.

In the decade from the mid-1970s, the main emphasis of Alan's work was on trying to convince the health policy establishment of the logic of the QALY approach. These efforts met with mixed success. He gained an important ally in Sir Douglas Black, the Chief Scientist at the Department of Health between 1973 and 1977 (and later author of the controversial 'Black Report' on social inequalities in health). Black invited Alan to serve on various of his advisory committees. By 1976, Alan had made a sufficiently favourable impression on the medical establishment to be deemed a suitable person to be a member of the Royal Commission on the NHS, set up in that year.

This proved to be a low point in Alan's career. Perhaps his impatience with compromise and preference for action over words were not adapted to the mode of working of a Royal Commission. It seems clear that there was a personality clash between Alan and the Commission's chairman, Sir Alec Merrison, a nuclear physicist who had become Vice-Chancellor of the University of Bristol, and who had previously chaired committees of enquiry into box-girder bridges and the regulation of the medical profession. Here is Alan's account of the episode:

> I found myself totally at loggerheads with the Chairman, Alec Merrison, over the Commission's role. I saw this as doing for the NHS what the Robbins Report had done for Higher Education, but he seemed to see it as some kind of holding operation in which all we had to do was to re-state basic principles and hold the line at a general strategic level. After a couple of years the tension got

---

[14] The paper which is now usually credited with initiating this research programme is S. Fanshel and J. W. Bush, 'A health-status index and its application to health-services outcomes', *Operations Research*, 18 (1970), 1021–66. Another founding father of health-status indices is George Torrance; see, e.g., George Torrance, Warren Thomas and David Sackett, 'A utility-maximization model for evaluation of health care programs', *Health Services Research*, 7 (1972), 118–33. In their pioneering paper on 'social indicators' (see above, n. 10), Culyer, Lavers and Williams acknowledge that their approach is 'fairly close methodologically' to that of M. Magdeleine, A. Mizrami and G. Rosch, 'Un indicateur de la morbidité appliquée aux données d'une enquette sur la consommation médicale', *Consommation*, 2 (1967).

too much for me and I quit, with a strong sense of inadequacy and personal failure.[15]

Some of Alan's main achievements around this time were in institution-building. It was in this period that the structure of health economics as a distinct sub-discipline began to emerge, and the University of York established its position as the leading British centre for teaching and research in the field. Alan played a central role in these developments, together with two younger colleagues, Tony Culyer and Alan Maynard. Alan was a co-founder of the Health Economists' Study Group, which immediately became the main academic forum for health economists in Britain; he remained one of its most active members for the rest of his life. Research in health economics at York expanded rapidly, first under the umbrella of Jack Wiseman's Institute of Social and Economic Research and then, from 1983, in the Centre for Health Economics. This is now a major enterprise, employing around forty researchers at any given time. In 1978, a master's programme in health economics was launched, which to date has trained over three hundred students. The *Journal of Health Economics* began in 1982, with Tony Culyer as one of the founding editors. There are very few health economists in Britain today who have not been associated with York in one way or another at some time. The cumulative effect of all this has been to produce a cadre of health economists with a strong sense of collective identity and a common intellectual tradition—a tradition on which Alan's ideas are imprinted. Without these developments, the idea that health-service decisions should be guided by economic analysis could not have been transformed into a feasible prospect.

As far as the QALY is concerned, the most important breakthrough came in 1985, with the publication of Alan's first paper in the *British Medical Journal*.[16] Twelve years later, as part of the commemoration of the first twenty-five years of health economics, experts were invited to make nominations for 'most influential publication'. This health economists' Oscar was awarded to Alan's *BMJ* paper.

The paper is less than four pages long and, revealingly, it appears in the 'For Debate . . .' section of the journal. The editors seem to be suggesting that the ideas being presented are not quite safe enough to warrant the *BMJ* seal of approval. The paper summarises a cost-effectiveness

---

[15] 'Discovering the QALY' (see above, n. 1).

[16] Alan Williams, 'Economics of coronary artery bypass grafting', *British Medical Journal*, 291 (1985), 326–9.

study of coronary artery bypass grafting (CABG). This study had been carried out by Alan and presented to an NHS enquiry into whether provision of CABG should be expanded. It uses the Kind/Rosser/Williams index to estimate the net QALY gain per episode of intervention, for different categories of patient. These estimates are combined with cost data to produce 'cost per QALY' measures. These are then compared with corresponding measures for some other interventions—significantly, ones which treat quite different medical conditions. This is the prototype of the Williams approach to priority-setting. Implicit in the analysis is the principle that interventions should be ranked by 'cost per QALY' and the NHS budget should be allocated to those with the lowest scores.

In fact, most forms of CABG turn out to be quite cost-effective at around £2000 per QALY. In comparison, kidney dialysis comes in at £11,000, while hip replacement is a much better buy at £750. Alan liked using the comparison between dialysis and hip replacement as an illustration of the logic of his approach. Dialysis was a high-technology treatment for a life-threatening condition. Hip replacement was undramatic and did not save lives, but an expansion of this programme could bring great benefits in reduced pain and increased mobility at low cost.

The next decade—a time of life at which many academics have retired—was in many ways the most productive period of Alan's life. The CABG study had shown the potential of the QALY approach, but the Kind/Rosser/Williams classification of health states was quite coarse, and the weights were not derived from a representative sample of the population. If QALYs were to be put to serious use, it was essential to refine the index. In addition, it would be advantageous to have a single index which could be used across as many applications as possible and across national boundaries. Alan was the central figure in two projects which addressed these issues.

The first project, which started in 1987 at a meeting in Rotterdam, was a loosely structured multi-disciplinary collaboration, initially involving researchers from seven centres in Britain, Finland, the Netherlands, Norway and Sweden. The aim was to produce a common system of generic classifications of health-related quality of life. This collaboration grew into a permanent research network, the 'EuroQoL Group'. The group was eventually able to agree on a generic classification system based on five dimensions of quality of life—mobility, ability to provide self-care, ability to perform usual activities, pain/discomfort, and anxiety/depression, each of which can be reported at three different levels. This descriptive measure, called 'EQ-5D', is now widely used around the world, providing a simple language in which health states can be described.

The second project was a more structured research programme, funded by the Department of Health and directed by Alan, with Paul Kind as his right-hand man. The aim of this 'Measurement and Valuation of Health' programme was to generate weights for the health states defined by the EQ-5D classification scheme, based on responses from a large representative sample of the British population. The final product—a firmly grounded and operational QALY measure—was finally delivered in 1995.

The final piece in Alan's jigsaw was put into place in 1999, with the establishment of the National Institute for Clinical Excellence (immediately known more familiarly as 'NICE'), with Alan's long-standing colleague and ally, Tony Culyer, as its first vice-chair. NICE's main function was to develop clinical guidelines for the NHS. In particular, it was charged with the task of appraising new medical technologies in terms of their appropriateness for NHS use. This at last provided an institutional structure within which Alan's grand scheme for rational decision-making about health care could be put into practice. In its appraisals, NICE generally uses Alan's QALY measure to assess cost-effectiveness, typically approving new technologies which do not cost more than about £30,000 per QALY. In one of his last public lectures, delivered in 2004, Alan reflected on these developments, asking 'What could be nicer than NICE?'[17] Alan acknowledged that NICE was doing *almost* everything he could possibly ask, but urged it to extend its QALY-based appraisals from new technologies to clinical guidelines in general. Provocative to the last, he suggested that a shadow price of £30,000 per QALY was far too extravagant, and that a figure closer to per capita national income (currently £18,000 per year) might be more reasonable.

In the last decade of his life, Alan began to question whether, on egalitarian grounds, some people's QALYs should be given more weight than others. Previously, in his 'guide through the ideological jungle', he had espoused the principle of equal access to health care for those in equal medical need. But if (as he had always believed) the *raison d'être* of universal health care is to reduce health inequalities, and if health status is measured in QALYs, the natural implication is that we should seek to equalise QALYs across individuals. Having recognised this implication of his analysis, Alan—logical as ever—concluded that priority should be

---

[17] Alan Williams, *What could be nicer than NICE?* (London: Office of Health Economics, 2004).

given to improving the lifetime health of those people with the lowest life-time QALY expectancy.[18] Since (as the Black Report had documented) life expectancy and health status in Britain are positively correlated with income and social class, many of the implications of this priority principle are in accord with egalitarian predilections. But, since men have markedly lower life expectancy than women, one implication is that (other things being equal) men's QALYs should have greater weight than women's. Professional egalitarians found this conclusion hard to take. Amartya Sen insisted that non-discrimination between the sexes should be treated as a moral constraint on health policy.[19] Alan's response can be paraphrased as: 'But *why?*' His counter-proposal was that policy should be based, not on axioms postulated by moral theorists, but on evidence about the trade-offs that members of the general public would want to see made on their behalf.[20]

Alan's interest in the distribution of QALYs had been sparked off by reflecting on what John Harris had called the 'fair innings' argument.[21] The idea, as re-expressed by Alan (at the age of 69) is that 'someone who dies young has been denied the opportunities that we older people have already had'; thus, as egalitarians, we should give more weight to the QALYs of the young than to those of the old. Or, more philosophically:

> In each of our lives there has to come a time when we accept the inevitability of death, and when we accept that a reasonable limit has to be set on the demands we can properly make on our fellow citizens in order to keep us going a bit longer.[22]

As the twenty-first century got under way, Alan may have recognised that he was becoming old; but he showed no sign of wanting to retire, or even to slow down. He was proud of the academic honours he received, such as the honorary doctorate announced by the University of Kuopio shortly before his death, and awarded posthumously; he was particularly pleased at being made a Fellow of the British Academy in 2002. But he was not the person to accept the status of a distinguished scholar reflecting on old glories. He wanted to be in the thick of things, and looked for

---

[18] Alan Williams, 'Intergenerational equity: an exploration of the "fair innings" argument', *Health Economics*, 6 (1997), 117–32.

[19] Amartya Sen, 'Why health equity?' *Health Economics*, 11 (2003), 659–66.

[20] Alan Williams, 'Comment on Amartya Sen's "Why health equity?"', *Health Economics*, 12 (2003), 65–6.

[21] John Harris, *The Value of Life: An Introduction to Medical Ethics* (London, 1985).

[22] Alan Williams, 'The rationing debate: rationing health care by age: the case for', *British Medical Journal*, 314 (1997), 820.

new controversies to provoke and new problems to tackle. In the last years of his life he was taking part in Home Office discussions about an analogue of the QALY for the criminal justice system—a potentially massive project in which he would surely have wanted to be fully involved.

Still, despite all this, he did find time for life away from economics. His private life centred on his family. From their first days together in Birmingham, Alan and June were keen walkers. After moving to York, they spent most Sundays walking in the Yorkshire Dales or on the North Yorkshire Moors. With the same propensity for organisation that he showed in his working life, Alan liked to plan his walks carefully in advance, and had a huge library of walking books to consult. He enjoyed pub lunches, and drew detailed maps showing the pubs he could recommend to himself. Symphony music and opera were other interests: he and June always had season tickets to the concerts at Leeds Town Hall, and were regulars at the Buxton and Ryedale Festivals. Alan was curious about how things worked. As a result of his work on cost–benefit analysis in the water industry, he developed an interest in sewage-treatment technology. Traction engines, preserved railways and model trains all appealed to him. He retained his political commitments to the end; with his daughter Susan, he took part in the 2003 demonstration in Hyde Park against the impending invasion of Iraq.

When he discovered that he had terminal cancer, he acknowledged that he had had a fair innings and accepted with stoicism his own downward path though the EQ-5D classification scheme. His taste for organisation did not desert him: he made careful plans for his own funeral and took part in the preliminary planning of the conference that was to commemorate his life and work. In a last message to his academic colleagues and friends, he reported on the excellence of the care he was receiving from the National Health Service. He died on 2 June 2005.

ROBERT SUGDEN
University of East Anglia

Note. In writing this essay I have used information given to me by many people, but particularly June Williams, Susan Williams, Tony Culyer, Diane Dawson, Paul Kind, Alan Maynard and Alan Peacock.

BERNARD WILLIAMS

Bernard Arthur Owen Williams
1929–2003

WHEN BERNARD WILLIAMS DIED, in Rome, on 10 June 2003 at the age of 73, the loss was felt well beyond the refined world of academic philosophy. In a succession of obituaries, and at affectionate memorial events in Cambridge, Oxford, and Berkeley, distinguished contemporaries from many fields testified to his place as one of the great, inspirational humanists of his time. While all spoke of his terrifying brilliance, his dazzling speed of mind and extraordinary range of understanding, his zest and his glittering wit, many also tried to come to terms with the deep humanity that had infused his life and work, and the seriousness with which he had tried to transform the role of the moral philosopher. The paradoxical combination of exhilaration and pessimism, of complete facility in the academic exercises of philosophy juxtaposed with an almost tragic sense of the resistance that the human clay offers to theory and analysis, let alone to recipes and panaceas, made Bernard a unique, and uniquely admired, figure in his generation.

I

Bernard Williams was born on 21 September 1929 at Westcliff-on-Sea in Essex. He was the only child of Owen Paisley Denny Williams, OBE, an architect and chief maintenance surveyor for the Ministry of Works, and his wife Hilda. He was educated at Chigwell School, which was then a grammar school, later to opt for independent status. He entered Balliol College in 1947 to read Greats, where he gravitated towards philosophy, although he was also taught by two great classicists to whom he later

Proceedings of the British Academy, **150**, 335–348. © The British Academy 2007.

paid tribute, Eduard Fraenkel and Eric Dodds. His extraordinary brilliance was immediately recognised, and it is reported that he regularly held informal tutorials in Balliol during which he would assist less gifted students with their philosophical difficulties. His undergraduate career culminated in his entering the final examination on Roman History twenty-nine minutes late, one minute before entry was forbidden, allegedly having needed the time to mug up the subject, which he had hitherto found too boring to study. This did not prevent him from achieving a congratulatory First.

Immediately after graduating he was offered a Prize Fellowship at All Souls College. However, before he could enjoy this he had to perform the then compulsory National Service, during which he learned to fly Spitfires in Canada, an exciting activity filling what he later described as the happiest year of his life. Shortly after returning to Oxford he moved to a teaching Fellowship at New College in 1954. One year later he married Shirley Brittain (later Baroness Williams of Crosby, leader of the Liberal Democrats in the House of Lords).

After a year's Visiting Lectureship at the new University College of Ghana, Williams accepted the offer by Professor A. J. Ayer of a Lectureship at University College, London, in 1959. In 1961 a daughter, Rebecca was born, and in 1964 Shirley became the Member of Parliament for Hitchin. In the same year Williams accepted a Professorship at Bedford College, London.

In 1967, at the young age of thirty-eight, Williams was appointed Knightbridge Professor of Philosophy in Cambridge and Fellow of King's College. Shortly afterwards he met Patricia Skinner, née Dwyer, then a Senior Editor at Cambridge University Press, of which Bernard had been appointed a Syndic. They married in 1974, the marriage to Shirley having been dissolved the same year. Two children, Jacob and Jonathan, were born in 1975 and 1980.

During the 1960s, Williams had published relatively little. But his period as Knightbridge Professor saw three books of his own, *Morality* (1972), *Problems of the Self* (1973), *Descartes* (1978), and one, *Utilitarianism, For and Against* (1973), shared with J. J. C. Smart. His growing stature in philosophy was reflected in the wider academic community, witnessed by his election to the Fellowship of the British Academy in 1971 and to be Provost of King's College in 1979. In addition to his academic eminence, he played a considerable role in public life, most visibly as member or chairman of various official public commissions. He did public schools, then gambling, and from 1977 to 1979 he chaired the committee set up by the Wilson government to review the laws concerning 'obscenity, indecency and violence' in public media (excluding broadcasting). The report of the last committee in particular was widely admired, finding a receptive audience from the professionals in the police and social services concerned with such issues, although less so in Mrs Thatcher's incoming Conservative government. The report, heavily indebted to his analytical and imaginative abilities, and largely his own work, was later published in an abridged form by Cambridge University Press in 1981. It remains an important marker in debates about obscenity and censorship. His flow of work continued with the collection of papers *Moral Luck* in 1981, and the most important of his books on moral philosophy, the vivid and forceful *Ethics and the Limits of Philosophy*, in 1985.

In addition, from 1968 until 1986 he was first a member, then Chair, of the English National Opera (formerly Sadlers' Wells). Music was an essential part of Bernard's life, and one about which he thought and wrote with great sensitivity and insight.

This firm place on the pinnacles of British academic and public life increased the surprise with which many friends and colleagues greeted his decision to leave Cambridge for Berkeley in 1988. But the demoralisation of the academic world by the Thatcher government was by then in full swing, and American universities were not slow to seize their opportunity to attract world-class talent. However, various reasons soon brought Williams back to the United Kingdom, in response to Oxford's invitation to the White's Professorship of Moral Philosophy which he occupied in 1990, becoming a Fellow of Corpus Christi College. He retained his Chair at Berkeley, and returned every year to teach. He was particularly proud of having been invited to lecture as the Sather Professor of Classics in Berkeley in 1989, and in 1993 the lectures were published as *Shame and Necessity*, in many peoples' judgement his deepest and finest book.

His return to the United Kingdom was also a return to public life. He served as a member of the Labour Party Commission on Social Justice, established by John Smith, and was a member of the Independent Inquiry into the Misuse of Drugs Act, 1971. Drugs thus took their place alongside public schools, gambling, and pornography, enabling him to quip that he had 'done all the major vices'. He brought out a third collection of papers, the one whose title most succinctly sums up his own intellectual quest, *Making Sense of Humanity*, in 1995.

After retirement in 1997 Williams was re-elected a Fellow of All Souls College. He continued to garner academic honours including honorary doctorates from the Universities of Chicago, Yale, Cambridge, and Harvard. He produced the small but sparkling panegyric to his most admired philosopher, *Plato: The Invention of Philosophy*, in 1998.

A year later, Williams was diagnosed with cancer. He continued to work, and in 2001 provided an introduction and notes to a new edition of Friedrich Nietzsche's *The Gay Science*. Homage to Nietzsche, whom Williams came increasingly to admire, is also visible in the larger and many-layered *Truth and Truthfulness* which came out in 2002. He lived just long enough to enjoy some of its many glowing reviews. Up until his death he was also working on a projected volume of political philosophy.

Since his death three collections of his papers have been prepared by Patricia Williams and others. They cover political philosophy (*In the Beginning was the Deed: Realism and Moralism in Political Argument*, 2005, edited by Geoffrey Hawthorn), the history of philosophy (*The Sense of the Past*, 2006, edited by Myles Burnyeat), and a set of further essays from every phase of his career, *Philosophy as a Humanistic Discipline*, also in 2006, edited by Adrian Moore. *On Opera*, a collection of his writings on music, was published in the same year, edited by Patricia Williams.

II

Although it is natural enough to think of Bernard Williams as a moral philosopher, his work covered much more than this term usually implies. His earliest papers included a good proportion on metaphysics, while an ongoing preoccupation with scepticism and philosophical method produced work on Wittgenstein, and was crowned by his book on Descartes. He wrote extensively on the history of philosophy, particularly classical philosophy, although never divorcing it from the dialogue with contemporary problems. Myles Burnyeat records arriving in London in the early sixties and immediately becoming transfixed by the dazzling combination of historical and textual knowledge with sheer philosophical power, that Bernard exhibited in a course on Plato's *Theaetetus*. At the time this represented a new synthesis of history and philosophy, although one that, largely through Williams's own influence, is now the goal of all first-class work in the history of philosophy. His ability to transform a subject is perhaps most visible, in this early work, in his papers on personal identity, later collected in *Problems of the Self*, in which he brought out the delusive role that imagination plays in generating some of our deepest-seated illusions about ourselves. We think we can imagine ourselves being Cleopatra or Napoleon, and this generates the illusion that the 'I' can float free of its contingent embodiment, and therefore should be identified with something like a traditional soul. Williams pointed out, rightly, that what I call imagining myself being Napoleon is no more than imagining seeing things as Napoleon did—'images of, for instance, the desolation at Austerlitz, as viewed by me vaguely aware of my short stature, and my cockaded hat, my hand in my tunic'. It is akin to acting Napoleon. There is no supernatural self or soul that is transported in the imagining, so the imagining itself has no metaphysical weight. It is no guide to what is possible for us. Inevitably Williams went on to make connections that most other philosophers would have missed, for instance with the difference between seeing a character in a play and seeing an actor, or with the intriguing fact that you can film a scene which is nevertheless presented as being unwitnessed. His method in work such as this perhaps most closely resembles the approach to highly abstract issues through everyday examples that was found in Gilbert Ryle, the Oxford teacher of his time for whom he expressed the most admiration.

Williams's metaphysical interests also dominated his work on Descartes. In particular his defence of the ability of science to put us on the road towards an 'absolute' conception of the world 'which is to the largest possible extent independent of the local perspectives or idiosyncrasies of inquirers' proved influential, and perhaps unnecessarily controversial. The view is probably implicitly held by most scientists, but the climate in philosophy of science at the time tended to emphasise constructivism over realism, and to celebrate the thickness of the spectacles, or paradigms, through which the scientist peers at nature. Williams later commented on the 'remarkable assumption that the sociology of knowledge is in a better position to deliver truths about science than science is to deliver truths about the world'. By opposing that picture Williams raised controversy, although in later years he was particularly irritated by the travesty occasionally foisted on him that we could have a description of the world without deploying our own language or without employing our own concepts. This was never the idea. Rather, Williams thought that science had a title to knowledge that did not depend on the history, culture, values, or interests of those engaged in it, and in this was distinguished from other inquiries, including philosophy itself. He thought this difference showed, for instance, in the different relation science bears to its own history. The scientist can get by with a very slight knowledge of the history of discovery. But the philosopher cannot do the same, because our present ways of thinking and acting are only intelligible as historical formations. They are not the inevitable or universal products of uniform human nature facing uniform problems. The subject matter of the humanities is the nature of human life and thought, and that subject matter is necessarily only approachable by us from our own human point of view, albeit a standpoint infused with enough of the same culture, values, and interests as those of the agents whom we interpret for understanding to be possible.

The difference between science and the humanities is visible, Williams argued, in the way the history of science can be presented as a history of arguments that were actually won by one side or another. Whereas a human change, such as the displacement of the *ancien régime* by modernity, is not a history of arguments won, but a history in which one set of ideas has simply displaced another: the defenders of old ways are not refuted, but just die out. Science can write a 'vindicatory genealogy' of its history, couched in terms of progress towards the truth. Humanity cannot write its own history like this, or rather, if it does so it will simply be imposing the perspective of the present, adding another dismal chapter to the story of human complacency. This way of thinking, Willliams argued, changed our political relationships. Opponents, for instance in a debate about equality or liberty, should be seen not as simply wrong or mistaken, but as standing somewhere else, either where the future may take everyone, or perhaps forlornly on a set of values that history may be about to trample underfoot.

Of course, this kind of thought can lead either to the quagmire of 'relativism', or to a closely related scepticism about the possibility of knowledge and objectivity in political and moral matters. It also raises doubts about our understanding of others, and one of Williams's constant themes was the tension between the historical mutability of human self-consciousness and the need for us to find ourselves in others if we are to understand them. We cannot write the history or understand the thoughts of beings wholly alien, yet we have to work in the consciousness that the agents in history were not simply displaced versions of ourselves. The difficulty is that genuine pluralism ought not to imply that understanding is impossible, yet it constantly threatens to do so. In his political essays, and his work on Wittgenstein, Williams often lets the issue revolve around who the 'we' are as we oscillate between an abstract, universal aspiration (Kant, or Rawls, or liberalism in its more imperialistic guises) and a more rooted, 'communitarian' reality (Hegel, reincarnated in contemporary times by Charles Taylor or Alasdair Macintyre).

Williams never accepted a simple position in this area, any more than Wittgenstein did, and indeed cheerfully admitted that in this debate 'my contribution has been to some extent that of making myself a nuisance to all parties'.

Williams can be seen as drawn to Nietzsche largely because he found him the philosopher who had wrestled the hardest with this conundrum, although there were other temperamental affinities to which we will come. Williams himself, perhaps as a consequence of his endless interest in the human carnival, often emphasised plurality and was impatient with the universalising tendencies of the Enlightenment. As he remarked about writing the history of philosophy, while we have to interpret great and dead philosophers as having something to say to *us*, we should not assume that what the dead have to say to us is much the same as what the living have to say to us. Yet he was equally cautious about overemphasising differences. When he turned to the classical world, particularly in *Shame and Necessity*, it was firstly to take issue with scholars who had magnified the difference between us and the Greeks to the point of making them altogether incomprehensible. Williams gave a closely reasoned rebuttal of such pessimism, and his Homeric agents turned out to be quite like ourselves after all, or ourselves as we might have been without so much Christianity, history, and knowledge in our baggage.

III

Although the historical turn came to dominate more of Williams's later work, it is as a moral philosopher that he wrote his most influential books and essays. He was an uncompromising critic of two of the major movements that often dominate the subject: utilitarianism and Kantianism. As the doctrine that actions are to be judged solely by their consequences for human good or ill, however that may be measured, utilitarianism has always had critics, and all philosophy students are brought up to puzzle over whether it could be right to hang an innocent man if, through surprising circumstances, more good can be gained or more harm averted by doing so. Williams transformed the standard discussion by moving the issue to the nature of motivation, the nature of agency, and the nature of the good for human beings. By analysing examples where an agent could maximise goods or minimise harms, but only at the cost of performing actions that go deeply against the grain, he argued that we cannot coherently regard ourselves simply as conduits to greater general utility. What we do is more than what we produce. An agent's integrity is bound up with local spheres of responsibility, and it is the meaning of the actions performed inside those spheres that give us our identities. By trying to turn us into 'servants of the world' utilitarianism in fact destroys the very networks of care and responsibility that are required for life to have meaning at all. Williams's point was not that utilitarianism necessarily gave the wrong answers in difficult cases, but the much more subtle one that it goes about getting its answers in the wrong way.

His examples and his analysis dominated all subsequent work in this area, and were largely responsible for a general awareness of the complex clusters of values that actually determine our decision-making. He was well aware that sophisticated utilitarians, such as Sidgwick and possibly even Mill, advocated various indirect forms of the doctrine. They measured the motivations in a moral consciousness by their impact on utility, but admitted that by this measure the utilitarian consciousness itself might not come out as the best. Williams thought that this complexity produced an unacceptable dislocation or fracture in the theory, or in the psychology of any agent who embodied the theory. He mocked it as what he called Government House Utilitarianism, whereby a higher part of us controls the doings of lower parts for purposes which it is important to conceal from them. The subsequent collection he edited with Amartya Sen, *Utilitarianism and Beyond* (1982), accelerated the general flight from utilitarianism among many economists and philosophers.

Williams's opposition to Kantianism in ethics was also founded on a deep mistrust of the nature of agency as it is construed by Kantians. One issue was the Kantian emphasis on acting from the sense of duty, giving rise, as Williams put it with his usual genius for the memorable phrase, to the problem of 'one thought too many'. If you kiss your wife, or for that matter save her from the shipwreck, because it is your duty, then things have gone wrong: you are supposed to act spontaneously, out of affection, and if you drag duty into it you have one thought too many. The other issue he highlighted is one of what he equally felicitously called 'moral luck'. Kant, he believed, had sought to put right action beyond the sphere of happenstance and contingency. According to Kant, whether you do right or wrong is entirely voluntary, totally within the control of your will. It does not matter what your natural and cultural inheritance might be, nor your emotional nature, nor your circumstances, nor the consequences that actually come about because of your action. This fantasy of pure freedom is part of what Williams called 'the morality system', a system of thinking about guilt and responsibility that still dominates many of our attitudes. Williams argues, like Hume, that motivation cannot come from reason alone, and that the motivational forces to which agents are subject are never entirely within their control.

He went on to assault the morality system by concentrating upon the moral emotions of shame and remorse, and the many ways in which luck determines whether someone gets into situations in which those emotions are appropriate. Thus two people might behave in exactly the same careless way, and one of them may get away with it and walk away blithely enough, whereas the other, because of bad luck, meets catastrophe and remorse and shame may dog their footsteps. The morality system, Williams argued, can make no sense of this difference, since by its reckoning each equally did what was right or did what was wrong. Yet the emotional difference cannot be ignored: life would be unrecognisable without it. So the moral emotions, properly understood, suggest that human life both is, and ought to be, conducted in terms of a much more pluralistic and heterogeneous set of values, which Williams preferred to dub 'ethics' rather than 'morals'. This became known as the 'Gauguin problem' after the salient example that Williams gave of the painter's bad behaviour later vindicated by unforseeable success. In the eyes of many the discussion of luck attacked the Kantian picture just as effectively and influentially as his assault had attacked utilitarianism.

Williams thought that Kant offered an illusion or consolation of another kind: the realist or objectivist fantasy of a moral system that will trump politics, an 'argument that will stop them in their tracks when they come to take you away'. Like some of the opponents of Socrates, Williams had a keen eye for the moment when politics takes over from moral principle, and in the eyes of some critics the book flirted with the same radical scepticism about the entire enterprise of ethics that animated Callicles or Thrasymachus. The limits referred to in the title often seemed more like limits to the coherence of ethical thought itself, rather than limits to our philosophical understanding of what ethics is supposed to be. Thus, as legacies of the Enlightenment, both Kantianism and utilitarianism purport to provide a standpoint from which moral criticism can be made, to which in some sense the reasonable agent must listen or ought to listen. But while the brilliance of Williams's criticism of each was universally acknowledged, it was harder to know what positive system he intended to put in their place. Evidently an agent's 'projects' or deepest attachments, or even his integrity as an agent, can depend on something falling short of a common point of view with other people. It seemed as if they might issue in highly local and restricted concerns and loyalties, or in other words, a politics of identity. And then it remained unclear what resources Williams would have left for exerting pressure towards more universal or liberal values. It sounded as though he might be joining with 'communitarian' opponents of the Enlightenment, allowing people their traditional prejudices and partialities, but with a clear conscience. This criticism is doubtless misplaced, for much of Williams's later work is concerned exactly with the interplay between the universal and the particular, or the challenge that equality, liberty, justice, and the common point of view pose to the rooted and potentially blinkered perspectives of our everyday priorities and concerns. By refusing to countenance easy or self-deceptive solutions to this conflict, he was acknowledging its depth rather than turning his back on its importance. In his final book he talked of the 'intellectual irreversibility of the Enlightenment' and described any moral or political forces that might undo it as potentially catastrophic.

Philosophers travelling in roughly Williams's direction often fall into the arms of Aristotle. But Williams's profound sense of the varieties of human existence prevented him from subscribing to any complacent view of a single human nature and a single proper expression of it. Aristotelians try to derive what it is to be a good human being simply from what it is to be a human being, just as once we know what a knife is, we know what a good knife is. But Williams was not likely to be seduced into equating behaving well, even in ethically minimal ways, with flourishing 'by the ecological standard of the bright eye and the bushy coat'. There is simply too much slippage between being a good person and being a successful or healthy or happy person, and in spite of the endeavours of Plato and Aristotle, it is at least partly a question of luck whether circumstances are such that the two come close together. Hearing a colleague comparing being a good action to being a good knife, Williams once drily remarked that if a knife was bad enough it stopped being a knife altogether, whereas when someone does something really bad, they still do something. It is therefore simplistic to think that our human nature, all by itself, contains a template for living as we should, and Williams was the last person to lose sight of what he called the sinister downside to the injunction to 'be a man'. He characteristically placed Aristotle in his disturbed historical situation in fourth-century BC Athens, and regarded him as a 'provincial who became exceedingly impressed by a conservative view of a certain kind'. He described the vision of each thing striving after its own perfection, or as he called it, his 'pretty self-satisfied account of the virtues', simply as 'an astonishing piece of cultural wish-fulfilment'.

Whereas some of his stress on emotion in human affairs affiliated Williams to Hume, he could never accept a Humean account of our ethics as simply an expression of our passions or attitudes, given by nature and moulded by culture. He had a pronounced antipathy to the whole issue of whether with ethics we are in the domain of representation of moral fact, or whether we are in the domain of attitude and prescription. He held that issue responsible for what he somewhat unfairly regarded as the arid and boring substitute for real ethics that dominated the Oxford of his upbringing. His only interest was in the practical and political expression of the issue, for instance in the reasons we may have for diminishing our bigotries or for expanding our tolerations. In many of his writings he instead explored the centrality of 'thick concepts' in practical reasonings. A thick concept is used when we describe someone as modest, or just, or courageous, in which there are both elements of description and elements of evaluation. Fact and value are seamlessly entangled, and this entangling gives us a way of crossing, or perhaps ignoring, the distinction between fact and value that preoccupies so much ethical theory. Williams did not, however, see this entangling as a way of evading the perspectival nature of ethical thought; we must not jump to the other extreme, and suppose that with ethical concepts we describe 'what is there, anyway', or give an absolutely true description of things such as science may aspire to deliver. Again, the bogey of relativism or scepticism lurks in the wings, and the task is to reconcile the perspectival element with a satisfying account of the claim of ethics to be a subject about which knowledge is possible. In *Ethics and the Limits of Philosophy* the treatment of relativism even allows that the movement from an unreflective, primitive ethic towards something more reflective, and perhaps closer to a liberal, egalitarian ideal, might nevertheless represent an actual loss of knowledge, which in turn suggests that knowledge itself loses its status as the kind of commitment that cannot be undermined by real improvement in the subject's position. In a revealing interview shortly before he died, Williams said that most of his efforts had been concentrated upon making 'some sense of the ethical as opposed to throwing out the whole thing because you can't have an idealized version of it'.

A similarly perspectival and pluralistic attitude informed Williams's discussion of yet another topic that he made his own, that of the nature of tragedy and tragic dilemmas, as when Agamemnon must either betray his army or sacrifice his daughter Iphigenia. Williams again gave a central place to notions like remorse and shame. But he also suggested that these examples set a limit to the goal of consistency in ethics. Whereas consistency is the first virtue of theory that purports to describe how things stand, in response to tragic dilemmas the inconsistency of thinking both that you must do something and that you cannot do it, seems far from being a vice. Indeed, it seems to be a virtue, since not to think both things would seem to be crass and insensitive. Here too we have a contrast between an ethical response to the world and a description of its fabric. When we face two contradictory descriptions of 'what is there, anyway', we resolve the problem by settling for one, and the other disappears without trace. But in a tragic dilemma, even if we decide we must pursue one course of action, the other does not disappear, and typically a vivid sense remains that we have failed in the obligation that we did not meet.

Williams's final book, *Truth and Truthfulness*, weaves together many of these themes. The aim is described in Nietzschean terms as provision of a 'genealogy' of truth: an account of its place in our lives that would, he hoped, vindicate its importance, putting back some of the lustre supposedly rubbed off by postmodernists, relativists, and other 'deniers' of the very notion. The aim was ambitious, given Williams's fundamental sympathy with the principal thought that motivated postmodernism, which was the ineluctably historical and contingent perspective that any interpreter or investigator must bring to his activity, and which is only transcended, if at all, in the abstract area of scientific theory. In the upshot the work was not a full-frontal assault on postmodernism, but a discussion of the central virtues of accuracy in investigation and sincerity in transmission of information. Applied to plain facts about our immediate environments, these virtues will have their utility in anything recognisable as human life, which actually means that they are unsuitable subjects for a genealogy describing a possible history of how they might have emerged under natural pressure from a form of human life that lacked them. They would seem at best to have had an evolutionary biology, having emerged as variations on primitive animal signals. But the point for Williams is that their utility rapidly drops off as we depart from the here-and-now, until when we think of the scripts that make up our cultural and national identities, and indeed the writing of history in general, myth and fiction may serve our particular ends just as well or better than the truth. Hence it is a remarkable fact, a piece of what Nietzsche called our asceticism, that we can care about truth as much as we do, and that our concern extends to accuracy even in these regions where it may not benefit us at all. Williams in fact located the discovery of historical truth as a datable occurrence, occurring at some time between Herodotus and Thucydides.

The question he finally broaches is whether our commitment to truthfulness leads to tragedy, or whether it is possible for history to be both truthful and hopeful. Williams does not close the question, but his sympathy lay with the view he represented as Nietzsche's own, that 'there are very compelling true accounts of the world that could lead anyone to despair who did not hate humanity'. Significantly, the book ends with the passage from Conrad's *Heart of Darkness* in which the narrator admits that Kurtz was a remarkable man, and describes his despairing last words as the appalling face of a glimpsed truth.

IV

There is a deep pessimism at the heart of much of Bernard's writing, and one could catch a tone of nihilism underneath some of his very funny but frequently destructive remarks about almost everybody else (of a showy colleague: 'If you look carefully under the artificial tinsel, you will get a glimpse of the real tinsel'). But he never came across as bitter, perhaps because he was always too clear-sighted to have had large-scale hopes whose betrayal by time would engender that vice. He appeared a singularly happy man, especially in his private life, even if his world view was closer to that of his favourite Greek tragedians or to the stark historian Thucydides than to anything more reconciled to the nature of things. For him, as for Sophocles or Conrad, the order of what we call reason is a fragile and perishable veneer, barely covering for a time the kaleidoscope of divergent lights and darknesses, triumphs and horrors, that is the human condition.

The philosophical project of finding some deep bedrock on which to stand our own ordering of thought and conduct struck Bernard as bound to fail, and he could be savage in his contempt for 'the tireless aim of moral philosophy to make the world safe for well-disposed people'. His final word on the relentless systematiser Sidgwick was: 'The fact that Sidgwick's theory so clearly and significantly fails in these respects follows, I believe, simply from the fact that it is so clear and significant an example of an attempt at an ethical theory'; and he gloriously summed up Robert Nozick's influential libertarian theory of rights simply as 'a device for switching off the monitors to earth'. But the pessimism about theory did not go along with any Tolstoyan or Wittgensteinian celebration of the wisdom of the everyday: Bernard may have been an egalitarian and a social democrat, but he was unsentimentally aware of the 'emptiness and cruel superficiality of everyday thought'. Complacency was one of his principal targets, and he was careful to run no risk of joining those who offer an easy recipe or handbook of living, and thereby condemn themselves to fall into its capacious jaw.

Bernard offered no handbook and no consolation, but he was also far from resigned. His reaction was to seize life, horrors and all, with an energy that was the opposite of fatalism. We may live under the great indifferent thoughtlessness of the gods, but then the right response is to live. This energy, constantly expressed in his intense intellectual curiosity, goes some way to resolving the paradox that in spite of the tragic sense of life, he was the most exhilarating of writers and companions. It is not just that he was endlessly informed and endlessly hilarious; but that in spite of the bite of his wit, he was also intensely sympathetic, notably generous to those that needed it, and quick to notice who they were. I remember myself as a fledgling philosopher being mauled by one of his more violent colleagues at the Moral Sciences Club in the early 1970s, and after the meeting Bernard scooped me up, took me back to King's, opened a large bottle of whisky, and for around an hour turned my dejection into gales of laughter with his plentifully illustrated, detailed and scurrilous diagnosis of the psychology of my assailant.

Above all, both his writings and his presence forced everyone to tap their own resources more deeply, to raise their game. One had to try harder in Bernard's presence, not for fear of being eclipsed, since that was inevitable, but simply to repay the privilege, to rise to the occasion. He burned brighter than anyone, and the world seemed duller and darker when he went.

SIMON BLACKBURN
Fellow of the Academy

Note. I am very grateful for help in writing this memoir from Myles Burnyeat, Baroness Williams, Adrian Moore, David Pears, Tom Sebestyen, David Wiggins, and above all Patricia Williams, who answered my questions patiently, and who willingly made a great deal of material available to me.

JOHN WYMER   *Jim Rose*

John James Wymer
1928–2006

ON A WET JUNE DAY IN 1997 a party of archaeologists met at the Swan in the small Suffolk village of Hoxne to celebrate a short letter that changed the way we understand our origins. Two hundred years before, the Suffolk landowner John Frere had written to the Society of Antiquaries of London about flint 'weapons' that had been dug up in the local brickyard. He noted the depth of the strata in which they lay alongside the bones of unknown animals of enormous size. He concluded with great prescience that 'the situation in which these weapons were found may tempt us to refer them to a very remote period indeed; even beyond that of the present world'.[1]

Frere's letter is now recognised as the starting point for Palaeolithic, old stone age, archaeology. In two short pages he identified stone tools as objects of curiosity in their own right. But he also reasoned that because of their geological position they were 'fabricated and used by a people who had not the use of metals'.[2]

The bi-centenary gathering was organised by John Wymer who devoted his professional life to the study of the Palaeolithic and whose importance to the subject extended far beyond a brickpit in Suffolk. Wymer was the greatest field naturalist of the Palaeolithic. He had acute gifts of observation and an attention to detail for both artefacts and geology that was unsurpassed. He provided a typology and a chronology for the earliest artefacts of Britain and used these same skills to establish

---

[1] R. Singer, B. G. Gladfelter and J. J. Wymer, *The Lower Palaeolithic Site at Hoxne, England* (London, 1993), p. 1.
[2] Singer, Gladfelter and Wymer, *The Lower Palaeolithic Site at Hoxne, England.*

Proceedings of the British Academy, **150**, 351–367. © The British Academy 2007.

major sequences in South Africa. In doing so he ordered and energised what was a neglected and demoralised subject so that now it is one of the most vibrant communities in British archaeology.

The Palaeolithic tradition

Wymer belonged to the tradition of field observation begun by Frere with his provocative letter. The collection of flint artefacts gathered pace during the nineteenth century driven by the scientific investigation of human antiquity. These activities culminated in the landmark work of Sir John Evans, *The ancient stone implements, weapons and ornaments, of Great Britain*, first published in 1872. This remarkable volume drew together all that was then known about stone tools into a national archive. It was based on Evans's many visits to sites as well as his extensive correspondence with collectors from around Britain. Indeed his work inspired collecting on a massive scale by enthusiasts such as Dr Allen Sturge and Henry Stopes whose stone archives passed respectively to the British Museum and the National Museum of Wales in the early years of the twentieth century. Neither were they isolated examples. Members of The Prehistoric Society of East Anglia, founded in 1908, had under its dynamic President J. Reid Moir, a fanatical zeal to collect stone tools. A trend that continued until 1935 when, in a skilfully managed coup, Sir Grahame Clark, FBA, transformed them into The Prehistoric Society with an international agenda.

Evans was however much more than a flint collector. Along with Sir John Lubbock and assisted by Sir Charles Lyell, he propelled Palaeolithic archaeology into a lead role in the evolutionary synthesis that emerged in the second half of the nineteenth century. It was the young Evans who in 1859 on his visit to the Somme with geologist Joseph Prestwich had confirmed the observations of Boucher de Perthes that stone artefacts and extinct animals were indeed associated. Thus the high antiquity of humans was proved in the same year as the publication of *On the origin of species* where Darwin set out the mechanism of natural selection to account for biological variation. Prior to *Ancient stone implements*, Sir John Lubbock had in his 1865 *Pre-historic times* divided the stone age into Palaeolithic and Neolithic, a division that Evans followed. The majority of his chapters are devoted to Neolithic stone types; perforated axes, grinding-stones, scrapers etc. However, it was the final section on implements of the Palaeolithic periods that set the framework which

Wymer was to spend his life refining. In the second edition of 1897, Evans divided the material into those from caves and river deposits. He established a geographical approach to the archive and directed attention to the stratigraphical position and faunal associations of the material.

Evans died in 1908 and Lubbock, by then Lord Avebury, five years later. With them went a good deal of the common sense behind Palaeolithic archaeology and the subject quickly lost its pole position in the scientific pantheon. The quest for the oldest stone tools came to dominate the activities of flint enthusiasts and East Anglia proved a particularly happy hunting ground. However, not everything that was found proved to be humanly made. Reid Moir believed passionately in eoliths, or dawn stones, from the Cromer Forest Bed on the Norfolk coast, while others such as Hazeldine Warren pointed to mechanical explanations such as wave action to account for the patterns of fracture.

While the eolith debate grew ever more acrimonious with claims and counter-claims of artefact and geofact, one enthusiast who remained untouched by the invective was John Wymer's father. Indeed, his parents had been visiting gravel pits along the Thames near the family home in Kew for some years. They had a launch moored at Staines which provided an agreeable way to visit pits and appreciate the riverscape.

They had a passion to understand more about the geological setting for the abundant flint tools that came from Britain's major river. Their visits coincided with some of the last days of digging the sand and gravel pits by hand. Sections would be exposed slowly and stand for some time while the quarrymen also supplemented their income by selling-on the handaxes and other stone tools that they found, and in some cases made! The young John Wymer, born on 5 March 1928, therefore learned about Palaeolithic archaeology and Pleistocene geology as a result of family expeditions to a world of small-scale diggings for a necessary but poorly rewarded industry. He came to know the local landscape, and then England, through cycling expeditions with his brother. Fifty miles a day was their target, a 10 shilling note sewn into their jackets in case of emergencies.[3] A devotee of public transport and walking, his advice in later years was always to take the bus if you wanted to count the number of river terraces; going uphill in a city like Bournemouth or Southampton the driver would change gear with each new terrace step.

---

[3] A. Lawson and A. Rogerson, 'Bifaces, booze and the blues: Anecdotes from the life and times of a Palaeolithic archaeologist', *Stone Age Archaeology: essays in honour of John Wymer*, ed. N. Ashton, F. Healy and P. Pettitt (Oxford, 1998), p. 1.

Early years

Wymer received no formal training in archaeology. He never attended university. He wrote in his diary that the first archaeological book he read was in 1948 when he was in the RAF. It was Jacquetta Hawkes's *Prehistoric Britain* and it stirred his curiosity. After National Service he took a job as an audit clerk with British Rail and worked for Amalgamated Press as a screen printer. All three occupations were to fashion his thoroughness and attention to detail. He did not settle and in 1955 completed a certificate in teacher training, followed by a brief period spent teaching. However, in the same year, at the age of 27, those long searches in the gravel pits of the Thames had taken a remarkable turn. During work with his father in the disused gravel pit at Swanscombe, North Kent, Wymer found on 30 July, a Saturday, an *in-situ* piece of human skull in the Upper Middle Gravels. The Barnfield Pit at Swanscombe had been known for many years and had produced thousands of stone tools, in particular pointed handaxes. The long sequence also had evidence for an older non-handaxe occupation, named Clactonian after the Essex type site. But what was remarkable about Wymer's discovery, the result of patient, systematic searching and observation, was that the skull fragment (a right parietal) fitted perfectly with two other pieces from the same skull that had been found elsewhere in the same gravels in 1935 and 1936 by A. T. Marston. Wymer recalled that his skull fragment had the consistency of wet soap, but it fitted together with the other pieces, the stratigraphic context was precise and a paper in *Nature*, his first published work, quickly followed.[4] Such attention to detail was Wymer's trademark. However, it was also very necessary as this was only two years after the Piltdown hoax was unmasked and the edifice of human evolutionary anatomy laid out by Sir Arthur Keith and others had finally collapsed.[5] The Lower Palaeolithic Swanscombe find was much needed coming as it did at a moment when Palaeolithic and palaeontological studies were demoralised by the fallout from Piltdown. Swanscombe remains the only Middle Pleistocene skull from Britain and is now dated to about 400,000 years old.

This discovery, but above all his systematic approach to recording, led to the end of his teaching career when he accepted a post at Reading

[4] J. J. Wymer, 'A further fragment of the Swanscombe skull', *Nature*, 176 (1955), 426–7.
[5] J. S. Weiner, K. P. Oakley and W. E. L. G. Clark, 'The solution to the Piltdown problem', *Bulletin of the British Museum of Natural History*, 2 (1953), 141–6.

Museum in 1956. This was the perfect base for his continued study of the Thames terraces and with his first wife Paula he raised not only a family in Wokingham but also the profile of Palaeolithic studies in its post-eolith, post-Piltdown days.

In 1956 there were very few professional archaeologists and even fewer studying the Palaeolithic. Dorothy Garrod, the first female professor at Cambridge, and Grahame Clark, then a lecturer in her department, were rare examples. In addition there was Frederick Zeuner at London University who brought a European perspective to issues of chronology and glacial sequences. In the national museums only Kenneth Oakley at the British Museum of Natural History had any sustained impact on the subject through his scientific approach to dating and environmental reconstruction. By contrast, the Palaeolithic tradition in France was a much stronger national enterprise. It was led by its doyen Abbé Henri Breuil and backed by substantial funding in the Institut de Palaéontologie Humaine, while a new regional centre for Quaternary studies, headed by François Bordes at Bordeaux, now concentrated on the rich caves of the Dordogne.

Interest in the British Palaeolithic was further diminished by the work of the Leakeys at Olduvai Gorge in Tanzania. In 1959 their excavations of stone tools and early campsites were supplemented with the first of many fossil skulls. Crucially, in 1961, the volcanic tuffs that interleave the Olduvai stratigraphy were first dated by Potassium-Argon methods to almost 2 million years old.[6] By contrast the British ancient lake fills such as Hoxne and the gravel terraces of the Thames could not be dated by any scientific methods. Moreover, excavations were small, often casual and for the most part the artefacts that were recovered had been moved about by the rivers. It seemed that Continental Europe and Africa promised not only dateable material but also much better preserved evidence for the reconstruction of the lifeways of our earliest ancestors.

Four decades, four syntheses

The Swanscombe skull fragment was therefore welcome news indeed. Wymer, however, was never one to be discouraged by what others thought was unimportant. He set his own goal and that was to understand the

---

[6] L. S. B. Leakey, J. F. Evernden and G. H. Curtis, 'Age of Bed I, Olduvai Gorge, Tanganyika', *Nature*, 191 (1961), 478–9.

English river sequences which contained so many hundreds of thousands of stone tools. With the determination, but not the resources, of a Breuil or Bordes he set out to draw together all the available evidence to construct a reliable sequence. His archive was a 6 ins. × 4 ins. card index that fills 6 m of drawers and records every Lower and Middle Palaeolithic artefact from Britain. He was still adding to it a few months before he died. He will be the last person who saw nearly every Palaeolithic stone tool and noted it.

The many visits he made were meticulously recorded in his field notebooks and now represent an archive for Palaeolithic archaeologists as well as a photographic record of the social changes in the subject over the last half century. Through them we see not only his intellectual development but also his transformation into one of the great field archaeologists, as shown for example by his growing skills as a draughtsman and the development of his distinctive calligraphy. The draughtsmanship was applied to section drawings as well as to his exquisite drawings of the many flint artefacts. A Wymer drawing is instantly recognisable and they remain a benchmark of accuracy as well as interpretation.

Doing the homework; Lower Palaeolithic Britain

So, in 1956 equipped with a job, a purpose and the skills to reach his goal he began work on the first of his four major synthetic books, *Lower Palaeolithic Archaeology in Britain: as represented by the Thames Valley*.[7] He did not set out to entertain since it was 'full of what might be described as weighty archaeological and geological matters. It is, perhaps, the homework which, once done, allows us to indulge in unbounded flights of fanciful ideas about our ancestors, confident that it at least has some basis.'[8] The book is a description, site by site, river valley by river valley, of the Thames. It has the appearance of a gazetteer but to treat it as only that would be like calling Pevsner's *Buildings of England* an estate agent's catalogue. With every entry there is judgement as to significance and potential of the finds, based on their geological context and quantity; immaculately illustrated and structured by the chronological framework of the time.

---

[7] J. J. Wymer, *Lower Palaeolithic Archaeology in Britain, as represented by the Thames Valley* (London, 1968).
[8] Ibid., p. 4.

Wymer was working to the well-established model of four major glaciations and three intervening interglacials. This system had been proposed on the basis of Alpine glaciations and their associated river terraces in 1909.[9] Wymer followed the lead of Zeuner and tied the British system, with its local names, into the Continental system. He was able to identify the key sections containing interglacial and glacial deposits[10] and made the critical distinction between the sequences and deposits in the Upper, Middle and Lower Thames. The recent geomorphological and climatic forces that shaped the English landscape provided a relative chronological framework and he 'guessed' that the Clactonian, the earliest evidence for humans in Britain, was about 400,000 years old.[11]

This was homework indeed. In the same year Derek Roe published his gazetteer of the handaxe industries in Britain as well as a synthesis of the industries based on an innovative approach to quantification.[12] Wymer did not follow such a route. His approach to the distinctive handaxes that dominate the collections was a typology of forms rather than a metrical description.[13] He was a skilled flint knapper concerned with the technology of artefact manufacture. In particular he was interested in the distribution of material either at the scale of terraces and findspots in particular reaches of the rivers[14] or for the entire country.[15] However, Roe and Wymer had demonstrated the potential of the British sequence and pointed the way forward for the next generation of Palaeolithic archaeologists.

Mapping the muddle; Mesolithic Britain

Another decade and another significant project. Wymer's second major synthesis was a self-styled gazetteer that forms a companion to Roe's

---

[9] A. Penck and E. Brückner, *Die Alpen in Eiszeitalter* (Leipzig, 1909).

[10] Wymer, *Lower Palaeolithic Archaeology in Britain, as represented by the Thames Valley*, pp. 368, 371.

[11] Wymer, *Lower Palaeolithic Archaeology in Britain, as represented by the Thames Valley*, p. 388.

[12] D. Roe, 'British Lower and Middle Palaeolithic handaxe groups', *Proceedings of the Prehistoric Society* 34 (1968), 1–82; *A Gazetteer of British Lower and Middle Palaeolithic Sites* (London, 1968).

[13] Wymer, *Lower Palaeolithic Archaeology in Britain, as represented by the Thames Valley*, fig. 27.

[14] Ibid., fig. 60.

[15] Ibid., fig. 109.

work on the Lower Palaeolithic.[16] It was also sponsored by the Council for British Archaeology and covered the Upper Palaeolithic and Mesolithic periods in England and Wales. Wymer was the coordinator for all the regional groups supplying data and where there were gaps in coverage he plugged them. The task was equally massive in that Mesolithic stone tools are not only more abundant but also, due to the lack of subsequent glaciation, pretty much ubiquitous. The pace of Palaeolithic discovery has always been slower whereas field-walking and excavation habitually turn up Mesolithic material. He had known this since 1949 on trips with his parents to the Brecklands where they had picked up Mesolithic material. However, what has not kept pace is the discovery of sites worth excavating. Grahame Clark led the way with his investigations at Star Carr in the Vale of Pickering, Yorkshire.[17] He combined environmental and artefactual evidence, in a site where organic preservation was good, and used them to present an economic interpretation of a band of Early Mesolithic hunters and gatherers camping on the shores of a small lake. In doing so he raised the bar very high indeed since few other Mesolithic sites have such a combination of evidence. In fact it could be argued that Star Carr was the worst thing to happen to British Mesolithic studies since it was so unrepresentative of the vast majority of finds such as those recorded in Wymer's Mesolithic gazetteer. Ever since Clark's excavation, the hunt has been on for the next Star Carr, and with little success. Wymer understood the anomalous nature of Star Carr and was not going to suffer any inferiority complex. While at the Reading Museum, and starting in 1957, he excavated the Early Mesolithic site of Thatcham in Berkshire that for evidence and age closely matches Star Carr.[18] Today the brilliance of Clark's interpretation still shines, but it is Wymer in his Thatcham report who understood more clearly how excavation could assist us to understand those flint scatters that needed to be tied into the larger geographical picture. His excavations are now remembered for the coffer dam he built so that excavation could proceed and the hazelnuts and pig bones he found. Huts were reconstructed from the patterns of flints plotted by excavated square. The result was a picture of floodplain archaeology for hunters and gatherers that is indeed of more

---

[16] Wymer, *Gazetteer of Mesolithic sites in England and Wales* (London, 1977).

[17] J. G. D. Clark, *Excavations at Star Carr* (Cambridge: 1954).

[18] J. J. Wymer, 'Excavations on the Mesolithic site at Thatcham: interim report', *Berkshire Archaeological Journal*, 57 (1959), p. 1–24; 'Excavations at the Maglemosian sites at Thatcham, Berkshire, England', *Proceedings of the Prehistoric Society*, 28 (1962), 329–61.

relevance to the vast quantities of material collected from the surface of the fields of England, and so patiently recorded in his Mesolithic gazetteer.

Rivers and coasts: East Anglia and South Africa

In 1965 Wymer left Reading Museum and for the next fifteen years worked as research field director for Ronald Singer, a South African who specialised in Plio-Pleistocene mammals at the University of Chicago. Their plan was to return to key sites in Britain and South Africa to acquire environmental information, stratigraphic controls and absolute dates. Finding human fossils was also part of the plan especially as the 1970s saw the rise of a new debate in Palaeoanthropology concerning the origins of modern humans.

In Britain Wymer's two principal excavations were at Clacton, from 1969–70[19] and Hoxne, from 1971–8,[20] with some delay to the appearance in print of the latter which irritated Wymer considerably. These well-known localities had both been excavated many times before but what Wymer brought to them, along with Bruce Gladfelter his collaborator on geomorphology and dating, was a new scale of methodology and intellectual enquiry. For almost the first time in British Lower Palaeolithic excavations individual finds were carefully plotted and their association with faunal remains and other sedimentary features noted. At both sites Lawrence Keeley, then a research student at Oxford, examined selected specimens for traces of use wear on their edges. Such studies were possible because of the excavation strategy as well as the demonstration that much of the material had been gently deposited in fine-grained sediments and was in primary context. Through these two excavations the credentials of the British Lower Palaeolithic were re-established: well-preserved sites with a wide range of artefactual and palaeoecological data dating to the Middle Pleistocene. By the time Hoxne was published in 1993 there had been a critical revision of African sites such as Olduvai where more agents than early humans were now seen as responsible for the patterns among the bones and stones. The British Palaeolithic was beginning to

---

[19] R. Singer, J. J. Wymer, B. G. Gladfelter and R. G. Wolff, 'Excavation of the Clactonian industry at the golf course, Clacton-on-Sea, Essex', *Proceedings of the Prehistoric Society*, 39 (1973), 6–74.

[20] Singer, Gladfelter and Wymer, *The Lower Palaeolithic Site at Hoxne*.

shake off its inferiority complex and the way was prepared for major excavations, starting in the 1980s, at Boxgrove,[21] High Lodge[22] and Barnham.[23]

Between the two site publications came Wymer's third synthesis *The Palaeolithic sites of East Anglia*.[24] Many regard this as his most important since the entries for sites are even more infused with information and interpretation than those from the earlier *Lower Palaeolithic archaeology in Britain*. Here he concentrated on the counties of Norfolk, Suffolk, Essex and parts of Cambridgeshire, Hertfordshire and London. The lost rivers of the region formed his main focus and in particular the ancient Bytham River that had been discovered and described by Quaternary geologist Jim Rose who worked closely with him.[25] East Anglia is a happy hunting ground for Palaeolithic archaeology precisely because the successive ice sheets that extended across the area have buried much of the landscape and re-designed the drainage system. This process affected in particular the Bytham River that once rose in the West Midlands and South Pennines. The Bytham was the largest river in England until it was overwhelmed by the Anglian ice sheet that also resulted in diverting the river Thames to its present course through London.[26]

In his synthesis Wymer also incorporated the revolution in Pleistocene stratigraphy that resulted from the oxygen isotope record of climate change recovered from the deep sea cores. Sir Nick Shackleton, FRS, and others had shown from the isotopic analysis of microscopic foraminifera, incorporated into the sediments that accumulate on the ocean floors, that glaciations were far more frequent than the four based on the Alpine sequence.[27] In the last 780,000 years there had been no less than eight full

---

[21] M. B. Roberts and S. A. Parfitt, *Boxgrove: a Middle Pleistocene hominid site at Eartham Quarry, Boxgrove, West Sussex* (London, 1999).

[22] N. Ashton, J. Cook, S. G. Lewis and J. Rose, *High Lodge: Excavations by G. de G. Sieveking 1962–68 and J. Cook 1988* (London, 1992).

[23] N. M. Ashton, D. Q. Bowen, J. A. Holman, C. O. Hunt. B. G. Irving, R. A. Kemp, S. G. Lewis, J. McNabb, S. A. Parfitt and M. B. Sneddon, 'Excavation at the Lower Palaeolithic site at East Farm Barnham, Suffolk: 1989–1992', *Journal of the Geological Society*, 151 (1994), 599–605.

[24] J. J. Wymer, *The Palaeolithic Sites of East Anglia* (Norwich, 1985).

[25] J. Rose, 'Status of the Wolstonian glaciation in the British Quaternary', *Quaternary Newsletter*, 53 (1987), 1–9; 'Major river systems of central and southern Britain in the Early and Middle Pleistocene', *Terra Nova*, 6 (1994), 435–43.

[26] J. R. Lee, J. Rose, R. J. O. Hamblin and B. S. P. Moorlock, 'Dating the earliest lowland glaciation of eastern England: a pre-MIS 12 early Middle Pleistocene glaciation', *Quaternary Science Reviews*, 23 (2004), 1551–66.

[27] N. J. Shackleton and N. D. Opdyke, 'Oxygen isotope and palaeomagnetic stratigraphy of Equatorial Pacific core V28-238', *Quaternary Research*, 3 (1973), 39–55.

glacial–interglacial cycles. The timing and duration of these were known from palaeomagnetic dating in ocean and ice cores and in long sedimentary sequences on land; for example, lake basins in Southern Europe and the massive loess profiles in Central Europe and China. The challenge for all archaeologists was now to determine to which of the many interglacial stages sites such as Hoxne and Clacton belonged. Obtaining absolute dates was still problematic and the answer was through their stratigraphic relationship to such events as the Anglian ice advance and via biostratigraphy, that uses the rich faunal and floral records in these sedimentary archives, to refine the picture. Ahead of most of his contemporaries, Wymer now started to make this transition to the new Quaternary timescale and patterns of climate change. He was happiest with the old terms of Anglian, Wolstonian and Devensian for the glaciations but in *The Palaeolithic sites of East Anglia* he established, through an insightful series of sketch maps, how the rivers and their archaeology had changed as a result of the more fluid and complex picture of climate change that had now emerged. His summary maps stand as one of the break-throughs in Palaeolithic geography, turning the obscure science of river-terrace stratigraphy into a regional, changing landscape. It would be these insights and the homework he provided that in 2001 would lead to the *Ancient Human Occupation of Britain* project funded by the Leverhulme Trust and led by Chris Stringer, FRS, at the Natural History Museum.[28] Among the rewards for this project was the discovery in traditional eolith territory of a handaxe, found on the beach at Happisburgh by Mike Chambers, a local resident, and then through excavations the recovery of indisputably worked flints from Pakefield at the mouth of the pre-Anglian Bytham River.[29] Their age of around 800,000 marks the currently oldest traces of humans in Britain.

The second strand of Singer's Chicago based project had international ambitions and again Wymer delivered important results. This led them eventually to the coast of South Africa and the excavation between 1966 and 1968 of a massive cave at Klasies River Mouth, 400 miles east of Cape Town. In two long excavation seasons Wymer uncovered a sequence

---

[28] C. Stringer, *Homo britannicus: the incredible story of human life in Britain* (London, 2006).
[29] S. Parfitt, R. W. Barendregt, M. Breda, I. Candy, M. J. Collins, G. R. Coope, P. Durbridge, M. H. Field, J. R. Lee, A. M. Lister, R. Mutch, K. E. H. Penkman, R. Preece, J. Rose, C. Stringer, R. Symmons, J. E. Whittaker, J. J. Wymer and A. J. Stuart, 'The earliest record of human activity in northern Europe', *Nature*, 438 (2005), 1008–12.

25 metres in height through a vast midden of shells, animal bones and stone tools.[30] The site proved remarkably rich in traces of fireplaces, indicating repeated visits, and over a quarter of a million Middle Stone Age (MSA) artefacts were excavated. The size of these assemblages would have daunted many, but not Wymer, who divided them on the basis of typology and technology into four main phases with the distinctive Howiesons Poort industry stratified between the second and third phases. Singer was also rewarded with some human remains that had a distinctive modern appearance.

The work that Wymer undertook has been re-analysed on a number of occasions but these results are poorly published compared to Wymer's towering achievement. As a result, the primary archive has been repeatedly quarried and helped set an agenda for the study of modern human origins. With good timing the site was excavated as the debate in palaeonthropology that was to dominate the 1980s and early 1990s started. This involved proponents of an origin for modern humans in Africa and its opponents who argued for multi-regional evolution in distinct geographical regions.[31] This debate between a human revolution and human continuity provided the wider framework into which the Klasies River Mouth discoveries were placed. The development of science-based dating pushed the age of the Klasies human remains back in time. Moreover, their association with MSA tools, that in Europe would be regarded as the handiwork of Neanderthals, challenged the orthodox view of how culture and anatomy went together. Today it is Wymer's sequence at Klasies River Mouth, supplemented by other excavations along the same coast, as at Blombos Cave,[32] that has set the standard. While South Africa may be a continental size cul-de-sac for the wider issues of human evolution its status is comparable to that for another peripheral region, Britain. In both cases, as Wymer showed, the archaeology from these regions serves us well in pointing to the timing and direction of trends in human evolution that elsewhere are blurred by too much data because they lie at the centre

---

[30] R. Singer and J. J. Wymer, *The Middle Stone Age at Klasies River Mouth in South Africa* (Chicago, 1982).

[31] P. A. Mellars and C. Stringer (eds.), *The Human Revolution: behavioural and biological perspectives on the origins of modern humans* (Edinburgh, 1989).

[32] C. S. Henshilwood, J. C. Sealy, R. Yates, K. Cruz-Uribe, P. Goldberg, F. E. Grine, R. G. Klein, C. Poggenpoel, K. van Niekerk and I. Watts, 'Blombos Cave, Southern Cape, South Africa: preliminary report on the 1992–1999 excavations of the Middle Stone Age levels', *Journal of Archaeological Science*, 28 (2001), 421–48.

of such developments. This aspect of the record and the importance of both regions to the wider issues of human development were set out in his global survey of the period.[33] *The Palaeolithic Age* presented his first-hand experiences of stone age data in an uncomplicated narrative of technological progress and achievement.

Father of the British Acheulean, and FBA

In the acknowledgements to his last synthesis *The Lower Palaeolithic Occupation of Britain*, John Wymer characteristically recalled, 'I am very conscious of the statement I once heard in my youth from a wise man (actually a tramp with a philosophical and poetic frame of mind, on a 65 bus between Kingston and Richmond) that "the idea is more important than the execution". I think he was right.'[34] This was also the case when it came to employment. The Chicago grant ended in 1980 and after a year's Research Fellowship at East Anglia, Wymer was again looking for a job. His search coincided with the rise of regional archaeological field units funded at first through English Heritage and later by the developers themselves under the policy of 'the polluter pays'. The purpose of these field units was to record archaeological evidence before it was destroyed. The pace of destruction was unparalleled with deep ploughing destroying monuments that were last ploughed in the Bronze Age while infrastructure and building projects were making increasing demands for aggregates with new pits being opened on a mechanised scale in which archaeological remains were simply lost, and old pits were abandoned, overgrown or backfilled and restored.

But what archaeological unit would employ a Palaeolithic archaeologist? The subject in 1980 was still regarded as a warm-up to the main show; those standing-stone monuments of later prehistory, Roman towns, walls and roads, and the urban centres of medieval England. However, Wymer's previous career at Reading Museum now stood him in good stead. While he will be remembered for his time there by his excavations at Thatcham and the publication of his book on the Lower Palaeolithic of the Thames, he had also dug the Lambourn Neolithic long

---

[33] J. J. Wymer, *The Palaeolithic Age* (London, 1982).
[34] J. J. Wymer, *The Lower Palaeolithic Occupation of Britain* (Salisbury, 1999), p. xiv.

barrow,[35] drawn and described the Moulsford gold torc[36] and carried out a series of other excavations on a wide range of prehistoric sites.[37] Over the years he had flown in a Cessna to photograph and identify new sites from the air. These of course were not deeply buried Palaeolithic ones. Based now in Norfolk with his second wife Mollie, whom he married in 1976, his first position was with Essex County Council in 1981 and then in 1983 a job as a Field Officer came up at the Norfolk Archaeology Unit. Living at Great Cressingham, he was well placed to complete his 1985 *Palaeolithic sites of East Anglia* while being conscientious about, if not devoted to, the demands of rescue archaeology and the more commercially minded direction it was taking. He worked there until 1990 when he wrote in his archaeological diary, 'Resigned from the Norfolk Archaeological Unit in response to its organisation evolving along the lines of entrepreneurial management.' These pressures on units to become competent businesses did not fit with Wymer's view of what made a professional archaeologist.

Then the opportunity to put his skills to their best use arose when a dispute among Palaeolithic specialists as to the correct approach to a planning application at the old gravel pit of Dunbridge, Hampshire, highlighted the lack of reliable information on Palaeolithic archaeology to aid the planning process. Geoffrey Wainwright, Chief Archaeologist at English Heritage, was already supporting the long-term excavations at Boxgrove in Sussex but it was the gravel sites with less-well-preserved material, such as Dunbridge, that needed to be reviewed on a national scale. Andrew Lawson, who had dug at Klasies River Mouth in the 1960s, and was by now Director of Wessex Archaeology in Salisbury, put forward a proposal to English Heritage for a *Southern Rivers Palaeolithic Project* with Wymer as the principal investigator. Wymer jumped at the opportunity, writing in his diary, 'In the summer [of 1990] I am approached by Andrew Lawson as to whether I would consider conducting a survey of the Lower Palaeolithic . . . I am exhilarated at the prospect and assent.' The details were quickly sorted out and the survey, which involved visiting, along with Phil Harding, every gravel pit in southern England, was funded for three years. Now Wymer's 6 m of card index records came into its own. The 1968 survey of the Thames was updated

[35] J. J. Wymer, 'Excavations of the Lambourn long barrow', *Berkshire Archaeological Journal*, 62 (1968), 1–10.

[36] J. J. Wymer, 'The discovery of a gold torc at Moulsford', *Berkshire Archaeological Journal*, 59 (1961), 36–7.

[37] Ashton, Healy and Pettitt (eds.), *Stone Age Archaeology: essays in honour of John Wymer*.

and many new sites added to the archive. The audience for this ambitious work were the County Archaeologists charged with advising on the planning process. So successful was the project that it was extended for a further three years to become *The English Rivers Palaeolithic survey* in which Wales was also included. A key to its success was the involvement of David Bridgland as part of the advisory team and who to Wymer's general satisfaction had married up the process by which different terrace deposits were formed to the isotope record from the deep sea cores and its continuous chronology for climate change.[38] Combined with the work of Danielle Schreve on the bio-stratigraphy of the mammals contained in these deposits,[39] sites such as Swanscombe could now be confidently placed in Marine Isotope Stage 11, an interglacial period that spanned from 427,000 to 364,000 years ago.

Wymer's survey is one of the great achievements of British archaeology. Almost one hundred years after the second edition of John Evans's *Ancient stone implements* and two hundred years since John Frere's perceptive letter to the Society of Antiquaries, the work of one archaeologist presented a conspectus of 500,000 years of human prehistory that was simultaneously of professional, managerial, academic and public interest. The survey produced six large regional reports that went back to the County curators and where Wymer helped them by selecting sites of future importance. The results were distilled into the two volumes of *The Lower Palaeolithic Occupation of Britain*,[40] richly illustrated by the author, with the formation of terraces explained so that all could understand. But above all the book returns a sense of geography to the period, ordered by five landscapes; rivers, coasts, lakes, downland and caves. The long tradition started by Frere and archived by Evans had culminated in Wymer's great achievement.

Now the recognition flowed. He received an honorary doctorate from Reading University in 1993 and was elected a Fellow of the British Academy in 1996. In 2002 he received the British Academy's Grahame Clark medal for outstanding distinction in the study of prehistory. These awards were in addition to earlier acknowledgements of his contribution; an honorary MA from Durham University in 1969 and the Geologists' Association highest honour, the Stopes Medal, in 1973.

---

[38] D. R. Bridgland, *Quaternary of the Thames* (London, 1994).
[39] D. C. Schreve, 'Differentiation of the British Late Middle Pleistocene interglacials: the evidence from mammalian biostratigraphy', *Quaternary Science Reviews*, 20 (2001).
[40] Wymer, *The Lower Palaeolithic Occupation of Britain*.

What gave him equal satisfaction, and undoubted pleasure, was the stimulus he provided for the next generation of Palaeolithic archaeologists. Many passed through John and Mollie's front door at the aptly named The Vines, their home at Great Cressingham. Even more went with him to the pubs of East Anglia as they joined Wymer on a visit to a new site or to re-visit an old one. When Nick Ashton from the British Museum was digging the East Anglian sites of Barnham and Elveden, the barbecues thrown for his team by John and Mollie became legendary events. Good food, beer and fine wine were central to Wymer's interests because they provided the setting to meet those who would carry on the good work of Palaeolithic exploration; an opportunity to share his knowledge and learn from others. But the talk would eventually stop as the evening wore on and John would start playing his Blues guitar and his accomplished boogie-woogie piano.

This exuberant exterior disguised a modest man of strong principles. He would say that all he hoped to achieve was a bit of the homework for others to build on, and then argue passionately and decisively about the true status of the Clactonian or the age of the Caversham Channel. He held many positions in learned societies. He was President of the Quaternary Research Association and Chair of the Lithics Study Society. He was a Vice-President of the Prehistoric Society and could have been President but his principles would not allow him to accept after the Society supported a ban on South African archaeologists attending an international conference in 1986.

For a generation of archaeologists he was a father figure to their chosen profession. This position and his achievements were celebrated in a festschrift presented to him in 1998.[41] Following his death in February 2006 a special edition of the *Journal of Quaternary Science*[42] and a two-day conference held in September of that year at the British Museum marked his memory. Central to the memorial volume was work undertaken by members of the *Ancient Human Occupation of Britain Project*. Wymer had been closely involved and after Mollie's death in 1999 he moved back to Bildeston, near Ipswich, to the house where they had lived before Great Cressingham. He began searching the foreshore for palaeoliths because he thought they should be there and he was proved right. As a result, the publication of the Pakefield finds, illustrated by Wymer's

[41] Ashton, Healy and Pettitt (eds.), *Stone Age Archaeology: essays in honour of John Wymer*.
[42] S. G. Lewis and N. Ashton (eds.), 'The Palaeolithic Occupation of Europe: in memory of John Wymer, 1928–2006', *Journal of Quaternary Science*, 21 (2006).

drawings of the oldest artefacts in Britain and Northern Europe, has a symmetry to it.[43] His first and last papers were published in *Nature*, and in the intervening fifty years he had helped transform the Palaeolithic while keeping its heart intact. He died on 14 February 2006.

Our photograph shows him in his familiar trilby hat, holding aloft a small handaxe during a visit to Swanscombe in 2004. The professionals from Quaternary science, archaeology and human palaeontology, as well as a large number of independent archaeologists who surround him are there because of him. He once wrote of his hope that his work 'may inspire some to search for palaeoliths themselves, and it would be a dull person who could not enjoy the thrill of finding a handaxe and considering who held it last'.[44]

CLIVE GAMBLE
Fellow of the Academy

Note. I am very grateful to Andrew Lawson who supplied many details of John Wymer's rich and varied life, and to Jim Rose for his advice and permission to use his photograph. Nick Ashton and Paul Mellars, FBA, also commented on and corrected earlier drafts.

[43] S. Parfitt *et al.*, 'The earliest record of human activity in northern Europe'.
[44] Wymer, *Lower Palaeolithic Archaeology in Britain, as represented by the Thames Valley*, p. 5.